Michelle Morgan was the president of the Marilyn Lives Society, a UK fan club, from 1991 to 2007. She is the author of *Marilyn's Addresses* and *Marilyn Monroe: Private and Undisclosed*. She is the co-producer of the upcoming documentary *Gable: The Ties that Bind* with Prospect House Entertainment. She lives in Northamptonshire.

THE MAMMOTH BOOK OF

Hollywood Scandals

Michelle Morgan

ROBINSON

RUNNING PRESS
PHILADELPHIA · LONDON

ROBINSON

First published in Great Britain by Robinson in 2013

Copyright © Michelle Morgan, 2013

1 3 5 7 9 10 8 6 4 2

The moral right of the author has been asserted.

A CIP catalogue record for this book
is available from the British Library.

UK ISBN: 978-1-4721-0033-7 (paperback)
UK ISBN: 978-1-4721-0034-4 (ebook)

Robinson
is an imprint of
Constable & Robinson Ltd
100 Victoria Embankment
London EC4Y 0DY

An Hachette UK Company

www.hachette.co.uk
www.littlebrown.co.uk

First Published in the United States in 2013 by Running Press Book Publishers
A member of the Perseus Books Group

Books published by Running Press are available at special discounts for bulk purchases in the United States by corporations, institutions and other organizations. For more information, please contact the Special Markets Department at the Perseus Books Group, 2300 Chestnut Street, Suite 200, Philadelphia, PA 19103, or call (800) 810-4145, ext. 5000, or email special.markets@perseusbooks.com.

US ISBN: 978-0-7624-4946-0
US Library of Congress Control Number: 2013933735

10 9 8 7 6 5 4 3 2

Digit on the right indicates the number of this printing

Running Press Book Publishers
2300 Chestnut Street
Philadelphia, PA 19103-4371

Visit us on the web!
www.runningpress.com

Printed and bound in Great Britain by CPI Group (UK) Ltd., Croydon CR0 4YY

This book is dedicated to my dear friend, Claire Hollies Slater, who has been in my life since we were both eleven years old. She is one of the strongest women I know and will always be an inspiration to me.

To my grandparents, Bill, Lily, Cosimo Pacitti and Pearl, for teaching me all about "the olden days" and inspiring my love for times gone by.

And to the memory of my dear friend Ross McNaughton, who was really looking forward to this book.

This book is dedicated to my dear friend, Claire Hollies-
Sister who has been in my life since we were both
eleven years old. She is one of the strongest women I
know and will always be an inspiration to me.

To my grandparents, Gail, Lily, Cosmo, Pavitt and
Pearl for teaching me all about "the olden days" and
inspiring my love for times gone by.

And to the memory of my dear friend Kass
Melaughton, who was really looking forward to this
book.

Acknowledgements

I would like to thank my friends and readers who not only pointed me in the direction of various scandals, but also provided a lot of information, help and support along the way. In that regard I would particularly like to thank Eric Woodard, Richard Kirby and Hanna Nixon, who all sent items that they felt would inspire my work on this project.

To my agent, Robert Smith; all the staff at Constable & Robinson, and my wonderful editor Howard Watson.

Christina Rice from the Los Angeles Public Library helped me so much during the writing of this book; while it seems clichéd to say that it could not have been written without her, I honestly believe that to be true.

I would like to thank my wonderful husband Richard, who has supported and loved me for the past twenty-six years, and Mum, Dad, Paul, Wendy and Angelina for always being there for me.

And last but by no means least, my gorgeous daughter Daisy, for inspiring me every single day for the past nine years. I love you, baby; all my dreams came true because of you.

Acknowledgments

Contents

Introduction

"There are three sides to every story . . . His, hers and the truth." – Anon

Some people consider Hollywood a location; some an industry; others a state of mind. To me, and for the purpose of this book, Hollywood is a combination of all three. Some of the scandals in this book happened in California where Hollywood is located, of course, while others may have happened elsewhere but are included here because the people concerned were (or are) part of the Hollywood industry and legend.

Within these pages you will read about strange deaths, tragedies, suicides, sex scandals, robberies, murders and much, much more. These scandals run the gamut from the days of silent films right up to the present day, and show that while times may change, the extraordinary lives people live and the things they get up to are the same now as they were a hundred years ago. People are drawn to scandal; scandal is drawn to them. It all goes on no matter if the star is from the 1920s or the present day.

This book covers over sixty different scandals from the high-profile – Whitney Houston's death, the Fatty Arbuckle court case and the fatal stabbing of Lana Turner's boyfriend – to those scandals long since forgotten, such as the death of actor Albert Dekker or the colourful life of boxer/actor Norman

Selby. Some scandals are small; others so large I wondered if they would ever come to a conclusion, but all are revealing, tragic, outrageous and at times – such as the case of Zsa Zsa Gabor clobbering a policeman – somewhat entertaining.

When I first began writing this book, it became clear very early on that there was a huge amount of information to get through, and many areas to cover. With that in mind I decided that, rather than zip through every scandal with just an ounce of information, I really wanted to delve into the archives to bring out many facts about each and every story I wrote. With that in mind, each chapter is a story in itself – an investigation into the lives of the stars and the underbelly of Hollywood society – and it is my belief that no other book has been written which covers not only almost a hundred years of Hollywood scandals, but also in such an in-depth manner.

It has been an absolute pleasure to write this book; I have been introduced to many extraordinary stars and situations, and have really learned a great deal. In that regard I very much hope that you enjoy reading the finished book as much as I have enjoyed writing it.

Michelle Morgan

1

The Roscoe "Fatty" Arbuckle Scandal

Hollywood has seen hundreds – maybe thousands – of scandals during the course of the past hundred years, but the first and probably most memorable one was the Roscoe "Fatty" Arbuckle scandal, which brought Hollywood to its knees in the early 1920s.

Roscoe Conkling Arbuckle was born on 24 March 1887, in Kansas, to Mollie and William Goodrich Arbuckle. The saying goes that he weighed somewhere between fourteen and sixteen pounds at birth and his brother was so traumatized by the sight of him that he actually fled from the room. This was not the most positive of entrances to the world, and was made worse when his father wondered if such a huge child could possibly be his own. The birth – not surprisingly – was so horrific that Roscoe's mother never fully recovered and the health problems she encountered afterwards were said to be contributory factors when she passed away twelve short years later.

But long before death came to the Arbuckle family, they moved to Santa Ana, California, where Roscoe developed a strong interest in the theatre. His mother tried desperately to encourage her child to develop what seemed to be a very natural talent, but this did not sit well with his father, who took to telling the child that he would go nowhere in life; especially in "the show business". The frustrated Mollie complained bitterly that her husband was being too hard on the boy, but showing a strength of character that would do him good in the years to come, Roscoe carried on with his dream regardless and gained a job with the Frank Bacon stock company when he was just eight years old.

Shortly afterwards the child's embittered father decided to leave the family and move to Watsonville, California, saying he was going to look for gold. Devastation later hit when Mollie passed away and it was decided that Roscoe should go to live with his father, since by this time he was the only child who was still living at home. The child did not find much comfort in the thought of living with the man who had laughed at his dreams and abandoned him completely, but he went to Watsonville anyway, anxious to discover if his father had changed in any way since he had last seen him. Unfortunately for Roscoe, however, on hearing that the child would be moving to his new home town, the neglectful father fled once again. By the time the child arrived at the train station, he was well and truly on his own.

With no choice but to raise and support himself, it was not long before Roscoe found his way into show business once again, singing songs in local theatres and, by 1904, working for entrepreneur Sid Grauman, firstly as a ticket taker and then as an entertainer at the Unique Theater in San Francisco. Thus began a theatre career which saw Roscoe touring not only the United States but China and Japan too, where his funny routines, clowning and singing were a huge hit with the vaudeville audience and he loved the attention he received.

By August 1908 Arbuckle was in Long Beach where he met a seventeen-year-old woman called Minta Durfee. Short and petite, she told him she was not interested in men of his size, but he soon won her over with his personality and together they set up a comedy duo and married several months later. After that, both their careers began to take off and they often acted together in early Hollywood comedies, the first being *Fatty's Day Off* in 1913. But while things were going well in his life at last, there was still part of Roscoe

Arbuckle that never got over the early death of his mother and abandonment by his father, as witnessed by Minta on many occasions during their marriage.

> "He always said he would never live to be 50," she told reporters. "We were married when we were just kids and he used to drive me to distraction when he said this."

Roscoe's career went off like a bullet when producer Mack Sennett took a shine to him and decided to offer him a contract. The producer was especially pleased at how agile the actor was, particularly given his huge size, and was impressed by the amount of acrobatic moves he could make for comedy value: back flips, somersaults, tumbles . . . he could do them all. The joy went both ways, as given the opportunity of signing with a studio, Roscoe was able to meet and work with Hollywood star Mabel Normand, as well as later mentoring future stars such as Charlie Chaplin and Buster Keaton. Arbuckle's status as a comedic genius was now set in stone, and his future looked bright.

It wasn't long before other studios started to develop a keen interest in the actor and a bidding war began which saw Paramount sign Roscoe on an unheard-of-million dollar contract in 1914. Sadly, the marriage between Minta and Roscoe was beginning to break down and they became estranged around the time the Paramount contract was drawn up. Some say the breakdown in the marriage came as a result of a clause in Arbuckle's contract which forbade him to be married, which seems a little extreme but could nonetheless be true. However, the cause was more likely the fact that the couple had been through various personal tragedies in the recent past, including miscarriage and an inability to have children, and this most certainly would have added to their marital problems.

Talking about the end of the marriage some years later, Minta told reporters:

When we were married I was 17 and my husband was 21. That was back in 1908. Five years ago we agreed to disagree and I received a separate maintenance. Unfortunately – or perhaps fortunately, as you please, there are no children. We were not bitter against each other. We simply decided that we would remain good friends. Mr Arbuckle has been very generous in his treatment of me financially – I have not had to work during these years and last February he made me a present of a fine automobile.

As his marriage was breaking down, so too was the state of Roscoe's health. He began drinking heavily, and after suffering from an infection in his leg in 1916, he became addicted to morphine. He was also developing a big distaste for his nickname, "Fatty", which he had endured since childhood and was quickly overtaking his real name in terms of popularity. The characters he played were often also called "Fatty" and this was certainly the name by which the media and fans knew him, but it was something he wanted to get away from. He began encouraging everyone to call him Roscoe, and anyone caught calling him Fatty to his face would be met by the stern reply, "I've got a name you know!"

After a brief stint running his own film company, "Comique", the actor went on to sign another lucrative contract with Paramount, this time for $3 million to make up to eighteen feature films. To say this was a scoop for Roscoe would be an understatement; $1 million was a fortune, but three? He was on top of the world. Unfortunately, his new-found position as a top earner in Hollywood left him wide open for trouble and in September 1921 Roscoe Arbuckle found out that the higher you climb, the further you fall, when all hell broke loose at a party he hosted during Labor Day weekend.

On Saturday, 3 September, the actor drove to San Francisco with friends Lowell Sherman and Fred Fischbach (who Americanized his surname to Fishback). Once there the three men checked into the St Francis Hotel, where they occupied adjoining rooms 1219, 1220 and 1221; numbers 1219 and 1221 being used to sleep, and 1220 as a reception/living room located between the two. The weekend started slowly and quietly with the three men being joined by two male friends for dinner, and then the next day some relaxation on the beach, before they later enjoyed a spot of dancing.

Then on Monday, 5 September, Roscoe slept late and at around 1 p.m. was still dressed in his pyjamas, robe and slippers, about to have breakfast in room 1219. Another friend arrived at the suite of rooms and told Roscoe and Fischbach that he had just seen an actress in the hotel, who said she knew the men currently staying in the suite of rooms. On hearing the name of the woman, both Fischbach and Roscoe agreed that they were indeed acquainted and after telephoning downstairs, they invited her over. The woman in question was aspiring actress Virginia Rappe, who had been working on the fringes of Hollywood for some time, and who had known Roscoe for approximately six years. She was also accompanied by her agent Alfred Seminacher and friend Maude Delmont, a notorious, hard-faced troublemaker, known to the police for extortion, blackmail, bigamy and much, much more.

Delmont and Rappe were known to be a pretty wild pair, and Virginia had a reputation for an overindulgence with alcohol which caused her to embarrass herself at parties by tearing her clothes every time she became drunk. The reason for this would seem that she suffered greatly with cystitis and the alcohol brought about various stomach problems every time she partook. Added to that, shortly before the weekend of 5 September 1921 she had apparently undergone one of several recent backstreet abortions and was still very much recovering, though obviously not eager to advertise this fact to the other members of the party.

The men invited Rappe and her friends into the room, gave them breakfast and relaxed in their company. However, it was not long before somebody began serving bootleg alcohol and the quiet get-together was soon turning into an afternoon party, complete with Roscoe, his friends, Rappe and various other hangers-on. It is fair to say that Arbuckle had not planned the party and was not particularly keen to host it, and it would seem that he did not have that much to do with Rappe or her friends, other than being in the same room at the same time. He later made it clear to his attorney that he had not intended to invite either of the women into his rooms, and that the only people he did plan to ask over were a friend called Mrs Taube and one other, unnamed woman.

"They all kept stringing in," he later said of the people who arrived that afternoon. "I didn't know who they were then. I didn't invite them."

Virginia Rappe asked for there to be music in the room, and several of the party guests – including Arbuckle himself – danced for some time during the afternoon, though it has been said that the actress herself did not dance much and instead chose to watch from a nearby chair. However, while Roscoe was obviously enjoying the dancing to some degree, the party wasn't enough to convince him to change his plans for sightseeing with Mrs Taube, and by 3 p.m. he decided to go next door and dress.

Several minutes earlier, Roscoe had seen Virginia Rappe heading next door into room 1221, but unfortunately for him, by the time he had arrived in his own room – 1219 – she had found her way into his bathroom where she was on the floor; sick, hysterical and somewhat blocking the entrance. He later told the court of his first sighting of the woman in his room:

> I entered 1219 to dress, closed and locked the door. I went into the bathroom. Miss Rappe was sitting in there, holding her stomach and vomiting. I bumped her with the door when I entered. I picked her up and she vomited again. I was holding her head and wiped her face. She was still holding her stomach. I asked her if I could do anything. She asked for a drink of water and then for another drink of water.

It was at this point that some authors claim that Virginia confessed to the actor that she was having pains in her chest and had recently had an abortion. Having lost an unborn child with his wife, the actor was apparently upset to hear this revelation, but even so, he did not leave the woman to suffer alone. Instead, he placed her on the bed in order for her to rest, gave her a glass of water as requested, then went back into the bathroom in an effort to shave and change his clothes. While Roscoe was in the bathroom, however, Rappe managed to fall out of his bed and crash on to the floor, and on returning to the room, he began to get concerned.

"I found her rolling on the floor between the two beds, holding her stomach. I tried to pick her back up and couldn't."

Arbuckle eventually managed to help the woman back on to the bed, and headed into the next room to alert his party guests to the drama next door. Until this time, Maude Delmont had been with one of Roscoe's friends in the bathroom of room 1221, but she soon appeared on the scene, drunk and – true to her reputation – seemingly looking for an opportunity for trouble. Roscoe told both her and another guest about the sick woman and together they went back into the room to find Miss Rappe sitting on the edge of the bed, tearing her clothes from her body and frothing at the mouth.

"I pulled her dress down and she tore her stockings and a black lace garter. She was tearing on the sleeve of her dress," the actor later told the courtroom.

Roscoe left the room for a moment and at this point Delmont decided that she was going to take full charge of the situation. By the time he returned, she had completely undressed Virginia Rappe and was rubbing ice on her body. When Arbuckle tried to object, the bold woman ordered him out of the room, to which he replied that if she didn't shut up he would "throw her out of the window". Roscoe Arbuckle was no fan of Maude Delmont. She had already caused uproar earlier in the day by dressing up in a pair of pyjamas, drinking and partying so wildly that Arbuckle had demanded she leave the party. She had refused, but his disgust at her behaviour had left her fizzing, and she was not a woman to forgive and forget easily. In fact, the decision by Arbuckle to stand up to the woman was to have grave implications for the actor in the moments to come.

Virginia Rappe was still hysterical; rambling incoherently and sliding on to the floor, so Arbuckle picked her up and placed her back on to the bed. Delmont later lied to police that the actor had been violent towards the woman, and had thrown – not placed – her on to the bed. He denied this, and explained that he was merely trying to calm her down before the doctor arrived.

The hotel management was alerted to the fracas going on in the room and Delmont was first on the scene to greet the assistant manager, H. J. Boyle, with the words, "A woman is hysterical here and is tearing her clothes off. You had better do something about it." The manager entered the room and found Rappe on the bed, almost nude except for a hastily placed bathrobe, and by this time going in and out of consciousness. The room was full of partygoers, and they all told the manager that the woman had become hysterical after having two or three drinks. "I took it for granted that there was nothing more serious than a drinking party," he later told reporters.

Maude Delmont told the manager that she wanted to take Rappe to another room to recuperate and he then left room 1219 to organize it. Then guest Alice Blake and another, unnamed girl decided to place Virginia into a tub of cold water in a bid to relieve her hysterics. Not surprisingly, this did not help the situation one bit and so guest Fred Fischbach carried her back into the bedroom and placed her on the bed. Even being picked up was painful for Virginia at this point, and she complained that the man had hurt her in his attempts to get her from the tub back into bed. Unfortunately, this statement would be taken down and used in evidence against Roscoe, and twisted to make it look as though he had hurt her during an unprovoked attack, which was simply not the case.

Finally the nearby room was ready and Roscoe helped move the woman into it, and a doctor was called. Arriving a short time later, the physician could find no physical injuries on the girl and told Roscoe that it looked as though the problem was an overindulgence with alcohol.

"The doctor and I thought it was nothing more serious than a case of indigestion," Arbuckle later told reporters. "He said a little bicarbonate of soda probably would straighten her out."

Meanwhile, back in room 1219, Rappe's agent, Al Seminacher took it upon himself to gather up the woman's torn clothes and place all but two of the garments in a neat pile. The others he took down to his car in order, firstly to dust his vehicle, and secondly to tease Virginia about the state in which she had left her garments when she finally recovered from her episode.

Back upstairs, seeing that he had done as much as he could for the woman, and still presuming that the problem was not in any way serious, Arbuckle asked Lowell Sherman to clear the rooms of guests, before then leaving to go sightseeing around San Francisco with Mrs Taube. He later returned to the hotel, where he and his friends – including Seminacher – dined in his room, before he left to go dancing downstairs. The next morning he and his friends left the city and headed back to Los Angeles by boat. Later one of the party, Lowell Sherman, told the court: "I did not see Miss Rappe after that and never inquired about her because I did not take any of it seriously. I never asked Arbuckle what he thought was the matter with the girl. He seemed to have the same opinion as everyone else – that the girl had a bun on and was ill." He then went on to express that Roscoe did not seem upset about the episode, any more than anybody else at the party, and concluded, "I never heard Miss Rappe express an opinion as to what was the matter with her."

Unfortunately, while Roscoe and his friends were heading home, Virginia Rappe's condition grew worse and after several days of suffering in the hotel, the doctor was called once again.

He was sufficiently worried to order the woman to hospital where she was examined by a series of specialists, all citing her condition as acute abdominal pain with a fever. It was then decided that these symptoms were most likely caused by some kind of internal injury – perhaps an organ that had ruptured – which had caused peritonitis. They were right, as it was later announced that the actress's bladder had burst, causing infection, deliriousness, acute pain and, ultimately, death.

The odd thing about Virginia's trip to hospital was that instead of being taken to a general clinic where she could undergo emergency treatment, she was actually taken to a maternity unit instead. This strange occurrence would seem to go hand-in-hand with the fact that Delmont apparently brought her own doctor to look at Rappe – the same doctor who had performed the abortion just days before. Was Virginia taken to the maternity hospital as a result of complications from the abortion? It would seem possible. To add further fuel to this conjecture, when the actress passed away at the hospital on 9 September 1921, an unofficial autopsy was performed, allegedly by the doctor who had attended her, and all of her female internal organs – uterus, fallopian tubes and ovaries – were apparently removed before her body was taken back to Los Angeles. It would seem highly likely that this move was a deliberate attempt to hide the fact that she had undergone an illegal and dangerous abortion in the days before her death.

Both before and after Virginia passed away, Maude Delmont took great delight in telling anyone who would listen her own sordid version of what had happened on the afternoon of the party. Still angry from Roscoe's treatment of her, she placed the blame for her friend's death squarely on his shoulders and made sure everybody knew about it. According to her, this huge man had crushed her petite friend when forcing her to have sex, thus rupturing her bladder in the process. Since then other stories have been put forward which claim that Roscoe violated Rappe with some kind of foreign object – usually a coke bottle – and her bladder had burst as a result.

These stories are not only ludicrous but also come without any evidence whatsoever. Just how heavy would a person have to be to cause a bladder to rupture by lying on them? It is true that Roscoe was a big man, but he would surely have to have been considerably larger to rupture an internal organ. What's more, the bursting of Rappe's bladder, if it had been caused by a heavy weight, would likely not have been an isolated injury; the crushing would have led to other organs being damaged and possibly even bones breaking in the process. As for the coke-bottle story, there was no coke being served at the party that day. As there is no evidence whatsoever that a bottle of this nature was anywhere near the suite of rooms at that time, it too can effectively be ruled out.

While Delmont had been in the bathroom of room 1221 and could not have possibly heard anything when Virginia first collapsed in room 1219, this did not stop the police from believing the woman when she described how she had heard screams coming from Roscoe's bedroom. Perhaps the most outrageous thing about the Arbuckle scandal is that while Delmont had been known to police as a liar who had committed a variety of crimes, everyone suddenly sat up and took notice when she started spouting lies and innuendo about Arbuckle and Rappe.

It is interesting to note, however, that while her friends all stuck by her and agreed with her findings, the other guests denied that any of her stories and innuendo had the remotest bearing on the truth. Arbuckle himself later told police that she had made up the stories because "she is simply sore at me", and then told the tale of her becoming so wild at the party that he had tried to throw her out of the suite of rooms.

The fact that everyone in any kind of authority seemed to believe Delmont was incredible given her history, and yet it was true; in spite of there being not a scrap of hard evidence against Roscoe Arbuckle and no witnesses to any crime, the police decided that he was indeed to blame for the death of Virginia Rappe, and charged the poor man with murder.

"No man, whether he be Fatty Arbuckle or anyone else, can come into this city and commit that kind of an offence," Captain of Detectives Duncan Matheson told waiting reporters. "The evidence showed that there was an attack made on the girl." Except, of course, that there was no real evidence to show any kind of attack at all; and in fact doctors treating the woman had believed she was ill as a result of "natural causes". Had there been an injury, they surely would have seen it at that time.

Roscoe's arrest seems to be mainly as a result of finger-pointing from Delmont and a comment by a nurse, Mrs Jameson, who had attended to Virginia Rappe before she died. According to Jameson, the actress told her several stories: the first was that after a few drinks she could remember nothing at all about the party. "She did not remember whether Arbuckle asked or pulled her into his room," the nurse told police. The second story Rappe apparently told her was that Arbuckle was to blame for her illness; that he had attacked her. Then later she changed her mind once again and claimed that, no, she did not remember anything about what had happened that day.

The reason for Rappe's differing comments was very simple: as a result of high fever and infection, the actress was delirious and could not remember what had happened after she had become ill. However, while alone with the patient, Maude Delmont took the opportunity to feed the woman information of her own sordid account of what happened that afternoon, thus causing many false and misleading memories in the process. This would explain why Rappe's story kept changing, and why she had such confusion about whether or not she remembered anything that had happened at all.

Rappe was in no fit state to recall any event from the party; if she had been, she would have known that Arbuckle could not possibly have taken or pulled her into the room. There were witnesses in the reception room who had been talking to Roscoe during the time when Rappe disappeared; and since they were sitting just yards away from the bedroom door, it would have been impossible for them not to notice the actor forcibly pushing or pulling anybody into his room.

The whole thing very quickly got out of hand and Arbuckle was horrified that he was now facing the death penalty for a crime he did not commit. He refused to give any kind of statement to the police and instead chose to remain silent, except to say a few words to the reporters who waited with baited breath and their notebooks poised. "Well," he said with his shoulders sagging, "I guess you have enough for this time."

"Smile!" shouted photographers snapping his photograph, to which the distraught actor replied, "Not under circumstances like this." Moments later he was led from the building, en route to the city jail, his request for bail denied.

"It is not pleasant to take action like this," the Assistant District Attorney told reporters, "but under the evidence it was the only thing we could do."

Newspapers went wild with accusations against the actor, none more so than papers owned by the Hearst Corporation in San Francisco. It quickly became apparent to them that the Arbuckle story was going to sell countless copies of their rags, and it has been said that they even resorted to faking pictures of the actor – drawing bars across his face to make it look as though they had exclusive access to him in prison. Roscoe's films were pulled from the cinema; his fans deserted him in droves; and suddenly nobody wanted anything to do with the man who, just a few weeks before, had been known as a gentle comedy clown.

But Roscoe's friends still believed in him and chose to support their fellow actor through the case. Mabel Normand sent word that she and everyone else she knew all believed her co-star to be innocent; Charlie Chaplin released a statement to say that he had no doubt his friend had nothing to do with the death; while Buster Keaton was so upset that he wanted to give evidence as a character witness. This request was turned down by Arbuckle's lawyers, however, for fear that any kind of appearance by Keaton would somehow destroy his career too.

Meanwhile Roscoe's estranged wife Minta flew to California from New York so that she could support her ex-husband in any way she could. Reporters flocked to hear her opinion and she did not disappoint: "Roscoe Arbuckle is just a big lovable pleasure-loving, overgrown boy," she said, before adding, "His success and prosperity have been a little too much for him, but he is not guilty of the hideous charge made against him in San Francisco. I am going to him because I think it is my duty to be near him – I want to help him in every way I can."

Asked whether the couple were going to reunite, the woman answered, "A reconciliation? That depends upon whether, when he is acquitted of this charge, I find that my place is with him and whether he finds that he is ready for a return to the life we led when we were married."

Distraught that he had been unfairly accused of a crime he did not commit, Roscoe wrote to his friend and producer, Joseph Schenck, and told him that he was absolutely innocent of all the accusations being held against him. "I simply tried to help someone in distress, the same as you or anyone else with human instincts would have done in the circumstance," he said. He also assured his friend that he had done no wrong. "My heart is clean and my conscience is clear."

The trial of Roscoe Arbuckle began on 14 November 1921, by which time the charge had been changed to manslaughter, much to the relief of everyone involved. Every little detail was reported, from what actually went on during the proceedings, to what the women were wearing, to what the public were gossiping about in the gallery. Arbuckle's estranged wife arrived at the courthouse to support the comic and people were so incensed by her presence that it has been said she was abused and even shot at while entering the building.

The prosecutor during the trial was a man by the name of Matthew Brady who had great hopes and ambitions to become Governor of California and maybe even President later in his career. With that in mind, he went all out to try and prove that Arbuckle was not the sweet soul everyone thought him to be, but a monster, capable of rape and manslaughter in one foul swoop.

Tellingly, professional finger-pointer Maude Delmont was seen as such an unreliable witness that she did not take to the stand, but those who did made a good argument for Arbuckle's innocence. A doctor confirmed that Virginia Rappe had never mentioned that Roscoe had attacked her; a chambermaid at the hotel dispelled rumours of there being blood found on the bathroom door, while pathology experts were called to testify that Rappe's ruptured bladder was not caused by external events at all. In fact, it seemed pretty evident from their reports that it was the result of chronic inflammation coming from inside the body, not outside, which had caused the organ to burst.

Meanwhile, another doctor testified that Rappe had suffered from acute cystitis, while a friend was called to describe how the actress had often complained of severe abdominal pain over the course of their friendship. Then a Santa Ana saleslady threw light on Rappe's torn clothes by declaring that on three occasions she had witnessed Virginia tear to pieces items of clothing while in the throes of abdominal pain. A friend also described how once, during a party, Virginia had ripped off her stockings to give them to an admirer. The evidence given by the people who had witnessed such events was clear: Virginia Rappe was not a healthy girl, and she had certainly been known in the past to tear at her clothes when partying or in pain.

While listening intently to the evidence being piled up before him, Roscoe Arbuckle was nervously tearing paper into tiny little pieces. But finally it was time for him to take to the stand and, on hearing the news that he would be speaking that day, crowds gathered outside to such an extent that nobody could get into the building until the police cleared a pathway. Once on the stand he behaved in a calm, controlled and gentlemanly manner, while his estranged wife and mother-in-law both smiled and nodded their support to him from the gallery. His "performance" was impeccable; his delivery outstanding and even during what can only be described as a stressful and difficult cross-examination by the prosecution, he always remained composed and sure of every word that was coming from his mouth.

The actor told the prosecution how he had come into his bedroom to dress, locked the door for privacy and then discovered the sick woman crumpled on his bathroom floor. He then told how he went out to get help, and gave damning evidence against Maude Delmont when asked how he found Virginia Rappe when he returned to the room:

> Nude. Mrs Delmont had some ice in a towel. There was ice on the bed and a piece of ice on Miss Rappe's body. I picked the ice up from her body. I asked Mrs Delmont what the big idea was. She told me to put it back, that she knew how to care for Virginia, and ordered me out of the room. I told her to shut up or I would throw her out the window.

After a great deal of questioning, recess was called, after which time the ruptured bladder of poor Virginia Rappe was carried into the courtroom as evidence. The offending organ was gawped at by the entire room before the theory was presented that perhaps the women who had dunked the woman into a tub of cold water had caused the bladder to rupture. Then questions were raised about the possibility that it had burst during a violent vomiting episode, or by falling off the bed ... On and on it went, going round in circles with no obvious answer to any of the theories being presented.

After many days and much evidence had passed through the court, it was time for the case to be wrapped up, and Roscoe Arbuckle sat quietly, picking at the fluff on his coat, rolling his tie and squeezing his lip while the prosecution tried to convince everyone that he was guilty. In fact, so determined was the prosecution that they even twisted the evidence to back up their own theories, claiming that Roscoe had placed ice on Rappe's body, before telling her to shut up or he would throw her out of the window. This, of course, was a blatant lie – the ice had been placed there by Maude Delmont, and it was this woman who had been spoken to by Roscoe and told to "shut up".

Finally, they tried desperately to discredit every witness who dared take the stand in defence of Arbuckle, before resting their case and allowing the jury to go and make their deliberations. However, after forty-four hours of deliberation, the jury returned to the court and, on 4 December 1921, gave the news that they were deadlocked with a ten to two majority in favour of not guilty. Everyone was shocked, particularly when it was discovered that the woman who had initiated the deadlock was Mrs Hubbard, a woman who was married to a lawyer who frequently did business with the District Attorney's office. Not only that, the woman herself was a member of a feminist organization – the very likes of which had called for Arbuckle's films to be banned the moment he was arrested.

"I will vote guilty until hell freezes over," she is reported to have told the other members of the jury, refusing to listen to any information, reread transcripts or reconsider the evidence. Eventually another juror decided to join her in the call for a guilty verdict, and the entire trial was deadlocked and a mistrial declared.

Back at home, Roscoe tried to manage the hand he had been dealt and waited for the new trial to begin. Newspaper reporters were keen to hear his side of the story, and shortly after arriving back in Los Angeles he invited them into his home and shared his feelings on what had happened during the past few months:

> This case has put quite a crimp in my pocketbook. I resent the damage it has done me because I know I am a victim of circumstance. If I had had any connection with the

death of Virginia Rappe I would have said so, that is the kind of man I am. All of the dirt in this case was brought in by Mr Brady [the prosecutor]. The evidence consisted of what certain persons thought they knew – not what they were sure they knew – I have always tried to be a good scout and to treat people in the right way.

"Do you want to continue your career?" asked one reporter, to which a heavy-hearted Arbuckle replied:

I do not know whether or not I will ever appear in pictures again. Of course I want to. If the public wants to see me then I will go back to my work. If they don't I'll do something else. I won't act again unless the public shows that I will be well received. At present I have no position, no contract, and am not financially interested in any of my pictures released or awaiting release.

He then concluded with the words of an innocent man: "I have spent some very unhappy days, but my conscience is clear and my heart is clean. I have nothing to apologize for."

The second trial began on 11 January 1922 and took on the same routine as before, only this time the whole experience was an utter disaster. Arbuckle's team – for their own reasons – decided that their client would this time not take to the stand, and their whole defence seemed to lack any kind of energy and purpose. The, only shining light came when one of the party guests, Zey Prevost, decided that she could no longer remember ever saying that she had heard Virginia Rappe claim Arbuckle had hurt her. When presented with evidence of her first testimony she became hostile and bizarrely told the jury that she did not know if she had told the truth the last time she took to the stand. She then shocked everyone by presenting the bombshell that she had previously been arrested by the District Attorney and threatened with jail if she did not make a statement against Arbuckle.

This revelation brought claims of impeachment from the prosecution, claiming that Prevost was a hostile witness who was giving a "surprising" testimony. The motion was denied by the court but even this piece of startling information was not enough to help Arbuckle and when his team barely gave any kind of closing argument, some members of the jury took this to be a sign that the actor was guilty. True enough, after forty hours of deliberation they came back into court with a hung jury once again, but this time nine to three in favour of a guilty verdict. Roscoe was devastated and proceedings were brought for yet another trial, this time to begin on 13 March 1922.

Many lessons had been learned from the second trial, and when the third trial went ahead, this time things were very different. Roscoe was understandably wondering if he would ever be a free man again, and his defence team decided that they would be taking no chances; there would be no softly-softly approach and instead went full-steam ahead to prove his innocence.

Roscoe testified once again and special emphasis was made on showing that Virginia Rappe was not the healthy girl she had been made out to be in the previous trials, and instead had suffered from illness for quite some time. In this regard a new witness, a nurse by the name of Virginia Warren, was brought into the court to explain how she had attended to Rappe in Chicago when she had given birth to an illegitimate daughter some years before. This of course – rightly or wrongly – convinced the jury that the woman may not have been quite the innocent young girl they had been led to believe. Then another witness, Helen Madeline Whitehurst, took to the stand to explain how she had seen Rappe unwell on a number of occasions at her home in Chicago.

When the trial wrapped up, the jury took only six minutes to decide that Roscoe Arbuckle was an innocent man, wrongly accused of a crime he most certainly did not commit. In addition to that, they also made the unheard-of decision to issue an apology to the wronged man, signed by all of the jurors:

> We feel that a great injustice has been done him. We feel also that it was only our plain duty to give him this exoneration under the evidence, for there was not the slightest proof adduced to connect him in any way with the commission of a crime. He was manly throughout the case and told a straightforward story on the witness stand, which we all believed. The happening at the hotel was an unfortunate affair for which Arbuckle, so the evidence shows, was in no way responsible.
>
> We wish him success and hope that the American people will take the judgement of the men and women who have sat listening for thirty-one days to the evidence that Roscoe Arbuckle is entirely innocent and free from all blame.

Roscoe Arbuckle let out a long, relieved sigh and was deeply affected not only by the not-guilty verdict but also by the statement from the jury. He rose from his seat, shook hands with his team and then posed for photographs with the jurors; leaving the courthouse a free man. He then released a statement to the media which read:

> This is the most solemn moment of my life. My innocence of the hideous charges preferred against me has been proved by a jury of the best men and women of San Francisco – fourteen in all – rendering a verdict immediately after the trial. For this vindication I am truly grateful to God and my fellow men and women.
>
> My life has been devoted to the production of clean pictures for the happiness of children. I shall try to enlarge my field of usefulness so that my art shall have a wider service. It is the duty of all men to use the lessons that have been given them by experience and misfortune for the benefit of all, to make themselves more useful to humanity.

This I shall do. I can only repay the trust, confidence and loyalty bestowed upon me during my trouble by millions of men and women throughout the world by rendering service in justification of their faith.

Shortly after Arbuckle left with his estranged wife Minta to head back to Los Angeles. On the way they were met by many fans who threw their arms around the innocent actor and told him how much they adored him. Mothers even told Arbuckle that their children had been so concerned about his welfare that they had been forced to tell them he was sick but would return to the screen soon. Everyone wished him well and when the couple arrived back at Roscoe's West Adams home, the world's press were waiting for them.

Minta Durfee was quick to tell everyone just how relieved she was that her estranged husband had been acquitted and declared, "Though we have known each other since childhood and my mother has always been a mother to him too, still I think we never really knew each other until now."

Once inside the house, Roscoe Arbuckle had much to think about. The actor may have been cleared of the crime of which he had been so unfairly accused, but being hauled over the coals three times had taken its toll on his health and emotions. "His spontaneous laughter and kidding changed after the San Francisco trials," Minta later said, before adding that he was never again the happy-go-lucky person she had once known. Frequent requests by Durfee to encourage her estranged husband to write about his side of the story always went unheard.

Although remaining good friends, the couple had of course been separated for some years before the trial, and while it had looked hopeful that they would reconcile, they finally decided to separate for good, with Minta returning to New York, where she had lived for many years. At the time, Roscoe's manager denied that they had split and told the press that the two "are on the best of terms. Mrs Arbuckle simply went East with her sister on a pleasure trip. Do they still love each other? You ought to see the letters they still exchange! They're on happier terms now and understand each other better than ever before."

Actually while they may have been on good terms, the idea of them getting back together was a hopeful but naive one and the couple eventually divorced in Paris in 1925. After Arbuckle's death, Minta explained to reporters that their separation was not brought by a lack of love for each other, "but because of a clash of temperaments". She also added that her former husband was "a great artist, kind and generous and I will never forget my love for him".

Minta always believed that Arbuckle never got a "square deal" after the trial and she was right. Women's groups, church societies and other moral organizations began campaigning to ensure that the former star never worked in Hollywood again. The film industry was not keen on taking any chances on Arbuckle, aware that any kind of support would cause outrage among those organizations gunning for Roscoe. His films were banned and the broken man had to live with the fact that because of a crime he never committed, his career would never be the same again.

However, being in show business was all that the man had known since the age of eight when his mother encouraged him to take to the stage, and he was determined that he would not – could not – leave his career behind him completely. Almost all of his money had gone on his defence during the trials, and directly after his acquittal he ended up living as a guest in his former home, which he had sold to friend Joseph Schenck during the trial. A proud man, Arbuckle had no interest in living off other people and so decided to get himself together by embarking on a world trip in August 1922. Unfortunately, even this didn't go exactly to plan when he received a cut hand on the ship and had to undergo emergency treatment to prevent blood poisoning.

On his return to the States, Roscoe desperately wanted to make a living for himself in an attempt to recoup some of the money he had lost during the trial. He begged people to give him a chance and released a statement to the media, wishing to regain his former reputation. It read in part:

> No one ever saw a picture of mine that was not clean. No one ever saw a picture of mind that was not wholesome. No one ever will see such a picture. I claim the right of work and service. All I ask is the rights of an American citizen – American fair play. Through misfortune and tragic accident, I was tried on a charge of which I was absolutely innocent. A jury composed of eight men and four women all of whom were members of churches of the various faiths, found me innocent.

He then went on to quote from the original apology which the jurors had read in the courtroom, and added that unlike the jury, those denouncing his intentions to work had not heard any part of the evidence and were "without knowledge of the facts. The Scripture says that, 'As ye judge, so shall ye be judged.' How would my accusers like to be judged the way they are judging me?"

The statement went on at some length, though it was ultimately in vain, as church leaders and groups still continued to call for his films to be banned. But even this refusal to believe in his innocence did not stop Arbuckle from continuing with his career and he began directing under an assumed name, William Goodrich (and sometimes Will B. Good) and then travelling with a theatre group and entertaining in Chicago cafés. He undertook a variety of different stage roles, which earned him enough money to live on, and even appeared incognito in a film directed by his friend, Buster Keaton. However, it was apparent to everyone that the days of high finance and good living were far behind him, and even while undertaking these relatively low-key jobs, he still felt he had to be careful, very rarely revealing his name for fear of further disapproval from the masses.

He also had a second attempt at marriage, this time to a

woman called Doris Deane, whom he married in 1925. The pairing only lasted four years but during this time Arbuckle told his new wife that he expected to die young, just as he had predicted years earlier to Minta. "When I knew him he wasn't troubled with a heart ailment," Deane told reporters after her former husband's death, "[but] he always said his weight would cut off his years."

After the divorce from Doris in 1929, he lived three years as a single man before marrying a young woman called Addie McPhail in June 1932. Then by 1933 Roscoe saw something of a light at the end of the tunnel when he was given the opportunity to film a series of two-reel comedies for Warner Brothers. The actor was extremely excited and told reporters that being in films was like being home: "I can promise they'll be good, clean, wholesome pictures," he said. "Broad comedy with something for the children." Things were looking up both professionally and personally, though his health was giving some concern; he was still vastly overweight and had complained to Addie McPhail that he was suffering from some kind of heart ailment.

However, by June he was busy working in Long Island and on the 29th was celebrating not only the end to his latest comeback production, but also plans to do a vaudeville tour and celebrate his first wedding anniversary to Addie. "I've made my comeback," he told friends. "There are lots of stars not doing as well as I am right now." The actor was obviously in good spirits and dined out with his wife, before the two went to the apartment of their friend, William (Billy) LaHiff, who was hosting a party in their honour.

The evening was a success and later that night Arbuckle bid his wife goodnight and retired to bed. Shortly afterwards, around 2.15 a.m., she called to her husband from the next room to see if he was asleep. When no reply came the young woman went into the room and found her husband collapsed on the bed, the victim of a heart attack. Mrs Arbuckle became hysterical and summoned the doctor but it was too late to save the overweight entertainer; he had passed away at the age of just forty-six.

Arbuckle's body was taken to a church in New York where he lay in state until his funeral just a day after he passed away. The actor was cremated and his ashes scattered into the Pacific Ocean, while around the world tributes poured in for the once great star. Remembering how Roscoe always told her he would be dead before the age of fifty, first wife Minta Durfee emotionally told reporters, "I myself had a strange premonition of tragedy. He has been on my mind lately and on numerous occasions I have called other people by his first name."

Former friends and colleagues also expressed their shock, and Hollywood magnate Joseph Schenck summed up their feelings when he declared that everyone who ever knew the star, "will always treasure the memory of the great, generous heart of the man – a heart big enough to embrace in its warmth, everyone who came to him for help, stranger and friend alike".

Unfortunately it was this big heart, and a need to help others as he had never been helped in his own life, that led to the downfall of Roscoe Arbuckle. He had tried to assist a woman he believed to be in need, and instead of receiving praise, he only encountered hate, blame and a vast pointing of fingers. "I never did anything," he said just a year before his death. "I've got a clear conscience and a clean heart. They got all the money I had, and I ended up a quarter of a million dollars in debt." Arbuckle had lost everything because of the false accusations made against him but, in spite of that, the gentle giant never felt any hatred for what had happened to him. Instead, he did what only the strongest of people can do – got back up, dusted himself down and started again . . . and again . . . and again.

What is sad about the entire affair is not only the disgusting way Arbuckle was treated, but also that over the past ninety-plus years, Virginia Rappe, the girl who lost her life, has been interpreted as the "baddy" who caused all this trouble to happen to him. Her personal life and treatment of her body has been dragged through the mud, and while the way she lived is not to everyone's taste, that does not make her a villain.

Of course, had Rappe not died, then the trial and destruction of Arbuckle would never have happened, but that is hardly Virginia's fault. The real villain on that day in 1921 was, of course, Maude Delmont, who after being reprimanded by Roscoe for her behaviour during the party, saw an opportunity to make his life a living hell and grabbed it with open arms. Both Arbuckle and Rappe were the innocent parties; both just as used as each other in Delmont's wicked plan to get everything she could from what can only be described as a tragic, nightmare situation.

Perhaps Joseph Schenck said it best when he gave his tribute to Arbuckle after his death: "His was the tragedy of a man born to make the world laugh and to receive only suffering as his reward, and to the end he held no malice."

It is just a pity that the woman who pointed her finger in his direction had not done the same.

2

The Choy Ling Foo Dance Troupe

On 24 February 1923, an expectant audience at the Pantages Theater in Hollywood were waiting for the Choy Ling Foo troupe to make their entrance on stage. They were late appearing, and while the confused orchestra played their introduction over and over, little did they know that for some members of the Choy Ling Foo troupe the curtain would never rise again.

The five-strong troupe consisted of a fire-eater, a contortionist, a plate-spinner, a knife-thrower and – as described by the press – "one who hangs by his hair". Originating from China, the act had travelled around the world for seven years, entertaining audiences with their "mystic show", before finally settling in New York to concentrate in the United States.

One of the members of the troupe, Choy Den, was the fire-eater and dedicated boss of the show, while his cousin, Choy You Chung, was the contortionist. Choy Den was immensely proud of what they had achieved with the troupe, and spent hours refining the show and organizing rehearsals for himself and the others in the group. Choy You Chung, however, was getting tired of the constant travelling and entertaining, and wanted to leave the show completely. His cousin was not in the least bit impressed with this decision, however, and persuaded Choy You to carry on regardless, though as an act of rebellion he acquired a habit of not only being late to rehearsals but tardy in his entire approach to the show.

The unprofessionalism of Choy You was getting the entire troupe down, but as the boss, Choy Den felt that it was on his shoulders to take things in hand and he was frequently seen berating his cousin for the lack of concern he was showing for the others. Unfortunately, his demanding nature was to have tragic and dramatic consequences for Choy Den, as his cousin did not take kindly to being told what to do. He'd really had enough.

On the evening of 24 February, four members of the troupe went through their daily rehearsals before getting ready to take to the stage at Pantages. Choy You, however, was nowhere to be seen and his absence was noted by everyone but particularly Choy Den, who became more and more enraged as time wore on. As he had done before, the boss became frantic that as a result of the missed rehearsal, the show would suffer. To this end he sat on a trunk in the dressing room and complained bitterly to the other members about his cousin; he was not pulling his weight, he argued, and without every member putting in 100 per cent, how could they expect the audience to enjoy the performance?

The man complained for some time before Choy You finally arrived – unprepared, unrehearsed and in no mood to go onstage. Choy Den was incensed and immediately started lecturing him about the unprofessionalism he was showing not only to himself but to the other members of the troupe too. This time, however, their argument was different – more intense – and as it became heated, Choy Den accused his cousin of threatening to ruin their show with his constant lateness and refusal to take part in rehearsals.

The fight grew so bitter that it spilled out of the dressing room and into the passage beneath the stage, completely unknown to the audience who were still waiting in the auditorium, flicking through their souvenir programmes and wondering when the show was going to start. The shouting then became so heated that the other troupe members decided to take cover, knowing how infuriated Choy Den was with his cousin. They were not wrong, and as the argument continued to escalate, the furious man suddenly reached into his pocket, pulled out a revolver and shot Choy You straight through the heart.

Everyone around him could not believe what they had just witnessed, but before anyone could do anything about it, Choy Den shocked everyone by turning the gun on himself and shooting a bullet through his head. Astonishingly, the shot did not kill him straight away; instead, it caused him to lose consciousness. It took several days for the man finally to die from his injuries.

To say the other members were disturbed by the evening's events would be an understatement. The auditorium was immediately emptied and people spilled on to the pavements, wondering what on earth had happened, whispering to each other about the gunshots and wondering what had caused the screams and shouts they could not help but overhear. Rumours were rife but nobody knew exactly what had gone on until they read about it in the newspapers several days later, undoubtedly creating a great deal of discussion and intrigue at the breakfast tables of those who had witnessed the evening's proceedings.

It was never discovered if the shooting had been a heat-of-the-moment decision by Choy Den, or something he had planned as he sat fizzing in the theatre dressing room that evening. Had he taken the gun with him especially to shoot his cousin, or did he always carry the firearm and it was just sheer rage that had caused him to pull the trigger? We will never know, but certainly it would seem that both men had been pushed to the limit; both wanting different things from their careers and neither knowing precisely how to change the situation – until the heated argument had ended all sensible thoughts.

The remaining members of the troupe decided – not surprisingly – to cancel their shows and made plans to return home to China. However, various members of their entourage put a stop to these plans by telling them that it would be against their principles and culture to just give up on all they had achieved. Regardless of how they felt, the members were then told to release a statement which said they had undergone a change of heart and would go on without Choy You and Choy Den after all.

Meanwhile, at the family home in New York, Choy You's parents received a telegraph about the tragedy and refused point blank to believe he was dead. "Are we then fools to place our faith in the mutterings of a devil that speaks through a thin wire?" they asked, before adding that if it was true that their son was dead, they would have to see the body to confirm it for themselves.

As requested, the body was taken to New York, accompanied by a representative of the Choy Ling Foo troupe who announced his intention to search for Choy You's nearest heir. If an heir was found, he declared, he would immediately be conscripted into the troupe, regardless of his feelings on the subject. From California the remaining troupe made the bizarre decision to announce it was the heir's hereditary right to take over, regardless of opinion, desire or ability.

This was, of course, a strangely ironic decision, especially as the reason for the death of the original members had been because of Choy You's less than enthusiastic longing to be part of the show. The troupe seems to have disappeared shortly after the scandal that took over their show in 1923 and, unfortunately, it is not known whether the heir – willingly or otherwise – was ever roped in to their floundering show.

3

The Life and Death of Norman "Kid McCoy" Selby

Some Hollywood scandals involve full-time actors and actresses, while others involve those who have become famous in another area, only to find Hollywood stardom later in their lives. This is the case with our next scandal, focusing on Norman Selby, the boxer who had almost as many wives as boxing championships.

Norman Selby was born in Moscow, Indiana, on 13 October 1872, and went on to become an American world champion boxer. Winning no less than eighty-one times with fifty-five knockouts, he became a legendary middleweight fighter before turning his attention to acting, appearing in a variety of films during the early days of Hollywood.

However, his life out of the ring was far more colourful than the one he had in it, and Selby became something of a joke in the newspapers with his serial marriages. By 1920 he had been married seven times to five different women and was about to marry Carmen Browder (aka Dagmar Dahlgren), which would make it eight times. The newspapers tagged him the "Undisputed marrying champion of America", although he himself was adamant that his latest adventure would be the last time down the aisle. "I've been at it since 1895," he told reporters. "I feel entitled to retire from active marrying, although of course, I shall always retain an interest in the game." His reason for divorcing was, he joked, because he kept forgetting his wedding anniversary.

He married Browder on 19 April 1920 and by 5 September that year she had filed for divorce. According to the twenty-year-old dancer, her forty-seven-year-old husband had treated her with extreme cruelty; was abusive and violent; and had stayed out all night just three days after the wedding. During divorce proceedings, Browder's friend Frances Le Berthon said she had seen scars on the dancer's body; a result, she said, of spurning Selby's "excessive love-making". The disturbing story was that the two had lived as man and wife for just two weeks before Browder woke one night to find Selby forcing himself on to her. When she refused he threw his wife out of bed and hit her.

When Browder told the court that she believed Selby when he told her he wanted a "real girl he could love", Judge Jackson could not believe his ears. After seven previous marriages, did she not suspect there must be something wrong with him? "No I did not," replied Browder.

"Do you still believe he wanted a real girl to love?" he asked, to which Browder – not surprisingly – shook her head and said a simple, "No." The judge then granted the decree, but not before expressing his doubts about the serial marriage habit of Selby: "This man will get another wife if I grant the decree. This girl might as well act as a buffer for the rest of the community," he told the court.

He was almost right. In September 1922 Selby announced his intention to marry twenty-four-year-old Jacqueline MacDowell, who travelled to Los Angeles specifically to marry the "undisputed male vamp" as the newspapers were now calling him. After much hilarity while being turned down for a marriage licence due to the absence of the bride-to-be, the two were eventually granted permission to marry and posed happily for cameramen. Fortunately for MacDowell, however, she discovered Selby had been seeing another woman just days before the wedding, freeing her from a union almost certain to fail.

He spent the next few years in and out of the newspapers,

filing for bankruptcy and having several brushes with the law, including being investigated by police for firing a gun in the bathroom of his apartment on South Carondelet Street, Los Angeles. However, in August 1924 his scandalous life came to a head when he became the prime suspect in the murder of his married girlfriend, Teresa Mors.

Living as Mr and Mrs Shields, Norman and Teresa stayed together in an apartment at 2819 Leeward Avenue, where Selby told friends that he loved his girlfriend more than he had ever loved any woman before. However, the affair was not a quiet one, and although Mors was in the process of divorcing her husband, there were numerous fights about an antique shop they both shared.

The relationship between Mors and Selby was volatile. Mors' friend Ann Schapp, who owned the shop next door to the antique store, tried to persuade Teresa to leave the violent boxer on more than one occasion. However, this did not prove to be a sensible thing to do, as on one particular evening Selby approached Schapp and insulted her. It became clear to both Schapp and her husband that Selby somehow knew all about their talks with Mors about leaving the relationship, and they opted to be on their guard from that point on.

On 12 August, things took a disastrous turn when Teresa Mors was found shot dead in her and Selby's apartment. Determined not to be blamed for the death, Selby insisted that he had wanted to marry the woman and that he would never be happy without her. He told police that they had been for a drive and then returned home, where Mors became downhearted over trouble with the antique shop. According to Selby, she suddenly declared she was going to end it all, grabbed a knife and tried stabbing herself with it. When that did not work she took out a revolver, and despite his attempts to stop her, she committed suicide right there in front of him. Quite bizarrely, Selby then said he covered her with a blanket, washed up the dishes and headed out to kill Albert Mors, Teresa's estranged husband.

In a violent rage, Selby reached Mr Mors' home, where he was told by the maid that he was not in residence that evening. He left, travelled around hotels in a vain attempt at finding him, and then in the early morning went to the antiques shop to confront his rival. But Mr Mors was not present at the store, and instead Selby encountered a shop full of customers and staff; robbed them all and forced some of the men to remove their trousers so that they could not escape. One gentleman who tried to leave was shot by Shelby, before he turned his attention to Mr and Mrs Schapp, the couple who owned the shop next door.

Police questioned why he would do such a thing as hold up a shop full of customers and then shoot the neighbours, while Selby tried to convince them that it was all done to avenge his girlfriend's death. "My lights went out when I saw Teresa dead at my feet," he said. Police descended on his apartment, where they found the place in utter disarray; a copy of his will was on the table, along with liquor bottles. It did not take them long to decide that Selby had been the one to kill his girlfriend. They also believed he had left the will on the table as he intended to kill himself after he had shot Teresa's estranged husband, Mr Mors. "If I had caught him at home I would have killed him and then killed myself," he admitted to officers.

"There is no doubt in our minds that McCoy killed [Teresa] Mors," stated police. There were some doubts in the jury's minds, however, and after seeing Selby demonstrate a dramatic re-enactment of his girlfriend's last moments, as well as a surprise appearance by ex-wife Dagmar Dahlgren, they remained split between first degree murder and acquittal.

Finally, Selby was convicted of manslaughter and stayed in prison until 1932. When he left, he spoke to reporters. "I'm through with the prize ring, the matrimonial ring, and the ring of ice in glasses," he told them, before leaving for Michigan and a job with the Ford Motor Company.

He was not quite finished with women, however, as he married Sue Cobb Cowley in 1937. Unfortunately the new start he had hoped for in Michigan was never a peaceful one and eventually, on 18 April 1940, he decided to end his life in the Hotel Tuller in Detroit. Before taking a fatal overdose, he sat down to write a short note: "To all my dear friends, I wish you the best of luck. I'm sorry I could not endure this world's madness." He then signed it with the simple words, "My very best to you all, Norman Selby."

4

Lucille Ricksen, the Adult Child Star

While it is always sad when someone dies young, no matter who they are, the tale of Lucille Ricksen is particularly distressing, especially as at the time of her death she had barely reached puberty. However, she had been acting as an adult for some years prior to her passing. Hollywood is a land of make-believe – of fairy tales and glamour – but for Lucille Ricksen it was the stuff of nightmares, and it ultimately broke up her family and cost her life.

Born as Ingeborg Ericksen in Chicago, Illinois, on 22 August, her actual birth year is something of a mystery, but is most likely 1910. Almost from the day she was born, Lucille (as she became known) was working in the industry, first as a baby model and then, aged five, as an actress. Rather disturbingly, however, while some of the photographs she posed for were "cute" and show the smiling Lucille sporting ringlets in her hair, others are slightly less appealing. For instance, in one photograph of the child aged about five, she is seen posing provocatively next to a window, a lace scarf being the only thing covering her tiny body. How or why this disturbing photograph was ever taken is something of a mystery but it certainly shows the shape of things to come as she got older and moved into her movie career.

By the time the child was eight years old, the pressures of running Lucille's career and a home were becoming extremely tiring for her mother, also called Ingeborg. Normally one would expect that if the child's career was getting in the way of family life, the mother would perhaps scale down the amount of work she had, but not Ingeborg. She was one of the first real showbiz mothers, and instead of taking her daughter away from the camera, she decided that the best thing to do would be to divorce her husband, leave Chicago and move herself and her two children to the bright lights of Hollywood where she planned for Lucille to be more successful and even busier than ever before.

It is not known if Lucille was happy with this situation, but we do know that once in the city, the young girl's career took off in a big way. Her name was changed to Lucille Ricksen and she was chosen by producer Samuel Goldwyn to appear in a series of comedy shorts with titles such as *Edgar's Hamlet*, *Edgar Camps Out* and *Edgar, the Explorer*. These films ran from 1920 to 1921 before there then came the chance not only to act in a feature, but also to work alongside her brother Marshall when she was cast in *The Old Nest*, a film based on a story written by Rupert Hughes, the uncle of Howard Hughes.

Lucille impressed everyone with whom she worked. She had the opportunity of not only working with Rupert again several years later, but also becoming extremely good friends too. She was also a hit with movie fans and would often tour the country, chatting to children, appearing in theatres and attending celebrity events. The child seemed to enjoy the attention and the work, and as a result recorded her news meticulously in her scrapbook whenever she had a spare moment. She was living a lovely, fairytale dream; yes, she was busy and her childhood was not like that of other children, but she was having fun with it anyway. For a while . . .

As Lucille turned twelve, her work on camera began to change and the studio altered her image from that of a cutie-pie, ringlet-wearing kid to a sophisticated adult player, before casting her in films such as *Human Wreckage* (1923), a film about drug addiction, as well as allowing her to play the "sweetheart" role in *The Judgment of the Storm* (1923). In

February 1923, the *Covington Republic* newspaper called Lucille "The youngest leading lady on the screen", and described her as having big brown eyes and a wealth of blonde hair. They even printed her real age – twelve – but this would not last for long. In an attempt to make it more acceptable that she was now being offered grown-up roles, the studio had to make her a fully fledged "woman" and, before she knew it, they were saying that she was sixteen years old, when in actual fact she was still four years younger.

Disturbingly, the studio did not seem to see anything wrong with this, and would often cast her as the "devoted but excessively jealous young wife" alongside much older stars. In one particular film she was even cast as a young woman who is beaten up and generally abused by her bully of a husband; while on the cover of *Picture Play* magazine, she appeared wearing a large hat, with her bare shoulder, arm and some of her back visible. The wrong signals were clearly being given out and with so many fully fledged adult actresses and models around there was, of course, absolutely no need to use a child in a grown-up role. The reason the studio insisted on doing so remains a mystery, and it is equally concerning that it appears that at no time did her mother step in and tell the studios that Lucille was far too young for such dramatic roles.

The leap from child actress to adult at the age of just twelve very definitely had a lasting effect on Lucille Ricksen and it is clear that the types of parts being given to her only succeeded in priming the vulnerable young girl for all manner of disturbing real-life situations. It is interesting to note that at this point in time, Lucille stopped carefully cutting out and lovingly presenting her newspaper clippings, and now began tearing the pages out and just throwing them into the scrapbooks. Something had changed both on and off the camera, and for young Lucille Ricksen the glamour had ceased and her life would never be the same again.

If anyone had the least bit of concern for the child actress, nobody seems to have come forward to say so, and the adult roles and scripts continued to arrive at her door. Tragically the young girl seemed to develop a succession of crushes on her co-stars during this time, which – it has been said – were possibly even reciprocated, although the actors in question knew that Lucille was not yet past the age of consent. A case in point is an announcement in the pages of *Billboard* which said that Lucille had married actor Sydney Chaplin in the autumn of 1923. This seems absurd considering her age and there is no absolute proof that it happened, especially considering that no official comment was ever made about the "marriage" and, after the announcement, there was never any mention of it again.

Still, *Billboard* must have had some reason to believe that the thirteen-year-old actress was marrying thirty-eight-year-old Chaplin. The two must surely have been close enough for people to think they could have been an item, and Lucille herself once told an interviewer that while working together, they had a "perfectly screaming time".

By the time 1924 arrived, the child actress was being put into one film after another, and working long, hard hours at the studio. After completing no fewer than ten films in seven months, she was absolutely exhausted and in desperate need of a rest, but still Hollywood called and insisted she work. Sadly, this was the beginning of the end for Lucille Ricksen, whose young body could handle no more of the gruelling schedule that had been thrust upon her since almost the day she was born. As a result of exhaustion, the poor girl collapsed and was confined to bed at home, where her concerned mother kept a vigil and vowed to keep the studio and newspapers away from her daughter until she was better. It was too little, too late, however, and her condition just got worse and worse. The story of her breakdown was eventually leaked and it fell to her doctor, J. F. McKitrick, to announce exactly what he believed to be wrong with the child:

> She crowded too much work into too short a time, and
> overtaxed her capacities ... The result is that she has had
> a complete physical and nervous collapse – so complete
> that she has not rallied from it as she should.

Lying in her bedroom – or as she called it, her "sunshine room", Lucille enjoyed receiving visitors such as her brother Marshall and the actress Lois Wilson. "Please won't you all be so happy," she told them, "I know I will be well soon."

Unfortunately the child just grew worse and worse, and in February 1925 things took a tragic turn when her mother suddenly collapsed in Lucille's bedroom, dying in front of the stunned child and her brother Marshall. The shock of this tragic event was too much for the child to bear, and several days later she sank into a coma, from which she sadly never recovered.

With their father not living with the children, and their mother now passed away, it was decided that family friends, actor Conrad Nagel and producer and author Rupert Hughes, would become the children's guardians. However, this arrangement was not to last long, as sadly on 13 March 1925 Lucille Ricksen passed away, a victim – according to the newspapers – of a broken heart. Her death certificate stated that the girl died of pulmonary tuberculosis though sadly this has not stopped disturbing rumours that her breakdown, illness and death were all really the results of a botched abortion undertaken shortly before her initial collapse.

Of course, no newspaper reported such a thing at the time, and instead they were full of articles and tributes from many of Lucille's co-stars and friends. Lois Wilson led the way by claiming that she had "never known anyone so full of joy", while many others described her as a sweet-natured girl who gave happiness to everyone she met.

Flowers flooded into the home, and a simple but impressive funeral was planned at the Gates, Crane and Earl Chapel, where Lucille's memorial was to take place. On the day of the funeral itself, the venue was full of celebrities who had known or worked with Lucille Ricksen. Flowers from Mary Pickford, Sydney Chaplin, Rupert Hughes and Lois Wilson surrounded the coffin, while many more lay in anonymous tribute around the church. In accordance with her wishes, Lucille Ricksen's body was cremated, and then both her ashes and those of her mother were interred at Forest Lawn Memorial Park, where many other stars would be laid to rest in the years to come.

Just days later came the news that while still only a teenager, Lucille Ricksen had left an estate of $50,000 in the form of life insurance and $10,000 from personal property. This shocked everyone as she was relatively poor at the time of her death and, in fact, Hollywood producer Paul Bern had stepped in to pay for her nursing care for quite some time. Tragically it would seem that the child was now worth more in death than she had been in life, and her father Samuel was set to inherit it all.

Although she had not lived with him since she was eight years old, Samuel Ericksen had recently moved to Los Angeles – presumably to be close to his children. After losing firstly his ex-wife and then Lucille, the man had had enough of the so-called bright lights of Hollywood and was now intent on gaining back custody of his eighteen-year-old son, Marshall, who was still under the care of Rupert Hughes and Conrad Nagel. Samuel greatly distrusted the two men and made it clear to Marshall that he wanted him to give up his own acting career and concentrate on his education instead. To that end he decided to use the majority of his inheritance from Lucille for the education of his son, but first he would have to win him back.

To help in his quest, he hired a lawyer, Griffith Jones, who told reporters that Samuel Ericksen had objected to his children being associated with older people within the movie industry, and had "proved himself to be an extremely kind and loving parent and intensely interested in the welfare of the children". Both Hughes and Nagel were surprised at these developments, and Hughes released a statement to explain why they had stepped forward as guardians in the first place.

It read in part, "Mr Nagel and I were named in the petition with the full consent of the father. We were actuated by sympathy and a wish to help the children in their difficulties. I have had no information that Mr Ericksen desired to enter a protest to our guardianship."

But protest he did, citing the fact that the guardianship had never been legally sworn as Lucille had passed before it could be heard. The custody case for Marshall Ricksen went to court on 16 April 1925, with Samuel Ericksen's main charge being that Rupert Hughes could not be a suitable guardian, since he had recently written a piece entitled "Why I Quit going to Church". In the article Hughes had said that anyone who believed in the Bible had either never read it or was actually lying; Ericksen took great offence at this, stating that Hughes must obviously be an atheist and therefore an unsuitable candidate for looking after a teenage boy.

However, he did not bank on a revelation from Hughes himself, who told the court that before Lucille's death both she and Marshall had summoned him to their home and begged him and Nagel to take charge of their affairs in order to protect them from their father. Ericksen was obviously shocked to hear such a thing, but it was enough to swing the vote in Hughes's favour, and Judge J. Perry Wood gave him and Nagel joint custody of Marshall Ricksen.

During the coming years, the boy was given emotional support from the two men and he went on to attend university and later became a lawyer. He never spoke about his early life in Hollywood or his sister – the memories of both being far too raw in his mind. His father Samuel, meanwhile, tragically passed away on 25 April 1928, just over three years after his ex-wife and daughter.

Described by the *Los Angeles Times* as having an "enthusiasm as strong as her frame was slight", Lucille Ricksen gave everything to her career and lost her life and family to the trappings of Hollywood. She was perhaps the first example of the tragic consequences of putting a child into the limelight, but she most certainly was not the last. The exact circumstances surrounding her death will never be known, but one thing is for sure, if she had just been allowed to be a child instead of an adult at the age of twelve, her short life would have inevitably been far happier.

5

The "Almost Perfect" Murder

As covered in the first chapter, in 1921, Roscoe "Fatty" Arbuckle was accused of raping and killing a young actress called Virginia Rappe at one of his infamous parties. The court case that followed is still talked about nearly a hundred years later, yet another huge Hollywood court case that took place just six years later has long since been forgotten. Until now.

In 1927, Paul Kelly was an up-and-coming actor, described by the media as "dashing" and "debonair". Born on 9 August 1899 in Brooklyn, his career began as a child actor aged seven, and he quickly became a big star at the Vitagraph Studios. Unlike many actors since then, Kelly made the transition from child actor to leading man very successfully and went on to star on the New York stage in plays such as *Seventeen* and *Whispering Wires*. Still, as a result of his looks and talent, Hollywood came knocking on his door and it was not long before he was working at Paramount, making something of a splash in *The New Klondike* (1926) and *Special Delivery* (1927).

By March 1927, the gossip columnists were announcing the news that the hot young actor was destined for huge success and that Warner Brothers were anxious to sign him for their next picture. He was about to become one of the biggest stars in Hollywood, but sadly nobody could have predicted just what atrocities were going to happen next . . .

Ray Raymond was a stage actor and singer, who by 1927 had been married to actress Dorothy Mackaye for seven years, having met her in New York when they were both appearing in a production called *Blue Eyes*. Together they lived and worked in New York and Hollywood, and welcomed the arrival of their daughter Valeria who by 1927 was four years old. However, by all accounts the marriage was not a happy one, and this was confirmed by Mackaye herself who later declared: "I know it's not right for me to say, but he was unkind to me. He was always accusing me about Paul Kelly, but his accusations were untrue."

The accusations involving the actor stemmed from a friendship they had began in New York long before Dorothy had met Raymond. The two had kept in touch for many years, but while she claimed it was purely platonic, Raymond was convinced she was having a passionate affair and forbade his wife from seeing the actor any more. He was shocked by her response, however, when not only did Dorothy refuse to give up her friendship, but also blatantly continued seeing him in the full knowledge of her husband. "Paul was my friend," she later told police. "Our friendship was so clean, lovely and beautiful that I didn't want to give him up."

This refusal to cool her association with Kelly (which she described as "a sort of sisterly love") did not go down well with Raymond, particularly when it was rumoured that the actor had asked Dorothy to divorce her husband and marry him instead. Mackaye later laughed off the whispers by declaring that if there had been any talk of marriage with Kelly, it was purely a joke, although she did admit that her marriage to Raymond had been under strain but that they had been unable to divorce because of financial problems.

While Dorothy dismissed any marriage talk between Kelly and herself as a joke, Ray Raymond did not see the funny side. Once again he told Dorothy that under no circumstances must she ever see him again, though in the end this seems to have been a great mistake, because instead of deterring her, it only succeeded in making Mackaye even more determined to keep the relationship going. If she enjoyed humiliating her stressed husband in a very public way, she was certainly making a good job of it.

Although Dorothy later claimed that she and Kelly would always have chaperones when together, it was obvious to everyone that the two were spending more than enough time alone, going on motorcycle rides together, visiting his apartment and attending parties. One of the said parties was actually at her marital home on Holly Drive, where Raymond became so angry to see Paul Kelly there that he threw him out in front of the other guests. "He took a violent dislike to Kelly from the start . . . He was so silly, ridiculous and absurd about our friendship, and insanely jealous," Mackaye later said.

Raymond obviously had a temper and a drink problem to go with it – Mackaye's flaunting her "friendship" with Kelly was like playing with fire. "He wasn't in his right mind," Dorothy later said, which made her decision to keep the relationship with Kelly going in such a high-profile way even more questionable. But go on she did, and several months before the fateful last encounter between the two men, Paul Kelly was at the house when Raymond unexpectedly came home. Disturbed and furious to find his love rival sitting in his own living room, the upset man took no time in throwing out the young actor once again.

"I know exactly what your problem is," Kelly shouted at his rival as he hit the sidewalk. "You think I'm in love with your wife."

"That is exactly the reason," replied an angry Raymond, to which Kelly boldly said: "Well, you're exactly right."

This information did not sit well with Raymond, though at this point Dorothy was still denying to everyone that the pair were anything but good friends. Still, Raymond and his wife continued to live together and even moved house, this time to 2261 Cheremoya Avenue, Los Angeles, before Raymond went on tour with his play, *Castles in the Air*. This, of course, left Dorothy free to conduct her "friendship" with Kelly and the family maid later said that the actor was often at the house during parties and on his own in the company of Mackaye.

Whether or not Raymond knew anything about these get-togethers is not known but what is certain is that at the time he returned to Hollywood on 15 April 1927, he was still convinced his wife was in love with Paul Kelly and had begun to share his suspicions with friends. On the afternoon of his coming back from tour, there was an obvious strain between the couple and Raymond was in no mood for talking. Instead, he spent time drinking heavily before dramatically breaking a glass over his head, cutting his scalp in the process. He then left the house in a state of despair.

The next day, Dorothy Mackaye visited Paul Kelly and apparently told him that his love rival was spreading rumours about their affair all over town. Furious, Kelly telephoned Raymond to demand if it was true.

"I understand you have been saying things about me," he said.

"You're damn right I have and I wish you were here now so that I could give you what you deserve," Raymond screamed into the telephone.

"I'll be right over," Kelly boldly told him. Leaving Dorothy in his apartment, Paul Kelly arrived at the Cheremoya house around 7 p.m. Once there, he was greeted by the family maid, Ethel Lee, and asked her to go and get Raymond so that they could talk. The concerned maid immediately smelled trouble and relayed a message that if he wanted to see Raymond, he must enter the home himself, which Kelly did. He sat down next to the man in the dining room in order to have it out with him once and for all.

"What do you mean by talking about me?" Kelly asked, to which Raymond replied once again that he knew the actor had feelings for his wife. In scenes that could have come straight from a 1920s movie, the six-foot tall Kelly then punched Raymond on the jaw before challenging him to a fight. The smaller man refused the offer, saying, "No, I have just spent twenty-four hours on a train and I'm tired out. I'm in no condition to fight."

"You're not tired, just yellow clear through," replied Kelly, before Raymond then changed the subject and began questioning the actor on the whereabouts of Dorothy Mackaye. The official line was that the actress was out shopping for Easter eggs and visiting her dressmaker, but Raymond was in no position to believe this.

"I don't know where she is," lied Kelly.

"Yes, you do," answered Raymond, and at this point Kelly leaned over and struck the singer on the jaw once again. He then calmly got up and went to the kitchen where he proceeded to ask the maid for a cigarette. Raymond followed him, screaming, "I'll get you! I'll get you!" before Kelly turned and hit him several times.

According to the maid, Ethel, Raymond begged Kelly to stop, saying that he was a sick man and wasn't fit to fight as he had been drinking.

"That's just your alibi," shouted the actor and, according to Ethel, it was at this point that Paul Kelly really started to beat his rival severely, knocking him down several times in the process. "Mr Raymond got up and Kelly grabbed him and put one hand behind his neck and beat him with the other," the maid later explained. "He then threw him on the couch and he fell to the floor."

Watching from the door was Raymond's four-year-old daughter Valeria, who shouted for her dad to come to her. "Poor little Valeria wept and wept," the maid later told police. "The poor little thing was frightened to death by the noise."

Despite being totally aware that there was a child in the house, Kelly continued the beating and he ignored Ethel's cries for him to stop. "Raymond's face was cut and bleeding," the maid later described. While Mackaye's husband did try desperately to fight back he was no match for the younger Paul Kelly and finally, after taking a blow to his left eye, the singer fell on to a table, while Kelly hit him again and again until he was forced to the floor. Once there, the ailing man put both hands to his bloodied face.

"Oh my God!" he sighed, as Ethel finally told Kelly to leave.

"You have done enough," she said. "Go on home, this is his house."

Kelly shook his head and then quite bizarrely told the maid that he hadn't believed it to be Raymond's house. It was only after Ethel explained that Raymond was the one paying the rent that Kelly seemed to pull himself together and apologized to his adversary.

"Will you shake hands with me, Ray?" Kelly asked. The singer understandably refused and ordered him out of the house. "I turned around and took my hat and got in the car and went home," Kelly later said.

The shocked maid helped her boss up and took him to the bathroom where she put a wet towel on his head and tried to stop the bleeding. Meanwhile, Kelly went back to his apartment, although it is claimed that Dorothy had left by then. She arrived back at her own house around 9 p.m., accompanied by her friend, Helen Wilkinson. By this time Ray Raymond was wearing dark glasses and tried to brush off the whole, humiliating episode, but the same cannot be said for four-year-old Valeria, who was visibly upset by the scene she had witnessed that afternoon. "I picked her up and comforted her," Dorothy later told the court.

Dorothy stayed at the house for an hour or so before heading back out to see Paul Kelly and get his version of what had gone on that afternoon. She returned at midnight to find that Valeria had cried herself to sleep and Raymond was still in great pain from his beating. He eventually went to bed at 1 a.m. but by 3 a.m. he was up and, according to Ethel Lee, he seemed disorientated, "as he didn't seem able to see and had his hands out as though he were feeling his way".

Then by 7 a.m. the next morning, the severity of Raymond's injuries were becoming more pronounced when he collapsed on the bedroom floor and bent double with the pain before finally falling into a coma. Dorothy was witness to this disturbing scene and screamed for Ethel, who came running into the room and was shocked by what she found.

There was Raymond, lying on the floor, frothing at the mouth and shaking all over. The maid tried desperately to wake him up but it was no use. "I knew he was unconscious," she later said, and she helped Dorothy put him back on to the bed before running to call a doctor.

When Dr W. J. Sullivan eventually came to the house, he saw straight away that the man was in a serious condition.

"What happened to him?" he asked Dorothy.

"He's been drinking heavily and was in a fight."

"With who?" asked the doctor.

"I don't know," lied Dorothy.

The actress requested that Dr Sullivan look after the patient at home, but he could see that this was not a possibility. Despite Mackaye's protests, Ray Raymond was taken to hospital where it was hoped he would eventually recover. According to Dorothy, later that day she visited Paul Kelly at his apartment on North Gower Street in order to "bawl him out" over the beating he had given her husband.

"He said he was terribly, terribly sorry. I told him that could not make amends, that he shouldn't be so hot-tempered." Interestingly, when later questioned by the court, Paul Kelly denied all knowledge of having any visits from Mackaye after the fight, and maid Ethel Lee further confused proceedings by claiming that Kelly had actually visited the Raymond household after the singer had been taken to hospital. There, according to Ethel, Kelly, Mackaye and Helen Wilkinson all had dinner together.

Meanwhile, Ray Raymond's condition became worse and worse until finally, on 19 April, the singer sadly passed away. It was at this point that things became even hazier than they already were. Despite Raymond being beaten to a pulp, his doctor, Dr W. J. Sullivan, quickly declared that the death was natural, caused by "nephritic coma as a condition of neuritis". Dorothy Mackaye was right there to uphold his decision, saying

"I have absolute faith in Dr Sullivan's statement that Ray's death was due to natural causes. He hadn't been well for some time and we had been afraid of a nervous breakdown." A funeral was quickly arranged and things were all going rather smoothly until Coroner Nance got wind that something was going on.

Up until that point, Nance had no idea that the singer had even died, and it was not until newspaper reporters began knocking on his door that he eventually found out. Not happy with the decision that the death was "natural", Nance ordered the body to be removed from the undertakers immediately, and an autopsy was performed which revealed that Raymond had actually died as a result of a brain haemorrhage.

The police then heard that Kelly had fought with the singer shortly before his death, and so travelled to his home in order to arrest the actor on suspicion of causing Raymond's death. The previously tough man actually swooned on being told of his arrest, before being hauled off to face questioning and being held on suspicion of murdering his love rival. Strangely, Kelly then stifled a sob before smiling and telling officers, "Gee, I hope I can have somebody come and visit me. This is the first time I've ever been in the jug."

This attitude did not impress officers, who were sure the death was unnecessary and had been caused by a cad who was trying to seduce an innocent man's wife. Meanwhile, an inquest began which did not go well for Dorothy when she claimed that under no circumstances did four-year-old Valeria see the fight, before bizarrely adding – as if to make everything okay – that in any case, the child had always been keener on her than on Raymond.

This won the woman no fans, especially when Ethel Lee stood up to tell the court that, "The baby was crazy about her father. I have never seen a more beautiful affection between father and child." The maid also said that her boss had been a punching bag for the much stronger Kelly and disputed Dorothy's claims that the child had not seen the beating. She told the court that Valeria had said, "Kelly's a bad man to hit my daddy," and broke her heart crying for at least an hour afterwards.

Dorothy Mackaye tried to repair the damage by sending a telegram to her mother-in-law, Lottie Cedarbloom, offering to fly her from New York to Hollywood for the funeral. However, this ultimately backfired when reporters became inspired to track down not only Mackaye's mother-in-law, but also Matt Kelly, Paul's brother, who just happened to be a police lieutenant based at the Forty-First Precinct in Brooklyn. He told reporters that Kelly had always been a wild kid, while Cedarbloom declared that she just could not understand anything about the episode at all. "Dorothy and Ray were always so happy . . . I never heard of this Paul Kelly; they never mentioned him here."

Meanwhile, the newspaper columnists showed no concern for either Kelly or Mackaye and proceeded to tear them to pieces, much to the embarrassment of both. They were amused that while Paul had declared Raymond "yellow" when he wouldn't fight, he had cried like a baby and collapsed when locked in a cell; they also poked fun at Mackaye for saving a fainting spell until she just happened to be in front of the world's press.

The inquest into the passing of Ray Raymond was quickly wrapped up, and the reason for his death explained as hypostatic pneumonia following an extensive brain haemorrhage with acute alcoholism being a contributory factor. The overall conclusion was that Paul Kelly was most certainly responsible for the man's death: "This is the most brutal [murder] that has ever come under my notice as Coroner of Los Angeles county," Coroner Nance told reporters. "The evidence shows that Kelly is devoid of all sense of decency and ethics."

Another interesting development came when Nance added, "I am also informed that Mrs Raymond was in Kelly's apartment when he left his home for the purpose of going to her home to beat up Raymond," before adding that it was his belief that she had influenced Kelly's decision to beat up her ailing husband. Not only that, but he also added his belief that despite claims to the contrary, when Kelly had returned to his apartment after the fatal beating, the besotted Mackaye had been waiting for him.

Questions arose about the credibility of Raymond's doctor, W. J. Sullivan, who had attended the patient and declared his death "natural" despite the fact that the man had quite obviously sustained a terrible attack. The coroner was keen to know if Dorothy had promised to pay him well if he could ensure there was no publicity surrounding the death.

"Absolutely not," replied Dr Sullivan.

"How much did you receive for your services?" asked the coroner.

"Five hundred dollars."

"Do you think five hundred dollars' worth of services were rendered?" asked the coroner.

"Yes, sir," replied Dr Sullivan.

The coroner was not quite convinced, however, and asked the doctor if he thought that sum of money was perhaps an unusual charge. The doctor then argued that he had received more in other cases, and that at no time did he cover anything up, and was offered no extra money by Dorothy Mackaye in an attempt to falsify the death certificate. The doctor was adamant that what he was saying was correct, but Coroner Nance was not so sure.

His suspicions became even more profound when it was discovered that when the doctor visited Deputy Coroner Frank H. Schoeffle, he had not told him that Raymond had been in a fight and instead claimed during the autopsy that the bruises present must have been caused by a fall when he was drunk. This had been an unusual move on the part of the doctor and one that raised concerns throughout the department. Further concerns came when stories reached the coroner that before the department had heard of Raymond's death, Mackaye had busied herself trying to organize a quick cremation in order to destroy the evidence forever.

Nance was horrified that such a cover-up was going on right in front of his nose and ordered a thorough investigation into the entire matter, stating, "I am satisfied that Dr Sullivan has not given us all of the facts of the case and appropriate steps will be taken." The media were quick to declare that Paul Kelly, Dorothy Mackaye and the doctor were all involved in something rather distasteful, and rushed to the home of Dr Sullivan for an explanation. However, if they thought he would admit any wrongdoing, they were mistaken.

"Everything and every phase of the case was above board," he told them. "There was absolutely nothing to hide and nothing was hidden."

Dorothy Mackaye, meanwhile, was too ill to attend the inquest or make any statements to the police. Instead, she stayed at home with her best friend, Helen Wilkinson; they were both said to be so upset over the death of Ray Raymond that they were under the care of a doctor and on constant medication. With Mackaye's father by her bedside and friends declaring she had suffered a nervous breakdown, she made sure the media knew she was in no condition to comment about the case. But if the woman believed that by feigning illness she could just fade into the background, she was very wrong. The shock announcement came that both she and Dr W. G. Sullivan were being indicted as "accessories after the fact". Not only that, but the police believed that both she and the doctor had been paid by Paul Kelly himself to keep quiet about what he had done to the singer, and that Dorothy was even at Kelly's apartment at the time Raymond eventually died, drinking gin with her lover.

This announcement caused a sensation in the media, especially when Raymond's mother seemed to agree that Mackaye was in some way responsible for what had happened the week before. "Dorothy could have prevented the fight that took my son's life," Mrs Cedarbloom declared. "I feel that she didn't do it."

The grieving woman then travelled to her son's former

home – where he had been beaten just days before – and had a meeting with her daughter-in-law. The official reason for her attendance was to discuss funeral plans, and later Mrs Cedarbloom denied that there had been any talk about the circumstances surrounding her son's death. A statement from Mackaye's nurse, declaring that the woman was in a state of utter collapse after the meeting and surrounded by doctors, seemed to suggest otherwise.

The animosity between the pair became evident a few days later at the funeral of Ray Raymond, which took place at Forest Lawn on 26 April and was attended by both women. At no time did either of the two even look in the other's direction, and each caused a sensation when they collapsed at separate times, weeping loudly and becoming hysterical after viewing the body.

The rumours of Mackaye's whereabouts during the beating, coupled with gossip about her affair with Kelly, were so humiliating for the actress that she decided to release an official statement once and for all, through her attorney, Roger Marchetti. In the speech he denied that his client had been drinking gin fizzes with Paul Kelly as her husband lay dying, and that:

> "She will not try to delay her case in the least and if anything, will insist upon an immediate trial to prove her innocence of the charges against her." The attorney then added that all his client was asking for was fair play, and that the public should withhold any judgement "until she can tell her side of the story and deny all these false accusations."

He then went on to say that Mackaye had not been at all well and that, "Mrs Raymond's prominence on the stage has made her the unmerciful victim of a lot of things which would not have been discussed had she been an ordinary person."

The cases against Kelly, Mackaye and Sullivan were all

being prepared when suddenly a new twist occurred as two witnesses came forward to tell their version of the death of Ray Raymond. Mr and Mrs Perry Askom – friends and colleagues of the deceased – told police that on the day of the beating they had called in to see Raymond and were shocked to discover that the man had been physically assaulted.

"Raymond told me that Kelly came over and beat him up and that he never had a chance," Mr Askom told police, before adding that Mackaye had arrived home right before they were about to leave, saying she had been to the dressmaker, drinking gin and was in a "pugnacious mood". At that point, as if to predict his fate, the singer had turned to Askom and said, "Take me home with you, Perry. I'm all washed up."

By the time the trial of Paul Kelly began, the press, the public and friends and family of Ray Raymond were on tenterhooks. The first day got off slowly, with Kelly's attorney announcing that anyone hoping for scandal was in for a great disappointment. "The trial will turn out to be very humdrum," he announced, though anyone who saw Dorothy Mackaye pass by the back of her lover and touch him gently on the shoulder would not have been so sure.

The next day things became even less humdrum when the jurors and Kelly himself were escorted to 2261 Cheremoya Avenue where the scene of the crime took place. Kelly was visibly uneasy at being back in the house, silently following the jurors from room to room, with who-knows-what going on in his mind. At one point he encountered the maid Ethel Lee with the family dog, although his attempts to speak to her were thwarted when he was moved on by his accompanying attorney. By the time he left, spectators outside described him as "pale" and "glad to be out" as he was led back into the waiting police car.

Back in the courtroom, Wagner, the surgeon who had performed the autopsy on the body of Ray Raymond, was called to the stand. There he gave the crushing evidence that not only did he see two injuries on the victim's forehead, but also a black eye, a haemorrhage on the left side of his head and bruises all over his right shoulder, left arm, legs and chest. Gasps were heard when it was also declared that he had found both fractured and cracked ribs on the body, and the defence shuffled uncomfortably when the doctor proclaimed that the bruises and broken ribs could have been caused by crashing blows or kicks.

Questioning the doctor, Kelly's attorneys tried to determine whether the cause of death could in fact have just been Raymond's apparent alcoholism and, in particular, a problem with his heart.

"No," replied the doctor. "His heart and other organs were normal, with the exception of the kidneys which were fatty."

The defence team, however, were not prepared to accept that Kelly had been in any way responsible for the singer's death, and in their jury statement declared, "There was no murderous assault and young Kelly struck him just enough to end things and then went on his way. No blows were struck sufficient to produce death and Kelly used no more force than was necessary."

Still, in spite of the defence team's efforts, it became more and more apparent as the days went on that Kelly was not the innocent young man they were trying to portray him to be. Despite Mackaye's denial of an affair, love letters between the actor and herself were reported to be in the hands of the district attorney and whispers that the two had been conducting a passionate affair were flying around the media. Things were made no better when Ethel Lee took to the stand and said once again that when Raymond was out of town, Kelly was often at the house, and that if Mackaye ever failed to come home from work, she could always be found by telephoning Kelly's apartment.

The defence team were incensed that such information had come to light, and Kelly blushed and sweated his way through the damning evidence, while women in the gallery were seen dramatically wiping tears from their faces.

"How many times did she fail to come home at all during Raymond's absence with his theatrical company?" the maid was asked.

"There were many times," she replied, before adding that even when her employer did come home, it was almost always in the company of Paul Kelly. Furthermore, on the evening of the fight, just prior to Kelly's arrival at the house, she had seen Raymond crying and his daughter was sitting next to him, wiping tears from his eyes with her handkerchief. "He appeared mentally ill," she said.

Excitement came to the courtroom when Dorothy Mackaye took to the stand and explained that on the afternoon of 16 April, she had indeed been at Paul Kelly's apartment, but she had not been alone. Instead, she said, she was with her friend Helen Wilkinson and Kelly's flatmate, Max Wagner. They spent time together and enjoyed drinking gin and water before Kelly made a phone call and then left for an appointment.

"Isn't it a fact that you knew Kelly was going over to your place?" she was asked.

"No sir. The first thing I knew that he had had a telephone conversation with anyone was when Miss Wilkinson told me she thought she had heard him mention Ray's name. I said to her, 'You're silly.'"

Interestingly, Mackaye admitted that Wilkinson had jokingly told Kelly that Raymond wished to see the actor, though she was adamant that the whole thing had been said in jest and that Kelly did not really believe it to be so. However, she did admit to speaking about her husband with Kelly that day, telling him that things were "the same as usual" and that they had agreed to separate, but she denied that he had become angry with anything she had told him.

"Mr Kelly never discussed my husband or my affairs in the presence of others or my friends," she answered, clearly irritated, even though she had just described that they had been discussing her marriage in front of Helen Wilkinson. She then denied that she had waited for Kelly to come home from his "appointment", saying that she and Helen Wilkinson had instead gone shopping for Easter eggs before heading back to the Raymond family home.

Then came a bombshell, when love letters between Kelly and Mackaye were presented to the court. Despite Dorothy's claims that the two were just friends, the letters showed that Kelly's version of events was closer to the truth. In several letters Paul told the actress that he loved her, while in others he remarked how much he missed her, how he was miserable without her and how he was being awful to everyone because all he could think about was her. "I thought I'd die," he dramatically declared. Meanwhile other letters were disclosed: "Darling Mine," began one, while another included a row of kisses and a note which said, "Count them and that's not enough." Dorothy had responded during a trip to San Francisco with a wire which read, "Crazy to get home, our home. Love and everything that goes with it." And she signed it Mrs K.

The love between the two was further proven when Kelly's "house boy", Yobu, confirmed to the court that there were frequent visits by Mackaye to the house, and that the two shared a "love language" that he had been unable to understand. Gasps were heard when he then described taking water to the couple in Kelly's bedroom, and confirming that Mackaye had stayed overnight on several occasions.

Then it was time for Kelly to take the stand, which he did with great fanfare in the newspapers. During the testimony it became clear that Paul Kelly truly believed he had been provoked by the drunk Raymond, who was described as the aggressor and the one eager to fight. Kelly did admit, however, that he had swung the first punch. "He said, 'Where is my wife? You ought to know, she has been living with you.' I slapped him in the mouth. I said, 'That is a nice way to talk about your wife, isn't it?'" He then went on to explain how he had asked for the child to be taken out of the room, and had refused an invitation from Raymond to come back to the house later on, for fear that he planned to get friends to come there and beat him up.

The trial of Paul Kelly continued in a rambling way, with testimony repeated and incidents described time and time again. Even the newspapers grew tired of the case and started filling their columns with comment about Kelly's lawyer falling asleep, lady flappers in the audience who were giving the accused "the eye" and popping chewing-gum bubbles in his direction.

Finally, however, the case was wrapped up and it was time for the jury to give its verdict. Kelly was found guilty of causing the death of Ray Raymond, though he quickly announced that an appeal would be made. Meanwhile, the trial of Dorothy Mackaye began, though that too followed the route of the Kelly trial, with an added element of drama when she announced that she had reconciled with her husband on his deathbed.

Eventually Mackaye was found guilty of concealing the facts after her husband's death and the case against Dr Walter J. Sullivan was dropped for lack of evidence. The actress announced that she would appeal, though in the end both she and Kelly resigned themselves to their fate and lived out their sentences quietly at San Quentin Prison. In January 1929, Dorothy was released from prison. On her departure, she spoke to reporters and declared, "I'm leaving immediately for Denver to look after my baby daughter. I bear no ill will to anyone but I am determined to clear my name of the stigma that has been attached to it since the death of my husband of which I am, and Paul Kelly is, innocent."

Meanwhile, Kelly followed just seven months later and said, "I'm going straight to New York. I'm headed straight for the comeback trail. I've got a job with the New Century Play Company and I'm going to hit it hard."

For the next few years, both Kelly and Mackaye declined to speak about each other in the press, though by January 1931 they could hide their love no longer. The two were rumoured to be very much together and finally in February of that year they were married. Quite amazingly, Kelly then successfully adopted Valeria, Dorothy's daughter by the man her new husband had slain just a few years before. He then concentrated on his acting career while his wife wrote a play about her experiences in prison, which became a 1933 film entitled *Ladies They Talk About*, starring Barbara Stanwyck.

Dorothy Mackaye then decided to leave her Hollywood days behind in order to concentrate on being a mother. This seems to have been a decision she had come to back in 1927, just after the tragedy had unfolded. At the time she had announced, "I am willing to sacrifice everything for my daughter's sake. There is no excuse whatsoever of my baby being dragged into this mess and I don't want her ever to hear of the tragedy that has wrecked her home."

With the hopes of a happy life in front of them, the new family moved to a ranch in the San Fernando Valley which they named "Kellymae". Together they lived a quiet life away from the spotlight, although the marriage that Kelly had literally fought for lasted only nine years before disaster struck. On the evening of 2 January 1940, Dorothy was driving her car towards the ranch when she encountered another vehicle coming towards her. It was a foggy night and, as she swerved to miss the oncoming vehicle, Mackaye hit the edge of the pavement and her car overturned. Passers-by ran immediately to her aid and the former actress was able to drag herself from the vehicle. She was taken home by a neighbour.

While it seemed that initially she was going to be okay, the day after the accident she began to feel unwell and was taken to hospital, where the doctors predicted her injuries were not life-threatening. Sadly they were wrong, as internally there were problems with Dorothy's bladder and on 5 January 1940, after speaking breezily to her husband and doctor, it ruptured and the former actress collapsed and died, leaving Paul Kelly absolutely devastated.

After the initial period of bereavement, Paul Kelly returned to New York where he starred in several plays such as *Country*

Girl, Command Decision and *Bad Girl*. He also met a former actress called Zona Mardelle and together they moved to California, where they made their home at 1448 Club View Drive, Los Angeles. It was here, on 6 November 1956, that the actor collapsed and died suddenly, shortly after returning from casting his vote in the 1956 presidential election. He was fifty-seven years old.

The story of Paul Kelly and Dorothy Mackaye is one of scandal, intrigue, murder and love but, above all, tragedy. A man died in order for them to be together, but in the end it was something as simple as a car journey that would keep them apart forever. Was it karma that made sure they were never able to live out their lives happily together, or just a tragic case of coincidence? Alas, we will never know for sure.

6

Clara Bow's Scandalous Love Life

Where does one start when describing the life of Clara Bow? Known as "Crisis a Day Clara" because of the colossal number of scandals that came her way, the actress probably had more newspaper headlines in her career than just about any actress of the 1920s and 1930s. Everything from court cases to emotional breakdowns were covered, but probably the most publicized were her scandalous relationships with the many men that came her way (although contrary to popular belief, this does not include sleeping with the entire University of Southern California football team – that was merely a rumour.)

Born on 29 July 1905 in Brooklyn, Clara Gordon Bow was raised in a violent and highly unbalanced home. Her mother Sarah was an extremely unhappy and deranged woman, who had no desire for marriage or children, and frequently suffered from seizures and manic episodes. She could be extremely cruel to the child and throughout her infancy Clara never felt as though she was in any way loved by either parent. Indeed, it was later discovered that her father was even more psychotic than her mother, and would be violent and sexually abusive towards the child on a regular basis. He would also take off for long periods of time, leaving mother and daughter without any means of support, and the days alone would be cold, hungry and filled with horrific outbursts from Sarah Bow.

In 1921, keen to escape the horrors of her home life, Clara won a nationwide "Fame and Fortune" contest which she hoped would launch her into the world of showbiz and an eventual move to Hollywood. Unfortunately, this did not sit well with her mother, and one evening in 1922 the fledgling actress woke up to find the woman holding a knife to her throat. "You'd be better off dead," Sarah told her terrified daughter, and while Clara was able to escape physically unharmed, the nightmares of that evening would live with her forever. Shortly afterwards, Sarah Bow was taken to a mental hospital and she died in early 1923.

Things looked bleak for the fledgling actress, with the "Fame and Fortune" organizers not in the least bit interested in her now that she had won the competition. However, she did receive a positive comment in the January 1922 issue of *Motion Picture Classics* magazine – shortly before her mother tried to kill her – which described her as very young but full of confidence and ambition. They also added, "She has a genuine spark of divine fire."

They were not wrong. Clara was a courageous and determined young woman and despite her nightmarish background and abusive parents, she was positive that she would one day become a star. Casting directors were not so confident, unfortunately, but despite being told over and over again that she was not right for the part she was going for, the young woman continued to knock on doors and attend auditions. Eventually her persistence paid off and she started to win a variety of small roles in low-budget movies. This led to a move to Hollywood in July 1923, where her career really started to take off.

Despite being very young, Clara became the ultimate flapper girl, a symbol of what everyone believed 1920s Hollywood women looked like. With her flame-red hair, she began making a real name for herself among cinema-goers everywhere; and young girls tried to emulate her look and copy her style. She was extremely hard-working and appeared in dozens of films such as *Poisoned Paradise* (1924) and *The Plastic Age* (1925).

It was her 1927 appearance in *It* which cemented her fame

(making her the first ever "It Girl") and, for the first time in her life, Clara was actually a happy woman. During an interview in 1951 she described that period: "In my era, we had individuality. We did as we pleased. We stayed up late. We dressed the way we wanted. I'd whiz down Sunset Boulevard in my open Kissel with seven red chow dogs to match my hair. Today they're sensible and end up with better health – but we had more fun."

By the late 1920s, the fun Clara was having was getting a little too intense, however. She was now a huge star and soon found herself involved in more affairs than even the gossip columnists could remember. Her first real public relationship came in the form of a much publicized engagement to director Victor Fleming. He hoped it would lead to marriage, but Clara had no intention of allowing it to get that far. Instead of planning a wedding, the actress finished with her fiancé just weeks after they had announced their engagement because she found him "too much older than I. And gosh, he was too subtle. I couldn't live up to his subtlety."

She was not single for long, however, as film star Gary Cooper was next, and according to Clara it lasted for about two years. Of the relationship, she later told columnist Alma Whitaker that he was a "nice boy. But the studio objected to us keeping late nights and running around."

While the gossip columnists may have found her affairs and comments ever-so-amusing, there was one affair that studio heads hoped would disappear without trace, as it actually had the potential to derail Clara's career altogether. The romance in question was a 1928 affair with Dr Earl Pearson, who she met during a stay in hospital. Dr Pearson fell for the red-headed actress as most men did, and bombarded her with telegrams and notes, declaring on 27 September 1928 that he hoped his night-time loneliness would not be for long, and begging her to write to him. Then on 31 March 1929 he exclaimed, "Swiftly my love flies back to you, my own sweet darling. Earl."

Pearson was obviously more than a little smitten and in return Clara found him intriguing, later describing him as dominating but gentle, before adding, "Sometimes I feel as if he might spank me if I seriously annoyed him." In the 1920s, comments like these most certainly raised the eyebrows of both the newspaper readers and studio bosses, but that was nothing. Soon an even bigger scandal threatened to erupt when it was discovered that Dr Pearson was actually a married man with a wife who was not about to hand him over without a fight.

Despite Clara's claims that Dr Pearson and his wife were actually separated, this seems to have been news to Mrs Pearson, who turned up in California and proceeded to threaten to sue Clara for $150,000. Clara later described her shock at being told of Mrs Pearson's plans: "Blam! Like that! One hundred and fifty thousand smackers. Why, I had never seen that much money before."

Clara was called to Paramount Studios, where she told furious bosses that she had every intention of fighting the case. However, instead of pleasing the executives with this revelation, they were absolutely mortified. If the scandal got out it could not only completely ruin the reputation of their biggest star, but also the studio itself, so there was no way they would agree to her going to court. They insisted that to keep the case away from the press, Clara should pay Mrs Pearson as much as she could in order to settle out of court. The actress was not at all pleased but felt cornered by her bosses and acceded with their wishes. Against her better judgement, she gave Mrs Pearson $30,000, which she insisted was as much as she could possibly afford.

But the covered-up scandal was not over, as the couple continued seeing each other, much to the dismay of Mrs Pearson, the studio and Dr Pearson's family. Furious at the lack of respect from either her husband or Clara Bow, the wife hired private detectives to spy on the pair, while the studio told their star that they would be withholding $26,000 on the grounds of a "no scandal" clause in her contract, and $30,000 from several bonuses which came with the same stipulation. Clara was furious.

The concerned family of Dr Pearson decided in their wisdom to bundle him off to Europe in the hope that he would forget all about Clara. He didn't, of course, and instead continued to write to his beloved, but after losing so much money she had no intention of ever seeing him again. Instead of responding with love letters of her own to Pearson, she instead wrote and told him that it was over, that she was not willing to see him any more and to just move on with his life. But while Clara may have lost a great deal of money over the past few months, as far as Dr Pearson was concerned, he had lost more when robbed of the love of Clara Bow. He continued to bombard her with letters, all of which she apparently ignored.

The studio executives were pleased that their star had ended the relationship, and breathed a sigh of relief when the scandal passed over the gossip columnists without even a sniff. However, it was a short-lived joy, as several years later, in June 1930, Clara Bow got wind that Mrs Pearson had never taken any of the $30,000 she had been offered as an out-of-court settlement. As far as Clara was concerned, she wanted to know exactly what had happened to her hard-earned cash and jumped on a train to Dallas to see her ex-boyfriend, Dr Pearson, and "straighten things out". Meanwhile, the press found out that the actress was meeting someone in Texas, so happily met her at the station to see what was going on.

The thought of revealing her personal affairs to a pack of newsmen should have been enough to send Clara running back to Los Angeles but, unbelievably, she instead decided to give a full-on conference to the world's press. There she told them everything from how she met Dr Pearson, to how she had been made to pay $30,000 to his wife (made up of $26,000 from a studio trust fund and $4,000 of her own money), to a blow-by-blow account of everything that had happened during the formerly covered-up scandal.

News quickly got back to executives at Paramount Studios that their star had entertained dozens of reporters with her revelations, and they were absolutely livid. The scandal had been successfully hidden back in 1928, and here was Clara Bow quite happily admitting everything to anyone who would listen. Still, they were determined to play down the confession, and when asked about her statement, B. P. Schulberg, the general manager of the studio, brushed the entire thing off as one of her little pranks. He refused to make an official statement but in his carefully worded reply said, "Miss Bow always has been inclined to make extravagant statements to interviewers. All newspaper men who have ever gone to see her on stories must know this."

Not surprisingly, Clara received a good telling-off from Schulberg about her behaviour, and was ordered to return to Hollywood immediately. As she left for California via New York, the actress was forced to go back on her claims to the press that she had paid $30,000 to the wife of William Pearson, and backtracked on everything else she had said as well. "I was terribly misquoted," she complained. "The reporter said things I didn't say and just put two and two together. Why, I didn't even know that the doctor was in Dallas until she told me."

As for the pay-off itself, she was quick to offer this explanation: "I didn't even have the money to pay such a thing," she told reporters. "My money is tied up in a bonus trust fund which the studio established, and it can't be touched by anybody." This unfortunate statement was a complete contrast to what she had said previously, and sent the press scuttling to their telephones to research exactly what the trust fund was and how it worked. They established that, sure enough, an amount of approximately $25,000 was withdrawn from the California Trust Company on 17 October 1928, the very day Mrs Pearson had filed for divorce.

When asked about it, Clara replied, "Why, that's ridiculous. I never paid off any lawsuit. As far as the doctor's wife is concerned, I never met her or saw her . . . How was I to know

Dr Pearson was married? Is it for me to inquire into their personal affairs?"

The press thought the whole thing hilarious. "She's denying everything she claimed on her arrival!" reporters laughed in their editorials. Clara Bow was fed up by this point, especially when current boyfriends began phoning her to see why exactly she was hanging out with Dr Pearson in Dallas. The studio was still on her back and the press continued to camp on her doorstep.

"My contract is up a year from next October, and perhaps after that I can lead my own life. I am going to retire from pictures then," moaned the tired actress.

Turning the clock back to 1929, when the scandal had not yet been leaked and was very much still brushed under the carpet, Clara Bow was at the very top of her game and enjoying thousands of fan letters every week. But with the advent of talkies, her career was being tested, as she sadly told reporters: "I hate talkies. They're stiff and limiting." She then declared her plans to take a long rest at the beach once her contract was over, "and just play and eat and sleep", as well as settle down with a husband and children.

A new beau in the shape of nightclub-owner turned actor Harry Richman was a welcome distraction from her busy work schedule, though it is true to say he seemed more in love with the publicity she brought than Clara herself. Hungry for headlines, Richman paraded his new girlfriend around like a trophy, and if there was a party to be seen at, they would be there; if there was an opening to go to, he would be grabbing his coat.

The nightclub-owner was besotted with the fame and notoriety that being Clara Bow's mate brought to his life, though in all honesty if he thought he was being discreet about his true intentions, he was sorely mistaken. Clara's friends all became highly suspicious and worried that Richman was using the actress as a ticket to fame, rather than genuinely being in love with her.

It would seem that they were right. Richman's hunger for fame was unfortunately demonstrated towards the end of 1929 when Clara was admitted to hospital for a gynaecological operation. The surgery was to remove an ovary – a dreadful operation for any woman to go through – but rumour-mongers started whispering that they believed the actress was secretly having an abortion. Any man worth the title of gentleman would have jumped immediately to his partner's defence, but not Harry. Instead, he remained quiet in order to enhance his own reputation: that of a stud who was capable of getting the "It Girl" pregnant.

Why would he do such a caddish thing? It was all very simple really. Harry Richman was sterile and thoroughly enjoyed the idea of people thinking he was able to father a child. His ego was such that he would never acknowledge the fact that he could not father children, so he went along with the rumours to enhance his own libido, while allowing his girlfriend's reputation to be thoroughly discoloured.

Several months before her surgery, however, Clara surprised friends by announcing her engagement to the unscrupulous nightclub-owner. This raised many eyebrows, primarily because Clara had a long list of failed romances, but gossip columnists were nevertheless happy to hear about her plans. "As soon as we complete our pictures, [Harry and I] are going to be married," she told them. She refused to name a date though, which prompted several newspapers sarcastically to comment that she had been in this situation before – several times.

Richman responded to the negativity by declaring that the wedding would take place shortly before the honeymoon, which would be celebrated on a ship setting sail from New York on 12 September 1929. Wanting to attract the most attention he could, he also announced that the wedding would be a huge affair, attended by many prominent entertainers. Harry was ecstatic about this, of course, but to detract from his headline-grabbing ways, he made sure to add that he and Clara had wanted a small wedding, but friends would hear of no such thing. Then, just for good measure, he also added that he had won his fiancée's heart with his "caveman tactics".

Clara was absolutely furious. Not only did she object to Richman talking about their relationship to the media, but she had also never agreed to an actual date for their wedding. Yes, she admitted to reporters, they were engaged, but most certainly they had never discussed a ceremony or a honeymoon location. She then added, "If there is such a thing as love then I am in love with Harry Richman. But I am not going to rush into marriage because I do not want to do anything hasty."

Quite oddly for someone supposed to be on the brink of marriage, Clara then said, "Our marriage depends on whether we really find we love each other", before adding her feelings on the "caveman" comment by stating that she could not understand why Richman would make such "ridiculous statements".

Fearing he was about to lose his fiancée (and the constant source of his new-found fame), Richman in turn released his own statement: "I was thoroughly misquoted," he claimed, before going on to explain that he was madly in love with Clara and "I think she loves me too." It wasn't exactly the most committed of quotes, and newspapers were quick to challenge just how much the couple did actually love each other, and whether or not a marriage would take place at all.

Indeed, it did seem as though the couple were constantly bickering both in the press and at home; and things were made no better when Richman was accused of assault and battery by a dancer called Ellen Franks. According to the woman, the nightclub-owner had drugged and held her prisoner for four hours in his car in March 1929, beating her so much that she was now an invalid. Richman retorted that he did not know the woman in question, but by this time a weary Clara was getting rather tired of her beau's behaviour and temporarily began a secret affair with her old flame, Gary Cooper.

In October 1929, Clara was in Lake Arrowhead, while

Richman was in Hollywood. Lonesome, he decided to send her a telegram which told the actress just how much he missed her and that his greatest wish was to be with her at that moment. "I hope the place is terrible so you will come home to one who loves you more than anything," he declared, and while her response remains unrecorded, he wrote again shortly afterwards to tell her, "I love you, I love you, I love you."

But while Harry Richman was declaring his undying love for Clara in telegrams, she was readying herself for the operation to remove her ovary, something which worried her no end. To dispel the gossip about an abortion, and to keep their star's privacy intact, the studio released a statement saying that she had been operated on due to complications from an appendicitis surgery. Richman as we know, decided to stay very quiet about what the operation was for, but he bizarrely released a statement anyway, not about his fiancée's health, but about the state of their relationship.

"We will get married," he happily declared once again, before this time announcing that it would take place in New York in April 1930. Clara was not happy with his latest revelations, but she had so far weathered the storm. However, her patience was very much tested when it was announced in the newspapers that several years before his engagement to Bow, Richman had been involved with a married woman in New York. Now, seeing the nightclub owner with his photograph in every newspaper, the woman's estranged husband had been spurred on to take his revenge. He may have lost his wife, but he could regain his dignity by hitting Richman where it hurt – in his wallet. With that in mind, the man contacted the press to announce what the cad had done to his marriage, and to threaten a lawsuit.

This episode certainly did nothing to persuade Clara to marry Richman, and by January 1930 he was back in New York, much to the relief of Bow. But while they may have been on different sides of the country, it still did not stop Richman from continuing to make a fool of himself, this time by boasting that he had recently bought his fiancée a limousine and a diamond bracelet. However, by now even he was suspecting that Clara was having second thoughts about the engagement, though when she finally agreed to come east for a visit, he was still so excited that he hinted to the press that they might just go through with a wedding this time.

"If we do marry it will be in secret," he told reporters, and anxiously awaited the arrival of his love. Unfortunately for Richman, however, he was in for a shock: Clara had only agreed to come to New York because she had decided to break the engagement, once and for all.

Richman had been so engrossed in the publicity brought on by his relationship with Bow that he had failed to see that there was never any chance of her marrying him. She had refused to name a date, publicly told him off for declaring his love in the newspapers, and even had an affair with Gary Cooper, but still Richman refused to leave her. Clara was struggling to see how she would ever rid herself of her unwanted beau, but in the end she decided to use her fertile imagination. Gathering together reporters in her suite at the Park Central Hotel, she let out a long sigh. "I cannot marry Harry Richman," she sadly announced, "as I am expecting a nervous breakdown."

Reporters were bemused that the actress could possibly predict her nervous breakdowns in advance, but Richman at last seemed to take the hint. On 17 February he accompanied his former fiancée to the station to see her off, kissed her on the cheek and left quickly before the train had rolled out of the station. Clara told reporters that publicity had stopped their wedding. "We couldn't be alone long enough to be married," she told them, while Harry Richman pretended to be upset about the press situation by declaring, "We were on the front pages all the time – and the things they said about us!" He forgot to mention, of course, that he had revelled in the publicity and had taken every opportunity to propel both himself and his relationship into the headlines.

Despite several meetings and attempts at reconciliation, by

June 1930 the "engagement" was well and truly on its last legs. The last nail in the coffin came when Clara was spotted with her former flame, none other than Dr Pearson, which infuriated Richman to such a degree that he immediately requested the return of his engagement ring. Clara travelled to New York to negotiate with him, and in an attempt to sweeten the deal, described him as "a darling" to the waiting press. "We can never be married as long as I must remain in Hollywood and he in New York . . . But we are still engaged," she quickly added, though the cynical could be forgiven for thinking this was just her attempt to keep the ring.

But while Richman was quite happy to think he might still be engaged to Clara Bow, another threatened lawsuit was bubbling; this time from his former sweetheart, actress Flo Stanley. She had dated the nightclub-owner some eight years before, but in spite of the fact that the romance had been over for a long time, she still had feelings for her lost love and hoped one day to reconcile. Like a scene from a bad romance movie, the spurned woman took the decision to contact Clara Bow and demand she "keep away from my man". The actress paid no heed to the request, of course, so Stanley then contacted the newspapers with an outrageous story about planning to sue Clara for $100,000 and Richman for $250,000.

The numerous threatened lawsuits, the rumours of a renewed romance with Dr Pearson and the demands of the studio finally took their toll, and Clara eventually called time on the romance, giving a statement to columnist Alma Whitaker, which said, "No, I'm not going to marry Harry Richman. He's a nice fellow and was very kind to me, but he is older and so critical." She then went on to complain that he had been too stubborn, wanted to dominate her all the time and chastised her when he felt she had too much make-up on, or was wearing clothes that were "too loud".

She added, "I don't mind a little domination, but I object to being made over after it's me they fell for. Any girl would . . ." And then as a nod to the rumoured affairs with Gary Cooper and Dr Pearson, she added, "Gee, he couldn't stand me making goo-goo eyes even in fun with anybody else. So I think that's all off."

Clara sent back Richman's ring and he later attempted some revenge by beginning a romance with actress Lina Basquette, declaring that while he had seen Clara Bow during a recent visit, "she means absolutely nothing to me any more". This cutting remark was obviously aimed at Clara Bow's heart, but it ultimately missed, as by this time she had met Rex Bell, the love of her life. Clara described him as, "A boy out on the coast in pictures [who] I like awfully well. He played my lead in the last picture I made. Gee, he's a swell fella!"

Rex's love enabled her not only to settle down at last, but also gave her two sons and a life in the country away from the Hollywood glare of publicity. But first she would have to endure another year of unwanted headlines, in the shape of a very public lawsuit and, sadly, a nervous breakdown, both of which are explored in a separate chapter within this book.

7

Lottie Pickford: Mary's Naughty Sister

When one hears the name Pickford, one automatically thinks of America's Sweetheart, Mary, or "Pickfair", the studio and home she built with her husband, Douglas Fairbanks. Today the name Lottie Pickford is almost completely unknown, and yet in the 1920s and 1930s she caused uproar with her wild parties and multiple marriages.

Born as Charlotte Smith on 9 June 1893, Lottie was exceptionally close to her brother, Jack, but not so much to her sister, Mary, seeing her as controlling and far too strict for her liking. The children all started acting at a very early age and moved from their native Canada to make their name in New York. The siblings all won parts, but Mary was considered a star while the others merely tagged along on the back of her success, happy with whatever part they were able to obtain.

In 1915 Lottie married Alfred Rupp, a New York broker, and shortly after gave birth to a daughter whom she chose to name Mary after her sister, despite their apparent distance from each other. The marriage was short-lived, however, and the couple divorced in 1920, which resulted in the first real scandal in Lottie's life when she decided to hand over her daughter to be raised by her own mother, Charlotte. Why Lottie would chose to do this is not known, though some believe it was because she was by this time heavily into drugs and alcohol.

To avoid any confusion with her aunt Mary, the child was

renamed Gwynne and officially adopted by Charlotte Pickford in August 1926. Newspapers were aghast, enjoying the idea that some unusual relationships had been created with this move, including the fact that the young girl was now her own foster-aunt. She was also, according to newspapers, the niece and foster-sister to Mary Pickford, and niece and sister-in-law to Douglas Fairbanks. Reporters also relished in wondering why the child was given up in the first place, though Lottie stayed quiet on the matter, never publicly stating why the child was being raised by her mother – and later her sister – instead of herself.

Another marriage followed in 1922 to the actor Allan Forrest, and then another scandal hit in 1926 when Lottie was named in divorce proceedings between a woman called Thelma Leonard and her husband Charles. Apparently Mr Leonard had taken his wife to one of Lottie's renowned wild parties, where the actress had reportedly got drunk and pulled Mrs Leonard to one side. "I am not in love with your husband," declared Lottie, which immediately made Mrs Leonard highly suspicious since she had never accused her of being so in the first place.

Needless to say the Leonards' marriage soon broke up after this incident, and Lottie's followed shortly after. She then went on to become one of the most scandalous actresses of 1928.

Lottie Pickford had many friends, as her frequent parties proved. During this time she became acquainted with Jack Daugherty, one-time husband of Barbara La Marr, and the two attended numerous parties during 1928. On one November evening, the pair teamed up with a friend and the three attended a party together, where they all revelled until the friend decided to call it a night, followed by Daugherty and Pickford at approximately 3 a.m.

Driving through the streets of East Los Angeles, the car they were travelling in unfortunately suffered a flat tyre. The couple stopped to investigate and as they were examining the damage, four men approached them, knocked Daugherty unconscious and stole $15 from his pocket. Then, they dragged Lottie into their car and drove off.

However, they got more than they bargained for with Lottie Pickford, and while being driven through the dark streets, she managed to hide some of her rings in her shoes for safe-keeping. Unfortunately she could not hide everything, though, and a diamond bracelet was later badly bent when the gang unsuccessfully attempted to take it from her wrist.

The car drove through the night until reaching a secluded spot, where the attackers bundled the actress out of the car, tore at her clothes, physically assaulted her and stole some money. Lottie fought back, however, shouting at them in their native Spanish and begging them to take her back to her car. This was a brave and successful decision on Pickford's part, as shocked at hearing the woman speak Spanish, the gang leader seemed to feel a twinge of remorse and immediately told the other men to let her go, which they did. The leader then bundled her into the car and drove back to where they had left Daugherty; he was found still sitting at the side of the road, slowly coming round from the beating.

Once reunited, the pair somehow managed to drive back home and report the incident to the police, requesting that the matter be kept quiet to avoid any press attention. They then assisted them in trying to find the spot where the mugging and kidnapping had happened, though ultimately the pair were unable to make any sense of the streets and failed to find the exact location.

Despite their appeal to keep the episode quiet, as with most things related to Lottie's life, the story hit the news. It all came out several days later and Lottie posed for pictures while declaring that the robbers had bruised her wrists, ankles and legs while kicking her body "until it was a mass of bruises". The incident made headlines across the United States, but it was not to be the last scandal she endured in 1928.

On 5 November, gambler and rumoured Mafia member

Arnold Rothstein died after being shot the day before at New York's Park Central Hotel. Several weeks later, detectives discovered Lottie's name on promissory notes for $100,000 in the apartment of Rothstein's friend, Sidney Stager. Unfortunately for Pickford, Stager also happened to be the head of an international dope syndicate and the discovery of her name in his files once again brought her name to everyone's lips for all the wrong reasons. Police tried unsuccessfully to tie in her kidnapping with the murder of Rothstein, and although she initially chose to keep quiet about the incident, Lottie eventually gave a statement, declaring: "Why, how ridiculous, I didn't even know the man and as for writing a note for $100,000 – don't be foolish."

Christmas Eve soon arrived and Lottie decided to host one of her wild parties at her home at 6622 Iris Drive, Los Angeles, which was attended by her friends and admirers Daniel E. Jaeger and Jack Daugherty. The party lived up to Lottie's reputation and quickly became so out of hand that fed-up neighbours called the police to complain about the noise. Detectives arrived at the home but were more interested in determining whether or not the alcohol laws had been violated, rather than noise pollution. However, their investigations into the alcohol situation petered out and the party seemed to calm down. The police asked the group to keep the noise down, before heading off into the night.

Unfortunately for Lottie, not long after the police departed, friends Jack Daugherty and Daniel E. Jaeger decided to have a stern talk with one another about their attentions towards the actress. A fight broke out on the lawn between the jealous pair, which climaxed when Daugherty sank his teeth into the middle finger of Jaeger's right hand, almost severing it completely.

The resulting fracas once again attracted the neighbours' attention and the police were called again, arriving just after Daugherty had left, last seen slipping out of a side door with other parting guests. The detectives discovered Jaeger bleeding profusely and swiftly sent him to hospital, where he refused to make any formal complaints against his love-rival. Several weeks later Jaeger was arrested on suspicion of forgery, which, although completely unrelated to the Pickford party, nevertheless dragged Lottie's name into the mud once again.

When Lottie spoke of the party incident to reporters, she tried to laugh the entire thing off, claiming, "Oh the boys just raised a little whoopee, but they're good friends now." She also tried to assure them that she had not been privy to most of the row, had no idea what the "scrap" was about and, besides, "I didn't get here until it was about over."

Detectives continued to investigate the incident and neighbours told them that they had been frequently disturbed at night by noise coming from Lottie Pickford's home. On New Year's Eve 1928, however, the case was closed when the complainants were unable to identify for sure that it really was Lottie making the noise in the house; an outcome that must have frustrated the entire neighbourhood.

After the scandals of the last year, Lottie decided to settle down in July 1929 and married an undertaker, Russell O. Gillard, although her sister, Mary Pickford, declined to attend the wedding. Perhaps she had heard that when filing for a marriage certificate, Lottie gave her name as Lotta Rupp and then became furious when she was recognized by reporters: "I don't want anything about this in the papers," she shouted. "I was trying to keep this marriage secret." Then quite bizarrely she turned to the head of the marriage licence bureau and angrily told her, "I've changed my mind, tear that application up."

Her shocked fiancé tried to calm her down, and as she left the building Lottie shouted back to the registrar, "All right, let it ride!" She then demanded to know how the reporters knew that Lotta Rupp was the same person as Lottie Pickford, and when they explained that her parents' names were the same as the ones given on her last licence, she was unfazed. "That's just a coincidence," she snarled. It was not the most positive of starts for a happy marriage and, sure enough, three years later she filed for divorce, charging cruelty and claiming that her husband embarrassed her, called her vile names and abandoned her at the home of friends.

In June 1933, before the divorce from Gillard had even come through, Lottie wedded another admirer, John Locke, paying no attention at all to the fact that she was now a bigamist. "If this gets back to Los Angeles there'll be trouble," she laughed. "But of course the California authorities must prove where our secret marriage took place before they can separate us," she added.

By 1935 Lottie's party days were almost over and she spent much of her last years in and out of hospital, battling influenza among other ailments. Finally, on 9 December 1936, she suffered a massive heart attack and passed away at her home at 577 Burlington Avenue, Los Angeles. She was buried at Forest Lawn Memorial Park where 150 friends attended a private ceremony to say goodbye. In life she had been an outrageous figure, never far from scandal but loved by her friends and associates. Sadly, in death she is all but forgotten, her colourful life being overshadowed by her estranged sister Mary's legacy, which continues to this very day.

8

Christine Collins and the Wineville Chicken Coop Murders

Christine Collins may not have starred in a movie, won an Oscar or received a star on Hollywood's Walk of Fame, but her story is most certainly tied to the world of Hollywood scandals, due partly to her living in Los Angeles, and because of one young boy's obsession with film star Tom Mix. But before we can talk about that, we must first learn a little more about Christine Collins and the tragic circumstances that led to her losing everything during a dreadful, dark period in 1928.

Born in California during 1888, Christine Ida Dunne grew up to marry a gentleman by the name of Walter J. Collins, aka Conrad Collins, and settled in Los Angeles where she went on to give birth to a son, also named Walter, in September 1918.

Unfortunately, life was not easy for Christine Collins, as her husband did not prove to be the reliable person for whom she had hoped. He had previously spent two terms in prison, though had conveniently forgotten to tell his unsuspecting fiancée this information at the time they were married. There could have been two reasons for this: either Walter Senior wanted to forget his past and move on as a law-abiding citizen, or else he wanted to keep his prior indiscretions quiet as he intended to go on with his life of crime in the future.

Sadly, it would seem that it was the latter. Walter Sr had no intention of becoming a respectable citizen just because he was a husband and father, and he was unable – or unwilling – to hold down a regular job. It didn't come as a surprise when the couple's finances quickly began to spiral out of control and Christine was left wondering what on earth she had got herself into.

Added to her worries came news that Walter Sr's mother had fallen ill, which seems to have been a catalyst for him to gear up his shady business deals by gaining employment with an illegal drinking establishment. As if this wasn't bad enough, he then took the decision to be part of a robbery, which ultimately would be Walter Sr's undoing and led to his third incarceration, this time for forty years at Folsom Prison, Represa, California.

Christine was heartbroken but in spite of everything she still continued to believe her husband was innocent and assured everyone – rather short-sightedly, it would seem – that in all the years she had known Walter, he had always lived a straight life and been a good provider. When friends pointed out his many shortcomings, Christine brushed them aside, saying that perhaps he had temporarily lost his mind as a result of the debts and worry over his mother.

In spite of what the woman believed about her husband, the simple fact was that she was now the breadwinner of the family, and Christine very quickly had to come to terms with this fact. The mother of one had always been of a nervous disposition but now – in between bouts of sickness – she acquired a job as a supervisor at a telephone exchange where she was often forced to work long into the evening hours, just to make ends meet.

In spite of her nerves and the exhaustion she felt as a single, working mother, Christine was a very determined lady and took it upon herself to write endless letters to the prison where Walter Sr was held, begging officials to obtain his release. Every spare moment she had away from her job and son was spent writing notes to anyone she believed could help, including Thomas Gannon from the prison board. Unfortunately, writing to Gannon did not have the outcome she wanted, and instead of securing Walter Sr's release, the official was instead saddled with informing Christine of her husband's shady past.

When Christine read the letter telling her that Walter Sr had been in prison several times before, she was utterly bewildered and devastated. "I was very unaware of Mr Collins' previous offenses," she wrote to Gannon in 1925. "I was really surprised as well as greatly disappointed."

In spite of this, Christine still believed her husband should be released from prison, and upped her attempts in this regard. She continued to write to the prison as often as she could, but then also made the mistake of hiring a lawyer in San Francisco, who assured her he would be able to help with the case. Of course, in advance of his assistance, he would need $250 sent to him as soon as possible, and unbelievably Christine decided this was a good investment and forwarded the money, which she had borrowed from one of her friends.

Sadly, after six long months of letters, there remained no contact from the lawyer, who had conveniently disappeared the moment he received the cash. She tried for a long time to get the money back, but eventually Christine was faced with the inevitable reality that in spite of the lawyer's claims to be able to help her, she was now – more than ever – on her own.

Still depressed from being scammed by the lawyer, Christine then made the awful mistake of sending a sum of money to Thomas Gannon, in order to show her "appreciation" for his help. Utterly appalled, when Gannon received the cash he immediately wrote back to Collins and chastised her for trying to bribe him in some way. "Please understand," she wrote back, "I meant it as a personal appreciation and not as compensation in the least." Whether her "appreciation" was as innocent as she said remains to be seen, but certainly she was desperate enough to try anything at that point in order to have her husband returned to the family home.

By the time January 1928 rolled round, Christine Collins was on the verge of a nervous breakdown and had been ordered to rest by her doctor. Unfortunately, this was not possible, given that she had rent to pay and a child to support, so instead she continued to work long hours at the telephone exchange and kept on writing letters in the hope of freeing her husband. "We really need his support," she wrote to the chairman of the prison board, adding how very sincere she was in stating that fact.

Finally, in February 1928, Christine received some hopeful news when George B. Anderson, Transportation Manager at Los Angeles Railway (and Walter Sr's former employer), agreed to approve any request for parole. Unfortunately, no parole hearing ever came and she had to continue with her work, which often involved working weekends. Neither Christine nor her son Walter enjoyed the weekend work but as a single parent she barely had a choice if she wanted to provide for her family. As a result, on Saturday, 10 March 1928, the young woman was called into work at the telephone exchange and she was forced to leave her son to fend for himself until she got home.

In order to entertain the child while she was gone, Christine gave him some pocket money and told him to go to the cinema. "I'll be back later," she said as she headed out of the door. The child then dressed himself in a red plaid lumber jacket, brown cord trousers and grey cap, and headed off to see a film before his mother was due to return home.

At 5 p.m. the young boy was spotted briefly by his neighbour, Mrs A. Baker, but when Christine returned home later that evening, Walter was not in the house. This came as a surprise to her, since he was supposed to return home as soon as the movie had finished, and in the past he had always been an exceptionally straightforward child who always did as he was told. Fearing the worst, Christine immediately panicked and phoned the police, though they were of no help to the concerned woman, saying they were reluctant to look for the child as he would most likely turn up eventually by himself.

Told to call back if the "runaway" had not returned within twenty-four hours, Christine then spent the next day in utter despair before she had an idea. Telephoning the police again, Christine gave them the information that her husband was incarcerated and that she was worried the child had been kidnapped as revenge by one of his old criminal enemies. This disclosure prompted the police finally to take the woman seriously and they began investigating where on earth the child could have gone.

They did not have much to go on. Apart from the neighbour who had seen Walter at 5 p.m., there were no other clues or sightings, so they took the decision to report the disappearance in the *Los Angeles Times* in order to encourage people to come forward. The report in the paper prompted all sorts of people to contact them, though inevitably the calls they received often led to more questions than answers. Some people claimed they had seen the child with an "Italian-looking man", others said they spotted him with a man and a woman, while one – a service station attendant – reported rather disturbingly that he had seen a child meeting Walter Jr's description, dead in the back seat of a Nash sedan.

Everyone had begun to panic by this time and the Lincoln Park lake was dragged in an effort to find the boy. Added to that, many false leads were investigated and people continued to come forward with "sightings" which never came to anything. Finally, after months of investigation, the police were no further forward in finding Walter Collins, and Christine was distraught but – as always – refused to give up hope. "Mrs Collins is confident that no harm has befallen her boy and that he will be safely returned to her," police told reporters.

Then suddenly, after five months had gone by, Christine Collins received the news for which she had been waiting. Walter had been found, and not only that, he was safe and well. The story went that the child had been found wandering alone in DeKalb, Illinois, and after some prompting, he eventually admitted that he was the child for whom everyone had been looking. Christine was ecstatic and relieved. She paid $70 for his train fare to Los Angeles, and travelled to the train station, where the Los Angeles Police Department had called together many reporters and spectators to witness the event and revel in the fact that they had finally found the missing boy.

Unfortunately, as the passengers began to depart the train, it soon became apparent to Christine that Walter was not aboard. Confused, she looked along the platform, and there, coming towards her, was a boy who had a slight passing resemblance to her son, but nothing more. He clearly was not her child; she knew it from the moment she set eyes on him, and his appearance at the station was confusing to say the least. Nevertheless, he was the boy who had come home as her son, and when the police thrust "Walter" into her arms, flash bulbs popped and everyone was happy – except Christine.

"I do not think that is my boy," she said. "I do not think that is my boy."

But unbelievably, instead of becoming embarrassed by the lies he had told in order to get to Los Angeles, the imposter immediately flung his arms around his "mother" for a much longed-for hug. The woman was uncomfortable and told the police so, but they chose to ignore her cries of confusion. Instead, she was encouraged to smile sweetly and pose for the cameras, all the time being told that she must simply be mistaken; that Walter recognized her so of course he must be her son.

The child's recognition of his "mother" was all the police needed to see, and although she continued to tell them that he did not belong to her, they shrugged off her concerns and quite astonishingly sent Christine home to "try him out" for a couple of weeks. No one can possibly imagine just how gut-wrenching this decision must have been for the woman, returning home to 217 North Avenue 23 with a boy who was clearly not her own.

What must they have spoken about during the journey home? Did Christine ask the boy what was going on or did she choose to remain silent? We'll never know, but it is exceptionally clear that Christine Collins was distraught beyond belief in the knowledge that not only was she now looking after a child who was not hers, but that the police had given up their search for the real Walter Collins.

On the next day the newspapers beamed photographs of the mother–son reunion and while they reported Christine Collins's remarks, they also assured readers that they were only as a result of confusion. Walter was emaciated and drawn due to the harrowing time he had endured at the hands of his kidnapper, they said, therefore it was – according to them – only natural that Christine would not recognize him straightaway. They also added that there was absolutely no doubt in Walter's mind that Christine was his mother, and that over the course of the reunion she had gradually become convinced of the matter too. This was not true, of course, but at that point nobody seemed to care.

While Christine Collins remained convinced that her child was still missing, the new Walter gave a performance worthy of an Oscar during concise and informative interviews, covering every detail of how the kidnapping had taken place. According to the child, he was playing with some children at a vacant lot near to his home, when a man approached and told him he had been sent to get him by his mother. "He said mother had given him $15 to go and buy me a suit of clothes," "Walter" told police, before adding that he had been expecting to get a new suit and, as the man had promised he was a friend of his mother, he had believed it was perfectly fine to go with him.

The child then went on to invent an elaborate tale where he was taken to the home of a Mexican woman and then they all moved to Hollywood, where they stayed for several days. The man apparently told "Walter" that his parents were not really related to him and he was then introduced to his real father, who took him "way east, getting rides when we could and sometimes riding on trains when daddy had enough money to pay for our fares".

Finally, he described how they eventually reached DeKalb, where he was picked up by police and questioned as to who he was and what he was doing there. The boy then told the Los Angeles police that at first he had not wanted to say anything about his real identity because his "daddy" had told him not to.

The entire story was a lie, every tiny part of it, though where the child acquired the guts and cheek to make up such an elaborate tale is anyone's guess. What is tragic, however, is that while "Walter" enjoyed telling everyone about his harrowing experience and revelled in the attention it brought, Christine Collins had to witness the spectacle, knowing that the child was an imposter and lying in front of her very eyes. But the police were happy to listen to and believe his lies, it would seem, and for three weeks Christine and "Walter" lived together in the home she had once shared with her real son.

While it seemed to those in authority that Christine had finally accepted the child as her own, the reality was that at the very time she was sharing her home with the imposter, she was quietly but efficiently researching how best to prove that the boy was not her own. Here was the woman who fought for years to get her husband out of prison, who would not accept no for an answer, and who worked all the hours she could to keep her family together. There was no way she was ever going to give up trying to find her son, and she put all her energies into her research.

At first it seemed a daunting task, but finally Collins was able to obtain absolute proof that the boy was an imposter by accessing official documents relating to the real Walter Collins Jr. The child in her care had been circumcised, and medical records allowed her to prove that her Walter had not, while dental records showed that Christine's child had completely different teeth to the new Walter. This was not all. Christine spoke to her son's teachers and friends and not one of them would believe that the new child in class was the original Walter Collins.

The distraught mother finally had something positive to work with and she compiled everything she had found in order to convince the authorities of their mistake. Shockingly, even at that point, the police still believed that the new Walter was the child they had been looking for all those months and instead of believing Christine's research, she was chastised and called a cruel-hearted woman who wanted to shirk her responsibilities. Then, as if things could not get any worse, the police decided they'd had enough of Christine Collins's constant bombardment and declared her insane because of her refusal to accept the child as her own. She was packed off to the Los Angeles County General Hospital on a Code 12, reserved for what the police described as "bothersome people".

Still, in spite of the fact that they had now disposed of Christine Collins, the police were beginning to worry that maybe she was telling the truth. They sat down with the new Walter and asked him to write a paragraph of text, which was then compared to a sample of the real Walter's handwriting. Surprise, surprise, the two did not match and the imposter was exposed. But faced with such damning evidence, the child still did not crack. Instead, he wrote a note saying his name was Billy Fields and he had pretended to be Walter Collins to get into the movies. When questioned further he then changed his mind and pretended to be called Tommy Danny Ozburn, before finally confessing once and for all that he was actually Arthur Hutchins Jr from Marion, Iowa.

As soon as the truth came out, suddenly Arthur Hutchins wanted to tell the entire story of why he had impersonated Walter Collins. He told police that he had always dreamt of moving to Hollywood, gaining fame in the movies and meeting his idol, Western actor, Tom Mix. He had originally run away because he hated his stepmother Violet, and it seems the feeling was mutual as she had been in no rush to find him. However, she did decide to travel to California to collect Arthur once he had made headlines around the world and, as they were reunited, posed happily for the photographers, revelling in her new-found Hollywood fame.

The devastating consequences of Arthur's actions must surely have been realized by the boy as he grew older, but for now the child travelled back to Iowa with his stepmother, feeling no remorse for what he had done. When asked about it by journalists, he replied that it had all just been a game.

But for Christine Collins, the whole experience had been nothing like "a game". On 13 September 1928, she was finally released from the psychiatric ward. She later wrote in a letter that she had been held for five days and five nights "among the maniacs" in the hospital because "I would not accept him . . . I was called a liar, damn fool, crook . . ." She also painfully revealed that while she had lost her son, she had also lost her job, too, due to the stigma of being admitted to the insane ward.

The episode had caused great trauma in her life, but Christine was at least relieved that she had been right about Arthur Hutchins all along. However, the question on everyone's lips was that if Arthur was not Christine's child, then what on earth had happened to the real Walter Collins? Whole books have been written on the subject, but it would seem that, more than likely, Walter had tragically become involved in what were to become known as the Wineville Chicken Coop Murders.

The case is a long, complicated and confusing one, but in short, it involved a psychopath by the name of Gordon Northcott, who kidnapped many young boys, held them captive on his chicken ranch, raped, tortured and finally murdered them with the help of his mother and nephew, Sanford Clark. Sadly, it was later revealed that Sanford was himself a victim of Northcott and was forced to take part in the events very much against his will.

Gordon Northcott would have gone on kidnapping and abusing young boys if it were not for Sanford's sister Jessie who arrived in Wineville to visit her brother. Sanford was originally from Canada but had been brought to the ranch by the deranged Northcott under false pretences, and then had been too terrified to leave. Jessie noticed a real change in her little brother but at first he denied that anything was wrong. However, one evening shortly before she returned to Canada, Sanford finally had the strength to tell the girl exactly what had been going on at the ranch, and how he feared that his uncle was going to kill him too.

Though she was shocked beyond belief, Jessie pretended to Northcott that she knew nothing of the crimes, for fear he would kill both herself and her brother if she spoke out. However, on her return to Canada she immediately contacted the American Consul, who in turn contacted the Los Angeles Police Department. On the pretext of visiting over an immigration issue, inspectors travelled to the ranch. As they approached along the dusty road, Northcott caught sight of them and, along with his mother, fled to nearby trees, but not before telling Sanford that if he dared tell the officers what had been happening, he would shoot him from his hiding place.

After two hours of questioning, Sanford finally felt confident enough to share his horrific story with the men, and a warrant was immediately taken out on Northcott and his mother. By this time the pair were heading towards Canada, which is where they were both eventually picked up and brought into police custody.

Police were absolutely appalled to learn exactly what Northcott had been up to. Sanford told them that his uncle had apparently used quicklime to dispose of some of the bodies, while burning others, and that any further remains had been buried in shallow graves on the ranch. The police then showed the boy a photograph of Walter Collins and, on close inspection, Sanford sadly confirmed that the little boy had been just one of those murdered and buried on the property.

When police scoured the area, they did indeed find the shallow graves described by Sanford, though they never found complete bodies. As Sanford had previously told them, the evidence had been destroyed with quicklime and burning, so all that remained were various body parts and personal items from the missing boys. Added to that, it was also claimed that Northcott and his mother had exhumed some of the bodies and buried them in the desert during August 1928.

Because of Sanford's identification of Walter Collins, it was believed that the boy had indeed been at the ranch, and had more than likely been murdered and buried with the others. However, after his arrest and during his subsequent trial, Northcott's testimony about exactly what he had done and who was involved was shaky to say the least. Smiling wildly for the cameras, it soon became apparent that he enjoyed the fame and notoriety brought by the case, and he changed his story frequently.

Even the announcement that he would be sentenced to death for his crimes did nothing to deter his confidence, and much to everyone's surprise, he agreed to be visited by Christine Collins while he was awaiting his death sentence. The strength shown by Walter's mother was enormous, but the monster she encountered behind bars showed no remorse for what he had done. Instead, he actually seemed to enjoy toying with the grief-stricken woman, making comments that would boil the blood of the calmest of people. A photograph of Christine meeting the cold-blooded killer is hard to look at; the uncomfortable woman is sitting in a chair, hands in her lap and lips closed tightly; Northcott, who was recovering from flu at the time, looks slightly out of it, his eyes rolling upwards to the ceiling, his body covered in a cheap blanket.

It had been widely reported that Northcott's mother (and later Northcott himself) had confessed to killing Walter, but when Christine asked the murderer straight, "Did you kill my son?" he replied, "I did not kill your boy." The confusing meeting ended with Christine telling Northcott that she still believed her son was alive, and with that she left the room.

Christine Collins showed the strength of her resolve when, shortly afterwards, she sued Captain J. J. Jones of the LAPD for the unlawful confinement that had led to her being sectioned, and in September 1930 she won her case. Just two days before Gordon Northcott was hanged for his crimes, Christine was awarded $10,800 in damages, and told reporters that she had not pursued the case for money for herself. Instead, she declared with utter conviction that she had never been satisfied with the belief that Northcott had killed her son, and that "I intend to spend the money obtained in this judgement in seeing my lost son, if he still lives."

Just before Northcott was hanged, Christine Collins had the opportunity to question him again, but was left distraught when the "awful person" (as Christine described him) continually teased her and contradicted himself, happy in the knowledge that Christine would never know the extent of his involvement with her son. Northcott then went to his death knowing all the answers, and confident that the families of those he had murdered would never know anything but the scantest detail.

The grief caused by the crimes of Graham Northcott and his mother led to the renaming of Wineville to Mira Loma, in order to rid itself of the awful legacy he had left behind. The house where it all happened, however, remained, though over the years the surrounding area has been vastly redeveloped.

As for Christine, after the whole tragic episode had concluded the woman tried to get on with her life as best she could, campaigning once again for her husband's release and trying in vain to find her son. Unfortunately she would see neither of them again: Walter Sr died in a prison hospital on 16 August 1932 after suffering from atrophy of the liver, brought on by jaundice. The plans she had made to use Captain Jones's money to help fund her search for Walter also came to nothing when he shirked his responsibility to pay the bill and she was left with nothing. To the end of her days, Christine Collins searched quietly for her son away from the media spotlight. She passed away in 1964.

Her story was later told in the 2008 film, *Changeling*, which starred Angelina Jolie as Christine. Given time constraints in the film, her story could not be told in full, exactly as it happened, but nevertheless her strength, determination and compassion shone through to the very end. She may not have known it in life, but in death Christine Collins has become a true inspiration, a symbol of what a woman will go through for the love of her family.

9

Clara Bow, the Lawsuit and the Breakdown

"People are always bringing suits against me and printing scandals about me," complained Clara Bow in June 1930. She wasn't wrong. Clara, the original "It Girl" after her leading role in the film *It* (1927), was the most scandalous star of the 1920s and by the early 1930s she was about to experience her most scandalous – and her saddest – period yet.

In September 1930, Clara Bow was reported to owe a Cal Neva casino $13,900 in gambling debts, which raised many eyebrows in the Hollywood community. Word soon spread that the star had played and lost at the roulette wheel to such an extent that she had to write four cheques for her losses. Unfortunately for the casino, however, each one was returned to the resort as being "stopped" before payment was ever issued.

Clara denied this and laughed off the story, stating that she always paid honest debts promptly, and declaring, "If anyone in the world feels he has a rightful claim against me for any sum of money whatsoever, which I deny, I will gladly accept service of any legal documents."

As described in an earlier chapter ("Clara Bow's Scandalous Love Life"), "Crisis a Day Clara", as she was known, had been in and out of the headlines for the past few years on account of her scandalous love life with a publicity-hungry nightclub-owner and a married doctor. Now happy with her new beau, Rex Bell, both she and the studio wanted to put the last two years behind them and hoped this new scandal – and any future ones – could disappear without incident. Unfortunately for Clara, however, the casino gossip was just the tip of the iceberg; less than two months later the scandal of all scandals would erupt, thanks to her long-time secretary Daisy DeVoe.

Clara had met DeVoe on the set of her movie, *Wild Party*, where the woman had been assigned to take care of the actress's hair. They quickly became chummy, and Clara enjoyed her company so much that it was not long before DeVoe was asked to work for her full-time as a secretary.

"I studied it over for a day or two," Daisy later said, "because everyone said Clara was kind of a hard girl to work for and I didn't want to lose my job."

It was true that Clara had something of a reputation, but still, the money was better than she was earning at the studio, so DeVoe was certainly interested.

"But if you discharge me, I probably won't get my job back at the studio," DeVoe warned the actress, to which Clara laughed.

"If you work for me you'll never have to worry about your job at the studio," she said. So despite her initial concerns, DeVoe did indeed give up her job, with a promise that Clara would employ her for five years as a personal assistant and companion, starting at $75 per week. However, they also agreed that she would receive a raise in the very near future, which unfortunately never materialized, no matter how much DeVoe reminded her boss.

"I asked her for it numerous times," Daisy later complained. "She always said no."

The working relationship gave her many responsibilities, some of which – as it turned out – were not related to being a secretary at all. This may have been okay if her salary had been raised as agreed, but as it wasn't, DeVoe began to get more than a little irritated. "Clara is a funny child," she later said. "She wanted my companionship and everything."

It would seem that as well as being a secretary, DeVoe was

also saddled with routine tasks such as doing Clara's hair and nails, and dressing, undressing and inspecting the actress's clothes every time she intended to go out. She was also given the task of shooing away unwanted male admirers; grocery shopping; mending clothes; and seeing to it that "her clothes were not left piled on the floor".

The first real rumblings of just how much of an influence DeVoe was having on Clara's life came when Bow was out of town for six weeks, and the secretary took it upon herself to have the entire house not only cleaned but completely reorganized too. "Her house was terribly dirty," she said. "I had the drapes taken down and the rugs taken out and cleaned; floors polished; furniture gone over and everything." What Bow thought of the matter remains unrecorded, but certainly it would seem that as far as a working relationship went, DeVoe had her feet well and truly under the newly polished table.

The biggest example of how much DeVoe took over Clara's life comes in the discovery that the pair took the decision to set up a bank account together. They nicknamed it "The Clara Bow Special Account" and it was opened with $1,500 of Clara's money, giving DeVoe the ability to take cash out for household expenses. She later explained the purpose of the account to police:

> I couldn't draw anything on Clara's [personal] account unless I had a cheque with her signature, and each week I would take a cheque with her signature to the bank and put money into the special account for the household expenses. Almost all the money Clara spent was out of the household account. She very seldom wrote her own cheques.

But while it was nice for Clara to be looked after, the secretary went too far at times, such as the day when she found love letters to her employer from ex-boyfriends Dr Earl Pearson, Harry Richman, Gary Cooper and Victor Fleming.

"She had two drawers of letters that she had gotten from them," explained DeVoe. "I knew she would want them but I took them and burned them because I didn't think it was advisable for a woman in her position to have things like that lying around."

On that particular occasion, Clara arrived home just in time to see her beloved letters burning to a crisp in the back yard. "What have you done?" she screamed at the secretary, but it seems that DeVoe was not in the least bit apologetic. Clara was furious that her secretary had not only found her letters, but had seemingly also decided to read and destroy them. The two women fought for days about the episode.

Unfortunately, although she was torn to pieces for touching Clara Bow's personal property, astonishingly this still did not stop DeVoe from finding and destroying even more letters, without the knowledge of her employer. "As far as I know she doesn't know it," DeVoe later said. "She would be as mad as the devil about it."

These shocking incidents proved once and for all that DeVoe was stepping over the line between a professional and an obsessive interest in her employer's affairs. It is little wonder then that Clara's boyfriend Rex Bell grew to dislike her immensely, and it would seem that the feeling was mutual, with both parties becoming extremely suspicious and jealous of the time spent with the vivacious Clara. Bell's frustration came when he suspected that as well as general nosiness, DeVoe was also guilty of stealing from her employer, while in return DeVoe believed Bell was trying to persuade the actress to invest money in a phoney get-rich-quick scheme. To say that the hatred of one another was adding to Clara's already heightened stress levels would be an understatement.

On 29 July 1930 – Clara's birthday – DeVoe gave the actress a beautiful, silver dresser set with the initials CB engraved on it. Clara was absolutely delighted. "I thought she was being sweet and kind to me," she later told police. However, sweet and kind wasn't what she thought of her later, when it was claimed that the set had actually been paid for out of Clara's "Special Account" using a cheque authorized by the actress herself. Although Bell did not know for sure that Clara's money had bought her own present, he was suspicious enough about her behaviour to share his concerns with his girlfriend.

Clara was far more trusting, it would seem, and brushed away his comments, refusing to believe that her secretary was being in any way dishonest. However, when she later went to her safety deposit box and noticed several items had gone missing, the actress was mortified. When questioned later, DeVoe claimed to have removed Clara's items from the box in a bid to protect her employer from Bell's dodgy investment scheme. But that was later, and for now, on finding the items missing, Clara told Bell that he must be right; DeVoe really wasn't as honest as she had once believed her to be.

Rex told Clara he thought she had no option but to fire DeVoe, but the conversation between the two was fraught; Clara did not want to let her secretary go, but at the same time she knew she could no longer trust her. The couple began a rather heated debate about how they should tell DeVoe the news . . .

"If you want her to go, Rex, you can tell her yourself, because I won't tell her," Clara told him.

"When will I tell her?" asked her boyfriend, to which Bow replied:

"Any time within the next few days."

"Fine," answered Bell. "I'll tell her Saturday or Monday."

But while this discussion was going on, what neither of them realized was that the secretary was actually resting in the next room. Lying down on her bed, DeVoe had overheard the entire conversation and was absolutely mortified. How dare Clara Bow plan to fire her after all they had been through and everything she had promised? DeVoe was confused but still believed that at the very heart of the matter lay her nemesis, Rex Bell, urging Clara on in matters that DeVoe frankly felt were nothing to do with him.

Later, as he had promised, Rex went to Daisy's room in order to give her the news of her termination, which sent the furious secretary scuttling straight to Bow for an explanation. Shockingly for her, the actress did not deny that DeVoe was losing her job, and instead she told the woman that what Rex had told her was quite correct; she was to leave the house and Clara's employ, effective immediately.

According to DeVoe, when she was ready to leave the Bow house, her employer was so drunk that she decided not to announce her departure; that it was "more ladylike" not to say anything at all. This decision was made, she said, for fear that "she would have tried to kill me", before adding – quite dramatically – that the actress had actually tried to do that on a previous occasion. "I thought it would be better to walk out and later on straighten out her affairs. I wanted to get things settled as quietly as possible," grumbled the secretary.

For DeVoe, "as quietly as possible" meant returning to the house once the dust had settled in order to demand her job back. The answer was a definite no. She was stunned, believing that once Bow had sobered up, she would have seen things differently. Furious, DeVoe then naively contacted Clara's attorney in a misguided attempt to blackmail his client and demanded she receive $125,000 for the very items Daisy had illegally acquired in the first place. If they didn't comply, she added, things could get "complicated".

The lawyer retaliated by telling the secretary that instead of paying the ransom money, his advice to Clara would be to tell the entire, sorry story to the proper authorities. The disgruntled woman then left the office, but did not go home. Instead, she turned up at Clara Bow's house once again, by which time the actress had been advised of the blackmail attempt.

"Give me back my job!" DeVoe screamed at Bow.

"Didn't you just try to blackmail me?" Clara snapped. After which the shocked Daisy apparently admitted everything. "Yes, my best friend; that was the way she answered me," Clara Bow later said in court.

The actress had no wish to give the woman her job back or pay the money being demanded; but at the same time she also had no desire to have a full-blown argument, and refused to listen to Daisy's explanations as to how Clara's personal items had ended up in her possession. Instead DeVoe was sent on her way; the locks to the house were quickly changed; and Clara brought in District Attorney Buron Fitts to investigate the entire matter.

The investigators listened to what Bow had to say, then travelled to the home of DeVoe's sister to interview the secretary about the theft. They questioned her extensively and made notes as she gave her explanation of taking the items for safe keeping. Nobody believed her story and, instead of giving her a warning, they demanded she open her safety deposit box to let them see what was inside. DeVoe did as she was told and the police retrieved a stash of jewellery, a large amount of personal papers and a cashier's cheque.

"I was never going to cash the cheque myself," DeVoe cried. "Clara knows as well as everybody else that I could never have cashed it. I intended giving it back the same as everything I had that belonged to her."

Also included in the box were telegrams from boyfriends Rex Bell, Earl Pearson and Harry Richman, which surprisingly had not been included in the burning ceremony that DeVoe had given the others. All of these remaining notes were of a loving nature, and bound to cause a sensation if publicly released, so when the police turned them back over to Clara, she was exceptionally relieved. Her only hope now was that DeVoe would just disappear quietly, never to be heard of again. Unfortunately for Bow, the former secretary had other ideas about her future.

Instead of putting the whole thing behind her and moving on with her life, DeVoe started grumbling that she wanted answers to why she was fired from Clara's employ. This was surprising considering she had just been relieved of Bow's personal belongings from her safe, and she must have been able to remember the numerous quarrels, the mutual dislike between her and Bell, the conversation she had overheard which explained most of her questions, and finally the threats of blackmail after she had heard her fate. Yet, quite bizarrely, none of this seemed to provide DeVoe with any idea of why she was no longer required in Bow's home. It was all quite astonishing, particularly when, in a misguided effort to gain attention from Clara, DeVoe decided to contact the press to tell them her story – leaving out the parts about blackmail and theft, of course.

"For two years I have pulled Clara out of plenty of messes and saved her plenty of money," she joyfully told them. She then turned her attention to the gambling debts in Nevada, claiming that, sure enough, Clara did indeed have debts there, as well as approximately $12,000 more at other resorts. And still the revelations went on: "She suffers from insomnia and she doesn't sleep," a gleeful DeVoe revealed. "As a result she kept me awake all night. I worked twenty-four hours a day for her and if there were forty-eight hours in a day I would have worked forty-eight . . . I could never leave her alone at any time."

The reporters were riveted. "Crisis a Day Clara" was always good press, but with an insider now on their side, they were in heaven. Once the press conference was over, the reporters scuttled back to their typewriters to pen what they hoped would be the first of many juicy articles on the It Girl's private life. The first article was published the next day and, needless to say, Clara was blindsided. Not only was she shocked that there were revelations about her private life in the papers, but also she was utterly gobsmacked that her former secretary could spill the beans in such a way.

Never one to be quiet when it came to commenting in the press, Clara decided to issue a short statement of her own, claiming:

The more I talk the worse it gets, so I'm not saying much. If I cannot let go a secretary without a lot of fuss why should I talk? I fired Daisy for a personal reason and this reason is nobody's business but my own. So that's that.

The star also denied a recent rumour that she had now employed a male secretary, and then privately hoped very much that the whole sorry affair could now be forgotten once and for all. But it was not going to be that easy. DeVoe was a woman scorned and she took no time in telling reporters that if the actress refused to see her and give an explanation about why she was fired, she would have no option but to visit a lawyer.

Sure enough, the very next day Daisy hired attorney Nathan O. Freedman, who was instructed to file a suit against District Attorney Buron Fitts and his aides. This was a bold gesture, especially when it was revealed that the reason she hired him was to recover jewellery and items that she claimed had belonged to her, but were taken from her safety deposit box during the raid for Clara Bow's belongings.

"I have returned everything that belonged to Clara," she grumbled. "I also gave her back her fur coat, but why do they keep my cash and jewels and insurance papers? My attorney has made demand for them and they will not return them. We are going to sue." She also assured reporters that not only would she go after the District Attorney's office, but Clara Bow too, who she claimed had kept back salary and expenses owed to her.

In the end, the persistence of Daisy DeVoe led not to a lawsuit against Bow and Fitts, but to the arrest and prosecution of the secretary herself, who was accused of thirty-seven counts of grand theft, adding up to $16,000 in total. She was absolutely astounded and determined to fight her corner with all her might. She had lost her job; been accused of theft; and had her safety deposit box rummaged but DeVoe was a fighter and this time she was determined that if she was going to fall, she would be taking Clara Bow down with her.

The much publicized trial of Daisy DeVoe began in

January 1931 and from the very beginning of proceedings, the world and waiting press were transfixed. DeVoe seemed to revel in the attention her stories brought, but for Clara, the trial would reveal much more about her personal life than she ever feared, and from day one, it was a stressful and at times hurtful episode.

From the very outset, Clara's finances were brought into the frame when it was revealed that in a period of twenty months, the actress had spent $350,000 on everything from household expenses to cars to tips in restaurants and much more. This raised eyebrows, but audible gasps were heard when it was also argued that some of the money was not spent by Bow herself, but by Daisy DeVoe, who was accused of ordering jewellery for herself using her employer's own money. This wasn't all. It also transpired that a cheque for $400 was cashed for her benefit, and a glamorous fur coat had been purchased – all at the actress's expense.

Clara Bow arrived at court wearing dark glasses, which friends later claimed were to hide a recent operation on her face. She was also suffering from a bad cold and was seen crying and frequently coughing during the proceedings, while the ex-secretary glowered and smirked from her position in court. It inevitably wasn't long before Clara looked over and saw the faces being pulled by her former friend, and this drove the short-tempered actress to the point of explosion. Much to the shock of everyone, the actress suddenly shot forward in her chair and dramatically shouted at DeVoe, "Go ahead and sneer Daisy, that's all right!" This impromptu outburst caused the shocked Deputy District Attorney to shoot to his feet in order to caution Bow for interrupting the court.

Once it was her turn to take to the stand, Clara was asked if she had ever authorized cheques to be written by Daisy DeVoe and in particular if she gave permission for a series of whisky purchases. "I authorized Miss DeVoe to spend whatever was necessary to maintain the household," she replied, before adding, "I trusted her. If she wanted to buy whisky, why, I supposed she made out the checks and signed them."

"Didn't you ever check the books?" DeVoe's attorney asked. To which Clara replied sadly, "No, that's why I was so silly. I trusted her."

When asked if her ex-secretary had ever spent her own money on household expenses, Clara could not believe her ears, resorting to her Brooklyn slang in order to answer the question.

"She never spent anything out of her dough for me!" she replied. "She didn't have a cent until she worked for me."

At one point Clara broke down when asked about the birthday present that had been bought with her own money, and a cheque for $825 which had been signed by the actress and used by DeVoe to buy herself a fur coat.

"That is my cheque, I signed it myself," Clara sobbed. "But Miss DeVoe brought it to me and said it was to go on my income tax and I signed it because I trusted her."

More sorrow and embarrassment came when the telegrams from various beaus were introduced into evidence and read aloud in court. Why the private contents had to be revealed was a mystery, and much to her dismay, Clara found that not only were the telegrams heard by everyone in attendance, but there were also plans to reproduce them in the newspapers the next morning. The actress was in obvious dismay; her private life with ex-partners were about to be made public and there was nothing at all she could do about it. But that wasn't all, as later came a dramatic turn of events when a document was read to the court which apparently showed Daisy DeVoe being asked how much of Clara's money she had appropriated for her own use. Shockingly she had boldly replied:

"About $35,000. I can't tell exactly."

When the unapologetic woman was asked when she started to acquire the money, she revealed in the document that it had been around September or October 1929, and gave a half-hearted attempt at an explanation:

"It's so hard to see a girl like Clara with everything and no respect for anything. It was her fault. If she had paid attention to business I wouldn't have taken a dime from her because she would have known about everything."

The woman then went on to complain that the actress refused to write her own cheques and as a result, "she put me in a position to take everything I wanted. Of course I didn't blame her."

One example of the "no respect" that DeVoe attributed to Clara came in the shape of a diamond-studded vanity case which the actress was said to have cared so little about that she let her dogs play with it. The secretary was horrified to see such an expensive item treated this way and took it upon herself to rescue it from their canine clutches and place it in her safety deposit box. It would appear, of course, that this was not after any negotiation with Bow, who seemed oblivious to the case ever being taken.

Then more damning testimony came when it was claimed that shortly before her arrest, DeVoe had arrived at the bank and drawn out $22,000 from the "Special Account". She then told staff that she was withdrawing the money as she did not wish Clara to invest in any of Rex Bell's "wild schemes". "I'm going to place it in the safe deposit box where Clara can't find it," the secretary told an officer at the California Bank. It would appear that in this instance, the safety deposit box she was referring to belonged to Clara, though the money did not appear to have ended up there, as when Clara requested to see the box several days later, it was apparently empty.

All these revelations and titbits of information were compelling and the court was transfixed by what they had heard. However, this was nothing, as when Daisy DeVoe took to the witness stand herself, all hell broke loose. In the space of an hour Clara's world imploded when the secretary declared that her employer played poker at least six nights a week; drank extreme amounts of alcohol; and bought jewellery as presents for a variety of different men. Of the latter, Daisy claimed that her ex-employer had spoiled married Earl Pearson with a $4,000 watch, while Harry Richman received a $2,000 ring. She also claimed that Clara bought herself a $10,000 engagement ring, though declined to tell the court to which man she planned to become betrothed.

All these revelations were too much for the fragile actress, who was still suffering from a serious cold. Sent to bed by her doctor, Wesley Hommel, her condition was described as "not serious", though she was revealed to be running a high temperature and suffering from nervous exhaustion. Sadly, the emotional distress put upon Clara during the trial was very much the shape of things to come and it would seem that she never fully recovered from her days in court.

On 23 January 1931, after dozens of revelations about Clara Bow's love life, personal habits and financial affairs, as well as two days of deliberation and disagreements, the jury were ready to give their verdict. It had been a hard slog, with many arguments behind the scenes, but finally Ralph H. Boynton, foreman of the jury, stood up to speak.

"Have you reached a verdict?" asked the judge.

"Yes sir, we have, your Honour," replied Boynton.

Thirty-five slips of paper were then handed over to the judge, who read them to himself over the course of the next few minutes. Finally the drama of the court case and the stress of waiting for the verdict took its toll on the normally bolshie DeVoe, who lay her head on the table and sobbed uncontrollably to herself.

After reading the outcome, it was announced that the former secretary was not guilty of thirty-four of the counts brought against her, but was guilty of one: the charge that Daisy had bought herself a fur coat with money Clara believed was to pay her income tax bill. The jury pleaded for a recommendation of leniency, but even this was too much for DeVoe to handle. As the verdict was read out, her sobs became even more violent and then, unbelievably, members of the jury dissolved into tears too.

The entire episode was like something from a bad movie, and at this point many spectators jumped on to the backs of their seats in order to get a better look at what was going on. The whole court was erupting into hysteria and bailiffs tried to restore order and get people to sit down, but it was an almighty task. As bedlam ensued, Daisy's sobs could be heard echoing all around the courtroom.

Then finally, her sobs began to turn into disgruntled words, and Daisy began shouting her displeasure between the tears.

"If they were going to convict me at all why didn't they convict me of everything? I'm just as guilty on all counts as I am on one."

Then the time came for her to leave the courtroom, which she did while leaning heavily on the arm of a bailiff and a newspaper reporter.

"I can't stand it; I can't stand it," she cried, as she was led to the jail.

When the room eventually emptied, one of the jurors earned her fifteen minutes of fame by speaking to reporters outside the courtroom; telling them that "I'm sorry for Miss DeVoe, but I felt that pity should not be allowed to interfere with the necessity of upholding the laws of the State of California." She then went on to speak for many minutes, declaring that DeVoe needed to be made an example of and that justice would only ever be served by a conviction. She then added, "In the end, Miss DeVoe will see herself that it was best for us to convict her", though in reality it was pretty clear to everyone that Daisy would never agree with that remark.

Back in Beverly Hills, Clara was still ill as a result of flu and stress. Contacted by reporters, her statement was short and sweet: "I harbour no ill will against Miss DeVoe," she said. "For Daisy's sake, I hope the court will be lenient."

For the next few months, Daisy DeVoe tried to obtain her release from prison and at one point was let out on bond, though she was soon carted back after she failed to win an appeal. Clara, meanwhile, was going through hell in her Beverly Hills home, fighting depression and collapsing on set – a move which was to lead to her being replaced in at least two separate movies. Then another disaster came when it was revealed that publisher Frederick Girnau had been arrested for sending an obscene article about Clara through the US mail service.

The article was full of lies – terrible at best and libellous at worst – but for Clara it was the straw that broke the camel's back. She suffered a full-blown nervous breakdown and was immediately rushed to Glendale Sanatorium, where she was ordered to rest for six months, while at the same time being put through a series of cures to "relieve" her stress, including electric shock treatment and an abstinence from all visitors. "Absolute quiet is necessary for recuperation," the doctor told concerned friends, while Clara herself managed to get word out that she was planning to retire from pictures indefinitely.

Studio boss B. P. Schulberg pretended not to be too worried; after all, his star had made threats to leave at various stages of her career in the past, and nothing had ever come of it. He told reporters that no decision would be made until Clara was well enough to talk, but that "she is in no condition to talk business at the present time".

However, just days later came the shock news that Clara was adamant about her retirement and had requested that her contract be cancelled immediately. Paramount were beside themselves, as their star still had two more films to make before the projected end of her contract in October 1931. At the same time they knew that there was nothing they could ever do to control Clara Bow; they had never succeeded in doing so in the past, and they knew they wouldn't in the future. It was with a heavy heart, therefore, that they reluctantly agreed on the termination and Schulberg released a statement: "In accordance with Clara's wishes, we have consented to tear up her contract with Paramount." He then went on to say how difficult it was to discard an association he had enjoyed for many years, "particularly with one who has earned our personal liking and admiration . . . I am sorry to see her leave Paramount for she is a great and popular screen star."

While Paramount licked their wounds and wondered who would become the next It Girl, from her sick bed, Clara released her own statement:

"I am deeply grateful. Already I feel much better than I have for many weeks, as I struggled to regain my health so that I could carry on. I wanted my contract broken if Paramount saw fit, so that I might get back on my feet again . . . Now that this worry is over I can face the task of regaining my health with a free mind. It's like leaving home to leave the studio after so many years, but I know it is the best thing for me to do."

A few days later Clara Bow travelled to Nevada to spend time with Rex Bell and recuperate on his ranch, telling reporters, "I am going to forget anything and everything connected with pictures." She then added, "as soon as I'm able, I will become what is known as a freelance player, contracting for a single production at a time". She also denied rumours that she would sign with another studio, although she did admit to having various offers, all of which she had turned down, until the time was right that she could "stage a comeback".

In the end, Clara Bow never did make the big comeback she hoped for, though she did marry Rex Bell and gave birth to two sons whom she adored. She was never far from scandal and health problems, with another threat of a lawsuit from a casino and several breakdowns adding to her problems in future years. She also never obtained the full happiness she had always looked for, and she was unable to recover from the Daisy DeVoe trial, which had sent her over the edge in the first place. She died of a heart attack on 27 September 1965 at the age of sixty, and ex-lover Harry Richman was chosen to be one of the pall-bearers at her funeral.

Clara's life and career were over and, for some considerable years, her films were forgotten. However, in 2011 the producers of *The Artist* became inspired by the actress and looked at her style in order to create the look of one of the main characters in the film. Since then, interest in her has had something of a revival, with a new documentary broadcast in the UK during December 2012 and an exclusive showing of her movie *It* played to a packed-out audience in London in January 2013.

But what of Daisy DeVoe? Well, when she was released from prison in April 1933, the former secretary went to work in the aviation industry. Of her time in jail, she later declared, "I had a ball", while explaining that the prison wardens had loved her as she always volunteered to polish their nails . . .

10

Peg Entwistle and the Hollywood Sign

Although her career has been long since forgotten, Peg Entwistle gains the grisly and tragic honour of being the only person to ever commit suicide by jumping to her death from the Hollywood sign.

Millicent Lilian (Peg) Entwistle was born in Port Talbot, Wales, in 1908. She was brought up in London and New York, although her childhood was not a happy one. The details are still shrouded in mystery, but it is said that she tragically endured the death of her mother, stepmother and father, all by the year 1922.

Determined that her adult life would be better than her childhood, Peg became a stage actress, appearing in Boston and on Broadway, where she began to forge a busy career. She acted in plays such as *The Home Towners* and *Tommy*, and treated her career very seriously, studying hard and insisting that she would prefer to play roles that carry conviction rather than the standard Hollywood fluff. "To play any kind of emotional scene I must work up to a certain pitch. If I reach this in my first word, the rest of the words and lines take care of themselves," she told an interviewer early in her career.

As time went on, her career really began to take off, but unfortunately Peg was still unfulfilled in her personal life. This seemed destined to change in April 1927, however, as while acting in Eugene O'Neill's *The Great God Brown* she met actor Robert Keith and the two hit it off straight away. Incredibly, such was the attraction that the two decided to marry just four days later – a decision that she was later to regret.

Predictably, the marriage was not a happy one. The couple fought constantly, and when they divorced in 1929 Peg said that her life with Keith had been a continuous round of pain and suffering. According to the actress, he had torn her hair from her head and also failed to tell her he was the father of a six-year-old son from a former marriage. Suddenly marrying after only days of knowing each other did not seem such a good idea, and she would never make the same mistake again.

Free from the abusive marriage, in 1929 Peg visited California with the New York Theatre Guild to appear at the Geary Theater. Unfortunately, on her return to New York, her career seemed to slow somewhat and she ended up appearing in several plays that did not enjoy the same success as she had previously experienced. In April 1932, Peg decided to leave her Broadway career behind and instead travel back to Los Angeles in search of fame and fortune in the movies. Once there, she moved into her Uncle Harold's Beachwood Drive home and was ecstatic to win a part in the play *The Mad Hopes* by Romney Brent. Her joy was short-lived, however, when the play was not deemed a success and closed very quickly, taking Peg's hopes of stardom with it.

Still, she refused to give up on herself. Until the downturn she had experienced on Broadway, Peg's career had been relatively successful and she was determined it would be even better in the future. Her dreams looked set to come true when RKO offered her a part in their film, *Thirteen Women*, though after completion she heard rumours that most of her work had ended up on the cutting-room floor. As if that wasn't bad enough, the film itself was delayed during editing, preventing its release for some time to come.

Once again her confidence was shaken; her first big role had possibly ended up on the cutting-room floor and no other films were on the horizon. She became depressed, but this time Peg did not have the strength to pull herself and her career back together again. Her spirit was broken, her nerves shot, and friends blamed it all on the depressing part she had played in *Thirteen Women*. Aged just twenty-four, Peg believed her career was over and on the evening of 16 September she decided she could go on no more.

At her home at 2428 Beachwood Drive, a heartbroken Peg put pen to paper and wrote the following note: "I am afraid. I am a coward. I am sorry for everything. If I had done this a long time ago, it would have saved a lot of pain. P. E."

She folded the paper and placed it in her handbag, before telling her uncle Harold that she was meeting friends at a nearby store. If this was indeed her plan, she never made it, and instead walked two miles to the famous Hollywood sign – the symbol of hope for many would-be actors and actresses including, at one time, Peg herself.

We will never know how long Peg stood at the sign that night. Did she look out over the town, its lights glimmering with the possibility of glamorous film premieres and parties? Did she wonder where it had all gone wrong, and if there was any possibility she could put it all back together again? Who knows. All we know for sure is that at some point during the evening, Peg went to the back of the letter H, located the workmen's ladders and proceeded to climb up. What went through her mind and how long she stood there will forever remain a mystery, but at some point while standing looking out at the city below, Peg Entwistle took a deep breath and threw herself from the fifty-foot letter, sending herself careering down the mountainside, her body a mass of broken bones and dreams.

The next morning, an unidentified female hiker was taking a stroll through the Hollywood Hills when she came across a shoe, jacket and purse. There was no sign of the owner, so the concerned woman looked inside and discovered Peg's last note. Having read it, she immediately thought the worst, and started to look around for a body. She did not have to search long, as when she happened to gaze down the mountainside, much to her horror she saw a crumpled body lying there.

The last thing the hiker wanted was any kind of publicity, so instead of trying immediately to raise the alarm about the young woman who had fallen to her death, she decided to do things as quietly as she possibly could. She gathered up Peg's purse, shoe and jacket, wrapped them carefully and took them to the Hollywood police station, where she laid them neatly on the steps of the building. That done, she then walked to a phone booth, telephoned the Central Police Station, gave her statement and quickly hung up.

Police found the bundle of items on the steps of the station and immediately descended on the area of the Hollywood sign, looking for the woman's broken body. It was quickly found and after raising it back up the mountain, the corpse was taken to the morgue where sadly it lay unclaimed. At that point it was not known who the poor woman was, but the police decided to circulate the suicide note to the press, anxious to discover if anyone had any answers.

As Peg's Uncle Harold read his newspaper the next morning, his heart skipped a beat. The suicide letter was signed P. E. – could that possibly be a reference to Peg Entwistle? Surely not. But then he hadn't seen the girl since she had left home several nights ago, so while his heart prayed it couldn't possibly be his niece, his head knew different. Suddenly everything became clear and he raced to the morgue to see for himself. Once there he was shown the body and the horrific realization came that the poor broken girl before him really was the beautiful girl with whom he had been sharing his home in the recent past.

He was devastated, but now that the police had a name, they also wanted an explanation, so despite him being just as confused as they were, Harold told them all he possibly could. He told officers that although Peg had never confided her grief to him, he had become aware of the fact that she was suffering "intense mental anguish". He laid his head in his hands and sadly exclaimed, "She was only 24. It is a great shock to me that she gave up the fight as she did."

Now that the identification had taken place, it was time for

Peg Entwistle's funeral, which was attended by a small gathering of friends. Her body was cremated and her ashes were sent to the family plot in Cincinnati, where she became famous not for being a stunning actress, but for being the first (and likely only) person ever to throw herself from the Hollywood sign.

A sad epitaph came days later when rumours circulated that a letter had arrived at Uncle Harold's house, asking Peg to star in a new play. The accuracy of this story is open to debate, however; and so too is the rumour that Peg Entwistle's ghostly figure is frequently seen ambling around the letter H of the Hollywood sign, still desperately seeking her lost fame and fortune.

11

The Mysterious Death of Paul Bern

When Jean Harlow married older producer Paul Bern, she hoped she had met her partner for life. Tragically, two months later he was found dead, and the shock that rippled around the world was so dramatic that even today the incident is still widely discussed. Whole books have been dedicated to the case; articles have brought forward new theories; and internet forums are still buzzing with people desperate to know what really happened to the husband of the late, great Jean Harlow . . .

Paul Bern was born in Germany in 1889 as Paul Levy and relocated to the United States with his family when he was still a young boy. Deeply interested in the stage, he spent some time acting before moving behind the scenes and carving a career for himself in New York. However, he was ambitious and not content with just working on the East Coast, so eventually moved to Hollywood to work as a writer, producer and director at several studios, but in particular, MGM.

Known as the "Father Confessor", Bern was an extremely popular member of the film industry and was available whenever anyone needed advice, consoling or a good listening ear. His sister later described an incident which confirmed his generous spirit: "I once visited him when he was sick in bed with a high fever. The phone rang. After he was through talking he jumped out of bed and raced away in his car because somebody in need had called him."

This was the kind of man Paul Bern was. He championed

charities, escorted actresses to premieres and was known as a gentle, sincere man. A wonderful friend, yes, but very much a confirmed bachelor it seemed, so when it was announced that he and sex goddess Jean Harlow were to be married in July 1932, Hollywood was astounded. He was forty-two, his bride was twenty-one, and while they had been seen out together many times over the course of a year, nobody thought that the couple were serious about each other. Even when they eventually tied the knot, people who knew them both still could not quite believe it. Bern was a loyal companion, a reliable shoulder to cry on, but husband material? It was believed not.

However, despite what anyone else thought, actress Jean Harlow definitely saw him as someone she could rely on as a husband. Married once before to a man who was rumoured to be abusive and a heavy drinker, the gentle Bern was a welcome change, and they spent much time together before getting married on 2 July 1932 and moving into Bern's home on Easton Drive. At the time, the producer described his wife as the most upright and honest girl he had ever had the privilege of knowing, and friends noted that when they were spotted out together, he always seemed completely besotted and in love.

But despite the happy exterior, there were dark undercurrents in the marriage, and neighbours later reported that while Bern had always happily worked in his garden and talked to neighbours before the wedding, since Jean had moved in, he was distant, shy and almost reclusive. He seemed worried, they told police, as if something was "occupying his mind".

The comments were somewhat concerning, though it should be noted that these neighbours did not come forward until after his untimely death. Perhaps they were inclined to speak in order to enhance the stories surrounding his demise, and certainly it would seem that if people were worried for Bern's welfare in the weeks before his death, they most certainly did not make a big deal of it at the time.

On Saturday, 3 September, Bern was at the studio until 7.10 p.m., and then dined with friends at the Ambassador

Hotel before being driven home by Harold Allen Garrison. Quite bizarrely, according to the driver, it was Bern's custom to keep a gun in the dashboard of the car, but on this particular occasion, when Garrison reached in to retrieve it, it wasn't there.

"You haven't got your gun, Mr Bern?" asked the driver, to which he replied, "No, I didn't take my revolver with me today."

Garrison thought it was odd that the gun was not in the car, given Bern's custom for taking it, but said nothing. Instead, they arranged for the driver to come back to the house at 9.30 the next morning, ready to take Paul Bern out for the day.

That evening, Bern was in good spirits and read scripts in bed until 2 a.m., while his servants entertained friends in their quarters. Jean Harlow was not at home, so his butler, John Carmichael, checked on his boss before he went to bed, and then retired himself. The next morning, Sunday, 4 September, Garrison showed up at Easton Drive as instructed, but Bern did not come out of the house. Instead, the driver ended up waiting for most of the day, until finally at 4.30 he was told that the producer would not require him after all, and he was instructed to return the next morning.

After this time, the story of Paul Bern becomes a hazy mess that is still being debated some eighty-plus years later. After the body of the producer was found shot dead on Monday, 5 September 1932, his butler, Carmichael, told police that Bern was alone in the house on the night of 4 September, as Jean Harlow had stayed with her mother at 1353 Club View Drive. She had gone with her servants to prepare dinner that evening, but while Bern was supposed to have gone with her, he had apparently decided against it at the last minute, telling his wife that he would come along shortly. He never arrived, however, and Jean Harlow telephoned him later in the evening to advise him to stay at home, that it was late and she would remain for the night at her mother's.

According to Carmichael, "Goodbye dear, I'll be seeing

you" were the last words Jean said to her husband as she left for dinner that night, but gardener George Davis disagreed. According to him, there were cross words between the pair; the result, it would seem, of a difference of opinion concerning various financial plans he had with her stepfather Marino Bello and the deeds to their Benedict Canyon home.

Nevertheless, regardless of what was said the night before, by the time the butler opened the shades in Bern's bedroom at 11.30 a.m. the following morning, the producer was dead. As the light from the window fell on to his naked body slumped on the floor of the closet, the shocked butler promptly fainted, bringing the gardener running into the house to discover his boss's body too.

Shockingly, instead of calling the police, the staff decided to call MGM and almost immediately Production Executive Irving Thalberg, Business Executive M. E. Greenwood and RKO Executive David O. Selznick all sped to the home in order to decipher what had gone on and, inevitably, to tidy things up. Jean Harlow was their biggest star and the last thing they wanted or needed was her being tied into a suspicious death mystery. Something needed to be done – and fast.

It would seem that once in the bedroom, the men looked around for a suicide note but, disappointingly for them, could find no such thing. For the whole thing to be wrapped up as a self-inflicted shooting would be simple, quick and would gain sympathy for their star, so the lack of a note was disappointing. However, nearby lay Bern's notebook – a diary of sorts – and that seemed to be the answer to their prayers.

It is believed that studio bosses saw this journal as a way of presenting the death as a definite suicide, and flicked through the entries to see if there was something appropriate they could use. They were in luck, as a cryptic, undated entry had been scrawled in Bern's handwriting. They took the note, arranged it accordingly on the table next to the closet and left. The note read: "Dearest dear; unfortunately this is the only way to make good the frightful wrong I have done you and to wipe out my abject humiliation. Paul." And then underneath: "You understand that last night was only a comedy."

Meanwhile, at her mother's house, Jean was told of the tragedy and was in great shock. Newspapers later reported that on hearing the news, the actress became hysterical and cried, "Isn't this too horrible? Isn't this too terrible?" over and over again.

Police were finally called to the Bern house, and after examining the body and its surroundings, they headed over to the house of Harlow's mother in an attempt to speak to the actress herself. Although initially turned away because she was close to collapse, officers finally interviewed her, though they were disappointed to find they were unable to get much out of her due to the shock of the news. Harlow was accompanied by stepfather Marino Bello, MGM boss Louis B. Mayer, publicity chief Howard Strickland, her doctor and her attorney; the interview was short, with Harlow assuring officers that she knew nothing about the tragedy.

"I can't understand why this terrible thing should have happened," she said. When asked about the note, she replied, "I have no idea what it means. This frightful wrong he apparently believed he had done me is all a mystery. I can't imagine what it means."

The police then asked if Bern had ever mentioned killing himself, to which she said, "Paul often talked to me of suicide as a general topic, but never once did he intimate that he himself contemplated such an act." Would there be any reason why he would kill himself? "There was nothing between us that I can think of that would have caused him to do this."

It was then stepfather Marino Bello's turn to be questioned, and police officers were keen to know about the rumoured financial discussions between himself and Bern. However, whatever was going on between the pair, Bello had no intention of discussing it and instead assured police, "I have more money than Bern ever had and there was no occasion for any financial dealings between us." This seems a rather far-fetched statement considering Bello was something of a playboy who lived off Harlow's money, while Bern was a very successful and rich producer. However, this was Bello's story and he was sticking to it.

The whole episode was beginning to take on the feel of a 1930s detective novel, and was made all the more confusing when neighbours reported hearing a "powerful car" driving away from Easton Drive at 3 a.m. Even more confusion came when Bern's doctor, Ed B. Jones, sent a telegram to Louis B. Mayer, telling him that he understood the motive for the death and would come home from vacation immediately.

On his return he gave a statement to the hungry press: "Bern was suffering from acute melancholia, which brought on a terrific mental depression which developed into a suicide mania." He went on to describe his patient as an unusually sensitive man who was nervous and highly strung. "He was subject to fits of depression which often drive victims to suicide or other hopeless and desperate measures."

This was an intriguing statement on many levels, but the biggest question was why would Bern's personal doctor return from holiday and discuss private matters with a very public press pack? Decorum would have assured his patient confidentiality even after death, with a statement only being made to the police, but instead the doctor quite happily bandied about his patient's innermost problems to the world. It would later be wondered if his comments were made on the orders of MGM, who were desperate for the public to see the death as a suicide and ultimately to sweep the whole thing under the carpet.

Back at her mother's home, Jean Harlow was reportedly still so upset that she ran to the nearest balcony and shockingly tried to throw herself off. Saved by friends and relatives, the delirious actress was then sedated, returning her to a moment of calm.

Still wishing for the police quickly to wrap up their investigation, and the coroner to provide a verdict of suicide,

Louis B. Mayer began telling everyone stories of Bern's depression, which of course tied in rather nicely with the doctor's recent revelations. Mayer detailed that Bern was so depressed in the week before his death that Irving Thalberg believed he needed to take a holiday. "I thought this strange," said Mayer, "for he had only returned some days before from a short vacation." He then went on to say that Bern had acted strange and had "the queerest look about his eyes" during the week prior to his death. "If you knew Mr Bern you would realize this was unusual for him," he said.

Whether or not any of these stories were correct is another matter, and it is interesting to note that the same executives who claimed Bern was acting strange and depressed were also the ones who had entered the property before his death was announced, desperate to find a reason to pass the death off as suicide. To further support their suicide theories, the executives quickly gathered up various employees, unnamed sources and so-called friends to give statements to the press, during which they declared over and over that Paul was a melancholy man who discussed suicide many times. In reality, however, it all did not make much sense, since Paul had been known to be a happy person who everyone relied on in times of crisis.

Bern's MGM driver got in on the act when he later told the coroner that the producer just happened to mention to him that several of his family had committed suicide. "He said his mother had and that it ran in his family, but he hoped he never would," Garrison later told the inquest. This was later disputed by Bern's brother Henry, though on this occasion the story was actually the truth: Mrs Bern had indeed committed suicide by drowning herself, but it is understandable that in the midst of his brother's death, it was the very last thing Henry Bern wanted people to know about.

The arrival of Henry Bern in Los Angeles brought more headlines and questions. "Brother to Ban Death Secrecy" screamed the *Los Angeles Times*, and while Henry Bern boldly stated that he did not want to give a statement about Paul, he did manage to say a few words to waiting reporters. "I am simply a man come to the funeral of his brother," he told them. "I want no secrecy veiling the matter of my brother's death. He would not have had it that way in life; I wish to do as he would have done. He never had secrets from anyone."

This was tantalizing for reporters, who noted down every little detail in their spiral notebooks, but not so much for MGM, as having the brother of their "suicide" victim sniffing around was not a welcome addition to proceedings. And so it was that when Henry Bern headed off to meet with his sister-in-law, Jean's attorney was called to the house, while Louis B. Mayer rushed over with his secretary in tow, instructing her to take down full and detailed notes on her typewriter.

Several days after this tense meeting, Henry Bern was asked to reveal what went on at the house that evening.

"Imagine the condition of Miss Harlow and myself on that night," he told reporters. "I can't remember, under the circumstances, what we talked about. What the note he left means, I don't know. That girl has had a terrible shock, just as we all have had. When I was in the room with her I felt it would be cruel of me to ask about such things." He then went on to assure reporters that he fully believed the death was a suicide, "but as to the motive that prompted it that's all hypothetical".

Meanwhile, while Mayer may have been relieved by the comments of Henry Bern, his worst fears were beginning to come true when gossip columnists declared that Jean Harlow's career was about to implode. The snide comments in the press predicted that the actress was finished, that her career was through and she would never recover from the scandal. When asked about the stories by reporters, Mayer tried to laugh it off. The comments were simply not true, he told them, though what he really thought in the privacy of his office was definitely up for debate.

And then came another disaster.

The worst possible situation, a bolt out of the blue and a huge catastrophe occurred when it was revealed that a woman calling herself Mrs Paul Bern had lived in New York for the past ten years, and was known by friends as the producer's wife. The woman's name was Dorothy Millette, and since Bern had always been known as a bachelor, this came as a huge shock to almost everyone, particularly when it was revealed that he not only sent her cheques every fortnight, but also visited her once a year.

Then another story appeared which came from Bern's brother Henry, lawyer Henry Uttal and insurance man George G. Clarken. Clarken described how Bern held insurance policies, payable to a trust in New York, for care of a woman who was now in a sanatorium. Uttal backed this up by describing how he had drawn up a will for Paul which named a "wife" called Dorothy. Paul's brother Henry was asked about the woman and intriguingly told reporters in Kansas that, "His only secret was his last one. He was never married before he wedded the screen star, Miss Harlow, but he lived with a woman once a long time ago. Miss Harlow knew of it because Paul told her." Henry said, "He concealed nothing, but lived openly. Nothing was misrepresented when he married Miss Harlow; this I know."

Then, to add more fuel to the fire, the possible existence of yet another woman was brought to everyone's attention when it was rumoured that, at one point, Paul Bern had lived in Canada with a woman he called his wife. People began to wonder – were all of these women Dorothy Millette or three separate "wives"? For a time it looked as though it could be the latter, especially when Henry Bern's attorney Ralph Blum told reporters that, "We'll be able to announce something definite concerning Paul Bern's previous marital status within twenty-four hours. We are beginning to investigate the reports of the attorney in the East and the insurance man that said Paul Bern had provided for women said to have been his wives."

Reporters were intrigued by all this talk of mysterious death and countless wives, and determined to find out exactly how many women Paul Bern had in his life. MGM on the other hand were mortified and their plans to sweep the "suicide" quietly under the carpet were fast disappearing. The whole sorry episode was spinning out of control and, unfortunately for them, it was about to get worse – much, much worse.

After revealing the existence of "Mrs Bern", Paul's brother Henry suddenly went very quiet. He had unintentionally whipped the press into a frenzy, and then frustrated them to the point of fury by refusing to answer any more questions about the mysterious woman. Added to that, his planned statement was suddenly cancelled, and he announced "certain complications" which made it impossible for him to release any more information. "Please don't ask me what these complications are," he told the world's press. "Let's just say that when they have been straightened out I will tell all."

The coroner's verdict on Paul Bern's death came through very quickly – as MGM had hoped – concluding that the producer had "died from a gunshot wound which was self-inflicted with suicidal intent; motive undetermined". However, despite the quick wrap-up of events, next came a quizzical comment, released by county autopsy assistant Dr Frank Webb.

In the statement he reported that Bern may have had a problem with his nerves, judging by pills that were found in the house. This was not a surprise considering it had just been announced he had committed suicide, but the next part of the statement raised a great many eyebrows. Apparently, while examining Bern's corpse, Dr Webb had discovered characteristics of the body which he considered to be "subnormal". What these abnormalities consisted of was not immediately reported in the press though it was later revealed by various sources that Paul Bern's genitals were not the size of those of a normal man.

One ex-girlfriend declared that his penis was the size of her pinkie finger and then blatantly announced that Barbara La Marr had once turned down a marriage proposal from him because of this. The "secret" of his small appendage was apparently well known around gossip circles in Hollywood, though any sympathies for Harlow in this area were quickly thwarted when it was said that she actually knew about the abnormality before she married him and, what's more, told him she did not mind about it at all.

Spurred on by this, Bern reportedly convinced his bride that respect was much more important than sex, and having been pawed by overexcited film producers on more than one occasion, Harlow was happy to go along with it. However, the idea of not being able to have sex with his sex-symbol wife did seem to bother Paul Bern, despite his assurances to the contrary, and rumours later spread that he had committed suicide because he was impotent and unable to consummate the marriage.

Asked about his physical condition by the press several days after the first announcement, Bern's doctor, Ed Jones gruffly replied, "It is a matter between the patient and his doctor and professional ethics forbid me from discussing the matter. I intend to have a talk with Miss Harlow, however, and should she deem it wise I may have a statement to make at a later date."

Talking about her husband's lack of libido in the bedroom was most likely not something Jean Harlow relished, and the conversation between her and Dr Jones will forever be a mystery. Chances are she quickly put an end to the talk before it had even began, as Harlow had more pressing things on her mind – the mystery woman for one thing, and Paul Bern's funeral for another.

The memorial for the MGM producer was conducted on Friday, 9 September, at the Grace Chapel at Inglewood Park Cemetery. It was a private affair, with a specially invited congregation which included a devastated Jean Harlow, her mother and stepfather. Dressed from head to toe in black, Jean was visibly distraught and escorted down the steps of her mother's home by Marino Bello and her friend Willis Goldbeck. Once at the chapel, the actress wept openly at the sight of her husband's casket, and when it was all over, she left quietly to carry out her mourning in private.

However, 2,000 fans did not want her to go quietly and bizarrely begrudged her request for privacy. They surged forward, demanding autographs and photographs from the grieving widow, seemingly completely oblivious that at this point in time, she was not the sex symbol they had seen on the screen, but a frail, vulnerable young woman, trying to mourn her recently lost husband. Describing the sad day, Harlow later exclaimed, "To them I was not a person. I had no more personality than a corporation."

Meanwhile, Bern's sister, Mrs Friederike Marcus, caused a commotion when she was heard screaming hysterically in the chapel, shouting "He's gone, he's gone!" at the top of her voice. She was not on the best of terms with Harlow, having tried and failed to press her on the subject of why Paul would have committed suicide. Harlow assured her that she had no idea what had prompted him to do it, but his sister was not convinced, releasing a statement later that day which expressed her determination to find out exactly what had happened to her dead brother: "The dearest soul on earth is laid to rest today. He did not want to rest yet, he wanted to live. Life had everything for him to enjoy it to the utmost capacity." The statement then made a swipe at Jean Harlow by declaring that Paul was so madly in love with his wife that, if possible, he would have "snatched the stars from heaven for her, he would have done it to make her smile . . . What great grief, what great pain has torn his heart to pieces to make him take his own life?"

The frustrated Mrs Marcus also hinted that she was convinced Jean Harlow was withholding information from the family: "Why did he do it? What drove him to do it? What does it mean? Last night was only a comedy? We were not there to see it. But why don't the ones that know tell us about it? Aren't we entitled to know?"

But while friends and family mourned Paul Bern and tried to determine what really happened that fateful night, another scandal was rumbling all the way from San Francisco. Dorothy Millette, the mysterious woman rumoured to be Bern's first wife, was believed to have committed suicide, throwing herself from the *Delta King* steamboat on route from San Francisco to Sacramento.

Quite disturbingly, it seemed that the woman had boarded the boat just a day after the death of Paul Bern. However, this was no ordinary journey, and instead of watching the world go by from the privacy of her cabin or table, she had instead decided to discard her outer clothes and shoes, place them neatly on deck, and then quietly throw herself overboard into the murky depths below.

When the story first broke, no body had been found, so the story of Dorothy Millette and her possible suicide came with a huge amount of press speculation and discussion. It was still not apparent exactly who this woman was and how she was related to Paul Bern, and yet here she was making headlines around the world by throwing herself overboard on the very day after the producer's death. Questions needed to be answered, and finally it was left to brother Henry Bern to answer at least some of the queries. He called a press conference and, from the offices of MGM, he sat down with the world's reporters and finally revealed all.

According to Bern, Dorothy Millette and his brother had met each other while living in Canada. She had been a budding actress, he was involved in a new production company, and together they fell in love and decided to move to New York to continue their romance. Unfortunately, shortly after their arrival, Millette became mentally ill and there was nothing that could be done to rectify this. The decision was made to place the woman in an institution, and while Paul Bern was not her husband by law, nor the cause of her illness, he took the decision to look after her all the same. Always a caring and loving person, the producer told friends that he would care about the woman "as though she was his wife", and in this regard he kept his word.

Eighteen months later it was decided that Dorothy was well enough to be released from the institution, and while her condition was not entirely cured, she was certainly not considered to be a danger to the community. The romance between her and Paul was over, but sticking to his word he continued to provide for her, paying for her to live in the New York Algonquin Hotel, where she stayed for many years after her release from the institution.

During the press conference, an upset Henry Bern also revealed that up to the very last day before his death, Paul had continued to provide for Dorothy by writing cheques and visiting the woman in New York once a year. She had obviously struck a chord with other family members, too, it was revealed, as Henry described how he himself had kept in touch with Millette, though rarely went to visit her.

Quite revealingly, he declared that the last time he had heard from the woman was when she contacted him in early 1932. During the conversation she had told him of a plan she had to move to San Francisco. "What do you think about that?" she had asked.

"Not to disturb her mentality I did not oppose her suggestion," Henry Bern told reporters. "I told her that if she felt it would do her good, to go ahead." Millette had then moved to the West Coast in April, though Bern made it clear that his brother had never visited her while she lived there. When asked if she ever spoke of Paul, Henry replied, "She always said she had the profoundest respect for Paul, but never spoke of love."

These revelations finally tied up the three possible romances in Bern's life – the woman in Canada, the one in the institution and the woman he had lived with in New York. They were all one and the same: Dorothy Millette, the woman who had reportedly jumped to her death from the deck of a steamboat just a day after the producer's death.

When he had first heard about the death of his brother, Henry Bern had been understandably distraught, but found himself also concerned for the wellbeing of Dorothy Millette. She was a fragile woman and he knew the news would greatly upset her, so he had tried unsuccessfully to contact her in San Francisco. "I wanted to reach her and tell her of Paul's death," he explained. "I wanted to tell her to keep calm and not to worry about anything. That if Paul's will didn't provide for her it would have been his wish that she be taken care of in the future. I intended taking it on myself to provide for her."

While Henry Bern was trying to get his head around the disappearance of Dorothy Millette, a search for her body resulted in the dramatic decision to drag the Sacramento River. Everyone watched expectantly, though quite bizarrely, while no woman's body was discovered in the water, the body of a man was found wearing a suit which contained the key to a stateroom on the same boat from which it was believed that Dorothy Millette had jumped. It was all incredibly confusing.

Everyone wondered where Dorothy Millette could possibly have gone. If she had committed suicide, where was her body? Had she really thrown herself overboard, or had she sneaked off the ship incognito when it docked in Sacramento? Nobody had any idea but that did not stop false information flooding into the police department, with dozens of calls from people saying they had seen the mysterious woman walking around every part of California.

While everything seemed so muddy and distorted, the Bern family were becoming particularly outspoken and adamant that Paul had told Jean Harlow everything she needed to know about Dorothy Millette. The actress, however, denied that to be true. Returning to work on *Red Dust* with Clark Gable, Harlow had a few words to say to the press about a trip she had conducted to San Francisco, just a few weeks before Bern's death.

"I made no effort to see Miss Millette while in San Francisco," she said, "for the simple reason that at that time I had no idea that a Miss Dorothy Millette existed. I knew absolutely nothing of Paul's asserted interest in her until I read of it in the newspapers." She then went on to assure everyone that the only reason she had gone north to San Francisco was to buy clothes, though in the end she had only managed to stay for less than twenty-four hours, due to being called back to the studio on urgent business.

On 14 September, the search for Dorothy Millette was concluded when her body was found in the Sacramento River by a farmhand and his son. The two had been fishing on the banks of Georgiana Slough, and spotted the body underneath some brush, much to their horror. This grim discovery caused huge ripples in the Bern family, with Paul's brother Henry becoming so upset that he too went missing for several days.

Meanwhile, his sister, Mrs Marcus, released a short statement about Dorothy, stating, "The poor thing. I feel terribly about it and am sorry for her." But not everyone was so concerned about the discovery of the body, and Jean Harlow's lawyer actually saw the death as a good opportunity for some positive publicity. With that in mind he took it upon himself to make the spectacular announcement that his client would be taking care of all funeral arrangements for Ms Millette. The press went wild at this generosity, though eyebrows were raised when the statement was quickly followed by another declaring that Jean Harlow did not actually know anything about the prior announcement. "But I'm sure it will be fine," announced the forthright lawyer.

Several days later, the mysterious Dorothy Millette was buried, and as no proof was found by lawyers that Bern had been legally married to the woman, both estates were wrapped up quickly and Jean Harlow got on with her life. However, despite all attempts to convince everyone that the death was a straightforward suicide, the scandalous episode would rumble on for decades, with whole books being written in order to try and solve the case once and for all.

So was Paul Bern's death really a suicide as they said at the studio and in the newspapers? Did Jean Harlow know nothing as she had claimed, or did she know more than she ever cared to say? Certainly Bern's family seemed to think so, though the actress herself always maintained she was completely in the dark. And what about Dorothy Millette? Did she commit suicide because of her grief on hearing the news of Paul's death, or did she throw herself overboard after murdering him as revenge for marrying Jean Harlow?

This seems to be a likely scenario. After all, he had been there for her through thick and thin, and now this blonde interloper had appeared, threatening everything Millette held dear: her stability; her financial security; and the support of ex-partner Paul Bern. Certainly she had cause in her mind to be furious that her faithful friend had moved on, and over the years there have been many claims that she was most certainly not an innocent victim in the ghastly episode. But despite claims to the contrary, the mystery of Paul Bern's death has never been fully resolved or proved, and after eighty-plus years it is likely to remain that way. The case is now well and truly closed, and though it was briefly reopened in the 1960s, there is little hope that the matter will ever be fully wrapped up.

Perhaps the final word in this chapter should be from Jean Harlow herself, who just a month after the death of her husband, spoke to columnist Elza Schallert on what she had learnt from the experience of Bern's death.

"The best any of us can do in life is to try to build a strong foundation on which to stand," she said. "And then meet life as it comes, as courageously and honestly as possible. If we fall, well it is fate. It is destiny!"

12

The Tragic Death of Russ Columbo

Before Clark Gable whisked actress Carole Lombard off her feet, she had been exceptionally close to crooner Russ Columbo, but the romance ended in tragedy one dark day in September 1934 . . .

Born on 14 January 1908, Russ Columbo was famous to millions of moviegoers and radio listeners as the man whose beautiful voice brought them the likes of "You Call it Madness, But I Call it Love" and "Too Beautiful for Words". Not only that, but the hugely talented man was also a composer, violinist and actor; his film career saw him work with the likes of Gary Cooper and Lupe Vélez, to name but two.

Good-looking and charming, Russ was linked to various actresses over the years, including Dorothy Dell, who was tragically killed in a car accident just months before Russ's own death. However, it was his romance with Carole Lombard that caught the media's attention, and at people began to wonder if, at the age of twenty-six, the velvet-voiced crooner was about to settle down with the "Profane Angel", as Carole has often been called.

However, neither Carole nor the public would ever find out if the romance would become anything more serious, as their relationship ended under extremely tragic circumstances on 2 September 1934. While his rumoured fiancée was away on a short break to Lake Arrowhead, Russ popped in to visit an old school friend, Lansing V. Brown Jr, at his parents' home, 584 North Lillian Way.

The pair chatted for a while to Brown's parents before retiring to the home's library to look at the firearms collection, which had been bought from an antique store some seven years earlier. One of the items was an old duelling pistol which Brown kept in his desk drawer, and thinking his friend might like to see it, Brown took the gun out and started absent-mindedly to fool around with a match in one hand and the firearm in the other.

"We were talking about his next picture and his plans for the future," Brown later told the inquest. He then went on to say that he had been holding the pistol in his hand and snapping the trigger without paying much attention to what he was actually doing. "I don't know just how or why I got the match under the hammer. All I know is that there was the explosion," he said. He also told police that he had no idea there was any powder or bullets in the vintage firearm. "I had never made an examination to see whether they were loaded; they were so old. I had no idea at all they were loaded."

Unfortunately for both Brown and Columbo, the duelling pistol was indeed loaded and went off without warning. The bullet ricocheted off a mahogany table and entered Columbo's left eye, causing the singer to slide to the side of his chair, his skull fractured by the piercing bullet. After Brown had composed himself from the shock of the noise, he looked over at his friend, finding him motionless, slumped in the chair. "It was all mighty fast. I thought he was clowning," he later said.

But clowning he was not, and as soon as Brown realized that, he tried frantically to revive his friend. He was unable to, and by the time his shocked parents arrived in the room, they were horrified at the sight that greeted them.

"When we entered the room my son was bent over his friend, pleading with him to speak," said Brown's father, Lansing Sr, during the inquest. An ambulance was immediately called and the singer rushed to the Hollywood Receiving Hospital in a bid to save his life. There was nothing that could be done there, however, so he was then transferred to the Good

Samaritan Hospital, where special surgeons hoped they would have more luck.

Here, brain specialist Dr George W. Patterson tried in vain to halt the blood that flowed from Columbo's head, but found the wound too delicate to operate on. Knowing it was a losing battle, it was not very long before Columbo's family were called to the hospital. Sally Blane, a one-time rumoured love of Columbo, arrived and, although their relationship was over, she stood in the corridor with his distraught family, none of whom were allowed to see the singer. Finally, a doctor left his room and informed the waiting friends and family that there was only the slightest chance of survival. This was not what they wanted to hear, and their sorrow was clear for all to see.

On the evening of 2 September 1934, Russ Columbo was sadly declared dead. "I'm very surprised he lived so long in view of his condition," stated Dr Patterson. An X-ray revealed that sure enough, the bullet had entered the brain through the eye and lodged itself in the back of the skull, causing a fracture as it did so.

Carole Lombard's shocked mother heard the news and immediately telephoned her daughter at Lake Arrowhead. The actress was "shocked beyond words" and rushed to the hospital immediately, though she knew it was too late to say goodbye. The pair had planned to have dinner that evening at her mother's house, but instead she found herself grieving the loss of her close friend. As she left the hospital, a reporter asked how she felt. Through her tears Carole managed to give a brief comment. "It is impossible to express in words how deeply shocked I am to learn of the tragedy," she said, before getting into her car.

Later, once the news had sunk in a little, she managed to release a longer statement which was reported around the world:

"His death is a terrible shock to me, as it must be to all his friends and admirers. It is particularly tragic at this time, for I know Russ was destined for the most successful year of his career. He had told me of several offers he had and he was to take up a new radio contract within a few days. Only last Friday night we saw together a preview of his latest picture."

Carole Lombard never forgot her close friend and it is said that when she married Clark Gable in 1939, he banned all mention of the crooner in their home. Gable believed that before Carole had found love with him, the greatest love of her life had been Russ Columbo, and he could never bring himself to find peace with that idea.

After the death, Russ Columbo's friend Lansing V. Brown was questioned by police about the incident, and an inquest was held. However, no autopsy was performed and it was very quickly decided that no one was to blame: it was a tragic accident; a misadventure that had resulted in the loss of an emerging star. Brown meanwhile was so choked by the incident that he was in a state of near collapse and ended up handing all his guns to the police with instructions that he never wanted to see them again. Columbo's family, however, were more than forgiving towards the young man and released a statement to confirm their thoughts: "It was quite obviously an accident – an act of God. The pistol was possibly 100 years old, and its trigger had been snapped hundreds of times without an explosion." They added that nobody had known it was loaded and that the family could not possibly hold any kind of resentment against Lansing V. Brown. "He is taking the whole thing much harder than any of us," they said.

However, fans were less able to forgive and forget and a quick look at the online forums and websites dedicated to Russ Columbo reveals that there are certain admirers who even today believe that the singer's death was never actually an accident. Some have even called for a new investigation to be opened which would reveal once and for all if the bullet still lodged in Columbo's skull was actually shot from a vintage gun at all. The chance of an autopsy ever being performed is pretty remote, but it remains clear that, without a full investigation, there will always be fans and authors who will refuse to believe the death to be anything other than murder.

There is one final – and extraordinary – twist in the story of Russ Columbo's death. His mother, Julia (aka Julio) Columbo, had recently suffered a heart attack and was in hospital at the time of her son's passing. Doctors and family members decided that it was best not to tell her of the tragedy considering the state of her health. The news would be kept quiet for the immediate future, at least until she had regained her strength.

At first they told the enquiring Julia that her son was on location, with the intention of telling her the truth about his death when the time was right. However, it seems that there would never be a good time to tell the weak mother of her child's death, and unbelievably, for the next ten years the family devised a number of stories to keep Columbo "alive" in his mother's eyes, including an elaborate series of excuses as to why he could not possibly come to visit her.

It was a mammoth task but they succeeded by sending fake postcards from around the world and playing his records in a bid to fake his radio show. It has even been reported that the family told Julia that Russ and Carole Lombard had married and moved to New York; then postcards were sent from London to make it look as though they were happily on honeymoon together.

When Carole married Clark Gable in 1939, it threatened to blow their cover, but instead of coming clean, the family apparently doctored newspapers and made sure that Julia never saw anything that included a story about Clark and Carole. The ruse was carried on after Carole Lombard's death in 1942, until Julia's own passing in 1944.

13

The Fall of Karl Dane

In 2011, the highly acclaimed film *The Artist* was released. The movie told the fictional tale of George Valentin (played by Jean Dujardin) who finds the idea of making the transition between silent films to talkies absolutely unbearable. The reason for his resistance to the sound test becomes clear when you finally hear his voice and realize that he has a thick accent, completely unsuited to talking pictures. But like all good Hollywood movies, however, the story has a happy ending and by the finale the hero has a new role and a new love.

The film could, of course, be based on all the actors and actresses in Hollywood who found the transition into talkies impossible, but one actor's story stands out among all others for being similar to that of George Valentin. Karl Dane, who once earned a mammoth $1,500 a week, was a legend, loved by audiences around the country, but like George Valentin, he found his career imploding after the onset of sound. Unlike Valentin, however, there was no hope of a happy ending; it was tragedy all the way for the beloved Karl Dane.

Born in Denmark as Rasmus Karl Therkelsen Gottlieb on 12 October 1886, Karl grew up to work as a machinist before beginning military service and then marrying his girlfriend Carla in 1910. The couple had two children but Dane was not content with staying in his home country and decided to move to the United States in 1916, leaving his family behind in the hope that they would follow him shortly afterwards.

The journey to the States was a long one, but once he had arrived Dane wasted no time in setting up home in New York. However, a job was not easy to come by in the great city, so on hearing that he would have more chance of gaining employment in Nebraska, he moved to Lincoln where he found temporary work as a mechanic. He was happy for a while but working in a garage in Nebraska was not exactly his big dream, so as soon as the job was finished, he returned to New York, where he discovered that he could make $3 a day as a bit player in the film industry.

Dane auditioned for and got many small parts in the movies, and it was not long until he made his first film with Vitagraph Studios, though details of the shoot remain sketchy and his part was eventually cut out. Meanwhile, the long-distance relationship he had with his family back in Denmark had – not surprisingly – broken down, with his wife Carla becoming too ill to travel even if she had wanted to. The pair decided that it was best for them both to go their separate ways and they eventually divorced in 1918.

However, this small hiccup in his private life was not enough to deter Karl from making a living as an actor, and he worked successfully for a time in New York before marrying a young woman by the name of Helen Benson in 1921. Together they headed to the West Coast, but not to Hollywood to seek fame and fortune . . . Instead, they settled in Van Nuys, where Dane surprised friends by deciding to give up the acting business in favour of something more reliable – running a chicken farm. The couple also discovered they were to be parents, and concentrated for the next few months on running their business and readying themselves for the birth of their first child.

Unfortunately their joy was short-lived as complications arose in childbirth, and both Helen and their daughter sadly died. Dane was heartbroken, and after mourning his wife and child, he eventually returned to acting, this time in Hollywood. He also married a telephone operator by the name of Emma Awilda Peabody Sawyer, which was – to say the least – a decision made on impulse and most definitely on the rebound from the loss of Helen.

It would be fair to say that Dane knew he had made a mistake almost as soon as the ring had been slipped on to his fiancée's finger, and the pair separated after just six tumultuous months. Another relationship would come in 1928, with a Russian dancer, Thais Valdemar, but although they lived together for several months in Dane's home, their union was never officially sealed and Valdemar soon moved out.

For the moment Karl gave up on women and instead threw himself into his career. One of his successes came when he began work on *The Big Parade* with John Gilbert, a film which went on to make $6.5 million at the box office – a staggering amount of money at the time. This film boosted his career no end and it was not long before he had advanced to parts acting alongside the legendary Rudolph Valentino in *The Son of the Sheik* and Lillian Gish in *The Scarlet Letter*.

Great stardom came when Dane was cast alongside actor George K. Arthur to create a comedy duo, and together they appeared in both films and a vaudeville tour. They were a huge hit and fans followed them around the country while many newspaper articles were written about their work. Sadly, however, the walls were slowly but surely coming in on their success with the advent of sound, and it was not long before the requirement for the infamous test came knocking at Dane and Arthur's door.

During the subsequent sound tests, producers were happy to see that although Arthur's Scottish accent was rather unfortunate, it was still workable. Dane didn't have the same luck, however, when it was decided that his Danish accent was too thick and often could not be understood. Subsequently, the duo's days as a successful double act were numbered and they eventually parted in 1931.

Dane continued to struggle in the movie business, and by December 1932, his last film was released - *The Whispering Shadow* featuring Bela Lugosi. Unfortunately, however, after that film was complete, nobody seemed to want to hire the actor any more and he had to accept the fact that his beloved career might be over. Not afraid to undertake any kind of work that would ensure his livelihood, Dane then tried his hand at various other jobs, including forming a mining company, and working as a waiter and then as a carpenter.

He even tried going back to mechanics, the work he had done as a young man in Nebraska, but having only recently been a big MGM star, it was inevitable that no "normal" job would ever work out to his advantage. Both Dane and his colleagues found it exceptionally hard to adjust to having a film star in the workplace, and ultimately he was left unemployed. Lonely and without any means of support, Dane spent his time pottering around his apartment, thinking about old times and wondering if he would ever find acting work again. In those bleak, dark days, the likelihood seemed very far-fetched indeed.

In 1933, when he was down but not yet out, Karl Dane bought a drink-and-sandwich stand, and every day wheeled it down the road to stand outside MGM, the studio he had formerly called home. Once there, the sad ex-star would try to sell hotdogs and refreshments to passers-by, though he was left intimidated and embarrassed when his former friends refused to buy anything from him. It took strength and nerve to try selling hotdogs outside his former workplace, and perhaps deep in his heart he was spurred on by the hope that his former employers would see the stall and have the heart to hire him back.

But even though they were driven past his cart every single day, the executives neither invited him back into the studio nor ever bought anything from him. Dane was still determined to make a living, but the lack of custom inevitably caused his business to fail. He gave up the stand and went back to odd jobs, even applying at MGM to become an extra or labourer – he didn't mind which. However, it would seem that the great studio wanted nothing more to do with their former star in any capacity, and this knowledge caused Dane to fall into a deep and dark depression.

In April 1934, Karl Dane was understandably at a very low ebb. On 13 April he was robbed of what was to be the last of his money, and this seems to have been the event that caused his life to finally implode. The very next day, instead of meeting a friend as he had previously planned, he decided to retire to his apartment at 626 South Burnside Avenue. There he dressed himself in a shirt, trousers and slippers, and sat down to write a goodbye note to his remaining friends.

That done, Dane then took out his old newspaper articles, contracts, photographs and reviews, and looked through them one last time. Only he knows how long he thumbed through his past achievements before finally laying them down on a nearby table, reaching for his revolver and ending his life with a single gunshot to the head. Dane's body was later found by his landlady and the friend who was supposed to meet him that day. There was nothing they could do for the former actor; he was beyond saving.

Newspapers mentioned Karl Dane's tragic passing only in short articles, limited to one or two small columns. There was no real tribute to the once great star; no huge obituary or tearful comments from former co-stars. To make matters worse, no one came forward to claim the body since his family were all unaware of his death and living thousands of miles away in Denmark.

Reports surfaced that if the body was not claimed, he would be buried by the county in a pauper's grave; and with that announcement, people finally began to sit up and take notice. No matter what had happened in Dane's career at the end, there was no denying that he was once a big star and the thought of him being buried in an unmarked grave with no proper goodbye was horrifying.

Finally, a decision was made at MGM to take charge of the funeral themselves; while they had spurned their former employee just months before, they now proudly announced their plans to the press. Karl's funeral took place on 18 April and was a quiet but respectful affair. The goodbye – which nobody had been interested in just weeks before – now consisted of a plot at the Hollywood Forever Cemetery, a casket covered in roses and the help of Dane's co-stars as pall-bearers.

The tragic twist in the tale of the Karl Dane story is that just days after his death, it was revealed that Fox had been considering him for a part in their upcoming movie, *Servants' Entrance*. The only reason they had not told him, they said, was because the script was still in development and the casting had not yet been called.

14

The Life and Death of Lou-Tellegen

In life, Lou-Tellegen was the idol of many women and his love life was the talk of the town, often causing scandals in the press. However, ultimately his memory is kept alive not for the things he did in life, but for the tragic and unfortunate way he decided to take his own life after his star had begun to fade . . .

Born on 26 November 1883, Lou-Tellegen (the hyphen was intentional, though very rarely used) was a Dutch actor who was discovered by renowned actress Sarah Bernhardt in 1910. Lou (real name Isadore Louis Bernard Edmon van Dommelen) had endured a somewhat chequered career in Europe as a book salesman (which led to him being imprisoned for selling a "scandalous" book), circus performer, model and baker, before being introduced to the aging Bernhardt, who promptly booked him for an American tour on which she was about to embark.

The chiselled, athletic performer left behind an ex-wife, Countess Jeanne de Brouckère, their daughter, Diane, and countless broken hearts, and together with Bernhardt, with whom he was rumoured to be having an affair, travelled to the United States for the first time. Whether or not Tellegen was nervous about leaving Europe and travelling to a far-off country is not known, but in any case the tour was such a success that he decided to move to the United States permanently. From then on he put every effort into making a name for himself as an actor in numerous stage productions and movies such as *The Explorer* and *The Unknown* (both 1915).

As his star began to rise, Lou-Tellegen was lusted after by many women both on and off stage, but in 1915, rumours started to circulate that he had stolen the heart of opera sensation Geraldine Farrar, after meeting her on a Hollywood film set. For a long time they denied the affair, and though friends insisted it was serious, the only thing Tellegen would say was the extremely uninteresting, "I'm ignoring such a report."

Reporters were intrigued by his denials and the story of their romance was made even more tantalizing because of Geraldine's views on marriage which she gave during an interview with an overeager reporter in 1908. Desperate to discover if she had love in her life, the reporter asked Farrar if there was a wedding on the horizon, to which the outspoken woman announced that a singer must give up all idea of matrimony until she had become successful in her field. She truly believed, she said, that one could not be a good wife and mother and a good student at the same time. "One must be subordinated," she declared.

Rumours circulated that Farrar had once called a potential suitor – an unnamed member of royalty – a "silly boy" because of his eagerness to marry her, and in 1914 made her feelings extremely clear when she described romance as like a big bag of cakes. "After I have begun to nibble the cake with the pink icing I think perhaps I should rather have the cake with the green filling still in the bottom of the bag," she said, before going on to add that this way of thinking would never be acceptable within a marriage: "I'd have only one cake with the pink icing for ever and ever," she lamented.

Despite her negative views, Farrar surprised everyone – particularly herself – when she finally accepted Tellegen's proposal, and the two became man and wife on 8 February 1916. Unfortunately, the marriage was troublesome and it was not aided by their conflicting schedules, though Farrar later revealed that when she asked Tellegen if he expected her to give up her career, he answered, "I would not dream of it. I do not understand how any man can make such a demand of a woman."

He also declared himself immensely proud of his opera-singing wife, which impressed his wife no end. Speaking to journalist Nixola Greeley-Smith, Farrar declared, "I have known men of all nations and I find that they are all charming until they get some sort of hold on a woman. And then they begin to try to put her in their pockets. That would never do with me." When asked how their marriage was so successful, she replied, "We are very, very happy. The secret? Good comradeship, I think. And of course, similar tastes, an equal interest in art and complete confidence in each other."

Unfortunately it would seem that the singer was holding something back in the interview, and in spite of claims of similar tastes and interests, it was not enough to keep the couple together. Not long after the interview with Greeley-Smith, Lou-Tellegen and Geraldine Farrar separated, with the divorce becoming final in December 1923.

Despite his bad luck in relationships, Tellegen's star continued to rise and he found admiration not only as an actor, but also as a writer, sculptor, athlete and linguist, being able to speak six different languages. 1924 and 1925 were his most productive years, with an impressive sixteen film roles in such movies as *With this Ring*, *Womanpower* and *Parisian Love*. These were quite appropriate titles considering he was fast becoming known as an Adonis – something which often overshadowed his dramatic talents – and was linked to many attractive women. The next woman fully to win his heart was Isabel Craven Dilworth, a society girl who acted under the name of Nina Romano. They married just days after his divorce from Geraldine Farrar, but they kept it secret from the public for almost eighteen months.

"Oh, but I did not keep it a secret for unworthy reasons," Tellegen told columnist Alma Whitaker in 1925. Nor did he admit to staying quiet for anything resembling "professional expedience". Instead, he disclosed that the real reason they had not gone public with their marriage was because they had sealed their relationship so close to the end of his marriage to Geraldine Farrar that "we dreaded the publicity so hard upon the heels of the other".

In spite of keeping the marriage close to their chest, the couple found it astonishing that they were never asked about their relationship, even after having a child together. Tellegen would take the child out in the pram, and find it extremely confusing as to why no one ever asked whose baby it was, and if he indeed was the father. "They never seemed to question it," he told a newspaper reporter. Still, the couple were not in any rush to announce their marriage, and when they moved to Beverly Hills shortly before being "found out", they actually acquired two different homes in an effort to keep their relationship secret for as long as possible. This they understandably found tiresome and inconvenient at best, and expensive at worse. "I don't quite know why we did that," commented Tellegen.

Once the news was finally out of the bag, the couple declared themselves to be happy, with Tellegen announcing that life was "more enchanting every year!" However, by 1928 his movie career had slowed right down and rumours were rife that the two were to divorce. This prompted Romano to deny any rift by declaring that they were both extremely happy, but complained that if anyone was out to ruin the relationship, it was the press. "They just won't leave us alone," she said.

Less than two years later, the newspaper gossip was proved correct when the marriage broke up and the two went their separate ways. However, that didn't happen until they had gone through a very sticky divorce which resulted in accusations that Tellegen had been unfaithful and had told his wife he was now living with another woman. Who the secret lover was mystified the ever-present reporters, but their attentions soon shifted from the actor's love life and on to his personal health, when an almost catastrophic disaster struck.

On Christmas Day 1929, Lou fell asleep in his room at Atlantic City's Hotel Jefferson, with a cigarette in his hand. Needless to say, it was not long before it had burned all the way down to the bed covers and the room filled with smoke; fumes overcame Tellegen, who was still asleep on the now flaming bed. Meanwhile, other guests in the hotel became aware that there was a distinct smell of smoke wafting its way through the corridors and notified the management, who came running to Tellegen's room. Unable to get any answer from the actor at all, and with smoke by now seeping out underneath the door, the staff forced their way into the room just in time to find his bed ablaze and the actor unconscious. An ambulance was called and Tellegen was rushed to hospital where it was found that the lower half of his torso had been badly burned, though his injuries were thankfully not serious.

Unfortunately, by this time Lou's bed was not the only thing going up in smoke. His career was almost burned out too. He had appeared in no movies between 1927 and 1929 (though he did direct *No Other Woman* in 1928), and reporters hurtfully started referring to him as "One of the great lovers of stage and screen . . . ten years ago". He wasn't ready to let go, however, and had plastic surgery to rid himself of under-eye bags and wrinkles. He also acquired a new wife, an actress called Eve Casanova who had played opposite him on vaudeville circuits in the late 1920s.

Unfortunately the next years were not happy ones. He appeared in only a handful of movies and, by 1934, Lou was broke and upset. Refusing to believe he was washed up, the actor moved to California, leaving his wife in New York in the hope that he could revive his career with the Fox picture, *Caravane*.

For a time things began to look bright again, but it was not to be, when Lou shockingly discovered he was ill with cancer. The devastated actor was operated on, though doctors at the time assured him there was absolutely no hope of a full recovery. Quickly his weight plummeted from 180 to 150 pounds and though Tellegen managed to recover enough strength to gain a small part in *Together We Live*, he was in a lot of pain and knew the end was in sight.

On 13 October 1934, the *Los Angeles Times* reported seeing the usually expertly groomed Lou with a beard and flowing hair, talking to his friend, the actor Willard Mack. That was one of his last public appearances and he spent the rest of the month depressed and in ill-health at 1844 North Vine Street, the home of friend Mrs Jack P. Cudahy. During that time he confessed to Dr C. L. Cooper that he thought he might be losing his mind. "I don't think he was," Dr Cooper said. "At least he seemed perfectly sane to me." In spite of that, Tellegen was "brooding deeply" over the fact that he was no longer the star he once was and told the doctor that despite everything, he still wanted to be an actor and a star. The doctor, however, had bad news for Tellegen and told him that even if he could find another job, it was physically impossible for him to work as his body just was not up to it. Tellegen was understandably devastated.

On 29 October 1934, the depression that had haunted Lou-Tellegen for many years finally became too much to bear. He was unable to work; his marriage was practically over; and the cancer that was invading his body was quickly ravaging him. Still, life went on as normal in the Cudahy home, and Mrs Eugene Coffee, the maid at the house, knocked on his door to ask if she could prepare breakfast for him. Tellegen turned her down; he did not require any food that morning, which Mrs Coffee found to be so disturbing that she decided to tell her boss immediately.

Rushing to Mrs Cudahy, the maid reported that Tellegen had refused to eat and what's more seemed extremely morose. The lady of the house took this information as suspicious and told her maid that she would take a look into Mr Tellegen's room immediately, eager to find out what was wrong with her boarder.

Meanwhile, Tellegen remained in the privacy of his quarters, dressed only in a bathrobe. His scrapbooks spread around him, he took one last look at the reports documenting his career on stage and screen, before carefully shaving his face and combing his hair. Who knows what was going on in his mind at that moment, but one thing's for sure: it wasn't anything positive. Once he had made himself look presentable, it was time for his last big role, and one that would go down in history: Death.

The once fabulous actor picked up a pair of sharp scissors and quietly but deliberately plunged them into his chest. Was it a spur-of-the-moment decision or one he had thought through for some time? We'll never know. One thing we do know, however, was that Tellegen did not kill himself with just one fatal blow; instead he stabbed himself an incredible seven times before finally collapsing on the floor.

Outside his bedroom door, an oblivious Mrs Cudahy was asking him if he might like some soup. She received what she considered to be a weak reply, and so summoned her butler, William Wynn, who soon arrived at her side. Apprehensively they opened the door together and found something so shocking that it would be a sight they would remember for the rest of their lives. There was Tellegen on the floor of the room, blood gushing from his chest, while he – quite disturbingly – was still alive but remaining completely silent. The two rushed to the actor's side and made frantic attempts to stifle the blood while calling for a doctor, but it was too late; Lou-Tellegen quietly and calmly slipped away on the floor of the bathroom, his scrapbooks and mementos of a once great life sitting just feet away.

When told of the suicide by reporters, Tellegen's ex-wife Geraldine Farrar snapped, "Why should that interest me? It doesn't interest me in the least!" and slammed the telephone down. Meanwhile his current wife, Eve Casanova, received a wire asking what to do with Tellegen's remains but she had no intention of helping out. "Contact my cousin in Los Angeles," she said, though no such cousin was ever found and Tellegen's body remained unclaimed in the mortuary.

Officials got back in touch with Casanova in the hope that she would claim the body herself but despite declaring that she was "horribly, horribly shocked", she still would not budge. Instead of taking a flight out to California, she told reporters that she would not be able to go to the funeral as she was about to start rehearsals for a play called *A-Hunting We Will Go*. "I know Lou would want me to stay here and stick it out," she told reporters gathered at her front door, though no one could say they honestly believed her.

Finally, when all other avenues were blocked, friends of Tellegen, such as Mrs Cudahy, Norman Kerry and Willard Mack, vowed to give him the funeral he deserved and made the arrangements themselves. On the day itself, scores of fans stood outside the chapel, while Lou's colleagues and associates came together to act as pall-bearers.

Tellegen's first wife, the jilted Countess Jeanne de Brouckère, did not attend, though she did tell reporters that if she had known of Lou's illness she would have been only too glad to help. Meanwhile, third wife Isabel Dilworth (now remarried and called Countess Danneskiold) arrived on the arm of her current husband.

"He had scores of deep and intimate friends who would have been glad to help had they known of his illness," she said, before adding that if she had known of his pain and despair, she too would have most certainly rushed to his aid.

But at the end of the day, in spite of the renewed interest from several ex-wives and dozens of fans, Lou's passing was a sad and very lonely affair. At the conclusion of the funeral, the body of the former matinee idol was simply cremated and his ashes were scattered quietly into the blue depths of the Pacific Ocean.

15

The Strange Death of Thelma Todd

"I hate people who are not natural, I hate people who are stuck up, and I hate hypocrites. Aside from that I get along with everybody," so said outspoken Thelma Todd at the tender age of just nineteen. A rebel in the days when it was pretty much unheard of, Thelma Todd was nobody's fool and definitely no dumb blonde.

"I think I must have a brunette personality," she once said, before declaring that she always believed blondes to be soft and pliable, ready to cling to the nearest male for support and protection. "They're just waiting to be taken care of and very sweet and easy to live with because they are so amiable," she said, before admitting that none of those qualities could possibly belong to her. She believed herself to be a fighter who had made her way in the world alone; she knew how to stand up for herself and woe betide anyone who said otherwise.

"You see, I'm not a real blonde inside or I'd be steadfast under any circumstances. No brunette was ever a doormat," she admitted.

A doormat she most certainly was not, as attested by her on-off boyfriend Roland West during the inquest into her death: "You could not keep Miss Todd out of any place if she wanted to get in," he said. And yet in the early hours of 15 December 1935, Thelma was kept out of her apartment after West dead-bolted the door from the inside, rendering her Yale key useless. This action was just the beginning of a series of events that led to Thelma Todd being found dead in her car approximately thirty hours later.

Born in Lawrence, Massachusetts, on 29 July 1906, Thelma Alice Todd was the daughter of John Shaw Todd and his wife Alice Elizabeth Todd. John was Irish, while Alice came from Canada, and together they raised their two children at 502 Andover Street in Lawrence. When Thelma's older brother was killed in a freak farming accident, John Todd was devastated and Thelma decided to make up to him for the absence of a son. She played with boys, was boisterous and daring, and planned to be an engineer when she grew up. One neighbour later remembered that the seven-year-old girl could often be seen riding a boy's bicycle through the streets, and never wore frills or lace, even though it seemed that every other female did so at the time. Little Thelma Todd was very definitely a tomboy, and while other girls were playing dolls and houses, she instead preferred to play on the boy's baseball team, hike, swim and climb trees.

Exceptionally pretty and always willing to go along with whatever the boys were playing at the time, it was no surprise that, as she grew up, Thelma became one of the most popular girls in town. However, while others were obsessing on how beautiful she had become, Thelma herself was completely unconcerned with her looks and freely admitted that she would "kill a man who started to 'neck' with me".

Thelma trained to be a school teacher in Lawrence, and for a laugh decided to enter a beauty pageant to find "Miss Massachusetts". She won and was invited to tour the East Coast Paramount Studios, where she was introduced to producer Jesse L. Lasky. He dazzled her with his plans to start a Paramount Pictures School on the East Coast and promised that if the school went ahead, he would contact her.

Shortly after the contest, sure enough, Jesse Lasky was back in touch to say that his Paramount Pictures School was now in operation and Thelma was immediately enrolled. While there she learnt her craft, took part in a photo story for an East Coast newspaper and encountered her first "scandal" when a fellow student, Robert Andrews, fell madly in love with her and printed the news of their "engagement" all over a New York newspaper. Since Andrews had forgotten to tell Thelma that they were engaged, she gave him a stern talking-to and he quickly dropped out of the actress's affections.

Although the reason she was initially invited to the studio was because of the beauty pageant, Thelma was always adamant that it was not as a result of the contest that she was later signed by the studio. In a 1931 interview, Thelma told reporter Alice L. Tildesley that the beauty pageant had nothing to do with her eventual rise to fame: "I never heard of a beauty-contest winner getting very far in any other line. I didn't crash the movie gate by way of a contest, because I was already under contract when I won my title. The fact that I was Miss Massachusetts had nothing to do with it."

Thelma's career quickly started to hot up, but just as she was enjoying success, her father suddenly passed away. He was buried on her birthday, and just two days later Thelma was rushed to hospital where her appendix was removed. It was another two months before she was strong enough to resume her film career, and she found herself travelling to Hollywood for the first time, working for Paramount Pictures, home of Rudolph Valentino, Pola Negri, Gloria Swanson and Clara Bow.

Returning to good health, Thelma continued her journey into film and carved out a successful career playing in comedies at the Hal Roach Studios and Paramount, working with the likes of Charley Chase, the Marx Brothers and Laurel and Hardy. She was a huge success, but as with many comedic players, she harboured dreams of becoming a serious actress too, so after making the transition from silent movies to talkies easily, she decided to try her hand at drama, starring alongside Chester Morris in Roland West's movie *Corsair*.

To shed her screwball comedy image, director West suggested that she change her name to Alison Lloyd, which she did, though only on a temporary basis, much to her director's disappointment. Strangely, it would seem that Roland West was so obsessed with her being called Alison that when she died he even put his flowers in that name, instead of her real name of Thelma, which she had gone back to long before she passed away. Sadly, the actress's venture into drama was not successful and *Corsair* was not the box-office favourite she hoped it would be. She went back to comedies, though remained a friend, business partner and sometime lover of Roland West until the end of her life.

Thelma was loved by everyone at the studio, and while she never reached the dizzy heights of Jean Harlow, Carole Lombard or Clara Bow, she certainly held her own. Thelma was a pioneer and an organizer; while filming in Lake Placid, New York, she decided that rather than sit and twiddle her thumbs between takes, she would organize skiing parties, bobsled trips and other adventures, forcing the cast to go along with her ideas just for something to do. She loved to laugh and joke, so much so in fact that when her co-star Patsy Kelly found out she had died, she did not believe it. "I thought it was one of her jokes", she said.

Thelma became linked to various men including the English actor Ronald Colman and Academy Award nominee Richard Dix. However, it was a man by the name of Pat DiCicco (originally Pasquale DeCicco) who captured her heart, and the two eloped in 1932 before settling in Hollywood together. However, the marriage was not a happy one, and was said to be filled with violence and emotional abuse. DiCicco was frequently described as everything from a sportsman to a theatrical agent, but in truth he was a lackey for gangsters such as Lucky Luciano, and her relationship with DiCicco became Thelma's first introduction to the seedier side of Hollywood.

Several years before her marriage, Thelma gave her views on matrimony, saying that she felt when people married too young, they were so intent on being in love that they often refused to look at each other in a truthful way, expecting far too much from one another. "They won't take account of her quick temper or his extravagance, his indolence or her excitability," she said, before going on to describe how men and women seem to be so in awe of a great and thrilling romance that the awakening from such rose-tinted slumber was inevitably not such a great experience.

This was almost a foretelling of how her marriage would work out, and it was not long before it came to an abrupt end after a particularly abusive episode at a party. Thelma filed for divorce from DiCicco and shortly after entered into a business (and rumoured personal) partnership with old friend Roland West. He was in a troubled marriage to movie star Jewel Carmen, and some say that it was rumours of his relationship with Thelma that led to the couple becoming estranged. In truth, however, the marriage had been on the rocks for some time, though Roland seemed to be keener to end it than his wife. Jewel did not give up on her husband easily, and stayed off and on in their home, just minutes from where West decided to open a beach-side establishment called the Sidewalk Café, with Thelma Todd.

The café was a big success and Thelma enjoyed working there herself, serving customers and occasionally cooking food. She had always enjoyed entertaining and she took to the job like a duck to water, greeting friends and making sure that everyone had a fantastic time. However, one thing that did not go down well with the actress was when gangsters showed an interest in the restaurant. Members of the Mafia had long since ruled many of the establishments in Hollywood and it was not long before they were in the Sidewalk Café, planning to open a gambling establishment in the rooms upstairs. "Over my dead body," Thelma is rumoured to have told them.

In 1935 – the last year of her life – Thelma began receiving threatening notes from someone calling himself "The Ace". The letters demanded money and threatened death and destruction of the café, but even after the accused note-writers had been arrested, the letters still kept coming. Thelma was concerned for her own life and when she was told that a mysterious man had walked into the restaurant, demanding her address, she was even more terrified.

A break-in at her Hollywood home followed, prompting Thelma to move into an apartment above the Sidewalk Café, where her neighbour and sometime room-mate was business partner Roland West. The arrangement of living and working at the café worked for a time, until the discovery that prowlers had been spotted on the terrace outside her bedroom did little to quell Thelma's fears. As a result of the episode, bars were placed on the windows and she no longer answered her telephone.

On 14 December 1935, twenty-nine-year-old Thelma Todd was guest at a nightclub party given by actress Ida Lupino, though she went on her own as Roland West decided to remain at the café in order to entertain guests. He had warned Thelma that the door would be locked if she was not home by 2 a.m., but not being one to comply with demands, the actress carried on partying until past her curfew. Guests commented later that she seemed very happy and in good spirits despite an encounter with her ex-husband Pat DiCicco, who turned up at the nightclub with another woman.

Finally, Thelma was exhausted and left the party in order to travel home in the care of her chauffeur, Ernest Peters. He dropped the actress at the front of the Sidewalk Café and watched her walk towards the apartment. As it so happens, this turned out to be the last confirmed sighting of Thelma Todd alive.

Although there were many doors through which one could gain access to the sprawling Sidewalk Café, Thelma had a key to only one door, which as luck would have it just happened to be the one Roland West had locked and dead-bolted from the inside. He later said that he just had not realized that Thelma did not have a key to any other door, and that he presumed she would come in by another entrance. According to West he had no idea his girlfriend could not gain access to her home; he told the coroner that he awoke in the middle of the night, heard running water and assumed that Thelma was in the building. He was wrong.

So what happened to Thelma when she couldn't enter her home? Well, all we know for sure is that on Monday, 16 December, her housekeeper went to the garage located 127 steps away from the café, and found her employer dead in the front seat of her car. This was obviously a grisly discovery for the woman, but what could have possibly happened in order for the vibrant young Thelma Todd to end up in the garage in the first place?

One theory put forward by Roland West is that when Thelma realized she was locked out of her home, she decided to walk up to her garage rather than wake him to let her in. Once there, she turned on the engine of her Lincoln in order to keep warm, not knowing the dangers of inhalation of the car's fumes, which engulfed the garage causing Thelma to expire quickly afterwards. This seems reasonable, if not a little too straightforward.

Another theory is that Thelma had seen enough of Roland West and his demanding ways, and was scared of the gambling plans for her restaurant. She decided to take her own life in the garage by turning on the engine and slowly waiting for death to come. This theory is a little unbelievable, however, especially since no note was ever found and, aside from a few down moments at the party, she was in relatively good spirits that evening and greatly looking forward to Christmas. She was also an exceptionally strong person who had never shown any suicidal tendencies before that night so the idea of her deciding to commit suicide after partying the night away quite happily seems a little off-the-wall.

Yet another story is that the actress was kidnapped from outside the building by gangsters, furious that she had threatened to pull the plug on the gambling plans for her restaurant. This version of events has several other stories attached to it, however, including one outlandish rumour that the gangsters drove Thelma around Los Angeles for an entire day, before killing her and dumping the body in the front seat of her garaged car, in order for it to look like a suicide . . . This all seems rather far-fetched: if the Mafia did indeed kidnap the actress (which could very well have happened), they would not have had any interest in taking her on a sightseeing tour of the city, and instead would have been more likely to kill her straight away and dispose of the body as quickly as they could.

All we know for sure is that once Thelma's maid Mae Whitehead discovered the body, she immediately drove to the Sidewalk Café to raise the alarm and awaken Roland West who was sleeping upstairs. She then went to pick up Thelma's mother, who rushed to the garage in order to see her daughter's body for herself. She was asked by reporters how she thought Thelma had died, and her response shocked them. "She was murdered," she exclaimed, though days later she notably retracted her claim and said the whole thing must have been caused by Thelma's weak heart.

The hunt was on for answers to this questionable death, and everyone dived for cover. In court Roland West swore he had not seen his lover since before she left for the party; Pat DiCicco said he had not seen her since the party; friend Mrs Wallace Ford claimed to have received a call from Thelma the day after the party; while Roland's wife Jewel Carmen went one better and swore she had actually seen the actress driving round town hours after the approximate time of death.

From all four corners, people were coming out to claim their sightings of the blonde actress, and the only people who remained quiet were the gangsters who were rumoured to have been taking over the café. Of course, the likelihood of them ever being called to testify was zero, since the 1930s Mafia were notorious for having moles and contacts throughout the Los Angeles Police Department. With that in mind, the coroner's investigation into the death of Thelma Todd was wrapped up quickly and without a firm conclusion. No one ever came forward publicly to announce an involvement with

Thelma's death, and all the characters involved got on with their lives. Roland West stayed at the Sidewalk Café though his directing career was over; Jewel Carmen declared that Thelma Todd had been her best friend, though few believed her; and ex-husband Pat DiCicco went on to have a violent and short-lived marriage to Gloria Vanderbilt.

But what of Thelma? Well, her body was cremated and her ashes taken back to her native Lawrence, though it is said that she does not yet rest in peace. Indeed, it has been rumoured that her ghost has appeared various times on the stairs and hallways of her famed Sidewalk Café, frustrated that even now, nearly eighty years later, her untimely death has never been solved . . .

16

Clark Gable's Baby Scandals

It was 12 March 1936 when forty-seven-year-old Violet Wells Norton sat down to write another letter to film star Clark Gable, after several other letters had been ignored. She was not the only one to be writing to Gable that year; indeed, his fan mail was through the roof and about to get even bigger over the next few years with the release of blockbuster *Gone with the Wind*. However, Norton's letter was no ordinary piece of fan mail, but instead an attempt to obtain money for the care of her teenage daughter, Gwendolyn.

According to Norton, Gable was the father of her daughter, the result of a relationship they had enjoyed in 1920s England when Gable was supposedly living in Essex under the name of Frank Billings. The frankly unbelievable story went that Norton had hired Billings as a tutor for her son, fell hopelessly in love with the man and ended up conceiving her daughter as a result. Norton claimed that so in love were she and Billings, that despite not being married, they had the baby anyway, though four months after the birth he left her heartbroken when he fled first to London and then to the United States.

In fairness to Billings, the man had offered to take Norton with him on his travels, but unfortunately for her, he refused to take her four other children along for the ride. The two split up; she never heard from him again and several years later decided to marry Herbert Norton and settle down to a new, simple life in Winnipeg. However, this peaceful existence all changed during a family trip to the cinema to see the Clark Gable picture, *It Happened One Night*.

As Norton sat in the darkened cinema, she became somewhat agitated and surprised. The reason? Well, it would seem that the man on the screen bore a striking resemblance to Billings, and so the woman immediately put two and two together and decided that her ex-lover had thrown in his career as a teacher, changed his name to Gable (or Gables as she constantly referred to him) and made it big as a film star.

For Clark Gable (and anyone else for that matter) the very idea was preposterous; he had never been to England and in 1922 and 1923, when the relationship was said to have taken place, he had been working as a tie salesman and lumberjack in Oregon. With this in mind, he decided to ignore this and other letters from the obviously mistaken woman and get on with his life.

"I did not consider them worthy of serious action," he later told reporters, a decision which would seem logical given the circumstances.

While others would forgive Gable for his lack of concern for the letters, being ignored by the famous film star was not something that pleased the already volatile Mrs Norton. She decided that if she was going to be taken seriously she would need to write to others, too, so she took out her pen and once again sat down, this time writing to columnists such as Walter Winchell and Jimmy Fidler, along with radio commentators and – for reasons known only to herself – the actress Mae West. The obsession quickly got out of control and her whole existence seemed to revolve around proving that Clark Gable and Frank Billings were one and the same person. So much so, in fact, that in November 1934, when it became clear that Violet would not give up her quest, her exasperated husband packed his bags and moved out of the family home.

Even this shock did nothing to deter Norton, however, and instead she continued her letters, enlisting her daughter to help, and even sending some notes to Gable's home. He later told Pete Martin in the *Saturday Evening Post*: "She asked if she could see me about a personal matter. I didn't know her. In fact, I had never heard of her." Once again the actor ignored the letters, but they kept arriving anyway, with the woman becoming more and more concerned that she was being mistreated once again by "Frank Billings".

Finally, when every letter went unanswered, both Violet and her daughter decided to travel to Hollywood from their home in Canada in order to confront Clark Gable in person. The trip was said to be financed by private detective Jack L. Smith and Winnipeg landlord Frank James Keenan, though it was ultimately fruitless and Violet Norton did not get anywhere near the actor, much to her chagrin. "As affairs go, the one described was a long-distance project," Gable told Pete Martin. "I decided she was nuts and forgot about it."

But while Gable himself was happy to continue ignoring the persistent letters and visits, his studio and the American authorities were not. After receiving a letter from the Director of Administration Services in Canada, officials were convinced that Gable's admirer needed serious help. Events were put in motion and Norton was charged with mail fraud in January 1937, while Keenan and Smith were accused of scheming with her to obtain money from Clark Gable.

Reporters were thrilled to hear the outrageous stories being pointed in Gable's direction and were anxious to hear what the actor had to say about the matter. He did not disappoint: talking to newspapers was never his biggest concern, but he did open up over what he considered to be a fabricated and preposterous story.

"Now that the authorities have decided to prosecute," he said, "I can only offer my fullest cooperation." Suffering from flu, he nevertheless was still able to declare his distaste for the whole episode, branding it ridiculous, and adding, "I have never been in England; never heard of this woman except through notes written to me and turned over to the authorities."

In spite of Gable's pleas that he had never met the woman,

he was warned by the US Assistant District Attorney that the burden of responsibility fell on him – not her – to prove that he had never been to England, particularly in the years Norton was accusing him of being there. Not only that, but he would also have to show his exact whereabouts at the very time the child was being conceived. This was not an easy task, especially since Gable had been pretty much a free agent during the early 1920s, and had been working many jobs to make ends meet. But determined not to be beaten by the mysterious woman, Gable went through his archives and began to pull out things he deemed relevant, such as old theatre programmes and pay cheques from the Silverton Lumber Company where he had worked for a time. His attorney handed them all over the District Attorney's office, who readied the evidence for the case.

When Norton appeared in court on 26 January 1937, she went back and forth between saying she had never tried to get money from Gable and then quite happily asking if he could give financial help with thirteen-year-old Gwendolyn. Quite bizarrely, Norton also asked if he would consider buying four romantic stories that she had previously written, which just ended up making her look even more unhinged. Things became even more fraught when she claimed that an investigator for her attorney, Hiram McTavish, had tried to adopt daughter Gwendolyn against her will. McTavish retorted by denying all knowledge of being her current attorney and claimed his investigator had only taken Mrs Norton and Gwendolyn into her home because she felt sorry for their impoverished circumstances.

Coming to Gable's defence in the bizarre case was his first wife, Josephine Dillon, who released a statement saying that she had known the star in 1923 when he attended her acting classes in Portland, Oregon. "To my knowledge he has never been in England," she said. "The entire story is silly and fantastic." Meanwhile employee records were released from the Silver Falls Timber Company to coincide with the pay cheques he had previously supplied, which thankfully showed Gable as having worked there in the winter of 1922–3.

However, even when she was presented with this evidence, it still didn't stop Norton from insisting her story was true. From jail she told reporters, "He looks like the Frank Billings I knew in 1923. I'd like to see him in person." Of course, practically every woman in America at that time would have loved to meet Gable in person, and he had absolutely no interest in coming face to face with the woman who had been bombarding him with disturbing letters for months on end.

Unfortunately for him, he was dragged even deeper into the scandal when the London *Daily Express* reported that factory inspector H. Newton had come forward to say that he too had known Frank Billings when he ran a poultry farm in Essex, England. According to Newton, Gable was "either Frank Billings or his double", and went on to describe how his brows, nose, temples and "twisted, cynical half-smile" were all the same as those of Gable.

Then out of the blue, in February 1937, the real Frank Billings actually came forward to declare that he was the father of Gwendolyn, and joyously bragged that he was also "a perfect double for Clark Gable". By now it was pretty clear to everyone that Violet Norton was either lying or just a very mixed-up woman, and that Clark Gable was an innocent bystander in the bizarre episode. However, even this was not enough to prevent him from being called to testify during her trial in April 1937, much to his dismay.

On 20 April Gable fought his way through hundreds of adoring women to take his place in the courtroom holding the trial of Violet Norton. In front of everyone, including Norton herself, he denied ever being in England, confirmed he had never met the woman in his life, and laughed off the very idea of being the father of her daughter.

Violet, meanwhile, stared intently at Gable throughout his testimony. One can only ponder exactly what was going through her mind at that moment. "That's him, I'd know him anywhere," she later told her attorney, who amusingly then made it clear to everyone that he did not believe a word his client was saying. "She acted in complete good faith," he told waiting reporters. "We expect to prove that Clark Gable closely resembled the Frank Billings she knew in England."

Nobody could take the proceedings seriously, especially when Norton tried to explain why Frank Billings decided to change his name to Clark Gable. According to her, he called himself after their local butcher, Clark, who owned an estate called "The Gables". "Hence Clark Gables," declared Norton, to the amused crowd.

The trial went on for three days, during which time Gable was called to the stand on several occasions, including on one occasion when Norton requested to view him close up. Approaching the moustached actor, she was the envy of thousands of fans as she pored over his looks intently. After the examination, everyone listened closely to what Norton had to say. "Yes, he looks like Frank Billings," she said. "And I still feel convinced that Clark Gable and Frank Billings are one and the same man!"

On 23 April, after dozens of witnesses including Clark Gable's father, his ex-girlfriend and Gwendolyn Norton herself had taken to the stand, Violet Norton was convicted of misusing the mail system, but not guilty of conspiracy. Mrs Norton dramatically almost fainted in the courtroom, before being led away to face her distraught daughter, after which she was sentenced to one year in the Orange County Jail, where she still insisted that Clark Gable was her baby's father.

Gable, meanwhile described the entire episode as "Unfortunate . . . particularly because of her children," before adding, "My conscious is clear." Unfortunately for him, that was not entirely true, as at that very moment in time, he was embroiled in a baby scandal of a very different nature. And this time he really was the daddy . . .

In 1935, two years before Violet Norton untruthfully declared that Clark Gable was the father of her child, the actor was working on *The Call of the Wild* with film star Loretta Young. Young was single; Gable was not. Although estranged, he was most certainly still with his second wife, Ria Gable, though many believe it was always a marriage of convenience for the actor and he was never truly in love.

During the making of the film, Young and Gable enjoyed a secret and short-lived affair, which ended with the actress discovering she was pregnant. Distraught and ashamed, she immediately went into hiding for the majority of her pregnancy, travelling first to England and then back to California in order to deter uncomfortable questions from friends, colleagues and most of all, reporters.

Restricted by the studio's moral codes and terrified that the scandal would be enough to shatter her career and reputation as a good Catholic girl, Young was determined to protect both herself and Gable. With this in mind, when people started to wonder where she was towards the end of her pregnancy, Young showed considerable chutzpah by holding a press conference from the comfort of her bedroom, hiding her stomach under mountains of blankets and comforters.

Finally the child – Judy – was born at home on 6 November 1935. Rumour has it that Gable paid one visit to the child and gave the mother some money to buy a crib, before she was unceremoniously placed in an orphanage, while Young returned to work.

Finally in June 1937, just two months after Gable had appeared in court to deny all knowledge of being a father to Violet Norton's daughter, Loretta Young announced her intention to adopt two children: Judy and James. She had spotted the two, she told reporters, while visiting the orphanage in December 1936. "I have always wanted children," she said. "And when I saw these two I just had to have them."

What she failed to declare, however, was that Judy was actually her own child whom she had placed in the orphanage well over a year before. As for James, nobody knows if he really did exist, but Young certainly did not adopt him. She later announced that there had been problems taking the child and that she had instead opted for adopting only Judy instead.

It was a well-known story around Hollywood that Judy Lewis (she took the name of Young's second husband, Tom Lewis) was the illegitimate child of Loretta Young and Clark Gable. But for the rest of the world, Young was seen as a hero: an angel who adopted a poor child and took her to live with her in the palatial hills of Hollywood.

Unfortunately for Loretta, however, Judy not only inherited Clark Gable's huge ears, but facially she was the exact image of her mother, a fact Young explained away as being because they lived together and had developed the same mannerisms. Loretta worried about the ear situation, however, and for years insisted that her daughter wear bonnets in public until finally it was decided to pin them back. When the child became a teenager, she endured gossip on a regular basis that she was not adopted at all – that she was really the child of Loretta Young and Clark Gable. These stories continued throughout her teenage years though Judy tried to ignore them and get on with her life.

Finally, however, Judy could ignore the stories no more when she became engaged and her fiancé, Joseph Tinney, took it upon himself to tell his future bride that everybody knew who she really was. She was stunned but it wasn't until she had become a mother herself that Judy finally had the nerve to demand the truth from her mother. In true dramatic style, Young promptly threw up, admitted that she was indeed her natural mother, and then called her daughter "a walking mortal sin". She also demanded that Judy keep the information from her own children – Young's grandchildren – which was something she rightly refused to do.

Sadly, the only father-daughter time Gable and Judy ever shared was one day when, as a teenager, Judy came home from school to find Gable sitting in her living room. Not knowing that he was her father at the time, she sat with him for a while, answered his polite questions about her life, then bade him farewell while accepting a kiss on her head as he left the house. By the time Judy found out her true parentage, Gable had long since passed away. Sadly it was never possible for her to get to know her true father.

17

Aleta Freel Alexander and Ross Alexander

By the time actors Aleta Freel and Ross Alexander married in 1934, she was a success on the New York stage, while he had carved out a career for himself on both stage and screen. However, it was the tragic manner of their deaths, not careers, that would live on in the public's imagination for many years to come.

Born on 27 July 1907, Alexander Ross Smith was a New York actor who was not only considered charming, but good-looking and capable of an incredible stage presence too. His film career had been rather haphazard, however, until he signed with Warner Brothers, for whom he made several successful movies, such as *A Midsummer Night's Dream* and *Captain Blood* under the name of Ross Alexander.

Aleta Freel was just over a month older than Alexander, and by the time the two met, she had played various leading roles on stage, such as performances in *Strange Interlude* and *Both Your Houses*. The couple were married in 1934 and set up home together in Hollywood, where Freel went under the name of Aleta Alexander, and hoped to make a great career for herself as a screen actress.

Having been such a successful and popular actress on the New York stage, it came as a surprise when Aleta's Hollywood dreams did not come true. She spent much time travelling to and from auditions for minor roles on screen, but as casting directors were not impressed by her past stage career, she quickly became disenchanted with the entire industry.

The actress's distress and depression over her failing career caused cracks in the marriage, especially when rumours began to circulate that her husband had been unfaithful. As a result, the couple argued constantly over their life in Hollywood and the downhearted Aleta threatened on numerous occasions to leave the marriage and return home to her parents in Jersey City. Ross found it extremely hard to believe she would actually go through with it, however, and quickly brushed her comments aside.

Regardless of what her husband believed, things came to a head on the evening of Friday, 6 December 1935, when the two got into a huge argument at their home, 7357 Woodrow Wilson Drive. They fought bitterly and it was not long before Aleta and Ross told each other a few home truths about the state of the marriage and their unhappiness within it.

Freel was furious at her husband's comments and threatened once again to go back to her parents' house, causing Ross to lose his temper once and for all. Having heard the same threat over the course of the past months, he swung round in anger and shouted, "Well, for God's sake go on back and quit nagging me about it." The shocked actress then rushed out of the room, leaving her husband behind, to wait – as he had done before – for her to come back.

Unfortunately, she never did return. Several minutes later Ross Alexander was mortified to hear two loud shots coming from the garden. In shock, he ran to the dining room and called out to William Bolden, his butler, to turn on the yard lights. Then with the servant following closely behind, he dashed out of the house and stumbled across his wife's body, stretched out on the ground with a rifle lying beside her.

In a fit of rage and frustration, Aleta had turned the gun on herself but amazingly she was still alive – albeit barely. An ambulance was called and Ross stayed with his wife while waiting for it to arrive, speaking to her about the future and promising things would be better if only she would pull through. Once the paramedics had arrived at the home, they carefully lifted her into the vehicle and rushed her to Cedars of Lebanon Hospital, though sadly it was too late to save her life. The actress struggled on through the night but died the very next morning, much to the distress of her shocked husband.

Wracked with guilt and refusing to believe that their fight could have any bearing on his wife's decision to end her life, Ross Alexander downplayed the argument as "of minor consequence" and insisted to police that his wife had instead been depressed over her career. However, this statement did not sit well with Aleta's father, Dr William Freel, who left his home in Jersey City immediately, demanding that an inquest take place to look into the entire episode.

The inquest was called and halted any plans Alexander had to bury his wife; instead, he found himself sitting in the same courtroom as Aleta's father, waiting for a decision about what the court thought had happened to his dead wife. When asked about the circumstances of his wife's last moments, Ross Alexander took to the stand and explained, "She was discouraged because screen tests she had taken here on several occasions were not successful and she was unable to get into pictures."

However, when it was time for Aleta's father to speak, he shocked those present by announcing that when the death happened, Alexander did not bother to telephone him personally; instead, he left it to his business manager, Vernon D. Wood, to break the news. This decision had understandably left the grieving father absolutely furious over the insensitivity shown by his son-in-law and, as a result, he refused to believe that Alexander could be anything but guilty for allowing his daughter to die. Comments and insults flew from both sides, though in the end the coroner felt that in spite of everything, the death of Aleta Alexander was a suicide and the case was closed.

Just nine months later, Ross Alexander shocked the public and media alike when he announced his swift marriage to actress Anne Nagel, whom he claimed to have started dating only three months before. Moviegoers could not believe it: first, he was rumoured to have been unfaithful to his wife during their marriage; then his wife's father believed he may have had something to do with her death. Now here he was, less than a year later, taking another wife without – it would seem – any concern for the memory of Aleta whatsoever.

But if the rumours and speculation over their relationship worried Alexander and Nagel, they certainly did not show it. Instead, the couple departed by plane to be married in Yuma, before returning to Los Angeles and setting up home on a ranch situated at 17221 Ventura Boulevard.

However, while the public believed that Alexander had moved on from his former wife far too quickly, it would seem that they were wrong, as the marriage between the actor and his new wife was not an easy one. It had still been less than a year since the suicide and the thought of how life had changed in such a short space of time disturbed him. He was continuously haunted by the memory of his former wife, the way she had died and the troubles they had endured, and he could not shake the feeling of despair no matter how hard he tried.

On the evening of 7 December 1936, just a day after the first anniversary of Aleta's death, Ross Alexander became intoxicated and told his visiting father that he wanted to go outside and shoot sparrows. Knowing full well that it had been a year since the bereavement and highly sceptical that he could possibly be planning to shoot birds in the dark, the actor's alarmed father called the butler and together they talked Alexander into staying inside. However, just days after New Year, everything took a tragic turn . . .

The day had started in what seemed to be a fun fashion, with a game of badminton between Ross and Anne, followed by the taking down of their first marital Christmas tree. Afterwards, the actor sang and played guitar for his wife, who later reported that her husband had been in a good mood all day. "He was happier than ever before," she later told the coroner, though if this was the case, it would seem the happiness came from knowing what he had planned for himself, rather than anything to do with their marriage.

After spending the day together, the couple relaxed in their front room, where Anne was crocheting and Ross was – rather disturbingly – toying with a pistol. If Anne had known of his father's concern over the "shooting sparrows" quote, she chose not to show it, and later told the coroner that after Ross had removed the cartridges, they both started playing around with the gun. Shortly afterwards, Ross disappeared upstairs to do something more conventional – write poetry – before reappearing to tell his wife that he was going out to the barn to shoot a duck for dinner.

During the later police investigation, Vivian Jones, the gardener, said that on two occasions that day Alexander had appeared at the barn, and climbed the ladder to the loft for no reason that he could think of. Then, after Jones had caught a duck for dinner, Alexander appeared with his gun and asked if he could shoot the creature. "I told him not to, it would be better to chop its head off," said Jones. The gardener killed the bird, which prompted Ross to turn away, grimacing that he did not like the sight of blood.

Since it had been his intention – he said – to shoot the duck, it was somewhat odd that Alexander now claimed to dislike the sight of blood. Still, he had been thwarted by Jones in any case, so instead he returned to the house. Just a short time later, however, the cook, Elta Stevenson, saw him heading back towards the barn and mentioned it to Jones. He in turn told her of his experience at the barn with Ross, and together they wondered what he could possibly be doing out there, but decided it was none of their business to enquire.

At 7.10 p.m. Jones left for the day and had only been home a short time when he turned on the radio to catch up with the day's news. The headline that greeted him, however, was not what he expected to hear at all: the announcement that his boss, Ross Alexander, had shot himself dead. Jones immediately grabbed his car keys and drove straight back to the house. "I wish I had gone to the barn before I left," he told police. "Maybe it wouldn't have happened."

Ross Alexander's new wife was absolutely devastated at the loss of her husband. She had been married for less than four months and could not understand why he had chosen to take his own life – particularly as she had not seen anything out of the ordinary all day. It later surfaced, however, that Warner Brothers had recently told him they were scaling down his roles, concerned that Alexander's personal life was not allowing him to focus on his career. Worried about his job, his finances and with the tragic death of his first wife still very much on his mind, Alexander was in too much pain to carry on.

The actor's parents, who had been visiting over the Christmas holiday, were driving back home to Rochester, New York, when the news came through that their son had committed suicide. The devastated couple had just reached Arkansas and had to turn their car around to drive back to Hollywood. They were sad in the knowledge that while he had been talked out of using the gun just weeks earlier, Ross ultimately succeeded in taking his life by using the very same weapon that his wife had employed a little over a year before.

18

The Knickerbocker Hotel

In Hollywood, some scandals revolve around the actors, actresses and wannabes who come looking for fame, fortune or both. But occasionally we stumble across a building that has made so many headlines that it deserves an entry all to itself in this book. The Shelton Apartments, detailed here in "The Suicide Apartments" chapter, is one such building, and the Knickerbocker Hotel is another.

Built in 1925 by E. M. Frasier, the hotel was once a favourite haunt of Rudolph Valentino, Lana Turner, Mae West and Frank Sinatra. Elvis Presley lived in suite 1016 while making *Love Me Tender*, and Marilyn Monroe drove Joe DiMaggio here after their first date in 1952. But while it attracted its fair share of happy Hollywood memories, the hotel also played host to more than a few seedier headlines over the years, before finally evolving into a retirement home for senior citizens.

The first story is more amusing than scandalous, though it certainly made the headlines back in 1936. During his lifetime, magician Harry Houdini often spent time debunking psychics and mediums. He wrote a book, *A Magician Among the Spirits*, which chronicled his efforts to unmask those he deemed frauds and charlatans, and told his wife Bess that if there was such a thing as communication after death, then he would come to her during a séance. The couple agreed that the secret code would be "Rosabelle believe" and that she would try for a total of ten years after his passing to get in touch. Sure enough, on

Halloween 1927 – the first anniversary of Houdini's death – Bess began her yearly tradition of holding a séance for her husband, though disappointingly he never came through for her.

Bess persevered for nine years, and then flew to Hollywood from New York in 1936 and checked herself into the famed Knickerbocker Hotel for one last séance. There she told staff of her plans to conduct the final séance on the rooftop, accompanied by her business manager, Edward Saint. As she prepared for the evening, Bess told reporters that she had received many messages from mediums over the years, all telling her that they had been able to get through to the other side and speak with Houdini. "They mean nothing to me," she said. "If he were to manifest himself to anyone, it seems it would be to me."

Unfortunately, it would seem that if the magician was speaking from beyond the grave, it certainly was not to Bess, and that evening's attempt at contact was – as usual – a disappointing failure. The only thing that could be heard from the roof of the Knickerbocker was the quiet hum of the occasional car heading down Ivar Avenue, and taking the silence as a final hint, Bess finally gave up trying to contact her deceased husband. Still, the lack of correspondence did not deter other mediums, however, and for many years the tradition of holding a séance for Houdini has continued, though the success of the proceedings is somewhat debatable at best.

The first real scandal to hit the famed hotel was in January 1943 when actress Frances Farmer was arrested after violating her probation by drink driving. Farmer was staying in her room and only semi-attired when police arrived at her door with a warrant for her arrest. Once inside there was such a fracas that officers ended up dragging the distraught, half-nude woman out of the room, along the corridor and down into the hotel lobby, where she vocally aired her displeasure at being arrested, much to the shock and scandal of everyone mingling around the front desk.

Her arrest made headlines around the United States. Shortly afterwards she was admitted to hospital and spent the coming years under the care of doctors and psychiatrists. The arrest of Frances Farmer and her treatment by the police as she was taken from the hotel helped make the Knickerbocker become known as a headline-making hotel, and is still talked about to this day.

The first Knickerbocker resident to make headlines by passing away while living there came in 1948 when the "father of the movie industry" D. W. Griffith died after collapsing in his room at the hotel. Griffith had been a pioneering director famous for the 1915 film *The Birth of a Nation* and many other early Hollywood successes. However, as time went on, he became disillusioned with the industry and eventually retired, claiming that he had always found directing to be a chore. "Believe it or not," he said, "I always considered it a temporary thing, a sort of springboard", before adding that his ultimate, lifetime ambition was always to be a writer.

During his last year, Griffith lived a simple life at the Knickerbocker Hotel, where he read his large collection of books, and wrote plays and short skits. In the evening he would leave his room and quietly stroll along the boulevard, where he would swing his trademark cane and anonymously take in the sights and sounds of his beloved Hollywood.

On 22 July 1948, Griffith collapsed in his room at the hotel, and was immediately examined by Dr Edward Skaletar. Suspecting a stroke, he rushed Griffith to Temple Hospital but his life could not be saved and sadly he passed away on 23 July. Friends and colleagues lined up to pay tribute to their mentor, and movie executive Samuel Goldwyn summed up the feelings of Hollywood when he said: "All of us in the motion picture industry owe to him and to his memory more than we will ever be able to repay."

The next famous Knickerbocker death actually took place in the hotel itself and was the most dramatic in its history so far. This happened in 1962 when famed dress designer Irene

Lentz Gibbons (better known simply as Irene) ended her life in dramatic fashion right in the middle of the building.

Irene had been a costume designer at MGM for many years, making famed clothes for the likes of Rosalind Russell, Carole Lombard, Joan Crawford and June Allyson. She was extremely successful and respected in the industry, and when she finally decided to retire from movies in 1949, her popularity ensured that she went on designing clothes for various stars over the course of many years to come.

But by 1962, the now sixty-year-old Irene was living in Beverly Hills and spending much of her time worrying about her husband, Eliot, who had recently suffered a stroke. A high point had come when she had shown her latest designs at a nearby fashion show, but worries were never far from her mind and she seemed to be constantly beset by financial troubles and concerns. Finally, on 15 November she decided she no longer wished to be burdened by the stresses that came with her life and checked into room 1129 of the Knickerbocker Hotel.

Once installed in her room, Irene began drinking excessively, gearing herself up for what she intended to do during the hours ahead. She wrote several notes, in one saying she was sorry to be taking her life in such a manner. "Please see that Eliot is taken care of," she said, before going on to ask her friends to "get someone very good to design and be happy". She ended by declaring, "I love you all. Irene." Somewhat bizarrely, the designer also apologized in a note to fellow hotel guests which said simply, "Neighbours: Sorry I had to drink so much to get courage to do this."

Finally, having drunk herself into intoxication, Irene gathered up enough courage to end her life. Newspapers reported that she had tried to cut her wrists, though if she had, it was not mentioned on the death certificate. What we do know for sure is that during the afternoon, the respected dress designer staggered to her eleventh-floor window, opened it as wide as it would go, and at 3.20 p.m. jumped to her death, landing on the roof of the hotel lobby.

It has been rumoured that, tragically, her body lay on the roof for many days before someone finally discovered it. This was not the case, however, as the sound made by the crash was extreme enough to have everyone wondering what on earth had just fallen from above. Her body was found quickly and an ambulance was called, though it was too late for anything to be done for Irene and the death certificate listed the cause of death as "Multiple fractures of all extremities with severe internal crushing injuries". It also listed "acute alcohol intoxication" as another significant condition; a result of the copious amount of drink she had gulped to gain the courage to make her leap.

Irene's funeral was held at Forest Lawn, cemetery to the stars, and was attended by clients, friends and family. Her life may have been full of amazing designs and costumes, but sadly for Irene – just like many others before and since – it was her death that went down in history due to the gruesome way she decided to conduct it.

The final famous death to come to the Knickerbocker was in 1966, when actor William Frawley passed away in the lobby of the hotel. Frawley was most famous for co-starring in the hugely successful TV series *I Love Lucy*, but after leaving the show he had also achieved further fame in the Fred MacMurray show, *My Three Sons*. Unfortunately bad health had besieged the aging actor and in 1965 he was written out of the show after undergoing prostate surgery.

On Thursday, 3 March 1966, Frawley was walking down Hollywood Boulevard with his nurse, having just watched a movie at a nearby cinema. The seventy-three-year-old actor was supposed to be meeting a friend, but unfortunately as he was strolling towards his destination, he began to experience severe chest pains. His nurse was understandably shocked but somehow beat the odds by managing to get Frawley to the Knickerbocker Hotel on Ivar Avenue. Once there, the nurse shouted for help and concerned staff ran to the actor's aid and phoned for an ambulance.

Sadly, while they were waiting for the vehicle to arrive, the actor suffered a massive heart attack and proceeded to collapse on to the floor of the hotel lobby. The ambulance crew rushed into the building but, despite their best efforts, there was unfortunately nothing that could be done to help him and by the time they had reached a nearby hospital, the ailing actor had already passed away.

Though he'd been ill for some time, the acting world was in shock at Frawley's sudden death, and his co-star in *I Love Lucy*, Lucille Ball, released a statement. In it she said that she had lost one of her closest friends, and that "show business has lost one of the greatest character actors of all time".

The ironic thing about Frawley dying at the Knickerbocker was that for many years he had actually lived in the hotel with his sister, Mary. However, when she passed away herself, Frawley made the decision to move out of the hotel and into his own apartment. In March 1966 he was living at 450 North Rossmore Avenue, and it had been merely a coincidence that on the very night he died, he should be walking so close to the building he had called home for much of his later life.

19

Jean Harlow, Hollywood's Baby

Out of the many hundreds of high-profile Hollywood deaths over the past hundred years, there are very few that have really caused a huge outpouring of public grief. Marilyn Monroe was one such case, and her idol, Jean Harlow, was another. She was mourned twenty-five years before Marilyn died, with thousands lining the streets to share their sadness with the world.

Born Harlean Harlow Carpenter on 3 March 1911, "The Baby", as she was known, was raised in Kansas City, Missouri, by her father, Mont Clair Carpenter, and her mother, Jean Carpenter (née Harlow). Her childhood was financially secure but her mother was unhappy in the marriage and eventually filed for divorce in 1922. This was devastating for Harlean as she adored her father, and even more upsetting when it became apparent that the controlling Mrs Carpenter was only prepared to allow limited access to him for the rest of Jean's life.

After the divorce, Jean Carpenter decided to take her daughter to Hollywood to find fame and fortune. However, surprisingly it was not for Jean that she wished fame: it was for herself. The mother and daughter arrived in 1923 and "Mother Jean", as she was known, started the long process of walking from studio to studio in the hope of finding work. She soon discovered, however, that acting in Hollywood was purely a young girl's dream, and since she was the wrong side of thirty, she was never going to become remotely famous in her own right.

Broke and downhearted, the two left Hollywood on the instructions of Mother Jean's father, who threatened to disinherit her if she continued with what he considered to be her ridiculous and failed quest to be a movie star. Neither woman was happy to leave California and when Mother Jean married Marino Bello – a man with a questionable reputation – in 1927, Harlean showed her disapproval by eloping with her boyfriend, Charles McGrew, and moving straight back to Los Angeles. The newly married Jean's plan to escape her mother and stepfather did not go quite to plan, however, as she soon found herself followed to California by the pair, who felt it would be far more entertaining to live in Hollywood than plain old Missouri.

Once in California, Harlean became friends with a young actress called Rosalie Roy, who was eager to find fame and fortune as an actress. One day, desperate for a lift, she asked Harlean to drive her to an audition at a nearby studio. She was happy to provide this service, though what neither of the young women knew was that it would be Harlean who caught the eye of the executives there, not Rosalie Roy.

Harlean thought the whole idea of being discovered was quite a joke, especially after witnessing the failed career of her mother, and promptly told the studio that she had no interest in their plans for her. However, several days later, her friend joked with the young blonde about what had been offered to her, and made a bet that she would never have the nerve to go further with the "discovery". Always game for a laugh, this prompted Harlean to prove her friend wrong, and after driving herself to Central Casting, it was not long before she had signed a contract using her mother's maiden name, Jean Harlow.

This new and surprising career was entertaining to Jean, who enjoyed a series of bit parts, including an appearance in *Double Whoopee* with comedians Laurel and Hardy. However, back in Missouri her grandfather saw a photo of Jean in a skimpy outfit and he immediately wrote to show his displeasure and encourage the young woman to give up any dreams she might have of becoming an actress. After all the "nonsense" he had been through with his daughter's dreams of screen stardom, he did not want to go through it all again with his granddaughter, and was determined to get her back home.

However, while Mother Jean had probably known she was on a failing quest to become famous at her age, Jean was still a young woman and, despite her grandfather's concerns, she persevered with her career. But with this success came a great deal of stress within her marriage, and it eventually collapsed under great strain from both sides in 1929. Thankfully the sadness at the end of her relationship did not last long when more small roles came her way, including in the 1929 movie *The Saturday Night Kid* with Clara Bow. Then she scored her biggest break when cast in the Howard Hughes film, *Hell's Angels*, which was such a huge success that it catapulted Jean to stardom; she followed this with hits such as *The Public Enemy* (1931) with James Cagney and *Red Dust* (1932) with Clark Gable.

However, the headlines she received for *Red Dust* were not quite what she expected, after the sudden and mysterious death of her second husband of just a few weeks, producer Paul Bern. So scandalous was the marriage and death that a whole separate chapter is dedicated to it in this book ("The Mysterious Death of Paul Bern"). For now, the shadow of scandal that lingered over MGM's brightest star was almost unbearable.

With Bern's death so fuelled by rumours, Jean's career was severely threatened, though quite surprisingly she managed to weather the storm and won a great deal of public sympathy through the way she handled the whole episode. She then went on to star in successful movies such as *Bombshell* (1933) and *Dinner at Eight* (1933), though her tricky personal life was always on the verge of scandal and took another tumble when she married and quickly divorced her third husband, cameraman Hal Rosson, in 1933–4.

By this time Jean was gaining a reputation as a serial bride, but it would seem that the end of her marriage to Hal was not the result of anything she had done, but instead the conclusion of a great deal of stirring and continued interference by Mother Jean. Never one to shirk from an overpowering interest in her daughter's life, the woman had crashed into the couple's marriage to such a degree that while Hal was said to be deeply in love with his wife, it just was not enough to hold the relationship together.

By 1937 Jean was dating William Powell, the ex-husband of Jean's friend, the film star Carole Lombard. Carole was known for her raucous behaviour, wild parties and liking for the odd swearword or two. In short, she was the kind of person Jean Harlow was known to play on screen, though away from the camera Jean was quite the opposite: gentle, softly spoken and not regularly known to curse. The relationship Jean had with Powell was not entirely positive for this reason, as it would seem that he mistook the person she played on screen with the person she actually was, and was often known to joke and tease her in the same way he did with Carole. The outgoing Lombard could handle it, but the softer Harlow could not, and she became confused sometimes when his jokes hurt her feelings.

Adding to Jean's confusion was Powell's reluctance to marry her, and by spring 1937 she was unsure as to where the relationship was going. When reporters asked if the two would marry, she would always laugh and tell them that after three marriages, she surely would not want to marry again. Privately, however, it would seem that she longed for Powell to take her seriously, make their union official and rescue her from the arms of her controlling mother who she was living with at the time.

Unfortunately for Jean, she would never discover what Powell's true intentions were as on 29 May 1937, while working on the film *Saratoga* with Clark Gable, she fell desperately ill. Complaining to crew members, the actress told them, "I don't know what's the matter. I feel so ill, I haven't the strength to hold my hand to remove my make-up."

Worryingly, the day before she had complained to director Jack Conway that she did not feel quite herself and people began to worry that there was something very wrong with "The Baby". Earlier that morning, Jean had sat back in the make-up chair and allowed artist Violet Denoyer to attend to her face. "You know, Violet," the star suddenly said, "I have a feeling I'm going away from here and never coming back."

"She felt the end was coming," Denoyer later told reporters.

When it became clear that she was not going to be able to work that day, Jean was sent home to rest. A true professional, she did not go easily, however, and assured crew members that she would return the moment she felt better. She even telephoned the studio in the days ahead to assure them she would be back as soon as possible.

The illness seemed to come on very suddenly, but looking back there had been signs that the actress had not been well for some time. Early in 1937 Jean had attended the presidential inaugural ball in Washington, DC, but on the return journey had become unwell and arrived home suffering from flu. Then in April she was admitted to hospital for treatment on a wisdom tooth, and at the time friends noted that she had recently appeared bloated and her skin was sallow and grey. She was drinking heavily at times, something which worried them, particularly when the alcohol seemed to make her ankles swell quite considerably. Photographers even started to notice dark lines under her eyes that needed to be covered by thick make-up before they could shoot her.

When she left the set of *Saratoga* on 29 May, Jean did not go immediately home. Mother Jean was out of town, holidaying with friends on Catalina Island, so rather than be on her own, the actress chose to stay at her boyfriend William Powell's house until she felt better. Unfortunately, over the coming days her condition only worsened, and a concerned Powell phoned her mother in Catalina, who returned to Los Angeles immediately.

Once back in town, Mother Jean hurried to Powell's house,

bundled up her ailing daughter and took her back home to 512 North Palm Drive, where she was put immediately to bed. Being a Christian Scientist who thus did not believe in the reality of disease, Mother Jean initially consulted her religion in an effort to help the situation. When that did not work, she called in Dr Ernest C. Fishbaugh, who examined Jean while she was lying in her bedroom. He was not sure what was wrong; while the actress had the symptoms of a bad cold, he was unable to identify why she had severe pains in her stomach, too.

After tests and further examinations, it was obvious to everyone that Jean was bloated and retaining water, but instead of draining the fluids, Dr Fishbaugh unbelievably insisted on giving Harlow more and more to drink. This decision was to have a hugely detrimental effect on his patient's ultimate health in the days to come. Indeed, when Clark Gable came to visit her, he was extremely shocked at the sight of his dear friend and said afterwards that it was like conversing with a rotting body; that when he bent down to talk to her, Jean Harlow's breath smelled of urine. This was definitely not a good sign.

However, for a short while it did look as though Harlow was rallying, and she actually sat up to read a little of her favourite book, *Gone with the Wind*. Then on 4 June 1937 a news report appeared in the *Los Angeles Times* that stated she was on the mend and the scare was over. According to reports, Dr Fishbaugh had nursed Jean through a heavy cold but she was very definitely now over the worst.

On the surface this was great news, but the newspapers were quick to point out that when she collapsed, her mother had described her illness as being related to her gall bladder, not a cold. This was true, and her problems in that area were worrying Mother Jean a great deal. When Jean's condition then began to go downhill fast, she knew it was more than just a severe cold, but being a Christian Scientist, she ignored calls to take her daughter to the hospital.

Mother Jean was the mother of all controlling mothers and

if anyone dared say she was doing the wrong thing for Jean, she would ban them from the house. However, although she declared herself a Christian Scientist, she was quite happy for medical staff to continue to work on her daughter at home, and even begged the family doctor Dr Chapman to come and see if he could diagnose exactly what was the problem.

When Dr Chapman finally arrived at North Palm Drive, he was able to identify what was wrong with his patient almost immediately – kidney failure brought on over the years after a childhood bout of scarlet fever. Unhappily for everyone involved, the misdiagnosis and treatment that she had experienced in the days prior to Dr Chapman's visit meant there was little he could do to save her life. Despite her mother's reluctance, Jean Harlow was finally transferred to the Good Samaritan Hospital where she was given two blood transfusions and placed in an oxygen tent. Sadly, it would seem that while everyone was still trying desperately to keep the star alive and praying that she would make a miraculous recovery, Jean herself knew it was impossible. When one family member told her to get well soon, the actress shook her head. "I don't want to," she replied.

Jean Harlow passed away on 7 June 1937, surrounded by relatives and friends such as Mother Jean, her ex-stepfather Marino Bello (whom her mother had divorced the year before) and the love of her life, William Powell. She was just twenty-six years old.

In the halls of the Good Samaritan Hospital, reporters waited for news, their pens poised over their notebooks whenever anyone went to or from Jean's room. It was a wait that seemed to go on forever, until finally the door swung open and out ran a distraught William Powell, heading for a nearby room. He did not say anything to reporters, but they knew a grieving man when the saw one and immediately feared the worst.

Finally Dr Fishbaugh came out to break the sad news. "She's gone," he told reporters, while inside the room family members tried desperately to come to terms with the hand they had been dealt. Jean's mother was particularly upset; her baby was gone; her reason for living had disappeared; and she had to be sedated to such an extent that MGM announced it was necessary for them to step in and take over all arrangements for the funeral.

After the news of Harlow's death became public knowledge, Hollywood was devastated. The press tried to get a statement from co-star Clark Gable but with his last visit to Jean still fresh in his mind, he declared himself too devastated to speak about his friend's death. However, dozens of other stars, studio heads and crew members queued up to release statements to the press, all anxious to let the world know just how much they would miss her.

Perhaps the longest statement was issued by Jean's boss at MGM, Louis B. Mayer, who described how this was the end of a personal friendship, and described Jean Harlow as "one of the loveliest, sweetest persons I have known in thirty years of the theatrical business. I have lost a friend. The world has lost a ray of sunlight. She was a delight to handle as a star. She was one of the most charming, thoughtful and reasonable players with whom I have been associated."

Actress Jeanette MacDonald remembered the actress as a friend: "Jean was my next-door neighbour. Our dressing rooms were right together. I am terribly shocked. She was so sweet, I shall miss her so much." Her last director, Jack Conway, was shocked beyond compare and stated that the industry had lost a great, unique star; the world had lost laughter, "and I have lost a friend".

Carole Lombard was deeply saddened and told reporters that her friend was a "vital, sweet and charming girl. We all feel the tragedy of her passing." The experience of Harlow's passing and the way she was mourned deeply disturbed Lombard. She insisted that when her time came, Clark Gable should give her a quick, quiet funeral, which he did, just under five years later when she was tragically killed in a plane crash.

But back in 1937, the funeral of MGM's brightest star was

arranged for 9 June at the Wee Kirk o' the Heather in Forest Lawn Memorial Park. The ceremony was very private, with entrance only allowed to those invited to attend. This did not stop fans mourning, however, and such was the show of public grief that guards and police officers were placed around the chapel, blocking entrances and walkways in order to keep the crowds at bay. People complained that there was so much protection that it was harder to see Jean in death than it had ever been in life, but it fell on deaf ears and the doors remained closed.

One fan, twenty-seven-year-old Henry Conner, was the first to arrive. He told reporters, "I left Riverside yesterday morning and hitch-hiked to Los Angeles. I had to walk twelve miles of the way and slept last night in a Hollywood park . . . I have an autographed photograph of her and honestly, I think she was swell." Conner was just one example of the people who travelled to Forest Lawn that day and in the end the police turned away a thousand spectators, all of whom had come specifically to have one last look at "The Baby". "She was a regular on the screen," cried one fan. "Everyone says she was regular in real life. We wish we could see her – one more time."

Inside the chapel, Nelson Eddy sang one of Jean's favourite songs, "Ah Sweet Mystery of Life", while Jeannette MacDonald performed "Indian Love Call". Friends and family piled into the building, and many were visibly upset and close to collapse. Jean's last lover William Powell was helped by a friend and his mother Nettie Powell, while Mother Jean appeared in a dazed state, supported on both sides and clearly devastated. Even Jean's third husband, Hal Rosson, arrived at the chapel along with his new wife, though the couple shunned photographers and refused to answer reporters' questions. The funeral was most certainly a Hollywood spectacle, and the pall-bearers included luminaries such as Clark Gable and Louis B. Mayer, while overhead, a low-flying plane scattered rosebuds on to the ground below.

Meanwhile, back at MGM, a minute's silence took place in

order to honour the lost star, though in reality nobody much felt like talking anyway. The level of grief around the studio was unprecedented, the sense of loss profound and the sadness unbearable. Such was the despair around the world that the *Hollywood Reporter* even painted a picture of the MGM lion carrying a wreath, with his head bowed before a picture of a smiling Harlow.

To this day, over a hundred years since her birth, the girl known as "The Baby" – who never had the chance to fully grow up – is still remembered with fondness and laughter. Due to the sheer volume of fans still celebrating her life through books and fan clubs, it is clear that while her life may have been far too short, her legend will live on forever.

20

The Sad Death of Marie Prevost

In January 1930, Afton Place in Hollywood was abuzz with news that a Spanish-style apartment block, the Aftonian, was set to open at number 6230. Employees of nearby film studios quickly filled the apartments inside, and the place became synonymous with the film industry, its residents all seeming to have something to do with the business. The building was seen as a delightful place to live, but it was not until several years later that it would become infamous as the unfortunate last residence of tragic film star Marie Prevost.

Born as Mary Bickford Dunn in Sarnia, Ontario, on 8 November 1898, she moved to Denver with her family while still a young child. However, they soon discovered that Colorado was not quite what they were looking for, and it wasn't long before they moved once more to settle finally in Los Angeles, California. Mary grew up to work as an office secretary, but being in Hollywood meant that acting ambitions were never far from her mind. She did not have to wait long to be discovered, and when the opportunity of working at the Mack Sennett studio arose, Mary jumped at the chance to further her dreams, and left her secretarial days behind her for good.

Becoming known as a bathing beauty under the name Marie Prevost, her star began to rise rapidly, and between 1915 and 1921 she appeared in movies such as *Secrets of a Beauty Parlour*, *His Hidden Purpose* and *Uncle Tom Without a Cabin*.

Marie was an ambitious woman with ideas of a great career in films, so by 1921 she had decided to draw a line under her bathing-beauty days, and was then taken under the wing of Irving Thalberg and signed to Universal. Marie worked hard at the great studio and made several movies there, but a desire to move on was never far away, and she soon dumped Universal in favour of Warner Brothers, where she signed a two-year contract at a staggering $1,500 a week.

Unfortunately, just as things were really looking up for Marie, her career threatened to end in scandal before it had properly begun when, in August 1923, a gentleman by the name of Sonny Gerke filed for divorce from his estranged wife, Marie Gerke. It was revealed that the pair in question had married in 1918 and separated in 1922, but while this very run-of-the-mill divorce should not have even caused a ripple in the newspapers, there was something about it that had the reporters intrigued.

The name Sonny Gerke was familiar and a quick glance in the newspaper archives revealed that he had once squired Marie Prevost around town. It was thought at the time that Gerke was no more than a devoted admirer – a beau who took Marie to the occasional dinner or film screening, but nothing more than that. However, it was intriguing that he was divorcing a woman who just happened to have the same first name as the actress, and it was not long before reporters were digging deep into their files to uncover who the mysterious Marie Gerke really was.

They didn't have to search for long when they discovered that not only was Sonny Gerke the same man who had once dated Marie Prevost, but that his estranged wife Marie Gerke was indeed the now famous actress. The reporters were in shock. They knew that Marie's current squeeze, actor Kenneth Harlan, was still married but that had been the only thing they knew. Nobody had any inkling that Marie was married and the idea that she had secretly tied the knot – and was now trying quietly to untie it – created a sensation.

Knowing that this revelation was going to cause a major scandal, the press grabbed their notebooks and raced to Coronado where the actress was casually spending some spare time visiting friends. Banging on the door, they were surprised when Marie opened it herself; and they had no hesitation in happily sharing news of the divorce with her.

Marie stood on the doorstep with her mouth open, not knowing exactly what to say; she had been keeping the marriage a secret for years but how could she continue to do so while confronted by hungry newspapermen? In the end, she decided that she had no choice but to confirm that, yes, she was indeed married to Sonny Gerke and it was true that she was now going through what she hoped to be a very private divorce.

Several days later, with revelations of her private life flooding the papers, Marie finally sat down and opened up to a *Los Angeles Times* reporter. "Really there isn't anything to tell," she said. "We were just two foolish children who ran away and married and then separated immediately. And now it's all over."

This was not quite the truth, since she had been spotted with Sonny on more than one occasion in the past, but even so, Marie tried to make it clear that everything was very straightforward in both the marriage and the separation. Still, in spite of that, she managed to raise eyebrows by flippantly declaring that she could not even remember the date of the wedding or the name of the minister. She did, however manage to recall that they had met in 1918 and "he was in the Navy at the time".

"You see," she explained, "It was during the war and everybody was marrying, but immediately the ceremony was over we both realized what a silly thing we had done." She then went on to say – quite bizarrely – that even though she had gone through with the ceremony, she had never actually realized she was married. "I never thought about it," she admitted.

The actress obviously wanted to make light of the marriage and the circumstances surrounding it, but her comments most certainly were not truthful. The marriage had played on her mind and for three months after the ceremony she had wondered how exactly to tell her mother, Hughlina, what she had done. She knew she would not be pleased, and was sure she would be absolutely appalled at the spontaneity of her decision, but finally Marie knew she had to come clean.

Taking a deep breath the young actress opened her mouth and admitted everything to her previously uninformed mother. The woman was astonished at what her foolish daughter had done, and plans for an annulment were immediately arranged. However, for reasons known only to them, it never came to anything, so the couple decided that they would just continue to be friends and occasionally date, though it was agreed that they would never actually live together.

As Marie's star continued to rise, the fear of a scandal stopped the couple going through with a divorce, as they did not want the newspapers to find out about their secret marriage. However, at one point their cover was almost blown when a reporter got hold of a rumour that the two were actually betrothed. "Don't be silly," laughed a nervous Marie, while her concerned mother took it upon herself to issue a complete denial.

Finally, while Marie was happily trying to pretend she wasn't married, Gerke had had enough of being just good friends, and telephoned the actress to tell her that he'd had enough; he would finally be going through with a divorce. "I knew he was going to sue, but nevertheless I was surprised, and yes – frightened," she told reporters. Several weeks later Gerke was true to his word and went to court to obtain the official separation. While there he told the judge that Ms Prevost/Mrs Gerke would not object to the proceedings, and admitted that "my wife's aversion to having the fact that she was married known for fear of injuring her career, was an insurmountable barrier to our domestic happiness".

What he had neglected to say, however, was that part of the couple's problem was that Marie loved alcohol more than she had ever loved her estranged husband. Years later, Sonny's daughter Arden Keevers told author Michael G. Ankerich that her father said very little about the marriage to Marie. However, what he did reveal was that it was very tempestuous and that the actress definitely had a drinking problem during that time.

The divorce between Mrs and Mrs Gerke eventually became final and the scandal died down. Quite amusingly, however, Marie's next film was entitled *The Marriage Circle*, which was to be directed by Ernst Lubitsch. She was very optimistic about the part and told reporters, "Mr Lubitsch's way of directing is so different. All he wants me to do is to be natural, just like I would in real life." Working with Lubitsch was a fantastic experience for the actress, and she gave him credit for giving her the chance to "get away from the usual, conventional way of doing things". She was learning much about her abilities as an actress and felt sure that her career was moving in the direction she wanted it to go.

She was right, and from then on Marie's career went from strength to strength, with starring roles in *Kiss Me Again* and *Up in Mabel's Room*. Not wishing to attract any more attention in the marriage department, she quietly and without fuss wed her sweetheart, Kenneth Harlan, and looked forward to their future together.

Unfortunately, however, everything came crashing down in 1926 when Warner Brothers refused to renew the contracts of both Marie and her husband Harlan. Neither of them could believe it and the couple were left reeling at the unfairness of the decision. They wondered what they could possibly do to rectify the situation, but unfortunately, as it turned out, the renewing of contracts was just the tip of the iceberg; they were about to see just how cruel life could really be.

Just as Marie was getting her career back on track with several film roles, she was left inconsolable when news came through that her mother had been killed in a car accident while travelling from Los Angeles to Palm Beach. Apparently the wheel of the car came apart as she was in New Mexico, causing the vehicle to lose control and eventually overturn. The other passengers were not seriously injured but Hughlina was pronounced dead at the scene after suffering a broken spine and fractured skull.

Marie had been close to her mother and took the news of her death very badly. She began drinking more heavily than ever in an attempt to blank out her pain, but soon found that the alcohol did nothing for her emotions or her nerves. Then just before Christmas, a young girl stepped in front of the car Marie was driving, and although she was able to avert any real disaster, the incident caused the actress to stop driving for a year, taking streetcars to and from work for fear of anything happening while she was behind the wheel.

Marie's nerves were on edge; thoughts of her mother's death still played heavily on her mind, and the marriage between herself and Harlan started to crumble. The problems led to a much publicized separation in 1927, and Prevost decided to file for divorce. In court papers, the actress stated that Harlan refused to show any interest in the things she enjoyed; he was inconsiderate; he failed to provide her with reasonable recreation; he did not speak the way husbands should speak; and he became unreasonably jealous and told her that he would have been far happier if he had married somebody else. Newspapers were full of the stories of their divorce but, quite astonishingly, by July 1928 all seemed to have been forgiven and the couple announced that the divorce was off and they were back together again.

Confused reporters crowded into their Beverly Hills mansion to take photographs of the "happy" couple, but reported that while Prevost seemed giddy with excitement, the only word Harlan uttered was "Goof", said quietly into his wife's ear. Still, they were anxious to make the relationship work and, hoping to become closer, the two actors embarked on a second honeymoon to New York, but it was not successful; they argued most of the time and by January 1929 the marriage was over for good. Kenneth was polite when asked by reporters what his thoughts were, telling them that Marie was a "fine woman", that they were still the best of friends, but "we simply could not get along together".

Marie was more forthright. When asked when she would be getting married again she screwed up her nose. "Not very soon I assure you. Anyway, that is how I feel about it."

By this time the talkies had come along and while Marie made the transition to sound fairly successfully, like many others she found the technique of acting in front of a microphone more complicated than straightforward silent movies. The pressure put on stars at that time to make the transition without trauma was excruciating for the already nervous actress and it was perhaps no coincidence that with the advent of sound, Marie Prevost was never again the star of a movie.

The actress's weight started to fluctuate due to her battle with alcohol and her career suffered even more as a result. Gone were the heady days of bathing-beauty roles and dramatic parts, and instead she seemed destined to forever play "the friend" of actors such as Carole Lombard, who worked with her in *Hands Across the Table*. In that particular film, Marie brought in an amusing performance as Carole's friend Nona, but it was a fairly small role, not particularly important and certainly not what she was used to playing when she had been a star.

In 1935 Marie hoped for a proper comeback when Warner Brothers agreed to call on her for future acting assignments. It was not the positive experience she hoped for, however, and while she was still only in her thirties, Marie found herself sitting on the "Old Timers' Table" in the Warners' Restaurant, chatting to former stars about the "good old days".

It was at this point that Marie started to realize that her weight would always be an issue if she wanted to obtain good parts. However, instead of cutting back on alcohol, she astonishingly decided to stop eating and instead continued to drink more and more. The actress must surely have known the long-lasting damage that such a habit could bring not only to her career but to her body too, but by this time Marie was completely addicted; she was an alcoholic, but seemed destined never to admit it.

In late 1936 she moved into the Aftonian, at 6230 Afton Place, and in the comfort of her new home Marie spent her time thinking about the old days of Hollywood and playing with her dachshund, Maxie. A dog lover, she filled the apartment with ribbons and pictures of her prize-winning animals, and pinned a note to the door which read, "Please do not knock on this door more than once. It makes my dog bark. If I am in I will hear you as I am not deaf." Unfortunately, some of the people knocking for attention were not friends but debt collectors, often seen by neighbours banging for attention and grumbling that the actress would not let them in.

Newspapers later reported that Marie Prevost owed money to everyone from dressmakers to tax collectors. In 1935 she had happily announced an inheritance of an estate in Scotland, but nothing came of it and her friend Joan Crawford had to lend her money to get by. She was far too proud to ask her family for help, however, and every time she wrote to her sister Peggy, Marie would always make sure she reported only the good things in her life: "She maintained a brave and cheerful outlook throughout," her sister later said.

Unfortunately, Marie struggled with her finances for the rest of her life, and several days before her death she was spotted walking down Afton Place to a nearby delicatessen, where she was seen discussing the possibility of redeeming a returned cheque with the sales assistant, Bernard Weiss.

Finally, on 21 January 1937, Marie's malnourished and alcohol-laden body was irreversibly breaking down. With empty whisky bottles in the sink and two gas heaters burning in the kitchen, Marie removed her shoes and stockings, and lay down on her bed for a nap. There she passed away in the presence of her beloved dog, Maxie; she was a victim of acute alcoholism according to the autopsy report.

Unfortunately, no one discovered that Marie was dead until

two days after she had expired, when her dog was heard barking wildly inside the apartment. The building manager, Henrietta Jenks, sent the cleaner, William Bogle, to check on their famous resident, and he let himself in with his pass key. What awaited him was extremely distressing.

Marie was face down on the bed, a robe pulled up over her, and there were significant bites on her arms and legs, where Maxie had desperately tried to awaken his mistress. It was later reported that the dog had actually eaten the legs of Marie Prevost, but photographs of the death scene prove this to be absolutely false. There were large bites, yes, but they look more like the kind of marks made by an animal desperate for his owner to wake up, rather than that of a human-eating canine.

Her sister, former actress Peggy Prevost, rushed to Los Angeles from her home in San Francisco and told reporters that "Marie was too proud to let anyone know of her circumstances. We were never advised." She then added tearfully that all she knew was that she had lost a wonderful sister, and was deeply sorry that she had been unable to spend the last few hours of her life with her. "There was never anyone who was more devoted to her friends," Peggy told reporters. "No one more kind and helpful."

Marie Prevost's funeral was a quiet affair. Her mother, who had been buried at Forest Lawn eleven years previously, was exhumed, and the two were cremated together in a private ceremony. Her last rites were as low-key as her last days; there were no flowers, no drama, no glitz or glamour. In fact, so quiet was the affair that there is still no proper evidence of where her ashes ended up, though Peggy later claimed that Joan Crawford paid for a plot of land at Hollywood Memorial Cemetery.

The actress had actually taken the news of her friend's death very badly and was said to have been inconsolable, feeling she was somehow responsible and that she could have – should have – done something to save her. This, it seems, was an emotion felt by many of the people who attended the funeral, most of whom seemed inconsolable at the early passing of their much-loved friend.

Marie's ex-husband, Kenneth Harlan, was saddened by her passing. "I was upset and shocked to learn of my former wife's death," he said, before remarking that he was particularly surprised to hear the circumstances of the way she had died. "We hadn't been in touch with each other for some time," he sadly told reporters.

Indeed, it would seem that while previously Harlan had said he hoped they would still be best friends after their divorce, the only real companion Marie Prevost had with her at the time of her death was her dachshund Maxie. It was a sad and tragic end to the life of the one-time bathing beauty, though unfortunately in Hollywood, not a wholly unusual one.

21

The Rape of Patricia Douglas

Patricia Douglas might not be a household name now, but in 1937 she was on the front pages of numerous newspapers, creating more headlines than even the death of film star and icon, Jean Harlow. Sadly her name and story were covered up in the years that followed, and you are about to find out why.

Douglas was born on 27 March 1917 in Kansas City, Missouri, before moving to Hollywood with her mother, Mildred Mitchell. Mitchell was a dressmaker determined to make glamorous gowns for movie stars, but during the course of pursuing her ambitions – and eight unsuccessful marriages – she was not an attentive mother and ended up neglecting her daughter.

As she was used to going to the cinema as a child, it was a natural progression for Patricia to make her way into the movies, which she did almost as soon as she left school aged fourteen. However, she had no dreams of becoming an actress; instead she performed in dance numbers where she was so good at learning the routines and teaching others that she made a good name for herself with dance directors and gained a lot of work in the process. However, after one particularly tragic night in 1937, Patricia's interest in movies ended forever and she never danced again.

On 2 May 1937, MGM started hosting a much anticipated convention for 282 of their sales executives, who had all arrived as VIPs at the Ambassador Hotel in Los Angeles. They were wined, dined and had private transport to the events; you name it, they got it. In fact, MGM were so adamant that the executives would be satisfied that MGM boss Louis B. Mayer announced at the beginning of the convention that they could have "Anything you want!" and this was repeated time and time again during the course of the next few days.

On 5 May 1937, Patricia Douglas had a 4 p.m. movie call-time at a remote barn on producer Hal Roach's ranch. Patricia was kitted out in a cowgirl outfit, consisting of brown felt hat, suede skirt and black side-seam boots, while 120 other girls were given a mixture of Western and Spanish costumes. They had no reason to believe that this call was for anything but a film, but they were very wrong. When they arrived at the barn there was no film crew, no lights, no cameras or sound equipment. Instead there were 500 cases of champagne, Scotch and lots of food; in short, it looked decidedly like a party was about to start, not a film shoot.

At 7 p.m., the girls were proved right in their suspicions when throngs of salesmen arrived at the barn, all of whom seemed happy to see that "party favours" had been left for them. But it wasn't the food they were interested in; instead, it was the young women who had been tricked into thinking they would be making a movie, not taking part in a free-for-all at the hands of hundreds of hungry salesmen.

Patricia Douglas was allocated to the table of David Ross, a salesman from Chicago. In 2003, she was filmed for *Girl 27* (2007), a documentary by respected author/producer David Stenn, and said on camera that Ross kept asking her to teach him how to "truck", a new dance craze that Patricia was particularly good at. "It never entered my mind that anyone would do me any harm," she told Stenn, adding that Ross was forever "copping a feel", and was slimy with bulging eyes that dominated his entire face.

When Patricia returned from the dance floor to the table, the teetotal dancer was asked by another salesman to try the Scotch and champagne. She refused, which prompted one of the men to mix both drinks together into a glass and proceed to hold her nose while another man poured the ghastly liquid down Douglas's throat. The young dancer almost choked on the liquid and it ran all over her face and down her clothes.

Patricia Douglas was not only horrified by what had just happened, but extremely ill from the liquor, so she went outside to vomit. Unfortunately she was followed by David Ross, who grabbed the virginal Douglas and appallingly proceeded to rape her, slapping the young dancer's face to keep her awake, after the alcohol threatened to make her pass out. One of the last things she remembered him saying to her was the ghastly remark, "I want to destroy you", a comment that troubled and confused Patricia for the rest of her life.

Finally, the attack was over and her screams for help brought car parking attendant Clement Soth to her aid. She was then taken to the Community Hospital, where she was given a douche, effectively destroying all evidence of the attack. Getting rid of anything that could put Ross at the scene of the attack seems a bizarre thing to do, but when you consider that the studio executives were furious that Douglas had made a fuss and determined that they would not be dragged into any kind of scandal, it all makes perfect sense.

It would seem that the studio executives were adamant that they would make sure it was Douglas, not them, who had a ruined reputation, and as a result, questionnaires were handed out to other dancers to see what kind of girl Patricia was. This was not all, as private detectives were then assigned to spy on her, and even her doctor was reportedly paid to claim falsely that she was suffering from a sexually transmitted disease. Meanwhile, if Patricia believed she would at least find love and understanding with her family, she was very wrong as at her home at 1160 South Bronson Avenue, she received no compassion from her mother at all. "It was never mentioned; it never happened," she told David Stenn years later.

It wasn't long, of course, before the scandal hit the

newspapers, with District Attorney Buron Fitts telling reporters that he intended to have a man with the same name as the attacker face Patricia Douglas to see if she could identify him. "I am taking no definite action until I am sure we have the right man," he said. At no time was David Ross or MGM mentioned in the article, though Patricia Douglas was named in the very first sentence, with her full address published on numerous occasions over the coming days and weeks.

In a twist, it turned out that the man they presented to Douglas in the District Attorney's office was not the right David Ross at all, but an innocent Hollywood theatre manager, whom Patricia had never seen in her life. Photographs were then sought to clarify exactly who the attacker could be and Patricia was once again called to the police station, where she looked through a file of "suspects" and eventually picked David Ross out of a group of twenty-four men. "This is the man," Patricia declared, before turning over the photographs and declining to look any further.

The case was eventually brought before a grand jury, and David Ross was finally named in the newspapers, though never officially served. However, he did appear in court to defend himself, and was led into the room for official identification. That day newspapers described Douglas as accusing Ross of "beating and attacking her when she repulsed his advances" and the word rape was not mentioned at all. Then in the recess, Douglas had the unfortunate experience of seeing Ross in the corridor, a situation most likely set up by the media as a good photo opportunity. She broke down and ran towards an open window before being consoled by her mother in front of the press photographers. Given that Douglas's mother had never shown any loving interest in the child before, one can be forgiven for thinking that her show of remorse was merely for the photographers.

Ross took to the stand to testify. He denied the attack except to say that he was introduced to Patricia Douglas with several other girls, danced and joined her for one round of drinks. He then claimed to have left with friends at midnight, while Douglas continued to party with another man at the event. It was all lies but that, coupled with the fact that a host of witnesses, including the car parking attendant, were apparently paid to change their stories and deny they had seen anything at all, resulted in the case being dropped.

This should have been the end of the matter, but actually it wasn't as the extraordinarily brave Patricia Douglas was not prepared to give up without a fight and announced plans to sue MGM herself. This was a huge decision for a young woman to do and she deserves nothing but applause for the strength and bravery displayed at that time, but unfortunately it all came to nothing. Patricia's plans to sue were buried without trace amid claims that both her lawyer and mother were paid off in order to let the matter drop quietly.

The outcome of the trial and her treatment at the hands of MGM, the media, her mother and the witnesses to her ordeal affected Patricia Douglas's life forever. She married numerous times; shared no closeness with any of her husbands; had no friends; endured a tumultuous relationship with her daughter (who only lived with her briefly during her life); and admitted in 2003 that she had never been in love nor knew what it was like to be loved. The entire event of what happened that ghastly night in 1937 was then buried along with all the evidence against Ross, and if it were not for the discovery of the story by writer/producer David Stenn, it would have remained so.

Instead, shortly before her death in 2003, Patricia finally got the chance to tell her story in David's article "It Happened One Night at MGM" (published in *Vanity Fair*) and his follow-up documentary, *Girl 27*. Her name was cleared, though her life had most certainly been ruined by the actions not only of David Ross, but the incredible forces who came together to help clear his name instead of hers. May she now rest in peace.

22

Florence Lawrence: Hollywood's First Forgotten Star

With the advent of film came the discovery of real-life movie stars, the first of whom was a young woman by the name of Florence Lawrence. She was loved by the public, respected by her peers, and had the unprecedented honour of being dubbed "The First Movie Star". However, she was also the first example of how fickle fame can be, and how quickly stars can be forgotten, no matter how much they once shone.

Born in Canada on 2 January 1886, Florence Annie Brigwood as she was then known, did not have the happiest of childhoods. As seems to be the way with many film stars, she came from a broken home, her father leaving when she was just four years old and her mother – a vaudeville actress – struggling to raise her family of one daughter and two sons. Being raised by a woman who loved the stage had an obvious effect on the young child, and it was not long before she was often seen performing with her mother; billed as "Baby Florence, The Kid Wonder".

The family moved to several locations before finally settling in New York where Florence continued her love affair with the theatre, and also developed a new interest in horse riding, athletics and film. She excelled at everything to which she put her mind, and in 1906 appeared in her first movie, Vitagraph's *The Automobile Thieves*, which saw the young woman playing one half of a couple who conduct a series of robberies. Her co-star, J. Stuart Blackton, was also the director, and together they shot a scene where they are both chased down and shot dead for their crimes.

At just eleven minutes long, it was not what one would call feature length, but it did give Florence a taste of movies that she was not in any hurry to forget, and when she was offered more roles by Vitagraph she wholeheartedly accepted. Her time at the studio led to great experience and though her real name did not appear on the credits, she was quickly nicknamed "The Vitagraph Girl" by both the studio and fans. Her on-screen anonymity did not stop Biograph Studios director D. W. Griffith from discovering Florence's talents for himself, and he very quickly gave her a starring role in his movie, *The Girl and the Outlaw* (1907), which led to dozens of other movies and a new nickname of "The Biograph Girl".

Florence's career had really taken off but she still remained largely anonymous thanks to the fact that her name continued to be kept from the credits. Her personal life was also on the up when she met actor Harry Solter while making *Romeo and Juliet* for Vitagraph. The two fell madly in love and were married on 30 August 1908, which not only gave them personal satisfaction, but also enabled them to be more of a powerful force in the movie industry.

As a result, they began working in 1909 for Carl Laemmle's film company, the Independent Moving Pictures Company of America (IMP), which renamed Florence "The Imp Girl" and set about making her into a huge star. Of course, the plans for this included a good amount of publicity and Laemmle came up with the unprecedented idea of spreading the "news" that poor Florence Lawrence had been killed in a dreadful streetcar accident.

Newspapers were full of this terrible scandal and fans were in uproar until Carl Laemmle himself stepped in and declared that the entire thing had been a dreadful mistake (aka a lie) and that his star was not only very much alive, but also about to star in a new movie, *The Broken Bath*. This got everyone talking about the woman who had seemed to rise from the dead, and moviegoers began bombarding the studio with sacks full of fan mail and greetings. Rumour has it that at one point the actress was so popular that her postman even injured his back in an attempt to deliver all of the mail to her house.

The much ballyhooed *The Broken Bath* was a big success and gave her a first taste at being hounded by fans in the flesh when she went on a publicity tour. The public surged forward and ripped buttons and whatever else they could from the star's coats and garments, but still, the experience was chiefly a positive one. Florence not only had her name on the billboards at last, but was also given a brand new nickname, that of "The First Movie Star".

In 1912 Florence had enough power to be able to form her own film company with her husband called "The Victor Studios". The deal was made under the guidance of Carl Laemmle and gave her an unheard of $500 a week as an actress, while Solter gained a great deal of success as a director. The couple made so much money, in fact, that they were able to buy their dream house, and a year later sold the company to Universal. Florence continued to act, and in 1914 made the ill-fated *The Pawns of Destiny*, which was directed by husband Harry Solter.

This film would see the beginning of Florence's health problems and the end of her marriage, when she fell and badly hurt herself in an accident on the set, and then suffered unbelievable trauma when a staged fire got out of control. Acting with Matt Moore, the two became trapped in a burning house and Moore was quickly overcome by smoke. Showing no concern for herself, and knowing that no help was forthcoming, Florence instinctively knew she had to rescue her co-star and managed to somehow carry the actor out of the building. This extreme bravery had dire consequences, however, as by the time they both got out, the actress was suffering from burns all around her face and neck, which required plastic surgery and a great deal of respite care.

Rightly or wrongly, Florence blamed Solter for the accident

and they separated for good shortly afterwards. Meanwhile, she tried desperately to overcome the trauma she had suffered, but found it impossible. Reliving the nightmare she had endured in her mind, and being in a great deal of physical pain, she was never able to recover completely and instead fell into a deep depression.

Florence's personality began to change and she started to act in a brittle, short-tempered way. Co-stars started calling her difficult and hard to work with, but in reality she was suffering immense amounts of depression and anxiety brought on by the accident, and actually collapsed after the making of her film *Elusive Isabel* as a result of her depression.

The actress rested for a time before going back to work in a movie called *The Slave*. However, her big comeback was only mildly successful and it was clear for everyone to see that her days as a huge star were very definitely over. For the rest of her life Florence was forced to take small parts in low-budget movies, and the newspapers revelled in telling their readers that "ex-favourites" such as Lawrence were now working for just $10 a day in order to keep the wolf from the door. The articles were insulting and downright patronizing, and while Florence was still eager to remain in the public eye, sadly the fans who had once flocked to her premieres and flooded her mailbox were long gone. So too were the many friends she had met along the way, all moving on with their film careers while her own had begun to crumble.

In 1927 Lawrence was interviewed for the *Appleton Post-Crescent*, during which time she sat strumming a ukulele and singing a song she had written herself entitled "Fairweather Friends". The song could have been an ode to those who had quickly departed after her career had fallen by the wayside. Telling the interviewer that most producers did not recall her name any more, she poignantly stated, "I don't hope for stardom again. I know that went glimmering in the years when illness kept me from the screen. But I do want to stay on the screen . . . The movies I helped to build into an industry are my life."

Sadly she was never to achieve the kind of roles she had once been able to win, and even her personal life was unsuccessful. On 12 May 1921 she had married salesman Charles B. Woodring and together they had set up a company, Florence Lawrence Cosmetics. Running the business from 821 North Fairfax, the couple tried to cement a decent income through Florence's former pull as a great movie star. They were somewhat successful in business, though as a personal partnership they were less so. Woodring disliked Florence looking anything but her best and insulted her, telling the actress that he had grown tired of her and, as she recalled, saying "that I did not keep myself as pretty as I used to".

Finally, the insults were explained with the revelation that he had actually met somebody else and, after admitting his new love to his wife, the couple separated on 12 December 1929. However, it was not until 11 February 1931 that the two actually divorced, and the cosmetics business was divided up between the pair. Woodring then continued to operate the business, while paying $100 a month to his former wife from the profits.

A third marriage followed, though not much is known about it, except that the gentleman was named Henry Bolton and rumour has it that he was a raging alcoholic who enjoyed beating up his wife on a regular basis. The disastrous marriage apparently lasted just five months before Florence had finally had enough and they separated in 1933.

Despite appearing in several tiny movie roles, and still being interviewed by newspapers and writing the odd article, by 1938 Florence was alone, unhappy and suffering from a rare and incurable bone disease. The Christmas period was depressing as she spent it by herself with only her thoughts for company. Finally, on 27 December, she took the decision to end her life and consequently the suffering she had endured for many years. In her small apartment at 532 Westbourne Drive, Florence sat down to write a note to her friend Robert Brindlow which read: "Dear Bob, Call Dr Wilson. I am tired.

Hope this works. Good-bye my darling. They can't cure me, so let it go at that. Lovingly, Florence." She then added a P.S. which told her friends they had all been "swell" and declaring that she was leaving all her belongings to them.

When the letter was written, the once-great star then took the decision to end her life in a most unconventional way – by poisoning herself with ant paste which she had previously bought to quell the legions of insects that had invaded her home. Not surprisingly, Florence's death was slow and painful and, before she finally succumbed, she was discovered by passer-by Marian Menzer who had heard her screaming in agony and ran into the house. The woman was shocked by the sight of Lawrence's poisoned body, writhing in front of her, but was unable to do anything to help, so she instead phoned an ambulance which rushed Lawrence to the Beverly Hills Receiving Hospital, where she passed away shortly afterwards.

Ironically, as with several other actresses that succeeded her, newspapers reported that at the exact moment she died, a phone call was going through to offer her a part in a Metro-Goldwyn-Mayer production, though this – as always – is questionable. What we do know for sure is that tragically the former star's death received scant column inches in the newspapers, and her funeral was announced with as few words as possible.

She was buried on 30 December 1938 and just days later her brother George H. Lawrence was involved in a fist fight with her friends, Norman and Robert Brindlow, outside her home, over who was to take possession of her personal belongings. That of course, the newspapers were happy to report on, and gave the story more inches than they had ever dreamt of giving her death.

Although Florence made more than 300 films in her short life, in death, as she had been in the last years of her life, Florence was then forgotten and sadly her grave at the Hollywood Forever cemetery was left without a headstone, such was the level of concern for her remembrance. Fortunately, in 1991 actor Roddy McDowall heard the tragic story of the forgotten star, and took the decision to pay for a memorial himself. The stone that was installed reads fittingly: "Florence Lawrence, The Biograph Girl. The First Movie Star." At last she can be remembered, if only in this small way.

23

Clark Gable Tackles a Burglar

Clark Gable was always known as something of a he-man in the movies. Women wanted to date him while men wanted to be just like him; able to throw a punch, beat the baddies and claim the woman all in one fell swoop. But while his tough guy attitude was mainly for the sake of his film roles, towards the end of the 1930s he was able to show the world just how hard he actually was when faced with an intruder right in the middle of his real-life home.

At the end of July 1939, Clark Gable and his new wife, actress Carole Lombard, were at their beloved ranch at 4545 Petit Street, Encino. They had been dating and secretly living together for some time but had not married earlier because of the reluctance of Gable's wife Ria to divorce her estranged husband. But now everything was above board and the two actors were happily living together, doing up the house and making a home for themselves. However, it very nearly became a murder scene on the morning of 31 July, when Gable waved goodbye to his wife on her way to the studio, before heading out of the house in order to dig ditches in the orchard.

What seemed like a normal, run-of-the-mill day was actually not quite what it seemed, as some time during the previous night, a young man by the name of Willard Broski had come to the ranch and begun peering into the couple's windows. Without anyone noticing what he was up to, Broski eyed up the impressive set of rifles and guns that Gable kept in his private gun room, and admired various other possessions as he gawped through the windows.

Seeing an opportunity to make some money, the eighteen-year-old man decided he was going to help himself to Gable's firearms, but there was too much going on at the property to enable him to get in and out without being seen. Incredibly, it was at that point that instead of just going home, the young man actually decided to stay on site until morning and made his way to the garage where he encountered the Gables' guard dog asleep inside the car. Thankfully what could have been a bloody situation actually ended peacefully, as somehow Broski was able to make friends with the dog and actually fell asleep in the car with the hound curled up beside him. This almost unbelievable turn of events led Carole Lombard and Clark Gable to later sarcastically rename the boxer, "Old Dependable".

The next morning, while Clark Gable was out in the orchard, Broski exited the garage and watched the kitchen windows. Eventually, the cook, Fanny Jacobson, came to the door in order to let out the cat, and while her back was turned for just a moment, Broski took the chance to enter the home. When Fanny turned back into the kitchen and saw the intruder, the shocked woman immediately asked what he was doing there. He told her that he was a friend of Gable and had come to visit, which was something she took to be an out-and-out lie.

Fanny tried not to let the man know she was nervous and instead asked him to leave the house which he did. She then went to find her boss but while she was gone, the butler, William Mildner, went out of the back door and not knowing that there was an intruder on the ranch, he left it ajar. Unbelievably, Broski still had not taken the hint that he wasn't welcome and seeing the door open, decided to enter after the butler had gone. He then snooped around the ground floor for a few moments, had a good look around Gable's gun room and then tiptoed upstairs to see what he could find up there.

Meanwhile, out in the orchard, a ring that Gable was wearing proved to be something of a nuisance while he was digging, so he retired from the garden to go back into the house and rid himself of it. At this point Fanny Jacobson was still looking for the actor and had not yet caught up with him by the time he had left the orchard. This meant that while walking upstairs Gable had no idea that there was an intruder in the house or that there was anything wrong at all. Feeling somewhat hot after digging the orchard all morning, he decided to take an impromptu shower and began taking off his jewellery in the mirrored dressing room. It was at that point that the actor was shocked to see a figure disappearing behind a closet door.

"I yelled for the intruder to come out," Gable later testified, and at that point, the door slowly opened and Broski entered the room. The actor was shocked to discover the intruder and even more so when he noticed one of his own guns sticking out of his jacket. Without a second thought – and living up to his he-man reputation – Gable wasted no time in showing his displeasure. "I let him have it behind the ear," he later told reporter Peter Martin of the *Saturday Evening Post*. According to court records he testified that in order to protect himself, Gable grabbed Broski, threw him to the floor and took the gun away from him. "That's about all there was to it," he added, very matter-of-factly.

Gable demanded the young man leave the bedroom and accompany him downstairs, to which the intruder apparently took great exception. Instead of coming quietly, he amazingly refused point blank to leave the bedroom, a decision which both confused and infuriated the already stressed Gable. When the man continued to resist, the actor finally lost his patience, grabbed the undeterred Broski by the collar and proceeded to drag him downstairs and into the kitchen. "It was a bouncy drag," Gable later exclaimed.

Once in the kitchen, the actor let go of Broski and noticed that the young man was little more than a kid, "He didn't look more than twenty-one," Gable told Peter Martin.

"Why are you here?" Gable demanded, to which Broski replied that he was in need of some money.

"Well, you have a peculiar way of asking for it," Gable told him. "There are better ways."

Seeing how young the intruder was, Gable decided to go easy on him and began lecturing Broski on why it was wrong to enter a person's house and snoop around. Telling him that there was no way he should be doing things like this to other people, the actor asked Broski, "Aren't you sorry?"

"No!" snapped the burglar and made a break for the door. He wasn't quick enough, however, and Gable tackled him to the ground and called the police. "If he had shown any remorse I wouldn't have called the cops," he later said.

The young man was carted off to the local station, where he was photographed by reporters behind bars and dressed smartly in a suit, shirt and tie. Later Gable was called to testify against Broski in a Van Nuys courtroom, where he was appearing on a burglary charge. Accompanying the actor was Carole Lombard, their cook Fanny and butler William, who all sat in the spectators' gallery and watched as Gable calmly told everyone in the court what had happened.

Eventually, the judge bound Broski over on a burglary charge and told him to come back to court on 19 August to be arraigned. Gable never heard from the young man again, but did surprisingly sympathize with him. "I am sorry it happened," he told reporters outside the courtroom. "He's only a boy who got off on the wrong foot. I hope he gets off without too much trouble."

24

The Suicide Apartments

The Shelton Apartments once stood at 1735 North Wilcox Avenue in Hollywood and, in the golden age of Hollywood, they were considered extremely luxurious. A number of actors and actresses lived there, but unfortunately it was because of two suicides that the building became notorious and was unofficially rechristened "The Suicide Apartments" by macabre members of the public.

The first suicide came in 1941, when dancer Jenny Dolly decided to end her life in a rented suite at the hotel . . .

Born on 25 October 1892 in Hungary, identical twins Roszika (Rosie) and Janszieka (Jenny) Deutsch immigrated to the United States in 1905, where they both developed an interest in vaudeville and dance. Perfecting their elaborate dance act before mirrors, they christened themselves "The Dolly Sisters" and joined the circuit as teenagers, debuting at the Union Square Theater in New York. So successful were they that the pair went on to appear in vaudeville circuits all over the United States before travelling to Paris and London, and finally signing with the Ziegfeld Follies in 1911.

The sisters became famous not only for their theatre and cinema performances, but also for their beauty. Dubbed "The Most Beautiful Girls in the World", the Dolly Sisters took good care of themselves and were always seen dressed to impress; they were sophisticated, glamorous and worldly-wise. They also had a love for gambling, winning huge amounts of money in Cannes and Deauville and gaining a reputation for themselves as being extremely lucky in the casino. Indeed, Rosie later bragged that she had made $400,000 playing roulette one evening, while Jenny went one better by being rumoured to have broken the bank at Monte Carlo.

To go with their love of glamour and clothes came an obsession with other material possessions, too, and Jenny in particular was a keen collector of fancy jewellery, receiving much of it from admirers and would-be boyfriends. One day she spotted a huge diamond ring that was worth a staggering quarter of a million dollars. She did not have to think long before she had acquired it for her collection, though she later regretted bragging about its value to the French media when she was forced to pay a fine of $758,000 for evading the luxury tax payable on such an item.

In spite of having all they needed in terms of possessions and social life, it was not all glitz and glamour for the sisters. Jenny was unhappily married three times and then in 1933 was involved in an automobile accident in Bordeaux, which left the devastated actress with a disfigured face. Not only that but she also suffered a punctured lung, fractured ribs and damage to her limbs, which sadly made it impossible for her to dance. In just one moment her entire life had changed; not only had she lost her stunning good looks but her career was tragically over. Jenny was inconsolable.

In unbelievable pain, the woman suffered for the next eight years, enduring plastic surgery to rebuild her once-beautiful face and having to sell her extensive jewellery collection to pay for treatment. By 1941, Jenny knew she could not go on that way, and her health started to become of great concern to just about everybody in her life.

Separated from her third husband, attorney Bernard Vinisky, Jenny moved into the Shelton Apartments with her two adopted daughters, Clarika and Manzie. There she tried to make things work, but everybody could see just how quickly the former dancer was sinking, particularly on one occasion just days before her death, when Jenny broke down in such a way that her panicked daughter called for a doctor. He came to the apartment, and after examining his patient, turned to the daughter to break the news that Jenny was most certainly on her way to a nervous breakdown. He prescribed her a sedative to help her cope and went on his way.

On 1 May 1941, Jenny had a plan to end her days of pain and distress. She waited for her daughters to go out for the day and then telephoned her brother-in-law (Rosie's husband), and then her aunt, Frieda Bakos, in order to complain that she felt unwell. On numerous occasions during the years, Jenny had told her aunt that doctors had not done her any favours by saving her life after the car crash. It would seem that on 1 May 1941, Jenny was ready to take back control and end it herself.

After speaking with her niece, Frieda Bakos was so concerned about Jenny's state of mind that she decided to rush round to the apartment with her daughter, Stephanie. Unfortunately, before they arrived, Jenny had prepared a sash strong enough to support her weight, tied it around her neck and proceeded to hang herself from an iron curtain rod next to her apartment window.

When Frieda and Stephanie finally arrived at the building, they rushed up to her floor and were shocked to hear Jenny's dog crying inside. Knocking loudly at the door and trying to open it themselves, the pair tried desperately to get Jenny's attention but it was no good, so they rushed to fetch the manager who was able to open the door with his pass key. The three people stumbled into the apartment to be met by a distressing sight: there hung the body of the once beautiful Jenny Dolly. She had been dead for just a few minutes and did not leave a note.

Jenny's funeral was held in the Wee Kirk o' the Heather in Forest Lawn Memorial Park. Her estranged husband was too ill to travel from Chicago where he was living, though seventy-five other friends and family gathered round to say their last goodbyes. Her sister Rosie wore a heavy veil and almost collapsed in the chapel, while friends such as theatre luminaries Fanny Brice and Gracie Allen wept as Jenny's coffin was carried into the chapel, covered in pink roses and a sprinkling of lilies of the valley.

Jenny Dolly's death and funeral had a great deal of press coverage around the world, but the next death at the Shelton received little attention at the time, though it has most certainly gone down in history as yet another victim of "The Suicide Apartments".

Actress Clara Blandick was an established actress of theatre and films, winning roles such as Aunt Polly in the 1930 film *Tom Sawyer*. However, it was her role as Auntie Em in 1939's *The Wizard of Oz* for which she is best remembered, though her part was actually very small in comparison to most of her work and only took her a week to film.

After the success of *The Wizard of Oz*, Blandick played various small roles, but by 1950 the work had dried up and she decided to retire. However, the former actress was unable to enjoy her retirement because of ill-health; she suffered from acute arthritis which left her in a great deal of pain for most of the latter part of her life. Still, Clara struggled on until finally things came to a head when her doctor gave her the tragic news that she was going to lose her eyesight. She was devastated and determined that she would not live to endure this; she could struggle to live with pain, but she was not prepared to suffer blindness.

In early April 1962, Clara disposed of all her medication and told her friend James Busch that she had done so because she did not want anyone getting their hands on it, "if anything should happen to me". He did not think too much about the comment at the time, but in hindsight it became clear that the reason Clara worried about such a thing was because she had been planning her death down the very last detail in the weeks and months leading up to it.

On Sunday, 15 April 1962, it was time for her plans to be put into action. It would seem that the last few hours of the eighty-one year-old Clara Blandick's life were relatively calm: she pottered around her Shelton apartment, styled her hair carefully and dressed herself in a royal-blue dressing gown. She then found a plastic bag, and sitting it beside her she picked up a pen and proceeded to write a short note. "I am now about to make the great adventure," she wrote, explaining that she could not endure the agonizing pain any longer. "It is all over my body," she said. "Neither can I face the impending blindness. I pray the Lord my soul to take. Amen."

Once the note was written entirely to her liking, Clara then placed it on the table next to the sofa and picked up the plastic bag. Lying down on the couch, she then covered herself in a gold blanket before proceeding to pull the bag down over her head and wait for her inevitable death to arrive.

Nobody knows just how long it took for Clara Blandick to pass away, but the next day her landlady Helen Mason was shocked to find her lifeless body, still covered in the gold blanket. Mason called the police who removed the body and declared the death a suicide.

The tragedy of Miss Blandick's passing was reported in several articles around the country, with the suicide method making the most comment. Sadly, it would seem that while Clara was once renowned for her performance in *The Wizard of Oz*, she is now only remembered for the tragic and lonely way she chose to end her life.

25

The Tragic Love of Peggy Shannon and Albert Roberts

An unexplained and early death always causes headlines in Hollywood, but when the passing is so great that it inspires a loved one to commit suicide, it goes from tragic to absolute catastrophe.

Peggy Shannon was born in 1907 as Winona Sammon, and was raised in Pine Bluff, Arkansas. She developed a love for the entertainment business from an early age and while visiting an aunt in New York during 1923, she met Broadway producer Florenz Ziegfeld, who took an immediate liking to the youngster and hired her as a chorus girl. From there she went on to dance professionally with the Ziegfeld Follies and worked extremely hard in various productions. She expressed an interest in serious roles and was ambitious enough to ensure that her efforts paid off, eventually playing not only in dance roles, but dramatic ones too. In 1925 her confidence was boosted when she was voted "Miss Coney Island", which not only gave her a huge amount of joy, but also exposed her to an audience who would not have gone to see her in the theatre.

In 1926 Peggy married an actor called Alan Davis, and then continued to work on Broadway in a variety of shows including "What Anne Brought Home". However, with her star rising rapidly, it was just a matter of time before she was discovered by B. P. Schulberg, production head at Paramount Studios, and whisked off for a glamorous life in Hollywood.

For most actresses uprooted from New York and brought to

California, success came slowly and steadily, but for Shannon, as soon as she arrived in the great state she was thrown into the deep end when the studio announced that the red-headed actress would be the new Clara Bow. Just two days later Peggy was employed on the set of *The Secret Call* after Bow suffered a nervous breakdown and was unable to work. Peggy could be forgiven for being completely terrified at the new situation in which she found herself, but instead she threw herself into the work, sometimes filming from early in the morning until late into the night. The experience was exhausting but gratifying and Peggy quickly became a Hollywood star; she was rewarded in her hometown of Pine Bluff by receiving a "Peggy Shannon Day" in July 1931.

Unfortunately, it was not long before Peggy became known as difficult on set, and rumours flew that she also had a drinking problem. This could be hidden in Hollywood, but not so much in New York, when she returned for the theatre production of *The Light Behind the Shadow* and was quickly replaced because of her behaviour. The official line was that Peggy was dropped due to her being under the weather with a tooth infection, though in reality it was most probably her struggle with alcohol that was the problem.

What many people did not know was that while Peggy was dismissed as a difficult, alcoholic actress, she was actually suffering badly at home at the hands of her actor husband Alan Davis. When she had first travelled to Hollywood, Davis had stayed in New York to concentrate on his theatre work. However, after a bout of illness, the actor travelled to Los Angeles where Shannon tried desperately to get him into the movies. It was a disastrous move and while the actress quite happily knocked on many doors for her husband, nobody wanted to hire him. "He tried to get in," she later said. "I tried to get him in, but no – he was Peggy Shannon's husband and nobody would give him a test."

The outcome of this was that Davis ended up going into a job that had nothing to do with the acting business, and he hated it with a passion. He became deeply unhappy and while he did occasionally receive the odd acting part, the marriage was under immense strain and had turned quite violent. Whether or not Peggy's drinking was as a result of the unhappy marriage is up for debate, but one thing is for sure: it became harder and harder for her to hide the problem and her film roles began to dry up.

Then on 13 July 1938 Peggy was driving with her sister, Carole Beckman, when disaster struck. The car in which they were travelling was hit head-on with that of one being driven by a gentleman called Robert Thoren. The actress received a severe cut to the nose, along with others on her legs, while her sister suffered injuries to her chin. Details of the accident are sketchy to say the least, and it is not known if Shannon was drinking at the time of the accident, though it is safe to say that at that point, her reliance on alcohol was becoming a bigger problem than previously thought.

Meanwhile, things at home continued to go from bad to worse and Peggy was growing distinctly tired of financially supporting her now unemployed husband. Added to that, he had also begun to humiliate the actress in public, which distressed the woman and only succeeded in making her unhappier than ever before. On one such occasion the couple were visiting the home of actress Wynne Gibson, when Davis and Shannon got into a slight argument. Instead of letting the matter go until they went home, Davis suddenly lost his temper completely; struck out and hit his shocked wife, hurting her physically and embarrassing her in the process.

Peggy's health started to suffer and she lost twenty-four pounds in less than a year – not because she was dieting but because of the stress caused by the marriage and her drinking problem. Things became so bad that finally in July 1940 Peggy Shannon decided to call time on her marriage to Alan Davis. "He was just lazy," she told the court. "He played all the time." She also told Judge Edward R. Brand about the incident at Wynne Gibson's house, and Gibson herself stood up to defend her friend, telling the judge that the actor had struck her friend "over something very inconsequential".

Shannon was relieved when the divorce was granted and she was finally able to walk away from her abusive marriage. She quickly fell in love with studio cameraman and actor Albert Roberts, and the two tied the knot in Mexico in October 1940, just three months after the divorce from Davis. Of course, the fact that she had married again so soon caused much debate and whispering, though Peggy was unprepared to comment on whether or not she had actually started dating the cameraman before her last marriage was over.

For a time it looked as though the new couple would live happily ever after, though this was quickly thwarted when Davis came back into their lives in an unexpected manner. One evening Peggy was spending the evening in a cocktail bar when she was spotted by her ex-husband. He came over to chat and before long they were talking about their lives, and the fourteen years they had been together. They had been through a lot and there had been good times in spite of the way they had parted, and it was not long before Davis was beginning to wish they had never gone their separate ways in the first place.

It would seem that Shannon may have returned home with Davis that evening, as the chauffeur's wife later told police that she had met the woman at that time. But if she did visit with the actor, she most certainly was gone by morning when Davis told the driver's wife that he was leaving to pick up some groceries. This was a lie and instead he asked the chauffeur to drive from his home at 747 North Wilcox Avenue to Shannon's home at 4318 Irvine Street. Details of the reason he went to the house are cloudy to say the least, but what we do know is that, once there, he wandered up to the front door, knocked furiously, and when the door was opened, was met by current husband Albert Roberts. The cameraman was surprised to say the least at seeing his wife's former love standing on his doorstep.

Roberts was shocked further when Davis began shouting four-letter expletives at him, and the tirade became so heated that the new husband punched the actor in the face, sending him flying flat on to his back as he did so. At this point chauffeur Ramón Larios saw what was going on and came running up the path to rescue his boss, while Albert Roberts ran to his neighbour's house in order to phone the police.

Struggling up from the floor, Davis and Larios then took the unprecedented decision to go into Peggy's home and start rummaging around. What they were looking for is not known, but by the time police arrived, they found Alan Davis talking on the telephone while his chauffeur was found in the garage in possession of two wristwatches, one of which had the initials PSD – Peggy Shannon Davis – engraved on it.

Both Larios and Davis were arrested immediately and hauled off to the nearest police station for questioning. Peggy Shannon was taken down later in order to give her version of events, though she could not help them much as it would seem that she was not at the house during the incident. Both Alan Davis and Raymond Larios were later released without charge, and what prompted the trip to the house and the events that followed have never been completely cleared up, though the story made great fodder for the newspapers at the time.

Less than two months later, Albert Roberts bid his wife goodbye and went off on a fishing trip with his friend, Elmer Fryer. Once on her own, Peggy planned to spend some time sunbathing, and dressed in a sun suit for the occasion. Barefoot, she sat at her kitchen table, smoked a cigarette and made her plans, though tragically she was never able to carry them out as she quite suddenly and without warning passed away. Her body slumped down over the table and the recently lit cigarette burned slowly but surely down to her now lifeless hands.

When Roberts returned from his trip, he was devastated to find his wife's body at the table, along with several empty glasses and a bottle of soft-drink. Understandably, Albert was beyond shocked and he did not understand what could possibly have happened to his wife to cause her to expire so suddenly. The police were called and the body was taken away for a post-mortem examination, though at first no immediate cause could be found and the coroner immediately ordered laboratory tests to determine exactly what had happened.

Peggy's funeral took place shortly afterwards at the Hollywood Forever Cemetery, where a tombstone was later installed which read: "That Red Headed Girl, Peggy Shannon." But this sadly was not the end of the tragedy, as on 30 May 1941 – just days before the results of the chemical analysis were due back – Albert Roberts decided he could live without his wife no longer, and that he had no option but to join her in death.

The signs of despair had been there ever since he had said goodbye to his wife, and he spent much of his last few weeks telling friends and family just how much he hated being without Peggy, and how determined he was to end his life. Members of his circle told him not to be so silly, that life goes on and he would find peace over time, but Roberts found their misguided comments to be insulting. He determined that no one understood what he was going through; he was confused about the death and began to feel extreme pangs of guilt that he had not been there when Shannon had passed away. The guilt also turned to paranoia and he began to think that the police believed he was responsible; he even questioned Detective William Burris about it.

"You've got something on your mind. You don't suspect me of Peggy's death do you?" the concerned man asked.

"Of course not," the detective told him, before explaining that he was merely waiting for the lab results before making a decision on what had really happened to Peggy.

Roberts listened intently and then gave his worrying reply. "Well, if you have anything on your mind, get it off now, because you won't see me again," he said. The concerned officer asked the man to explain what exactly he meant, before receiving a worrying reply.

"I'm going to commit suicide," Albert told him, which worried the officer so much that he took the time to tell him that perhaps he had just had too much to drink.

"Just don't do anything stupid," Burris begged him, before asking his officers to explain to Roberts that there was absolutely no evidence whatsoever to connect the grieving man to the death. But for Albert Roberts this was all just white noise. He had lost his wife in the very home where they had hoped to build their future, and in the days ahead he repeated his threats of suicide to various members of his friends, family and anyone else willing to listen.

In spite of the declarations, everyone seemed to ignore the signs, sweeping them under the carpet and telling Albert that everything would one day be okay. Perhaps they chose to disbelieve the threats because the alternative was too much to bear, or maybe the cameraman was prone to dramatics and no one believed he was really capable of ending his own life.

But capable he was, and just three weeks after Peggy Shannon's death, he took his dog to visit his wife's grave one last time. Once there he discovered that none of her friends or family had delivered any flowers at all, which made the widower absolutely furious. "They have never been near the grave," he wrote in a note to his sister. "Them dirty leeches, they wouldn't take her a pansy but they would take her clothes and say they loved her more than life."

Peggy had supported her friends and family for many years, and Roberts was only too aware of that. "You know how Peg supported them," he wrote. "Any denial, just ask them to prove how they lived all these years." Seeing no flowers on Peggy Shannon's grave was the final straw for the grieving man, and quite despondent he arrived back home at the house he had shared with his beloved wife, and took out his gun. He then sat down on the same chair, at the same table as the one where he had found Peggy, and wrote a sad and devastating note to no one in particular: "To Whom It May Concern, I am very much in love with my wife, Peggy Shannon. In this spot she passed away. So in reverence to her you will find me in the same spot . . ." He then went on to say that he believed no one would understand his actions, but that was as it should be. "Why don't you all try a little harder – it wouldn't hurt," he wrote. "Adios amigos, Al Roberts."

He then wrote two notes to his sister, Phoebe Genereux, one berating Peggy's friends and family for their lack of respect, and urging her not to allow them to take any of his wife's belongings, and the other begging her to take his dog and ship him to "Johnny". "If you don't," he wrote, "I will never forgive you." He then said that he knew the dog would get on well with his new owner as Peggy had told him so on more than one occasion. "So please, take him 'our child' and send him on. He certainly is entitled to that." He then left instructions to be buried in his grey suit, and signed the letter simply, "Al".

How long he sat at that table we will never know, but it was certainly a good few hours, because just as dawn was breaking, he picked up the telephone and rang his sister, Phoebe Genereux.

"I'm going to shoot myself," Roberts told her, which sent his sister into a blind panic.

"Al don't do it!" she screamed, but it was too late. Just seconds later a gunshot echoed down the telephone line, then his dog began to bark and Genereux could no longer hear her brother. Albert Roberts was gone.

By the time the police arrived at the home they were shocked to find him slumped in exactly the same manner as Peggy had been found just weeks before. His dog "Spec" lay next to the table, whimpering for his master to wake up, but it was too late. The next day, the coroner announced that "examination so far shows no traces of poison or any bruises or marks". Ironically just two days after that, it was announced that the death of Peggy Shannon had been caused by a combination of factors: low vitality, a run-down body and a heart attack. The passing had been entirely natural and any concern that the grieving Roberts had about his part in her death was entirely misguided.

A month after Peggy Shannon's death, Louis Sobol wrote in

the *San Antonio Light* that she must have been hit by the "Follies jinx" which had apparently blighted various members of the troupe for a number of years. The article then went on to list a huge variety of dancers who had died due to suicide or in some kind of mysterious way, and detailed others who had fallen on hard times. It cannot be argued that Peggy Shannon was most certainly the latest in a long line of Follies whose lives had ended badly, but had she been jinxed, or was it all just a tragic coincidence?

Her family perhaps did not believe in a jinx but they certainly thought there was some kind of foul play involved and this was hammered home when the shock news of Albert Roberts's death was announced. Two members of the same family dead in a matter of weeks – it all seemed too much of a coincidence – so to get to the heart of the "mystery" they hired a private detective to solve the case. Nothing was ever found, of course, and the deaths of Peggy Shannon and Albert Roberts were put down to tragedy and heartbreak, rather than anything untoward. Peggy had lived in a haze of drama, alcohol and pain for a number of years and perhaps the biggest tragedy of all is that at a time when she had finally discovered true love, it was sadly all taken away in the blink of an eye.

26

Mrs Gable: The Carole Lombard Tragedy

In 1942 Carole Lombard was one of the biggest stars in Hollywood, famed for her legendary parties and whacky sense of humour; she was also Mrs Clark Gable, making her part of one of the most beloved couples in entertainment history. However, the fairy tale would come to an end one dark January evening, when Carole Lombard's light was extinguished from the screen and the world forever.

Born Jane Alice Peters on 6 October 1908, she was raised for her first six years with her brothers, Stuart and Fred, in Fort Wayne, Indiana. However, the divorce of her parents prompted her mother, Elizabeth (Beth), to take her children away from their hometown and to move west in order to settle in Los Angeles, California.

Jane was a popular student who enjoyed acting and sports. She was an outdoor kind of girl who revelled in tomboy activities and adventures. However, acting was not far away from her mind and she made her screen debut aged twelve, when she worked in the 1921 movie, *A Perfect Crime*. She then went on to work for a time under both the names Jane Peters and Carol Lombard, before finally opting for the more permanent Carole Lombard.

With her star quickly rising, Carole had the world at her feet, but it all threatened to come crashing down in 1926 when she was involved in a terrible car accident that saw the actress's cheek being sliced to such a degree that she required plastic surgery. As if this wasn't bad enough, it was agreed that in order to avoid a huge scar, the procedure should be carried out without anaesthetic. Carole agreed and the operation was a success, though the scar can still be seen in her later movies. It did not, however, detract from her amazing beauty, and it is safe to say that during the 1930s Carole Lombard was one of the most – if not *the* most – beautiful actresses working in Hollywood at that time.

After taking some time off following the car accident, the young Carole was finally able to resume her career and her love life, dating several actors and marrying actor William Powell in 1931. Although the pair were later to divorce, they stayed the best of friends and even worked together later in their careers. Powell also went on to have a relationship with Jean Harlow, whom Carole knew well and she totally approved of the romance. It seemed that while the two had been unable to sustain their own relationship, they made very good friends and were very happy to remain this way until the end.

After the failure of her marriage, Carole concentrated on her career and her star continued to rise. She had made a smooth transition from silent movies to talkies, and in the early 1930s the upcoming star was showcased in a variety of movies including 1932's *No Man of Her Own* (where she met Clark Gable), *Bolero* (1934) and *We're Not Dressing* (1934). Later films included *My Man Godfrey* (1936), in which she played opposite her ex-husband William Powell, and *Hands Across the Table*, which teamed her up with tragic star Marie Prevost.

Romance was also back on the cards when Carole met "crooner" Russ Columbo. Russ was a very popular musical artist who had hundreds of women swooning whenever he opened his mouth to sing. However, it was Carole who won his heart and it was rumoured that the two would marry, though both played down the relationship, assuring the press that they were "just good friends". However, the rumours continued and everyone expected to hear wedding bells that would lead the beautiful Lombard to the altar for the second time.

Tragically, the romance came to a shocking end when Russ Columbo was shot dead in an accidental shooting in 1934, the details of which are covered in a separate chapter within this book. Carole Lombard was absolutely devastated with the loss of her partner and some say that she never fully got over his death.

Moving on from the loss of Russ Columbo, Carole slowly but surely rebuilt her life and, after becoming reacquainted with Clark Gable at a party, the two became inseparable. Just as she had done as a child, Carole loved to be in the great outdoors, and it was that, combined with a magnificent sense of humour, that made her all the more attractive to Mr Gable. He was known as something of a "he-man" and despite being married to the much older Ria Langham, Gable began an affair with Lombard which quickly became public knowledge and the talk of the town.

By the time Ria agreed to a divorce, Gable was involved in the making of the 1939 movie, *Gone with the Wind*. Taking a break from the production, he quietly married Carole on 29 March 1939 and the two settled down to life in their Encino ranch. The couple were quickly dubbed the happiest couple in Hollywood and became famous for snubbing glamorous award shows in favour of road trips, fishing, shooting and camping, capturing some of these activities on their home movie camera. In fact, they loved their trips so much that at one point they were even reported missing in the countryside, feared dead. The couple eventually appeared again, however, laughingly telling reporters that the only reason they had gone missing was because their car had broken down; nothing more, nothing less.

But while their joint public persona was one of constant happiness, there were various problems within the marriage, such as the couple's fruitless desire to have children and the rumours of Gable's wandering eye. He had long since been legendary for his love of female co-stars, and while it cannot be confirmed either way, there have been rumours over the years that despite his love for Carole, he never did give up his dalliances with other actresses. Added to that, there was the knowledge that before Gable had swept her off her feet, the real love of Carole's life had been Russ Columbo. Clark was well aware of this fact and became so paranoid that he is said to have banned all mention of him from his house during the course of the couple's marriage.

In January 1942, just after the United States had entered World War II, Carole took on the role of Defence Bond saleswoman, and travelled to Indiana with her mother Beth and Gable's press agent, Otto Winkler. The tour was an almighty success with Carole raising over $2 million in just one evening. However, while she was happy to take part in the fundraising, the actress was also concerned at leaving her husband alone at home. He was busy making *Somewhere I'll Find You* with Lana Turner, and Lombard was afraid that his wandering eye would meander in the actress's direction. With this in mind, she suggested to her mother that they should fly home instead of taking the train as originally planned.

Lombard's mother, a keen numerologist, was completely against altering their plans and was overheard talking to her daughter at Indianapolis Municipal Airport.

"Carole, don't take that plane," she said, though her daughter was determined to have her way. Eventually the actress decided to settle the decision on the toss of a coin, and after winning the bet she was happy to be flying back to California. The party – including Carole's unhappy mother – settled into a flight which was to take them from Indiana to Las Vegas, and then finally back to Los Angeles. Tragically, however, the plane was never to make it home.

After stopping to refuel in Las Vegas, the TWA aircraft took off for the last part of the trip, but shortly after the plane had left the runway, it plummeted head first into Mount Potosi, killing everyone on board, including Carole Lombard, her mother, and twenty-two passengers and crew. The pilot, Wayne Williams, had last reported from the aircraft at 7.07 p.m., but nothing was then heard until local residents reported to police that they had heard an almighty explosion and had spotted fire in the mountains. These residents are reported to have included silent-screen star Clara Bow, who is said to have seen a huge light in the sky as the plane burned, some ninety miles away from her ranch.

Back in Los Angeles, a devastated Clark Gable was informed of the crash, just as he was waiting for his wife to return home. He immediately chartered a plane to Las Vegas in order to help with the search, though once there, was ultimately stopped from going up the mountain by friends, who were concerned that he would find Carole's body in a distressing state.

As the search crew gathered at the mountain base, it soon became apparent that this was not going to be an easy rescue. The terrain was so tough that the search was considered impossible until the following morning when daylight came and the crew could finally climb the mountain. Even then, the journey was intense and very few of the party made it up to the wreckage at first and reported that even when they did arrive, there was virtually nothing left of the aircraft at all. Debris had been thrown for 500 yards on every side, and had fallen 45 feet to the slopes below, with clothes and personal items settling on the ground, trees and bushes. To make things worse, the mountain was covered in snow – some of it waist deep – hampering the search.

Searchers reported that six bodies had been thrown from the wreckage while the others were either burned or mutilated inside the cabin. The only thing that made the knowledge of their deaths bearable was the fact that it would have been extremely unlikely that they knew anything about the crash at all. The plane had gone head first into the mountain in the dark and while the pilot probably knew at the last moment what was coming, everyone else would have likely been oblivious.

Finally, after much time and effort in the rugged mountain area, the body of Carole Lombard was found and brought back down to the land below. Gable was waiting at his hotel for news, which was broken to him by Don McElwaine from MGM, who had received a heart-breaking note from the searchers.

"Is it bad news?" asked the actor.

"I'm afraid it looks hopeless," replied McElwaine, after which Gable was heard tearfully whispering, "Oh God," and collapsed his head into his hands.

Still, as there had been only a tentative identification of the actress from a piece of uncharred hair and some scorched documents found near to her body, there was still some hope in Gable's mind that Carole would be found alive. However, formal identification eventually came when dental records were flown from Hollywood to Las Vegas, and Gable was absolutely devastated.

Several days later, after the formal identification of Carole's mother, the two bodies were taken home by Clark Gable and given a private and very simple funeral at Forest Lawn Memorial Park. This had been Carole's wish after seeing the huge spectacle of Jean Harlow's funeral just a few years before. Everyone in Hollywood was devastated at the loss of the blonde star, and even President Roosevelt sent a telegram to Clark Gable, which was released to the worldwide press:

> Mrs Roosevelt and I are deeply distressed . . . She brought great joy to all who knew her and to the millions who knew her only as a great artist. She gave unselfishly of her time and talent to serve her government in peace and war. She loved her country. She is and always will be a star, one we shall never forget nor cease to be grateful to.

Clark Gable never really recovered from the death of his wife, and very rarely spoke of her in the years after. The marriage may not have been the absolutely perfect one they had wanted it to be, but he had loved her dearly and had many regrets about her death. Gable sank into a deep depression for a long time after her death, and although he was by this time in his forties, he decide to sign up to the war effort, telling friends that he did not care if he ever came home again. He did eventually return, of course, though he was never quite the same again.

Although married twice more, when he died towards the end of 1960, Clark Gable was buried next to his beloved Carole, the woman he never forgot or stopped loving. As for the wreckage, much of it still sits in the mountains above Las Vegas, though ambitious explorers have taken most of the smaller items as morbid souvenirs. But the bigger parts of the aircraft – the engines and landing craft – are still there, where they will probably lie forever, a tragically sad reminder of what occurred one dark, winter's night over seventy years ago.

27

Miss Hot Tamale, Lupe Vélez

There is a memorable scene during an episode of the hit TV show *Frasier* where Frasier's producer, Roz Doyle, tells the story of 1930s actress, Lupe Vélez. The way Roz tells it, Lupe is a woman whose career is over and so decides to take an overdose, in order that she will be remembered forever. She dresses up, lights candles and surrounds herself with flowers. She then lies down on the bed and takes the pills; but unfortunately for Lupe she has a bad reaction to the tablets and her recently eaten dinner, and ends up passing away in the toilet instead.

The portrait presented by Roz raises a mighty laugh from the *Frasier* audience, but in reality the story of Lupe Vélez is far more tragic than anyone could ever imagine.

Born in San Luis, Mexico, in 1908, María Guadalupe Villalobos Vélez was an outspoken young lady who attended convent school in Texas, where she learned to speak English. She loved to perform, took dance lessons and appeared on stage in her native country before deciding to move permanently to the United States, where she toured with vaudeville shows and appeared in the New York theatre.

One of her earliest appearances was in a production called the *Fanchon and Marco Show*, where the organizers discovered that although she could be shy, Lupe was also vigorous. Fanchon later laughed that during her first appearance on stage, she was so under-clothed that the entire audience almost fell off their seats when she first walked out on to the stage. For future performances he had to persuade her to put on more clothes so as not to shock the audience again.

While Lupe enjoyed her time on stage, eventually, however, Hollywood beckoned and the actress arrived in California in order to find fame and fortune. She was relatively successful, appearing in the Laurel and Hardy picture *Sailors Beware!* and *The Gaucho* with Douglas Fairbanks. She was also an amazingly beautiful woman – mysterious and sultry – and because she played many "exotic" characters, the press were quick to nickname her "Miss Hot Tamale". But while this moniker suited the beautiful woman, Lupe herself preferred to be called "Whoopee Lupe" and did not have to try hard to live up to the tag of being wild and fiery.

At the height of her career, Lupe began a love affair with film star Gary Cooper, and as they made an extremely handsome and entertaining couple, the press lapped up every personal appearance and comment they could get. In return the couple enjoyed winding up reporters who became obsessed with wondering whether or not they would ever get married. One day they would say that yes, there was a big possibility they would tie the knot, and on the next they would deny all knowledge of even going out with each other.

"Why would we marry an way?" Lupe teased one reporter. "We have much more important things to do." Then to another she said, "Gary is a very nice boy. He likes me I hope and I like him. People marry us off. They engage us. Well that is all right. They enjoy themselves talking about us. Let them talk."

In reality the marriage plans were only ever just talk, and rumours surfaced that Gary was romantically linked to various other stars including actress June Collyer. When asked about the rumours, Lupe giggled. "Gary meets lots of girls," she told *Los Angeles Times* reporter Muriel Babcock. "He talks to them. I meet people too . . . Why should it mean anything if Gary talks to a girl?"

By 1931 the romance had fizzled out, but Lupe brushed off

the break-up by quipping, "I got tired of Gary, but he is one grand person just the same." She later talked to columnist Alma Whitaker about the relationship, stating, "I will never marry. When Gary and I were in love it was terrible." When pressed further she admitted that he had taken her away from her mother too much and she had not enjoyed that at all. "Lupe must do as she likes. I don't believe in marriage," she quickly added.

But marry she did – to Tarzan star Johnny Weissmuller. The two settled down to what Lupe hoped would be marital bliss, but it was not to be. With two huge personalities, the pair fought frequently, splitting up so many times that fans could not keep up. There were at least two attempts at divorce, on 11 July 1934 and 2 January 1935, but each time the actress would be convinced by Johnny to give things another try and the proceedings would be called off.

Ultimately, however, it just did not work out between the two and in July 1938, after a five-month trial separation, they split for good. Lupe released a statement that said that, in the last few years, her husband had been morose, had not spoken to her and had a very jealous nature. The media was sceptical, however, with many believing they would reconcile once more, since it was beginning to seem as though that's just what they did for kicks.

"I hope we might be able to make up," Lupe was quoted at the time, but eventually it all became official when the actress entered the divorce court on 15 August 1938. Dressed in a demure brown gabardine coat with white skirt and brown hat, Lupe accused her estranged husband of wanting to kill her pet Chihuahua from the moment he set eyes on it. He also called her names, she said, left her alone while out together, and flew into rages and stormed out of their home. "It's a wonder I wasn't killed!" she shouted in court, as the reporters noted down each and every juicy detail.

Lupe's distress was lost on Judge Burnell, who frequently made jokes throughout the entire process. "He probably thought you didn't need it," he said, when Lupe told him of Weissmuller's refusal to let her go to the beauty parlour. "It must have been hard for you to keep a complete set of china in the house," he replied when told that the Tarzan star liked to throw plates. "Why didn't you buy paper plates?" he quipped.

"I don't know why," giggled Lupe.

On a more serious note, the actress reported that her husband had threatened to break her neck if he ever discovered she had gone out without him. Then he started staying out all night himself and proceeded to bring a string of women back to the marital home. That was the last straw. "I didn't want a divorce," she said. "I tried so hard, but when he brought other women into my house I couldn't stand it. I tried to protect his name."

Finally, it was all over and after Lupe had declared it "the only true performance in my life", she was granted a divorce. Afterwards she gave an interview to the *Los Angeles Times*, during which she said she hated admitting to the court such "nasty things", but added, "I guess the law requires it." Still, the actress made it clear that she had a definite place for Johnny in her heart: "He likes me. I like him. But we just couldn't click in marriage. I am so sorry."

After the failure of her relationship, Lupe said she had sworn herself off men for good. "There isn't a man on earth I like," she told columnist Read Kendall on the set of her new film. She threw herself into her career instead; and for a time things seemed settled but just over a year later, in December 1939, Lupe hit the headlines again when she was tricked out of $2,500 by an opportunist gypsy who told her she had been cursed . . .

The "friendship" had begun while Lupe was not working and was looking for something to occupy her time at her home, 732 North Rodeo Drive. While chatting to her maid Katherine Taylor one day, the conversation got round to the topic of psychics, and Taylor told her employer that a gypsy by the name of Miss X had done a reading for her not long ago. Lupe was intrigued and invited the fortune-teller into her home for some fun. "I took an interest in this woman because I'm not working right now and she gave me something to do, like going to a show," she later said. "So I fooled around with her."

Predictably, the "fooling around" led to Lupe being told by Miss X that she was cursed and that it could only be lifted by praying over $10,000. Of course, the person who had to do the praying was Miss X herself, though when Lupe scoffed at the amount of money concerned, the gypsy told her she would settle for $2,500. Alarm bells should have sounded for Lupe by this point, but amazingly she still thought the woman was decent and honest. The actress gave Miss X the money and followed her instructions, lying down on the bed to "concentrate" on having the curse lifted.

As one might have imagined, the only thing lifted that day was the money, which Miss X liberated from the home while the actress was lying down, eyes closed, on the bed. "The money is nothing," Lupe later told police. "But just wait until I get my hands on that woman." She later went down to the Beverly Hills jail in the hope of identifying the thief, but came away unsatisfied. "All I want is to catch that gypsy," she declared, after scrutinizing twelve innocent women who had been rounded up specifically for her observation.

Despite losing her money, Lupe was able to put the disappointment behind her after the success of a series called *Mexican Spitfire*, which showed the actress off as a fine comedienne and rejuvenated her career. Everything was looking up but an unexpected turn was soon to come.

Having famously sworn herself off men just a short time before, in 1944 Lupe decided that she was ready to try again when she met and fell in love with Harald Ramond, an actor almost ten years her junior. The two planned to marry, and the excited woman exclaimed to reporters, "He's the only man who knows how to handle Lupe." Unfortunately, however, this was just a fantasy and the romance suddenly floundered towards the end of 1944.

On 9 December, Lupe told waiting reporters that her engagement was off due to a huge argument about politics. "We had one grand big battle," she said. "I told him to get out." She seemed very blasé about the whole thing, but in reality the fight had nothing to do with politics at all, and everything to do with the fact that the actress was pregnant with his child.

After a series of arguments, misunderstandings and language barriers, it seemed as though her lover had no wish to marry or even be with her and the child, and Lupe was distraught. Could she raise the child alone? Not likely given the era and the scandal that would hit if she did. Could she terminate the pregnancy and start again with her life? She just could not bring herself to even think about the idea. Finally, with no happy ending in sight and with the shame of an illegitimate baby hanging over her head, Lupe decided there was only one way forward: to get out permanently.

On the evening of 14 December 1944, just before Christmas, Lupe entertained her friends, Estelle Taylor and Mrs Jack Oakie. She was depressed and full of remorse over her lost love and pregnancy. "I have had plenty of opportunities to get rid of it," she told the shocked Taylor. "But it's my baby. I could not commit murder and still live with myself. I would rather kill myself."

Her friends tried to talk her out of the mood but it was no use. After saying goodnight, Lupe dressed herself in her favourite blue pyjamas and sat down to write a note to her estranged lover:

"Harald. May God forgive you and forgive me too. But I prefer to take my life away and our baby's before I bring him such shame or killing him. How could you fake such great love for me and our baby when all the time you didn't want us? I see no other way out for me, so goodbye and good luck to you. Love Lupe."

She wrote another note to her secretary, saying goodbye and asking her to take care of her dogs, Chips and Chops. Then she sat down, took a bottle of barbiturates and passed away in her immaculate silk bed – and not, as widely rumoured, with her head in the toilet.

The next morning, secretary Beulah Kinder found her employer lying on the bed, at first imagining she must be sleeping, but sadly she was wrong. The distraught woman felt the actress's head, saw the notes beside the bed and realized that she was dead. Rushing to the phone she called the police and it was not long before Lupe's North Rodeo Drive home was surrounded by a mixture of officers, reporters, fans and the curious.

Someone took it upon themselves to tell Lupe's ex-boyfriend, and from his own home at 8324 Fountain Avenue, Ramond released a statement: "I am so confused. I never expected this to happen. The last time I talked to Lupe I told her I was going to marry her any way she wanted. She said then she wasn't going to have a baby, so we parted." Once he had calmed down slightly, he then personally met with reporters and gave his version of events. According to Ramond he had been informed by Lupe's doctor that she was expecting his baby. He said that for a time he had not known what to do about the unexpected news, but then, "I called her up and asked her to marry me."

He then went on to tell reporters that after the news of the baby had sunk in, everything had been great between Lupe and himself, and she had even given him her finger size for an engagement ring. However, shortly afterwards, according to Ramond, the actress suddenly decided to call the whole thing off just a few days before her death. "I loved her very much and wanted to marry her. We just couldn't agree on the date," he said.

Everyone was confused. Why would Lupe decide to call off the wedding and then kill herself when things had seemingly been going so well? It just did not make sense. Lupe's manager waded in and shed light on the entire episode by arguing that Harald Ramond had not proposed to the actress out of any sense of romance or loyalty. Instead, he had apparently asked that they conduct a mock ceremony, in order to fool everyone that they had actually tied the knot and that their baby could be born in wedlock. "He wanted the marriage annulled after the child was legitimized," the manager told reporters.

"No!" exclaimed Ramond in shocked response. According to him, he had merely said that they should announce that the wedding had already taken place so they could make it look as though their child was conceived legitimately within the confines of marriage. "It was not wise to use the word fake," he cried to reporters. "She apparently did not understand my full explanation – that we would go ahead with a fully legal ceremony, at a later date."

Whatever the truth of the situation, Lupe Vélez was dead, and the world mourned the loss of a bright, fiery star. Thousands passed by her coffin at Forest Lawn Memorial Park, just days before Christmas, and then she was taken back home to Mexico. There, thousands more paid their respects to "Whoopee Lupe", who despite her reputation of being wild and not caring about what anyone thought, had become heartbroken because she believed she was unloved and about to bring shame upon herself. It was a tragic contradiction, and one which ultimately cost Lupe Vélez her life.

28

Carole Landis, the Heartbroken Star

When a person dies in Hollywood, it automatically makes headline news, with stories, rumours and facts quickly filling the pages. However, for poor Carole Landis, the newspapers not only ran stories about her demise, but also printed a photograph of the dead woman, curled on her bathroom floor, for all to see. Her life was unhappy; her death a tragedy; and the reporting sad to say the least.

Born Frances Lillian Mary Ridste in Wisconsin on 1 January 1919, the child's early life was one of misery and utter turmoil. Although she was given the name of her mother's first husband, he had left the family by the time Frances was born and she was raised instead by her mother's boyfriend (whom some say may have been her natural father, though this cannot be proved). Added to the mystery of not knowing who was her father, Frances also suffered heartbreak when two of her brothers tragically passed away.

Her life was grim, and in order to escape from the world around her Frances threw herself into the theatre, and she took part in a variety of talent shows and beauty contests. By the time she was fifteen, Frances had fallen in love with her next-door neighbour, Irving Wheeler, and the two secretly tied the knot, though the marriage was quickly annulled after her furious mother discovered what they had done. Six months, later, however, the couple wed again, though it did not turn out to be a success; they separated for a second and final time after just three weeks.

Frances had bigger things on her mind than getting divorced, so while very definitely separated, she decided to stay legally married to Irving while carving out a career first as a hula dancer and then a singer in a band. Hollywood soon beckoned and after moving there in September 1936 to begin her modelling and film career, she decided to change her name to Carole Landis, in tribute to her idol, Carole Lombard. The young woman was determined to make it as a star, though her career did not take off in the way she hoped and she very quickly found herself in nothing but uncredited bit parts, playing the likes of "The girl in the beret" or "The blonde at the airport". Still, Carole had been through much in her life so a little thing like bad parts was not going to stop her fulfilling her dream. Instead of giving up she carried on fighting for parts throughout the late 1930s, always hoping and dreaming that her big break was just around the corner.

By May 1938, Carole was a busy but still relatively unknown actress, though she was becoming very well known as a model and cover girl. It was at this time that she experienced her first sniff of scandal when she became involved briefly with dance director Busby Berkeley. Her estranged husband, Irving Wheeler, got wind of this and decided to construct a story which said that his wife had been persuaded to leave the family home after being seduced by Berkeley. It made no difference to him that he had actually split with the actress some years before, and decided to take the strange decision to sue the dance director for $250,000. Because Berkeley was well known, the story was splashed all over the papers and Carole found her photograph printed for all the wrong reasons. Irving lost the case, of course, but the scandal prompted Landis to end the marriage once and for all, the divorce becoming final in 1939.

But as they say, no publicity is bad publicity, and the Berkeley scandal had at least got Carole noticed; in 1940 she was cast in the movie *One Million BC*, which succeeded in propelling her into nationwide stardom. Nicknamed "The Ping Girl", Carole hated the tag so much that she even took out adverts in newspapers to request that people not call her that. Still, apart from that minor detail, she was very happy with the way her career was going, and after marrying and divorcing a yacht salesman by the name of Willis Hunt, she began a relationship with the head of Twentieth Century Fox, Darryl F. Zanuck.

Suddenly Carole began appearing in a string of successful films and acted opposite Betty Grable in *Moon over Miami* and *I Wake Up Screaming*. Some sceptics may say that her relationship with Zanuck ensured that she was offered such good roles, and sadly it would seem they were correct, as unfortunately for Carole, when she ended her relationship with Zanuck her career started to suffer. Once again she found herself in a variety of B-movies amid whispers that if she had not parted with the studio head, she would still have been on her way to the very top.

Carole was famous enough to have her presence requested to entertain the troops during World War II, though she suffered a great deal of illness while touring, almost dying as a result of amoebic dysentery and malaria. She also married once again, this time pilot Tommy Wallace, though as with all her previous relationships, the pairing was not a happy one. In May 1944 – a matter of months before the break-up of this marriage – the actress became so despondent that she was hospitalized after a suicide attempt. A broken engagement to producer Gene Markey followed the breakdown of her marriage to Wallace, and she began another unhappy, short marriage to producer W. Horace Schmidlapp in 1945. Another suicide attempt came in 1946 when she finally lost her contract with Twentieth Century Fox.

The threat of losing her career, coupled with the fact that she was unable to have children, had been too much for the young actress to bear. She was saved on this particular suicide attempt, though her private life remained complicated when she began an affair with married actor Rex Harrison. She fell hard for the British actor and began divorce proceedings against Schmidlapp in March 1948 so she could be with him permanently, but unfortunately Harrison was not so obliging. He refused point blank to abandon his wife for the actress, and left Carole heartbroken.

Several days before her death, all seemed relatively fine in Carole's world, and the actress recorded a two-minute tape for Hollywood Star Records which described her life and career as very satisfying. However, it was all an illusion. Carole was desperately unhappy with most aspects of her life; her love for Harrison was on the rocks; her marriage was broken; and added to that, she had almost never been satisfied with her career. Yes, there had been a time when she was given many good roles, but in the last few years she had been cast in nothing but B-movies and her confidence had taken a very definite blow.

Landis spent most of the 4 July 1948 celebrations at her home on Capri Drive, which she had recently sold because she felt it was far too big for just one person. She also attended a Fourth of July celebration and was seen playing in the pool and in good spirits, before later dining with old flame Rex Harrison at her home. He later claimed that during the course of the evening they had been discussing a possible project in England, but rumour has it that the actor actually gave her the news that he was breaking off their relationship once and for all, as he wished to renew his affection for his wife. This left Carole in absolute turmoil, and while she was painfully aware that her love life had always been difficult, this particular news was just too much to bear. After he left the house shortly after 9 p.m., Carole was in such a state that she decided to write a note to her mother.

"Dearest Mommie," it said. "I'm sorry, really sorry to put you through this but there is no way to avoid it." The actress then went on to say how much she loved her, and that she had been the most wonderful mother ever before adding, "that applies to all our family. Everything goes to you. Goodbye my angel, pray for me, Your Baby."

The distraught actress then placed the note on top of her dressing-room table; took an overdose of sleeping pills; staggered to her bathroom; and collapsed some time on 5 July. Fully clothed, in a frilly shirt and checked skirt, the actress expired with her head resting on a jewel box and her hand holding a satin ribbon with the words of the Lord's Prayer in gold letters. The position of her body looked as though she were trying to pick herself back up from the floor. There was an empty bottle nearby, with a variety of pills found around the bathroom and dressing areas.

The next day her housekeeper, Fannie Bolden, knocked on the actress's bedroom door but received no response. Rex Harrison phoned to see how she was and was told that she was still sleeping. He went about his business, but when he called again at 3 p.m. and was given the same answer, he became concerned enough to rush over to the home immediately. Unknown to the maid, Harrison went straight to the actress's bedroom to see what was wrong, and on opening Carole's door, he was sick to discover that she was collapsed on the bathroom floor. Sprinting over, he tried to wake her up: "I felt her pulse," he later told the coroner. "It must have been purely my imagination but I thought there was a little beat."

It was indeed his imagination because Carole was dead and had been that way for quite some time. Harrison then went to find Mrs Bolden to tell her the news.

"Have you been into Miss Landis's bedroom?" he asked.

"No," she answered.

The actor then broke the news to the shocked woman and took her into the bedroom to see for herself. It was at that point, Bolden said, that the suicide note was found and Harrison, on reading it, exclaimed, "Oh darling, why did you do it, why did you do it?"

The actor was in such a state that it was later said that he waited at least a couple of hours before calling the police, and did not think to ring the woman's mother, Clara, who found out about her daughter's death on the radio. "Why didn't somebody call me?" the mourning woman demanded to know, but nobody seemed to have an answer. Carole's estranged husband Horace Schmidlapp was just as shocked, crying, "Oh My God!!" when told of her death by reporters.

The police began asking Rex Harrison questions, with the first being, what had happened during Carole Landis's last evening? He told officers that they had been dining together but he had left some time around 9 p.m., as Carole was feeling ill after a recurrence of the amoebic infection she had suffered from before. Otherwise, he said, she was in good spirits. He declined to tell them that the two had been lovers and no doubt hoped that neither the press nor the police would probe any further.

He was – of course – sorely mistaken if he believed the entire episode would just fade away, and reporters wasted no time in asking about the exact nature of their relationship. "She was a very close friend of my wife's and mine," he told them. "While my wife was in New York I saw Carole quite frequently. We were planning a picture we were to make together in Europe. Immediately after her death, however, I called Lilli in New York and she flew home."

Several days later, more controversy came when newspapers reported that the actress's last will and testament were being sought, and though a number of would-be documents were brought forward, no one could confirm at that point whether Landis had a more up-to-date will than the one she had written four years earlier. This was further complicated when her lawyer, entertainment heavyweight Jerry Giesler, told the press, "Miss Landis was a person who was most meticulous about her business matters and the keeping of her records", and the police disclosed that she had made reference to the will in her suicide note. It was in a file, she had said, though at that point, neither the file nor the will could be found.

In the end, they did indeed go with the 1944 will, with everything going to her mother, Clara. As with most things in Hollywood, however, it was not a straightforward affair, with estranged husband Horace Schmidlapp later deciding to reject a former property settlement and thereby locking horns with Clara in a dispute over an equity of $35,000 which he said was owed to him from the sale of Carole's home on Capri Drive.

Another element that caused controversy was talk of a second suicide note, which was rumoured to have been in the room at the time Carole died. The story around Hollywood was that Rex Harrison had destroyed the letter in order to deter people thinking they were having an affair, and Carole's friend and former stand-in, Florence Wasson, put her two cents in when she declared that she specifically remembered seeing a letter that asked for someone to take care of her cat.

Since the official note had not mentioned any pets, the word was that another note must surely have been written, though Wasson was quick to point out that if it had disappeared, she had absolutely no idea where it could possibly have gone. "I don't even remember what the rest of the contents were," Wasson said, "but it did not relate to motive or anything like that." This revelation confused things even more – if the second note really had just been about the care of a pet, then why would Harrison have destroyed such a thing? It was quite a mystery.

Denying to the coroner that he knew anything about the second note, the British actor wasted no time in trying to quell rumours of a relationship by announcing once again that his wife Lilli Palmer and Carole were "great friends", before adding that the tragedy should not be clouded by sensational innuendoes. Humorously, he also said that he wished the scandal to stop as he wanted to clear Carole's name. The fact that if the rumours did subside, it would take the heat off his name, too, was not missed by the eager columnists and reporters.

If onlookers at the inquest were hoping to hear the nitty-gritty of the actress's "friendship" with Harrison, they must have been sorely disappointed, but the actor's testimony did shed some light on Carole's state of mind at the time of her death. He disclosed that they had not argued in any way on the evening before her death, and while she had been embarrassed by some financial problems, she did not seem too depressed about them.

"Was she worried about her divorce?" the coroner asked.

"I don't think so," replied the actor. "I can't give any explanation for [her death] at all."

Meanwhile, the other party in the divorce, Horace Schmidlapp, had flown into California and was stopped by reporters at the airport.

"Do you know why Carole might have taken her own life?" they asked.

"No, no," he answered. "I can't think of any reason. She was certainly all right financially; her career was in excellent shape . . ."

"Have you seen her recently?"

"I talked to her over the phone last week and she was like she'd always been – gay and happy. The last time I saw her was in January in Europe. She was in good spirits then – and beautiful."

Reporters then asked if the marriage had still been on the rocks, to which he replied that the divorce action had certainly been continuing at the time of death. He then went on to say that he was sure the suicide was not as a result of finances, since his ex-wife never worried about money at all. "She wasn't that kind," he said.

This observation was backed up by lawyer Jerry Giesler who added, "I had just completed a property settlement with Schmidlapp. Miss Landis was very satisfied with it." He then went on to deny that his client must have been concerned about her finances, stating, "I believe that if Carole had been worried about money, she would have been found dead in bed. When a person worries about finances they lie awake at night and the worry continues to mount until it seems almost insurmountable."

But there were definitely at least some money issues, as

testified by Giesler while talking to the press. In his comments the lawyer stated that Carole had personally written to her creditors to assure them of her intention of paying bills as soon as the house had been sold. But he also added, "With her Eagle-Lion contract for two films and another deal to make pictures in England, she had a bright future ahead of her."

So it would seem that money was not an issue that could have caused Carole Landis to suddenly commit suicide. With that in mind, could the lawyer shed any light on why the actress would have wanted to take her own life?

"It is difficult to understand," he told the press. "I knew Carole was a person of impulse. This must have been an impulsive thing. She was fully dressed. Alone in that big house."

The run-up to Carole's funeral was a heart-breaking affair, made more so because she had been so young, and her death sudden and tragic. She lay for several days at the Wilshire Funeral Home, where hundreds of mourners, including family, friends and fans, all filed past in order to see her one more time. There were so many flowers that the funeral home had to direct most of them to Forest Lawn; such was the public outcry for a life cut so terribly short.

When it was time for the funeral, Carole's coffin was carried into the chapel by pall-bearers that included actors Cesar Romero and Willard Parker, as well as Carole's personal make-up man, Ben Nye. Although the formalities were brief, they still came with a fair share of drama, when the actress's mother, Clara, collapsed on to the shoulder of her granddaughter, Diane, just as they were making their way to the chapel. Then during the service she collapsed again on the stairs, sobbing loudly at the sight of her daughter's coffin. The whole thing was extremely dramatic and by the time Rex Harrison arrived with his wife Lilli, the crowds were so frantic that the funeral assistants had to hold them back so that the couple could enter the venue safely.

Once inside, the service consisted of a short prayer and Carole's favourite song, "In a Garden" before Bishop Fred

Pyman addressed the congregation. "Life is a dress rehearsal for the greater play which comes after," he said. "Actors all believe they will play their roles again . . . and perfectly."

Carole was buried on a hillside overlooking the city, just as the coroner announced that no further action would be taken in regards to the investigation into her death. In a statement he said that he could find no criminal action in connection with her passing, and was therefore closing the case. Shortly before the announcement, Francis Kearney from the homicide squad told reporters that "If there were any suspicions of foul play, then motive would be important, but since all evidence shows the death without doubt to be suicide, then the search for motive is hardly a police matter."

Although her family had opted not to confront Rex Harrison about the death of Carole Landis, and had told reporters that they had not heard anything about the existence of a second suicide note, rumours started to circulate that they were not entirely convinced of the story of her final hours, and even suspected that Harrison had something to do with the death and was somehow covering up what he knew. There was even talk of them hiring a private detective to find out exactly what had happened on the fateful evening, but if indeed that story was true, it seems that nothing was found.

The autopsy showed that Carole had five milligrams of barbiturate per 100 grams of liver tissue, and her blood contained a high level of alcohol. This showed that the actress had drunk a great deal prior to her collapse, and with that in mind, it is the belief of many that after Harrison left that evening, she drowned her sorrows before taking her final, fatal overdose. In the end, while some people may have had their doubts, it seems that Carole Landis's death was very definitely a suicide, though why she did it remains unclear. Public consensus would seem to suggest that it was as a result of Harrison ending their relationship, and Carole's lawyer, Jerry Giesler, hinted as much when talking to reporters shortly after the death.

"I think Carole suffered a sudden great shock from which she did not recover sufficiently to undress and retire," he said. "But perhaps she regretted her impulsive action at the last moment, and was going to get help so she could recover."

As for Harrison himself, while he denied anything other than friendship with the actress, Hedda Hopper shed more light on the situation when she wrote her 9 July 1948 column. In it she said that she had asked him about Carole just four months prior to her death, mentioning the rumours that his marriage was ending because of her.

"That's just Hollywood gossip – and you know what that is," Harrison replied. He then added that his wife Lilli had arrived back at the family home and they were "trying to work things out". With that in mind, he asked Hedda not to print anything about the rumours of his relationship with Carole. She did as he requested and later Harrison sent her a bouquet of flowers, thanking the columnist for "your cooperation. It is very, very much appreciated. Many, many thanks."

29

Marilyn Monroe's Nude Calendar Scandal

In today's era of semi-nude pop stars and paparazzi pictures of celebrity wardrobe "malfunctions", it is strange to think that something as innocent as a picture of a nude woman (with lower parts hidden) would cause anything more than a half-raised eyebrow. However, in the 1950s, when nudity was meant for the bathroom only (if at all), a risqué calendar caused an absolute scandal and almost crushed the career of up-and-coming actress Marilyn Monroe before it had really begun.

Born in Los Angeles in 1926, Norma Jeane Baker was the daughter of Gladys Baker, an unwed mother who was volatile and suffered huge emotional problems. At just a few weeks old Norma Jeane was sent to live with a foster family, before an unsuccessful attempt at living with her mother ended with Gladys being taken to a mental hospital. Norma Jeane was then raised in a series of foster homes and an orphanage.

In an attempt to escape the foster system, Norma Jeane chose to wed a young man called James Dougherty when she was just sixteen, though she found marriage stifling and took solace in a new-found modelling career at the age of nineteen. Norma Jeane's husband was away at war during this time and he insisted that, although he would tolerate her career while away, the moment the war was over he expected her to give everything up and become a full-time wife and raise a house-ful of children.

Norma Jeane rejected this idea immediately. She had by this

point become a successful model and enjoyed seeing her face on many magazine covers. Film studios were also knocking on her door and in 1946, after sending her husband a "Dear John" letter, she travelled to Nevada in order to obtain a divorce. Free at last, she then signed with Twentieth Century Fox, changed her name to Marilyn Monroe and launched full-steam into an acting and modelling career. Her photos ranged from the girl-next-door to classic glamour or "cheesecake" shots, and while her acting career was full of bit parts and walk-ons, her star quality nevertheless began to increase.

However, organizing her finances was never a strong point for Marilyn, and by early 1949 she had fallen behind not only with her rent, but also with the payments on the car she relied on to get to and from auditions. Threatened with repossession of the vehicle, Marilyn picked up the telephone and called Tom Kelley, a photographer who had asked her to pose nude for him several months before.

She had declined to take her clothes off at that time, but now, worried that she was about to lose her possessions, she changed her mind and arrived at his studio on 27 May 1949 in order to pose. There, in the company of Kelley's partner Natalie Grasko, Marilyn removed her clothes, reclined on a red velvet blanket, and was paid $50 for her efforts. When asked years later what it felt like, Marilyn replied, "Very simple . . . And drafty!"

Initially Marilyn had felt okay about posing nude, since she did certainly need the money and was somewhat (naively) convinced that no one would actually see the photos. If they did, she told herself, they would not know it was her anyway, since she had signed her name as "Mona Monroe" on the release form. However, as time wore on and her acting career started to gain more attention, she became increasingly concerned that the photos would somehow emerge and destroy all that she had worked so hard to achieve.

Rumours started to circulate that Kelley was in the midst of selling the photos to a calendar company, and Marilyn finally broke down and admitted what she had done to her good friend, Bill Pursel, who shared his story with me for the book, *Marilyn Monroe: Private and Undisclosed*:

> She told me she had done something she was ashamed of, and she wanted to tell me about it before I found out elsewhere. She said she wanted to apologize and started to cry, before finally telling me she had posed nude and had done it because her rent was way past due. She then asked if I would look at the pictures and when I said yes she produced them. My first reaction was that these photos were not pornographic at all and they were actually very good. She said the photographer had promised not to sell them but I told her that he probably would, since selling photographs was what he did for a living. I told her that I thought the pictures were in good taste and she asked if I was ashamed of her, to which I said no, but that neither she nor I could undo something that was already done and I was in no position to object to them anyway.

Several years passed and, to the relief of Marilyn, the photos were nowhere to be seen. She continued her career and enjoyed a small but important part in the Marx Brothers film, *Love Happy*, which took her on a major tour around the United States. Fans clamoured to see her and fan letters began to clog up the mailroom at Twentieth Century Fox. Unfortunately, this national attention guaranteed that the nude photographs would be in great demand, and sure enough, in 1952 they showed up on calendars entitled "Golden Dreams" and "A New Wrinkle".

Still, nobody at the studio seemed to notice the existence of the calendars, and life continued as normal for Marilyn, until one day in 1952 when she was approached on the street by a man clutching one of the calendars. "This ought to be worth quite a bit of money to you. Suppose I showed it around town?" asked the stranger. Marilyn refused to be blackmailed and replied: "Mister, I'd just adore for you to show it around Hollywood – would you like me to also autograph it for you?"

Although obviously more than a little worried that the calendar could cause a sensation, outwardly Marilyn played it cool and chose not to do anything until finally Twentieth Century Fox got wind of the situation and called her into the office. Asking straight out if Marilyn was the nude girl being gawped at around the country, they were shocked when she nodded her head and admitted everything. The executives were furious and a frenzy ensued with them first demanding that she lie about it, then changing their minds and deciding she should say nothing at all.

Unfortunately for them, Marilyn saw no reason to deny the stories and, after much discussion, a statement was prepared which allowed her to put forward her version of events – that she was broke and needed money for her rent. She played the sympathy card and won, with the public not only forgiving the nude scandal, but also loving her even more for her honesty and candour.

Marilyn was immediately relieved, and once it became apparent that the photos would not negatively affect her career, she actually became quite proud of them. In fact, so pleased was she that the actress actually autographed a great many of the calendars and gave them away as gifts for her friends, as well as to future husband, baseball star Joe DiMaggio.

Marilyn Monroe had survived the nude scandal and her career continued to blossom. However, it was only a matter of years before she would be caught up in another scandal, this time brought on by Joe DiMaggio himself . . .

30

The Wrong Door Raid

In 1954, Marilyn Monroe married baseball star Joe DiMaggio. It was a marriage made in heaven for the press, but not so much for the two stars, as from the very beginning, it was a depressing and often abusive affair. DiMaggio had just retired from baseball and was quite content becoming a family man with the woman he loved. Marilyn, on the other hand, was at the peak of her career and any fantasies of settling down, ironing her husband's shirts and bearing his children were just that – fantasies.

The marriage dragged on for nine months, during which time Marilyn entertained the troops in Korea and made *There's No Business Like Show Business* with Ethel Merman. Joe was not happy about his wife working so hard but he went along with it anyway, though he often refused to accompany her to red-carpet events and parties, preferring to stay at home instead. Unfortunately, while Marilyn was shooting *The Seven Year Itch* in New York, DiMaggio decided that on this occasion he would actually go along and see what his wife was doing, just in time to observe her standing on a subway grating, her skirt flying into the air and panties on full display.

The jealous and insecure DiMaggio was furious and a huge argument broke out that evening, which some say turned particularly violent on the baseball player's part. It was at that moment that Marilyn decided she no longer wished to be married to Joe, and once they were back in Los Angeles, she moved out of their North Palm Drive house and into 8338 De Longpre Avenue, where she intended to stay until her divorce was organized.

During this time the actress began a romance with her voice coach, Hal Schaefer. The two had been great friends for several years and during the marriage to DiMaggio they had been so close that the baseball player had started to have suspicions they were having an affair. It is true that Schaefer was in love with the actress and in the months just before separating from her husband, Marilyn cooled her friendship with him to such an extent that he attempted suicide. This shocking event sent Marilyn straight to her voice coach's bedside, and DiMaggio was once again enraged.

However, by the time a true romance began for the pair, Marilyn was on her way to becoming divorced and it proved to be a comfortable, carefree relationship, the complete opposite to what she had endured with the volatile and moody DiMaggio. For Monroe the romance was fun, but for Schaefer it was true love, as he said in an interview for the book, *Marilyn Monroe: Private and Undisclosed*: "We became lovers and were going to get married," said Schaefer. "She wanted to convert to Judaism because I was a Jew. She was still legally married to DiMaggio but had already moved out and had started divorce proceedings."

It is doubtful that Marilyn wanted to rush straight from one marriage to another, but she did enjoy Schaefer's company and their new romance nevertheless. Unfortunately, DiMaggio was not about to give up on his wife that easily, especially as he was still in love and hopeful that Marilyn would one day forgive the mistakes he had made within the marriage, and move back in with him.

DiMaggio disliked Schaefer intensely as a result of the friendship his wife had shared with him during their marriage, and on hearing that Marilyn might actually be involved with the man, he took the questionable decision to hire private detectives from the City Detectives and Guard Service to follow the couple around Hollywood. The company began surveillance on 20 October 1954, and trailed both Marilyn and Schaefer between various Los Angeles neighbourhoods, witnessing her picking up friends, visiting her attorney and calling on her acting coach, Natasha Lytess.

They even followed Schaefer alone to a nightclub, where they reported that he looked "very dopey", though he was not drinking. Bizarrely, the detectives claimed to witness him "doing something to his arm", and wondered if he was "shooting up". All of this was written down in their reports, though if the detectives thought they were inconspicuous they were very wrong, as Marilyn and Hal were very much aware they were being followed.

"It was a sick and hostile situation because of DiMaggio", remembered Schaefer. "He hired private detectives and bugged Marilyn's car, my car, and my apartment. We were followed everywhere and it was very scary. Marilyn was terrified."

When she appeared at Santa Monica Court House for her divorce on 27 October, Marilyn did not mention the surveillance, even though it was ongoing. Instead, she leant on the arm of her business manager, Inez Melson and told how her dream of marital bliss had turned into a nightmare of "coldness" and "indifference". She added, "My husband would get into moods where he wouldn't speak to me for days at a time – a week, sometimes longer, maybe ten days. If I tried to coax him to talk to me, he wouldn't answer at all, or he would say, 'Leave me alone, stop nagging me!'"

Joe, meanwhile, insisted that he still wanted to be friends with Marilyn, though in truth he was verging on the obsessive. On 5 November it came to a head when a private detective tailed her to 754 Kilkea Drive, the apartment block of Sheila Stewart, a friend of Marilyn and ex-student of Schaefer. Bizarrely Joe DiMaggio was tailing the detectives (an amusing fact that they later recorded in their report); determined to catch Marilyn "in the act" with Schaefer, he stormed the apartment, along with the detectives and DiMaggio's friend, Frank Sinatra.

Aside from the fact that this was a ludicrous and illegal act, it was made even more absurd when it was discovered that the foursome had broken into the wrong apartment – that of Florence Kotz, who later described it as a "night of terror", adding, "I was terrified. The place was full of men. They were making a lot of noises and lights flashed on. They broke a lot of glasses in the kitchen getting out of there."

Frank Sinatra later claimed that he had stayed in the car and smoked a cigarette during the proceedings, and when the case went to court in March 1957, Joe DiMaggio backed him up (though Sinatra was not in court himself). Private detective Phil Irwin, however, insisted that Sinatra was an active participant in the raid and had most certainly stormed into Miss Kotz's apartment that evening.

Active or not, the "Wrong Door Raid" shook every inhabitant of the apartment block, including Marilyn and Hal Schaefer, who were together in the flat upstairs. At the time, both parties denied all knowledge of being in the building, but some fifty years later, Schaefer came clean:

> The apartment belonged to an ex-student of mine who had become a friend. She knew about Marilyn and I, and when she went out of town, she gave me the key to the apartment so that we could use it. It was just Marilyn and me in the apartment when the raid took place and Marilyn was terrified. I don't believe I'd be around today if they'd found me in the apartment. They almost wrecked the building – rammed the door down of the wrong apartment and the woman ended up suing. Marilyn and I managed to get out the back door.

The relationship between Schaefer and Marilyn ended soon afterwards when she moved to New York at the end of 1954.

However, despite the fact that DiMaggio had followed her, hired detectives to spy on her and stormed an apartment block to find her, Marilyn was eventually prepared to forgive him. The two remained good friends throughout the years and were seen together to such an extent that reporters started to believe they might get back together again. "Is this a reconciliation?" they asked when the couple were spotted at the theatre. "Just think of it as a visit," replied Marilyn, though the look on Joe DiMaggio's face made it clear that he wanted the visit to turn into a permanent arrangement.

Still, Marilyn was adamant that they would not get back together again, with the Wrong Door Raid being more than a little fresh in her mind. She married playwright Arthur Miller in 1956, although when that marriage broke down and she suffered a nervous breakdown, it was DiMaggio who came to her aid. After making *The Misfits* in 1960, Marilyn was exhausted and, encouraged by her doctor to stay in a hospital for a rest, she agreed, although she had no idea that the hospital to which she was admitted was actually a psychiatric clinic and not somewhere to relax for a few weeks in peace. From the confines of the clinic, she telephoned Joe DiMaggio who turned up and threatened to take the building apart "brick by brick" if they did not release her into his care.

The hospital did indeed release her and the two became firm friends again, with memories of their failed marriage and the Wrong Door Raid fading into the past. There was talk once again about reconciliation but it was not to be. When Marilyn died mysteriously at her Brentwood home on the night of 4–5 August 1962, it was once again Joe DiMaggio who tried to come to her rescue. He may have been too late to stop her death, but he did claim her body and help to organize the private funeral.

The baseball player never stopped loving his ex-wife and for the next twenty years ordered flowers to be delivered to Marilyn's grave every week. He never remarried, nor did he ever talk publicly about his lost love, preferring to live his last years quietly in Florida, alone with his memories and mementoes of their time together.

Their marriage had been painful; the break-up led to scandal, private detectives, threats, intrusion and a law suit; but his love for Marilyn never ended. When Joe DiMaggio passed away in 1999, his last words were reported to be, "At last I'll get to see Marilyn . . ."

31

The Sudden Death of James Dean

It is now almost sixty years since the world lost James Dean, although like Marilyn Monroe and Elvis Presley, he is still all around us in songs, in movies and on posters, mugs and postcards. He was the first "Rebel Without a Cause" but certainly not the last. When he died so tragically in 1955, the world lost not only a great actor, but also a star who has come to epitomize the 1950s and, in particular, the jeans and T-shirt-wearing teenagers of his generation.

Born on 8 February 1931, James Byron Dean was raised in Marion, Indiana, and then Santa Monica, California, where he lived a rather normal and loving life with his mother Mildred and father Winton. Unfortunately for the child, his mother developed cancer and passed away when Dean was just nine years old, forcing him to be raised by his aunt and uncle as his father could no longer care for his son. He was not an exceptional student at school, preferring sports to the basics such as maths and literacy. However, James did enjoy drama with his teacher Mrs Nall, and it would seem that it was these early lessons that planted the seed of his acting talent and interest.

After he graduated in 1949, James moved back to California with his father, where the young man enrolled in college and majored in pre-law. This thrilled his family but it was not long before Dean grew bored of the subject and changed his studies to drama at University of California, Los Angeles (UCLA), much to the chagrin of his father who could not see any point in studying such a frivolous activity.

While at UCLA, he had the opportunity of acting in *Macbeth*, which gave the young man enough confidence in his abilities to believe that he no longer needed to study the craft full-time; he wanted desperately to put all he had learned into action instead. With this in mind he dropped out of college and endeavoured to work as a full-time actor, though in reality he found himself offered only bit parts and the occasional commercial. But despite the disappointments, Dean was not prepared to give up on his career and it wasn't long before he moved across the country to New York, where he studied his craft and gained work on television.

James was a complex young man – a seemingly moody character, a deep thinker who was complicated and emotional, and totally dedicated to his craft. He worked hard and paid his dues in all manner of acting roles on television and theatre, but in spite of that he actually only had three major films to his credit, the first being *East of Eden*, which he began shooting in April 1954. This film was a big success, and landed James Dean an Academy Award nomination for best actor. Unfortunately by this time the actor had already passed away and in the end the award went to Ernest Borgnine for his performance in *Marty*.

Dean's next movie was perhaps his most famous, and is still frequently broadcast on television nearly sixty years after its release: *Rebel Without a Cause* was the movie that really seemed to give teenagers a name and introduced the world to their angst and problems – particularly problems related to their relationship with their parents. Young people around the world identified with Dean's character, Jim Stark. They had their hair cut like his and took to wearing white T-shirts and blue jeans just like their hero. The film gave Dean a huge degree of success, and it would be fair to say that, without it, there perhaps would not have been the amount of publicity surrounding the actor that we still witness today.

Next came the movie *Giant*, which saw Dean playing Jett

Rink, an outcast who strikes oil and becomes a baron – a very different character to those he had played in *Rebel* and *East of Eden*. The film saw Dean cast alongside Elizabeth Taylor and Rock Hudson, and he grew very fond of Taylor during filming, so much so that it is rumoured he once told her that he had been molested as a child by a local minister. However, since neither person is around in order to substantiate this story, it is impossible to say if this really happened or is just a product of hearsay and gossip.

Regardless of whether he ever admitted such a thing, the two actors did become close friends and Taylor presented Dean with a cat that he called Marcus and who lived with him until his untimely death. When a reporter telephoned Elizabeth after Dean died, she was shocked and unable to find any words. "I can't believe it; I'm just stunned," was all she managed to say, before breaking down.

Giant was not entirely finished at the time of James's death and still needed to be edited and polished. With this in mind, Nick Adams, an actor from *Rebel* and Dean's friend, took on the task of dubbing some of Dean's lines during this process. Still, the fact that the film had not been edited or seen before his death did nothing to diminish its likeability, and in 1956 he was given his second Academy Award nomination, though he lost out to Yul Brynner for his portrayal of the King in *The King and I*. While he may not have won the award, James did manage to become something of a record breaker when he became the only actor ever to receive two posthumous and consecutive nominations for acting.

Away from his career, James Dean was a keen racing driver and had a deep love for motorbikes and cars. Friends worried about his hobby, however, as he would often take his interest off the race track and instead go pelting down the highways with seemingly no regard for his personal safety whatsoever. Warner Brothers were concerned enough by this to ban Dean from all racing during the making of *Giant*, which he did not appreciate at all.

He did, somewhat ironically, manage to record a "Public Service Announcement" during the making of the film, warning young people of the dangers of speeding on the highway, during which he shared his thoughts: "I used to fly around quite a bit and took a lot of unnecessary chances on the highways," he explained. "Then I started racing and now when I drive on the highway I'm extra cautious because no one knows what they're doing." He then urged the youngsters to take care when driving because, "the life you save might be mine".

On 21 September 1955, just after filming on *Giant* had ended, Dean invested in a new Porsche 550 Spyder and christened it "Little Bastard", though the inspiration behind such a name remains unclear. Some say it was a direct dig at Jack Warner who had once apparently called Dean such a name, while others insist it was a nickname given to him by a friend. But whatever the reason behind the moniker, there were several people who had an uneasy feeling about the vehicle, including British actor Alec Guinness, who met Dean just seven days before his death. The young actor showed Guinness his car and asked him what he thought, to which he reportedly replied, "If you get in that car, you will be found dead in it by this time next week." The macabre Dean no doubt thought this comment somewhat amusing, and instead of avoiding the car as Guinness suggested, decided to enter it into the Salinas Road Race which was to take place on 1–2 October 1955.

James Dean had something of an obsession with death and was once even photographed sitting inside a coffin. He confessed to friends that he did not expect to live long, that he wanted to do everything quickly because he knew that time was running out for him. "He was an extreme individualist," said an unnamed friend, just days after his death. "A non-conformist who believed in acting and living as he pleased."

On 30 September 1955, Dean climbed into his Porsche, together with friend and mechanic Rolf Wütherich, and they set off for Salinas, followed by friend Bill Hickman and photographer Sanford H. Roth who had photographed Dean shortly before they left. Those beautifully candid shots of the actor, with the customary cigarette hanging from his mouth, were the last to be taken of him.

The idea had been for all four men to travel in a station wagon with the Porsche strapped to the back, but moments before they left, Dean had a change of heart and decided it would be better if he drove the sports car in order to break it in for the race ahead. It was a decision that unfortunately would cost the actor his life.

As Dean tore down the highway with Wütherich, they were pulled over by California Highway Patrolman O. V. Hunter, who warned the actor that he was driving sixty-five miles an hour instead of the legal fifty-five. Hickman, driving behind, was also ticketed, and after the episode the party continued on their way, stopping briefly at Blackwell Corners for refreshments before heading towards Paso Robles in order to meet up with friends for dinner later that evening.

Shortly before 6 p.m., at about nineteen miles east of Paso Robles, Dean's car was involved in a head-on collision at the intersection of Highways 41 and 466. The crash happened quickly and came when a Ford coupé being driven by a young man called Donald Turnupseed suddenly turned in front of Dean's car. The force of the collision was so violent and at such velocity that Dean's car flew up into the air, while the Ford slid almost forty feet down the highway.

Both Turnupseed and Wütherich were injured in the crash, with the mechanic suffering a fractured jaw and hip, and numerous other injuries. On being taken to the hospital, he was described as being in a "moderately serious condition" while Turnupseed's car was a write-off. Its owner got away with fairly minor injuries; so much so, in fact, that when officers arrived on the scene, they interviewed the young man and then – quite bizarrely – told him to leave his destroyed vehicle at the roadside and hitchhike his way home to Tulare. He did as he was asked, and despite having just been involved in a head-on collision and all the shock that brings with it, found his way home in the dark, thanks to the kindness of strangers.

But while the two men were obviously shocked and physically hurt, they did manage to get out of the crash alive. The same cannot be said for James Dean, sadly, who suffered a broken neck, other broken bones and lacerations all over his body. His foot had been crushed between the pedals and he had internal injuries, too, so that by the time Hickman and Roth arrived on the scene ten minutes later, he was all but gone.

The two men were stunned to see the wreckage before them and Hickman spent time getting his friend out of the wreckage in order to try and help him, while Roth snapped some photographs of the mangled car, some of which can be seen on websites that have sprung up over the years. While the photographs are not pleasant to look at, they do show the extent to which the vehicle was destroyed on impact and what a mystery it was that anyone got out alive at all.

An ambulance finally arrived on the scene and rushed James Dean to Paso Robles War Memorial Hospital, where he was pronounced dead immediately. Later reports would surface that Dean's last words were, "That guy's got to stop, he'll see us", in reference to Turnupseed's vehicle, but this seems unlikely, especially as the crash happened so quickly. Wütherich later admitted that he was sneezing at the time of impact, and was therefore in no fit state to see or hear much at all.

Several weeks after the crash that killed the world's most famous up-and-coming young actor, a coroner's inquest was held to determine what exactly had happened. During the proceedings, witnesses Tom Fredericks and his brother-in-law Tom Dooley shocked everyone by claiming that it wasn't Dean driving the car at the moment of impact, but actually his mechanic, Wütherich. This raised eyebrows around the room, but was categorically denied by the mechanic himself, who was still in hospital, recovering from the impact of the crash.

According to him, he was very definitely just the passenger

of the vehicle, but nearly sixty years later, rumours abound that he was the driver. He wasn't, but he never fully got over the crash, suffering depression and staying in hospital for eighteen months immediately after the accident. A tragic twist occurred in 1981 when Wütherich really was driving a car that was involved in a crash – he lost control and headed straight into a house, becoming mangled in the wreckage to such a degree that special equipment was needed in order to free him. Like James Dean more than twenty-five years earlier, Wütherich tragically passed away at the scene; he had escaped one major collision in his life, but he could not survive another.

Turnupseed, meanwhile, spoke very briefly to a reporter after the accident and then never mentioned it again, deciding that he needed to concentrate on the future rather than the past. He swore that at the moment of impact, he had not seen Dean's small Porsche, and spent the rest of his life fending off reporters, authors, fans and passers-by determined to dish the dirt on the death of James Dean and Turnupseed's part in it. So intrusive was the attention, in fact, that people would often trudge their way up his garden path in the hope of being granted an interview. They were never lucky, however, and instead of being able to talk to the man at the centre of the scandal, they were instead met by furious family members and quickly sent on their way. The poor man lived under the shadow of the actor's death until his own eventual passing in 1995.

When the inquest into James Dean's death was complete, his death was ruled an accident and the case closed. Meanwhile, the actor's funeral was handled by his father, Winton, who travelled to Paso Robles after the death in order to oversee his son's body returned to Fairmount, Indiana. The funeral itself was held at Fairmount Friends Church on 8 October 1955 and was attended by 3,000 people – a staggering number and said to be more than the entire population of his hometown at that time. His pall-bearers were his friends from school and he was buried in Fairmount's Park Cemetery later that day.

This should, of course, have been the end of the story, but

actually it was far from it. The headstone that was chosen for the plot went on to have rather a chequered story of its own when in 1983 the simple marker was stolen three times from the cemetery. It was returned twice and then disappeared for good. It has not been seen since; if someone stole it as a ghoulish memento, they have certainly kept very quiet about it.

Another headstone was placed in the spot shortly after the first was stolen for good, only to go missing in 1998. This time, however, it managed to find its way back when a sheriff found it after it had been dumped on a country road some sixty miles away. It was returned to the cemetery, and two metal rods secured it into the ground to prevent further theft. This has still not stopped macabre memorabilia hunters, however, who have come to the grave over the years to chip away pieces of stone for their creepy collections. They do this, they say, because they are fans, though what Dean's friends and family think of this unsavoury and hugely disrespectful ritual is something else entirely.

A more appropriate way of remembering the tragic young actor was undertaken in 2005 on the fiftieth anniversary of James Dean's death. Despite the original accident intersection being restructured and moved over the years (though the original road can still be seen nearby), the new layout was named the James Dean Memorial Junction and a small plaque is situated at the spot where the accident occured. Now everyone who drives down that particular stretch of road is reminded of the man who lost his life there, and perhaps they drive a little more slowly too. As James Dean once said, "the life you save might be mine".

32

The Mysterious Death of Lana Turner's Boyfriend

In terms of Hollywood actresses, you do not get much bigger than blonde bombshell Lana Turner. A star in every sense of the word, Lana exuded glamour, sophistication and sex appeal, but when her boyfriend Johnny Stompanato was killed in her Beverly Hills mansion, Turner's career and reputation looked as though they would be tarnished forever.

Born in Wallace, Idaho, on 8 February 1921, Julia Jean Turner, the woman who would grow up to be known as Lana, was raised for the most part in California; first in San Francisco and then, later, Los Angeles. Her childhood was not the happiest of starts and at an early age she lost her father after he was mugged and murdered on his way home from a "craps" game. The crime was never solved and as a result of having no father, the family were impoverished and often split apart while Lana's mother, Mildred, worked all the hours she could just to put food on the table.

During times such as those, Lana would move in with friends until her mother was able to have her back in the family home, but it was often a gruesome few months, particularly when some of the families she lived with treated her as their own personal servant and dogsbody. Lana herself later wrote that "servant" was too good a word for how she was treated in the homes where she stayed, and described her life as like "a cheap Cinderella" but with no hope of a pumpkin. There were also times when she was beaten so badly that she bled, leading her mother into despair when she eventually found out what was going on.

As she entered her teens, Lana and her mother moved to Los Angeles where they hoped to live a better life. Things did indeed look up while they were there, and Lana enrolled at Hollywood High School while Mildred gained employment as a beautician, though the hours were awful – often eighty a week. This meant that the child became something of a latch-key kid, letting herself into the house after school and fending for herself until her mother came home from work.

Depending on whom you believe, Lana Turner was either discovered at the soda fountain at Schwab's drugstore or in the Top Hat Café. It ultimately does not matter where the location was, of course – the most important fact being that the sixteen-year-old was spotted by William F. Wilkerson, the publisher of the *Hollywood Reporter* and a successful talent scout. He asked if she would like to be an actress, to which she replied, "I'll have to ask my mother." She did; it was fine; and Wilkerson put her in touch with producer and director Mervyn LeRoy who cast her in a small role in his next movie, *They Won't Forget* (1937).

Although only on the screen for a matter of minutes, Turner made a big impression, particularly because of the way her breasts bounced in her sweater as she walked down the street. After that columnists began calling the young woman "The Sweater Girl", though this was a tag that Lana hated and, if truth be known, the part in *They Won't Forget* was not one of her personal favourites, branding it embarrassing after seeing herself on screen.

Lana worked hard on her career after she became "The Sweater Girl" and gained many parts, moving to MGM and signing her first contract just months after her debut movie role. However, her popularity reached a new level during World War II when she starred in such films as *Ziegfeld Girl* (1941) and *Slightly Dangerous* (1943).

She worked with Clark Gable on several occasions and their

chemistry was such that Mrs Gable – Carole Lombard – did not particularly like the pairing and would often visit the set to keep an eye on both Lana and her husband. In fact, as documented here in the chapter on Lombard, it was while rushing home from a bond rally in order to reunite with Gable, who was filming with Turner, that Lombard died in a plane crash. Her death encouraged Gable to put his movie career on hold and go into the military. Lana then threw herself into selling bonds herself, as well as visiting soldiers in order to raise their spirits. Once the war was over, she went on to star in the 1946 film noir, *The Postman Always Rings Twice*, which buoyed her confidence as she had fought for a dramatic role for some considerable time and it cemented her reputation as a Hollywood star.

However, away from the screen, it was always Turner's personal life that caused the most waves in the newspapers, and she was known from an early age as a rebellious party girl who loved nightclubs and dancing. So much so, in fact, that she was often seen hanging around at Mocambo and Ciro's, staying up late to drink cocktails, dance the night away and spend time with the various men who frequented both establishments. Lana, it can be said, was a huge fan of the opposite sex and by the time she passed away in 1995, the actress had been married a staggering eight times to seven different men. She later wrote that she found men to be exciting and could not understand any woman who did not think that way, describing them as ladies with no corpuscles or as statues.

A true romantic at heart, Lana believed she would one day get the classic Hollywood ending and live happily ever after, but unfortunately none of her marriages were successful, and a few even turned abusive and violent. She later described her first husband, band leader Artie Shaw, as the most egotistical man she had ever met, adding, "I hate him." Things were not much better – and often worse – with her future husbands, but out of all the men in her life, perhaps it was second husband

Stephen Crane who made the most impact as it was with him that she had her beloved daughter, Cheryl.

Stephen and Lana actually married twice – the first in 1942 was annulled after he admitted to the actress that the divorce from his last wife was not yet final. This information did not sit well with Lana and she decided to call the whole thing off, which caused shockwaves in the studio and newspapers, especially when it was discovered that she was pregnant but still determined to annul the marriage. However, six months later the couple reunited and married for the sake of their baby daughter, though ultimately the partnership was not a happy one. Of particular concern were the arguments they had about the health of their baby daughter, who had been born with a hereditary condition called RH Incompatibility. The baby needed several blood transfusions and stayed in the hospital for two months while she was treated, during which time Stephen unfairly blamed his wife for giving the condition to the child. This proved to be a factor in the break-up of their marriage just a year later.

Lana's career and failed love life rattled on, but by 1956 her acting roles had been lacking in a certain something for quite some time and MGM decided to terminate her contract after they failed to see any more potential in their star. Turner was devastated, and things did not get much better when she miscarried a child in the seventh month of pregnancy. Shortly afterwards she discovered that her then husband, Lex Barker, was abusing her daughter Cheryl, and that marriage – quite understandably – ended in divorce. This in turn led to a rebellion by the teenage child, which saw the relationship between mother and daughter strained to the limits.

In truth, the bond between the pair had always been less than perfect, with Lana often leaving for long periods of time to work and conduct her frequent romances. This had led the child to wonder if her mother really loved her, and after the debacle of the Barker marriage, Cheryl found herself not only acting up in front of Turner, but also running away after her mother ordered her back to boarding school. The story goes that on her way to her Flintridge school she jumped out of the taxi, bid a friend goodbye with the words, "I'm not going back to school", and headed off into the streets of Los Angeles. She was found by a man while wandering around Skid Row, apparently being followed by some undesirables, and was taken to the local police station. The situation was eventually resolved and Cheryl returned to school, but not before the entire incident had made headlines around the world.

Facing financial hardship and with her career in freefall, Lana threw herself into the search for a great role, which she ultimately found in the tremendously successful *Peyton Place* co-starring Lee Philips and Lloyd Nolan. This was a great moment for Turner, but while the film would ultimately win her an Academy Award nomination, it was once again her personal life that hit the headlines – this time in the most dramatic fashion she could ever have imagined.

Johnny Stompanato was known as a hard man who had worked as a bodyguard for Mafia boss Mickey Cohen, but it was his good looks and reputation as a fine lover that first attracted Lana. Unfortunately, he was also extremely violent and during the course of their affair not only abused Turner on a number of occasions, but also found himself deported from the UK after beating his lover during the making of her movie, *Another Time, Another Place*. So bad was the beating, in fact, that the set had to be closed until she recovered, leading the British government to intervene and throw Stompanato out of the country.

Later Lana told the coroner's court that on one particular night in London, Stompanato allegedly got a razor from the bathroom and threatened to cut her face, declaring that he would start with a small cut to give her a taste of what it was like, before doing worse later on. In the end he didn't slash his lover, but by this time Lana Turner was ready to say goodbye, though several attempts were ultimately unsuccessful. As much as he seemed to dislike the actress, Stompanato was in no hurry to leave her, and after the fiasco in London she met her lover in Amsterdam and together they flew to Acapulco for two months, where they spent time arguing instead of relaxing. In fact, it would seem that the actress had actually thought she would be going to Acapulco on her own, as she had written to the hotel a few months before, reserving her regular bungalow and making no mention of Stompanato. By the time they arrived together, it was rumoured that the two never shared a room, Lana preferring instead to have separate accommodation from her volatile lover.

The manager of the hotel, Ted Stauffer, later told the *Los Angeles Times* that Lana's lover had "stuck like glue" and nobody ever had a chance to speak more than a few words to the actress the entire time she was there. However, on one occasion when Stauffer was able to get her alone for a minute, Turner did apparently hint that she was worried about the situation with Stompanato and was desperately trying to jilt him. "Johnny acted as if he knew it," the manager later told the press.

When the couple returned to the States, they were met at the airport by Turner's mother and daughter. The actress was in no hurry to declare any kind of love for Johnny and, in fact, during a short interview with waiting press, made the momentous decision to state that there was absolutely no romance between the couple at all. What Stompanato thought about this declaration is not known, but given his reputation it probably wasn't positive.

On the evening of the Academy Awards, where Lana was nominated for Best Actress, she celebrated with her daughter Cheryl, who was home from boarding school. The evening had been fun but darkness lay ahead when they returned to their Beverly Hills hotel and a tremendous fight broke out between Turner and Stompanato, who was furious that he had not been Lana's date for the evening. For Cheryl, this was her first taste of the abuse being suffered by her mother and as Johnny was threatening and hitting her mother, she pulled the covers up over her head in an attempt to drown out the noise. "I'm not proud of that but I did," she told KMIR 6 News many years later.

Despite the violence, it seems that Stompanato had set his goal on marrying Lana Turner and on at least one occasion he apparently took Cheryl out for hamburgers in an effort to win her over. His intention was for her to persuade her mother to consent to a wedding, though given his treatment of the woman, along with her desire to get away, this would seem something of a pie-in-the-sky idea. Indeed, Lana was so terrified of Stompanato that she would shake terrifically every time a quarrel erupted between them. With that in mind, marriage was the very last thing she ever wanted with him.

Several days after the Academy Awards, on 31 March 1958, more violence erupted when Lana and Cheryl were staying at the home of the actress's mother, Mildred, where they were readying themselves to move into their new home. Johnny was with Lana that day and started an argument over nothing in particular, only this time it was different, as Cheryl decided to confront her mother about it after he had left. The actress admitted to her daughter that Stompanato had hurt her in the past, and when asked why she wouldn't leave the violent man, Lana replied, "It isn't that easy." She then went on to explain how possessive he was, that she didn't have a moment to herself without him wanting to know what she was doing and who she was with. Both Cheryl and Lana were beside themselves with worry and it looked at that point as if the actress was never going to get away from Johnny Stompanato.

On 4 April 1958 – which also happened to be Good Friday – Lana was planning on spending Easter quietly with her daughter at their new home, 730 North Bedford Drive, where they had moved just three days before. Unfortunately, the arrival of Stompanato changed all that, and it was anything but a Good Friday for anyone involved. Lana had long since known the rumours of her boyfriend's Mafia connections, but recently she had become aware that not only was he working for Mafia boss Mickey Cohen, but for some reason he was also lying to her about his age, saying he was forty-one when he was only thirty-two. She decided to address the issues that evening and told her daughter that she was going to end the relationship once and for all. She told Cheryl not to believe anything Johnny said and to pay no attention to him, which the child had no intention of doing anyway since she had by now decided that he was not the sort of person with whom she wanted to spend time.

Of course, while Lana was insistent that the relationship would end, Stompanato had proved time and time again that he was not the type to go quietly. It was not long, therefore, before things turned ugly and a violent argument broke out between the pair in Lana Turner's bedroom. Cheryl was doing homework in her own room at the time and heard the man shouting, but it was when she heard him threaten to destroy not only her mother's looks, but also her family (including the child herself) that Lana's daughter decided something had to be done.

Cheryl went to see if her mother was okay, but fearing for her safety, Lana told her daughter to go back to her room. Instead – and in a sudden burst of daring protectiveness for Lana – fourteen-year-old Cheryl ran down to the kitchen and picked up a knife from the counter. She then turned and dashed back upstairs and listened outside Lana's bedroom. It was at that point that the door flew open and – according to Cheryl – Stompanato walked out of the room just as she was going in, and ran straight into the path of her knife. He looked her in the eyes; asked what on earth she had done; and then fell to the ground, lying on his back and making terrible gasping sounds as he lay dying.

Seeing the severity of what she had done, a shocked Cheryl ran back to her bedroom while Lana Turner rushed over to see what was wrong with her lover. She had not seen the knife and it was not until she lifted his cardigan that she realized there was a wound. She ran into the bathroom to retrieve a towel in order to staunch the bleeding. She could not believe it. She had wished her lover to leave, wondering if she would ever escape his violent outbursts, but had never wanted him dead. And yet there he was, in the middle of the bedroom in her new home, looking like something from a horror movie.

Lana's first reaction was to call the doctor, but not being able to recall his name she then took the decision to phone her mother, who in turn telephoned the doctor herself. Cheryl then returned to the bedroom where she too tried to help staunch the bleeding, this time with her mother's wash cloths that were found in the bathroom. "I didn't mean to do it," she told her mother to which Lana told her not to worry, that her grandmother was calling the doctor and everything would be okay.

Running once again from the bedroom, Cheryl called her father Stephen who soon arrived at the house to be greeted by his daughter running down the path to meet him. She ushered him inside and he ran up the stairs to Lana's bedroom where the actress was still with her lover. Declaring the scene "terrible", he took one look at the dying man and asked what had happened. "I did it, Daddy," came Cheryl's reply, though she assured him that she didn't mean to; that the man had been going to hurt her mother before she had come into the room.

Crane then took his daughter back to her bedroom, trying desperately to calm her down and assure her that everything would be okay. Shortly after, Lana's mother Mildred entered the house and first of all calmed down her granddaughter, before then taking matters into her own hands as she tried frantically to rouse the wounded man, rubbing his hands and calling his name. It was no good, however, and when she returned to Cheryl's bedroom where she and Stephen were sitting, Stephen took one look at the face of his ex-mother-in-law and knew that all hope was fading.

By the time the doctor eventually arrived, things were looking worse than ever; he demanded the actress call an ambulance and then gave Stompanato an injection of adrenalin.

The entire house was in an uproar by then, with Lana trying to call for an ambulance but not being able to find the right words when the operator began asking questions. The doctor eventually took over and while he talked to the ambulance service and another physician, Lana and her mother took it upon themselves to try and get air into the dying man by giving him mouth-to-mouth resuscitation.

While waiting for an ambulance to arrive, Stompanato's heart finally stopped beating. The doctor continued to work on him, but everyone knew it was too late. By this time the house began to fill with people including Lana's lawyer Jerry Giesler, several other doctors, the police and the ambulance crew. Everyone played a part in trying first of all to save the man, and second, when it was too late, to try to figure out exactly what had happened. It was not an easy task, however, as by this time Lana's mind was a blur, but eventually a statement was taken and the body of Johnny Stompanato was taken away for an autopsy.

The decision not to telephone the police straight away deeply upset Stompanato's family, who later complained to the newspapers that if they had called the police and an ambulance as soon as it had happened, the man could have still been alive. This was immediately ruled out by the autopsy surgeon, however, who found that the knife had pierced the abdominal wall, liver and aorta, meaning that Stompanato would have been dead within a very short time of the stabbing.

Cheryl Crane was taken from her Beverly Hills home and sent to juvenile hall for questioning, where the police did everything by the book. They were determined not to be told that they were letting the daughter of the great Lana Turner away with murder. "She will be treated no different than any other girl," declared Deputy District Attorney Manley Bowler. "She will be booked like any other juvenile and will be kept in Beverly Hills Jail overnight."

Meanwhile, back at the house, Cheryl's mother shocked everyone around her by declaring her intention to go to the morgue to see her ex-lover, a decision which was met by a locked door and the refusal by her publicist to let the actress anywhere near the body of Stompanato.

In the days to come things only got worse, and by this time Turner's ex-husband Stephen Crane had told her that he intended fighting for custody of their daughter. When a nurse was seen going into her Beverly Hills home, the actress was described as being on the verge of collapse, though this still did not stop the media interest in the story. In fact, it only made it worse and Lana was inundated with requests for interviews and press conferences – all of which she turned down, deeming them inappropriate.

Instead, she instructed celebrity lawyer Jerry Giesler to protect her from the unwanted attention, and he immediately released a statement describing how Cheryl had acted out of extreme fear. He also said that on several occasions the young girl had been witness to the man threatening not only her mother's face, but also revenge on her and Lana's ex-husband, Stephen Crane. Shockingly, when the police began interviewing Turner as part of their investigations, she became so distraught that she apparently asked if it was possible for her to take the blame for the murder herself. "That is impossible," came the reply.

Stompanato's brother Carmine arrived in California in the hope of meeting Lana, but was refused an audience. He left in disgust shortly afterwards, but not before he'd had the chance to air his grievances with the press, telling them that he believed there had been a lot of lies told about the death of his brother, and while he said he had no interest in prosecuting Cheryl himself, he just wanted the truth to come out. He also said it was "incredible" that a fourteen-year-old girl could stab a six-foot man to death, and added that in all the time they were together, it had been Turner who had chased his brother, not the other way around.

His stepmother also got in on the act when she told reporters that she was appalled her son's name was being dragged through the mud, especially as he had written to her from Acapulco, desperate for her to meet Lana when she was in California and hinting that they would soon marry. "We talk about you quite often, and she would like to know you, too," he had written to his stepmother. Embarrassingly for Lana, these claims of love between the two were backed up by a bracelet supposed to have been found on the body, with a love note from the actress engraved inside. Then came a lock of blonde hair, said to be from Lana, accompanying a photograph found in his wallet with an inscription signed "Lanita" – Johnny's pet name for his girlfriend.

Before leaving Los Angeles, Carmine Stompanato visited the police to demand that they look into the killing of his brother thoroughly and completely. They said they would, though the Chief of Police later hinted that he believed most of the investigation demands were brought on by Stompanato's boss, Mickey Cohen, who had sent two "close friends" to the police station with the man. Cohen himself had a lot to say when the press contacted him for a comment, backing up the family's opinion of Turner and expressing his disgust at her refusal to speak with Carmine. He also added that he was in possession of some steamy love letters from the actress to her dead lover, and that he was bitterly angry with Turner, claiming that she had not offered to share any of the expenses for the burial, leaving Cohen to "borrow $2300 to pay the whole tab".

Just a week after the death of Johnny Stompanato came the inquest, during which Lana Turner gave testimony, which some say was the greatest performance of her life. Clutching a handkerchief and visibly upset by what was going on around her, Turner took to the stand and described how on the afternoon of the killing she had gone shopping with her lover and then returned to Bedford Drive where some friends were waiting to see her. She then told the court that the friends had asked if she would like to go out to dinner with them but she refused as she had no one to look after her daughter. However, Stompanato had taken offence at not being invited along in the first place, which had caused something of a disagreement between the pair.

"Mr Stompanato was upset that I had even considered the idea of having dinner with friends, but I had not seen them for a long time," she said. She then described how she had confronted the possessive man with the words, "Surely I have a right to be able to see some people without your always being there . . . It was friendships that were long ago that you didn't even know about." When the man returned to the home later in the evening, he asked what time the friends had left. "He objected that they had stayed even an hour after he had left and words started and he was verbally very violent," Lana described.

The actress's testimony went on in that manner for some time, describing how Johnny was swearing in front of her daughter and following the actress around the house, all the time getting louder and more objectionable. At one point he apparently told her that she would never get away from him and that in the future, if he said jump, she would jump; if he said hop, she would hop. When it looked as though he was going to strike her again, the woman stood firm, telling the man that he must never touch her, that she was "absolutely finished" with the relationship and wanted him to get out. Describing the killing, the actress went on to say that her daughter had walked into the room as the door opened, and she believed that the girl had hit her lover in the stomach. "I swear it was so fast," she told the court. "The best I can remember they came together and they parted. I still never saw a blade."

After the jury heard witnesses that included Mickey Cohen, Lana's mother Mildred, a doctor, police officers and ex-husband Stephen Crane, it took just twenty minutes for the jury to decide that the death of Johnny Stompanato was justifiable homicide. This should have been the end of the matter but, unfortunately for Lana, this still did not convince her ex-lover's brother Carmine of her innocence and he went straight to the press. "You'll never convince me [of the story of Johnny's death]. She lied right from the beginning," he declared before asking the police (unsuccessfully as it turned out) to make Turner take a lie detector test.

The other members of his family did not believe the outcome either and assured everyone that their relative was a quiet man who was very much in love with the actress. Not so, said the Beverly Hills Police Chief Clinton Anderson, who described him as a gigolo who had been involved with the police on various occasions in the past. Other sources claimed he had forwarded his European hotel bills to Lana Turner, while it was also said he owed thousands to at least one other woman and was also suspected of blackmail attempts. If anyone wanted Johnny Stompanato's memory to be a positive one, it was becoming apparent very quickly that this was not to be the case.

On 24 April it was time for Cheryl to take part in proceedings at the Los Angeles Juvenile Court, which saw her being asked if she would like to take on a new persona in the hope of not being recognized as the killer of Stompanato. She declined the offer and instead decided to fight it out in the glare of the spotlight, which prompted the judge to say, "that's courage", before adding that he felt her to be a very bright girl who had a wonderful future ahead of her. "Don't let this destroy your future," he said. "Don't let all this attention that has been devoted to you, your mother and father during this period disturb your balance."

"I'll try," replied Cheryl.

After being released from juvenile hall, Cheryl went to live with her grandmother and later recalled that it was a terrible time for her as she had no idea what was going on and had limited access to her parents. Not only that, but the shutters on the house had to remain closed for fear that the ever-present paparazzi would take photographs through the window. "It was such a feeling of being entrapped," she later said in the 2001 documentary, *Lana Turner: A Daughter's Memoir*.

Meanwhile, threats began to come into the offices of

celebrity lawyer Jerry Giesler, who had managed to secure Cheryl's release from prison. In four days he was the victim of at least four threatening phone calls, which at first he dismissed as being from cranks, but when a stranger telephoned Giesler's wife at home and threatened to kill not only him but Turner as well, it was time to sit up and take notice. Another call came several days later from a sobbing woman, demanding that the lawyer keep the curtains of his home shut because the gang were "coming to get him". Thankfully the threats ultimately did not come to anything. The police began keeping a twenty-four-hour surveillance of both homes, but were keen to assure everyone that they were not "overly concerned".

Away from the threats and the custody battle came a new worry, this time from Stompanato's family, who filed a suit for damages worth $750,000 on behalf of the man's ten-year-old son. Not only that, but the suit brought up new rumours that Lana's lover did not die in the way first presented at all, but while he was lying flat on the bed, and that it could have been Lana who inflicted the fatal blow, not her daughter. There was further gossip that the death could have perhaps been a result of both Lana and Cheryl stabbing the man, all of which was vehemently denied by Turner and her representatives.

As if this weren't enough, Cheryl later went through another teenage rebellion which led to various scrapes with the law and a spell in a reformatory for girls who had "gone off the rails". This was a trying period for everyone involved, but eventually everything settled down; the paparazzi disappeared along with the lawsuits; and Lana and her daughter were left to get on with their lives.

However, while the Stompanato killing was shown by the court to be justified, this has not stopped rumours from spreading over the years, with some people still refusing to believe that it was Cheryl Crane who held the knife that evening. Instead, they prefer to think that it was Lana Turner herself, and that she put the blame on her daughter to protect her reputation. Just as it was back in the 1950s, these rumours are no more than unfounded gossip, and it would seem that if it really was Lana who had killed her lover then surely her daughter would have stepped forward by now in order to clear her own name.

She has never done this, however, and instead has always been steadfast in sticking by what she originally told the court. She has laughed off the conspiracy theories with the simple words: "Nobody wants to believe the truth." It would appear that she is right.

33

Marilyn Monroe: Suicide, Accident or Murder?

It may be over fifty years since Marilyn Monroe passed away, but her star continues to shine as brightly as it did in the 1950s. Her life was full of ups and downs, with various scandals along the way, but nothing was bigger than the headlines created by her death one Saturday evening during the first week of August 1962.

Marilyn's life had been a series of fabulous achievements and tragic let-downs. Her marriages to James Dougherty, Joe DiMaggio and Arthur Miller had failed; her attempts at motherhood had gone unfulfilled; and by 1962 she was alone and living in Los Angeles after a period of creative fulfilment in New York.

At first Marilyn had been perfectly happy to rent an apartment; in fact, she had moved back into the building in which she had once lived in the early 1950s. However, knowing that she had never owned a home by herself, buying a house became something of the highest importance, and the perfect property was found at 12305 Fifth Helena Drive. It was a small, Spanish-style house on a very quiet cul-de-sac, nothing like what you would expect a worldwide star to live in, but it fitted Marilyn's needs and she felt safe there, which was of the utmost importance.

Being raised as an orphan (though her parents were still alive) and in and out of foster homes for her entire childhood, the actual process of owning a home was a monumental achievement for Marilyn, and during 1962 she busied herself by making big plans for the home. She travelled to Mexico in order to buy furniture, and scoured the market on Hollywood's Olvera Street for knick-knacks and ornaments. She loved nothing more than planning her home, and during times when she was not working, could often be seen pottering around in her garden, playing with her dog Maf and planting plants and herbs.

Sadly, however, in spite of the positive exterior, there were still dark forces in Marilyn's life; mainly her problem with prescription drugs; hangers-on; and persistent illness. In May 1962 she infuriated her studio, Twentieth Century Fox, by jetting off to New York during the production of her last film, *Something's Got to Give.* The trip was in order to sing "Happy Birthday" to President John F. Kennedy and the studio made no secret of their dissatisfaction, telling her point blank that she was not allowed to go.

This decision was a complete turnaround from one they had made just months before, when they actually gave the star their blessing for the trip. But when shooting on the film got behind schedule, they decided there was just no time for Marilyn to travel out of state and revoked their permission. Always a rebel at heart, this did not deter Marilyn, and instead of obeying their wishes, she shocked everyone by travelling to New York regardless, eventually giving one of her most famous performances at Madison Square Garden.

Back in Los Angeles she resumed work on the film, taking part in a nude swimming scene which she said was designed to "knock Elizabeth Taylor from the front pages". She succeeded, though her time on set abruptly came to an end not long after her thirty-sixth birthday, when she was fired due – the studio said – to her numerous absences from the set. The newspapers went wild and Fox unfairly blamed Marilyn for every problem encountered during filming. Crew members sold their stories and sarcastically thanked her for losing them their jobs; and Marilyn found herself the butt of many Hollywood jokes and stories.

However, while she may have been out of work, the star was most definitely not about to give up, and for the next few months she took part in various photo sessions, regularly saw her psychiatrist and entertained friends in her new house. She made an effort never to stray far from the public's consciousness, and appeared in many newspaper and magazines all over the country, giving interviews and declaring her distaste for fame and the studio. Her efforts to stay in the public eye paid off and in the summer of 1962 it was believed that her lawyers were on the verge of securing a new agreement, which would mean a return to the set of *Something's Got to Give*.

On 4 August 1962 Marilyn puttered around her home and lounged in bed in her white towelling robe. "She wasn't ill," said her housekeeper, Eunice Murray, "she was just resting." She drank fruit juice and spoke to Mrs Murray about household matters, such as the three shipments of furnishings expected from Mexico, and a carpet which was being specially woven there. "The development of the house was so important to her," said Murray, before going on to say that in the weeks before her death, Marilyn had everything to live for. "The plans we made were so wonderful," she later declared.

During the course of the day, Marilyn received several phone calls and visitors, and in the afternoon she telephoned her old New York friend, the writer Norman Rosten, who found her "rambling but pleasant". She talked of the future and was very excited about visiting New York in the autumn: "Let's all start to live before we get old," she told him – words that stuck with him for the rest of his life.

Several workmen came and went, among them Murray's nephew Norman Jefferies and local mechanic Henry D'Antonio, who had been working on Mrs Murray's car and returned it some time during the day of 4 August.

All seemed fairly normal until 4.30 p.m. when Marilyn's psychiatrist, Dr Ralph Greenson, received a phone call, asking him to come to the house. Arriving at 5.15 p.m. he was said to have found his patient in a "somewhat drugged" and depressed state; and was so concerned he decided to telephone Marilyn's physician, Dr Hyman Engelberg, asking him to come to the home. The doctor denied the request, however, as he was going through marriage problems and was unable – or unwilling – to leave his home at that time.

Concerned for her welfare, Dr Greenson suggested to Marilyn that housekeeper Eunice Murray drive her to the beach and then stay at the house that night – something she had done on numerous occasions in the past. The actress agreed and Mrs Murray prepared herself to stay for the night.

That evening, Marilyn received several phone calls from her friend (and President Kennedy's brother-in-law) Peter Lawford, along with her stepson Joe DiMaggio Jr. During one conversation with Lawford, however, he became extremely concerned when her voice started to "fade out". He relayed his worries to friend and showbiz manager Milton Ebbins, who told him he would put in a call to lawyer Milton Rudin, just to make sure everything was all right. Rudin later rang Marilyn's home himself, but was unable to speak with her. Instead, he was assured by Eunice Murray that the actress was fine. He in turn relayed the information back to Peter Lawford and everyone resumed their evening.

According to Murray, at approximately 9 p.m. Marilyn appeared at her bedroom door and called out: "I think we'll not go to the beach, Mrs Murray. I think I'll turn in now." The housekeeper nodded, bade her goodnight and watched as Marilyn closed the door for the very last time.

At 4.25 a.m., the emergency services received the following call from 12305 Fifth Helena Drive: "Marilyn Monroe has died. She's committed suicide. I'm Dr Engelberg, Marilyn Monroe's physician. I'm at her residence. She's committed suicide."

When Sergeant Jack Clemmons arrived at the scene, he was concerned to discover Eunice Murray operating the washing machine, even though it was the middle of the night. Meanwhile, doctors Greenson and Engelberg were in the bedroom with

Marilyn's dead body, which was lying face down in the bed; her hair was a mess and the bed-stand was littered with pill bottles.

From the start, the story of Marilyn's discovery was patchy, to say the least, and changed numerous times from the 1960s to the 1980s when Eunice Murray eventually passed away. At the time of the death, Mrs Murray told police officers that she had awakened at around 3 a.m. and noticed a light and the telephone cord under Marilyn's locked door. This was an odd statement as Marilyn's room had a thick white carpet, so it would have been difficult to see a light under the door. Bizarrely, although she was steadfastly adamant that the door was locked when she spoke to police at the time, years later Murray changed her mind and claimed it had actually been closed but not locked at all. This was a startling revelation and has baffled fans ever since. Was her new statement the truth or just the result of old age confusing her memories? We'll never know.

But back in 1962, when Murray was sure she could not get into the bedroom, the housekeeper said that she phoned Dr Greenson, who instructed her to pound on the door and look through the window. She did as she was asked, firstly knocking unsuccessfully on the door, and then walking round to the front of the house and peering through a gap in the curtain, where she saw Marilyn lying on the bed. This comment is an interesting one as the actress was a well-known insomniac who slept with her curtains drawn tight to avoid sunlight streaming through the window. How could Murray see through the curtains in those circumstances? Only if Marilyn had accidentally left the curtains slightly apart that evening.

However, for now let's believe that the woman did gape through the curtains and did see Marilyn looking not quite right. Although the window was apparently open, Murray could not push back the curtains by hand in order to get a better look, owing to the fact that Marilyn's bedroom had wrought-iron grilles covering the front window. According to the housekeeper, she then went into the house and took a poker from the living-room fireplace, made her way back outside and managed to push the curtains back with the rod. That way she managed to take a good look at what was going on inside Marilyn's bedroom.

Murray said she discovered that the actress was lying on the bed with the phone in her hand, and "looking strange". She phoned Greenson, who dressed and readied himself for the journey to Fifth Helena, and then Dr Engelberg, who did the same. When Greenson arrived at 3.40 a.m., he used the same poker that Mrs Murray had used to peek through the curtains, in order to break the side window (which did not have a grille) thereby enabling him to enter the room and examine Marilyn. Apparently he then discovered that rigor mortis had already set in and when Engelberg arrived at 3.50 a.m. he immediately declared his patient dead.

It did not take long for the news to spread, and Marilyn's heartbroken ex-husband Joe DiMaggio flew into Los Angeles from San Francisco, booking himself into the Knickerbocker Hotel where Marilyn had driven him after their first date in 1952. From there he proceeded to arrange his ex-wife's funeral and burial at Westwood Memorial Village, where numerous members of Marilyn's family had been laid to rest years before. The evening before the funeral, he is said to have spent the night sitting quietly with her body in the chapel of rest.

So how and why did Marilyn Monroe pass away? Well, after an autopsy was performed and an investigation conducted, the official verdict was probable suicide, following "acute barbiturate poisoning". However, there are many people who dispute this and every year more and more outlandish stories are revealed, promising to solve her death "once and for all".

Dr Ralph Greenson said he could not believe Marilyn purposely took her own life, while Milton Wexler, a psychoanalyst who looked in on Marilyn when Greenson was out of town, never believed it either. Despite some hard times in 1962, the professional future actually looked bright for

Marilyn. *Something's Got to Give* was possibly going back into production and numerous projects were in the pipeline for autumn 1962 right through to 1963.

On a personal level, however, there are pointers to the possibility that Marilyn may have been struggling emotionally, and that she was unhappy enough to consider suicide. There had been various personal bumps in the road that year, including the cooling of her allegedly close friendship with the Kennedy brothers and her dismissal by Fox being spun to depict her as a has-been with her career in free fall. Friendship was always an issue, and Marilyn had few people in whom she could confide: she had virtually no friends who were not employed by her in some way.

To cap it all, ex-husband Arthur Miller had recently remarried, and his wife was expecting a baby – news of which might have served bleakly to highlight Marilyn's own childlessness. She had suffered several miscarriages during the Miller marriage, one of which had been on 1 August 1957, almost five years to the day before Marilyn died. Could this knowledge have been enough to tip Marilyn over the edge? Alas, we can only speculate.

On the other hand, the possibility that Marilyn was murdered is awash with conspiracy theories that range widely. There is talk that she may have been killed to stop her publicly discussing her relationship with the Kennedys; rumours of Mafia involvement and CIA plots; and even the absurd notion that she had to be silenced because she had found out that aliens had landed in America. Speculation is incessant; the so-called expert witnesses never-ending; the stories ever more outlandish. Without exception, they each raise questions of credibility and often lead us further away from the truth.

So could it all have been a tragic accident? Possibly. There are certainly those who believe Marilyn wanted people to know how desperate she felt, and took an overdose before calling for help. She had been known to do that before, only this time she had not been successful in gaining the help she wanted. Another theory is that Marilyn just lost track of how many pills she had taken during the course of the evening. Perhaps contradicting the suicide story, medical evidence would lead us to believe that it would have been incredibly hard for the drugs entering her body to have done so through her mouth, as there was apparently an absence of pills in her stomach.

So how could the drugs have entered the system? Her autopsy suggested that there were no needle marks, but that is not to say they were not there, carefully hidden from even the most expert of eyes. Also, apparently Marilyn frequently used enemas, including for the administration of prescription pills. This is an interesting comment, suggesting that she may have overmedicated that way, either by giving herself an enema or from someone giving one to her. With that in mind, could this account for Eunice Murray operating the washing machine in the middle of the night? Could the housekeeper have been the one who mistakenly gave her too much medication, and then washed away any evidence before the police arrived on the scene? It doesn't seem too far-fetched.

But perhaps the truth is that despite everyone having their own theories and suspicions, we will never know for sure what happened on the evening of 4 August 1962. Over the years the stories, lies and fables have spun out of control to the point where the truth is blurred beyond all comprehension. In the end, Marilyn Monroe is the only person who could possibly tell us the real, true story of what happened on that fateful night, but unfortunately when she passed away, she inevitably took all the secrets with her.

34

The Murder of Ramón Novarro

Many silent film stars came to grisly or disturbing ends shortly after the talkies were introduced, and the death of another should come as no surprise. However, for Ramón Novarro, his demise came not because of the stress of transitioning from one medium to another, but many years later, and in the most hideous way imaginable.

Born on 6 February 1899, José Ramón Gil Samaniego moved to Los Angeles with his family to avoid the Mexican Revolution. Coming from a well-to-do and influential family, Ramón had an air of sophistication about him that appealed to movie directors, and in 1917 he began making small appearances in a variety of silent movies, in which he was often compared to Hollywood legend Rudolph Valentino.

In 1923 Novarro made an impact when he starred in *Scaramouche*, and then after his appearance in 1925's *Ben Hur* his elevation to stardom was complete. His career went from strength to strength, and after Valentino's death in 1926, it was Novarro who inherited his crown, going on to appear with the likes of Joan Crawford, Lupe Vélez, Myrna Loy and Norma Shearer in a variety of critically acclaimed movies.

However, as was often the case, his career slowed somewhat with the advent of the talkies, as a result of his thick Mexican accent. But the actor was not one to give up on his career easily, and instead of mourning the loss of his once great silent acting roles, he began appearing in films that required a heavy accent, such as in *The Pagan* and *The Student Prince*.

As though knowing that his career in films would not last for his entire life, Novarro had developed a shrewd business head and when he was at his peak in the 1920s and 1930s, he began making a series of lucrative investments. By the time his career slowed, therefore, he then had the opportunity of taking the odd small movie role when he wanted, but was also able to live comfortably off the money he had raised during the highs of his career.

As a result of this sensible approach to business, Novarro led a secure life with very few money worries, though he did suffer drink problems which often gave him unwanted headlines from the 1930s onwards. It was one of the biggest struggles of his life, and one that is said to have started due to his inability truly to accept that he was homosexual; a guilt very much brought about by his strict Catholic upbringing. His alcoholism also led to brushes with the law due to drink driving. However, in 1962 his drinking seemed to have been conquered somewhat when his lawyer announced that Novarro had solved any psychological problems he had previously suffered from. "He has not driven a car or taken a drink for several months," the lawyer told reporters.

Unfortunately, this was not strictly true, as by 1968, Novarro was living at 3110 Laurel Canyon Boulevard, where it was noted that the bins outside his home were filled with empty bottles of vodka, whisky and gin. But despite his advancing years, and troubles with alcohol, the actor was still busy, making occasional appearances in television programmes such as *The High Chaparral*, *Bonanza* and *Rawhide*. He had also started to write his autobiography, on which he was still working on the ill-fated evening of 30 October 1968.

For some time, Novarro had used gay escort agencies and he was well known in the "hustling" community. So it was that on that particular afternoon, two brothers, Paul and Tommy Ferguson, took it upon themselves to call the actor on the chance he would invite them over. According to testimony, Paul telephoned the actor and introduced himself as a relative of "Larry", Ferguson's brother-in-law. Novarro was acquainted with him and, as a result, he spoke to Paul for a while before the actor eventually agreed that both brothers could come over to his Laurel Canyon home. Shortly afterwards, at approximately 4.30 p.m., they arrived at the house, and found Novarro already prepared for them, wearing a smart dressing gown, with his beard and moustache nicely trimmed.

The actor offered the boys cocktails and a snack of chicken gizzards and cheese crackers. He talked and sang a little, and then ordered cigarettes from a nearby drugstore. As luck would have it, Novarro's secretary of nine years, Edward Weber, was enjoying his evening off, but just happened to be calling into the store when the order came through. Hearing his employer's name, he then told the shopkeeper that he would deliver the cartons himself, though he later admitted to being somewhat confused by the order, as he had never known Novarro to smoke.

Weber made his way over to Laurel Canyon and knocked on the door. There he was met by the surprised actor, who obviously had no idea Weber would be visiting him that evening and was somewhat confused by his arrival. The secretary gave his boss the cigarettes and, as he did so, noted the trimmed moustache and smell of lotion, though did not comment on it. "I had the feeling that he had guests," he later said. He was right, of course, and after bidding Weber goodbye, Novarro headed back inside the house, where the Ferguson brothers played around on his piano and smoked the cigarettes he had just bought for them.

The evening is believed to have turned more intimate as it wore on, but did not go the way Novarro – or anyone else for that matter – expected things to go. Sadly, by the time the brothers left, Ramón Novarro was dead, and one of the biggest Hollywood scandals was about to begin . . .

On the morning of 31 October, Edward Weber returned to work, let himself into the house and was greeted by a dreadful sight. It was obvious that there had been a struggle in the house: there were bloodstains splattered on the carpets, walls and ceiling; furniture was overturned and Ramón's eyeglasses were broken on the floor. Added to that, there were cigarette butts everywhere, burns on the furniture and other debris littered all around.

The secretary was in great shock and deeply worried about what had gone on and where his employer was. He looked around the house, calling out Novarro's name as he did so, but it was not until he entered the actor's bedroom that he was met by a sight he would remember for the rest of his life. There was the body of the 1920s film star, lying face up on the bed, completely nude. His wrists and ankles were tied with cord and it was evident that his body had taken a severe and brutal beating. "It all indicated a fight or struggle had taken place," Detective Sergeant Robert T. Smith later testified.

Police were quickly called and an investigation began. Meanwhile, reporters got wind that something serious had happened at the Laurel Canyon home and rushed to find out as much as they could. Gathered outside, the world's press waited for an explanation as to how or why the beloved actor had been so brutally taken away, until finally the police gathered them together and read out a statement. The hungry reporters took out their notebooks, poised to write down every ounce of information, but the comments handed over by the police somehow ended in more questions than answers.

The officers confirmed that Ramón Novarro was dead – it would appear murdered – but stated that they could find absolutely no motive for the killing. Yes, there had been a great struggle – the state of the house was testament to that – but on closer inspection it did not appear that any of the actor's possessions were missing. Still, they were unwilling to rule out any lines of enquiry at this stage, including the possibility that it could very well have been a robbery gone wrong.

At this point the police really did not know much at all, though they did reveal that they had found bloodied clothes –

believed to have been those of the killer – on a nearby fence. The reporters noted it all down but when no more answers were forthcoming, they were left with the possibility that the killing could have been as a result of not one but several motives, and it was all a confusing mystery.

However, while the police had been able to reveal certain aspects of the case, there was one thing that they chose to keep secret from the media: they had found the possible murder weapon. The actor's walking stick had been located near to the body, only it was not in one piece; it had been broken in two. Could it have broken while the killer was bludgeoning the actor to death? They believed so, but knowing the murderers would most certainly be keeping track of the case, the police decided they needed to keep this information to themselves until the moment was right to release it.

An autopsy was performed on the body of Ramón Novarro, which showed that his death was attributed to "suffocation due to massive bleeding due to fracture of the nose and laceration of the lips and mouth". Still, while the police now had a reason why his body had finally given up, they were no further forward in finding out how or why it happened. Extra detectives were assigned to the case while the body of the once-great Novarro lay in state, mourned by everyone from waiters who had served him in restaurants to a housewife forever grateful for a fan letter he had written some thirty years before. The outpouring of grief was immense, and his death was commemorated around the world by everyone who remembered his glory days in silent movies.

Just a week later, the world was surprised to learn that two brothers, twenty-two-year-old Paul and seventeen-year-old Tommy Ferguson were arrested and booked on suspicion of murder. Their names were released to the press and Paul apparently responded to the development by – quite disturbingly – trying to gouge out his eyes with nothing but his own fingernails. This dramatic episode did not gain the man any sympathy but did make headlines, and newspapers around the country were left wondering what evidence the police must have to be so sure the brothers had performed the crime in the first place.

Officers refused to comment on the case, but the arrival of Tommy Ferguson's girlfriend Brenda Lee Metcalf put the rumour mill into overdrive, and it was soon discovered that she might just be the missing link between the death and the subsequent arrests. Shortly after, the brothers were indicted for the murder of the aging star, and by January 1969 it was revealed that they had initially been investigated by the police after conducting a routine check of Novarro's phone records. There had been one number that particularly intrigued them as it had been called on the very evening of the murder for a staggering forty-eight minutes. An investigation was immediately conducted and, after finding that it belonged to Brenda Metcalf, police were quick to get in touch.

What they discovered was truly horrifying. Miss Metcalf confirmed that she had indeed received a phone call from the house that evening, and it had been from her boyfriend, Tommy Ferguson. She went on to explain that he had freely admitted he was with the actor, and that she then asked him what he was doing there.

"He's trying to get me into pictures," he replied, before oddly changing his mind and declaring he had made a mistake, that it was Paul who would be in pictures, not himself. According to Metcalf, Ferguson left her hanging on the telephone several times while he went off to talk to his brother, get cigarettes and drink beer. Then some way into the call he apparently announced that they knew there was $5,000 in the house and intended to tie the actor up to find out where it was.

Metcalf was said to be horrified. "Don't do it," she begged, "you'll get yourself into trouble." Then, quite disturbingly, the young woman told the police that at one point near the end of the call she heard screaming coming from somewhere within the house. When she asked Tommy what was happening, he replied, "Paul is probably just trying to scare him or hit him with something." He then told the woman that he had to go to see what was happening, as he did not want Paul to really hurt Ramón Novarro.

After the body had been found, Metcalf received one more phone call from Tommy Ferguson, this time asking if she had heard of Novarro's death and then telling her that, on the night in question, he had bent down over the actor and could tell immediately that he had died. Metcalf was horrified to think that her boyfriend was in some way associated with the murder but decided not to say anything to the police about the calls she had received. Her decision may have had something to do with the fact that Tommy had told her that he and his brother were planning to travel back to Chicago, rather than stay in California and risk arrest. Whatever her reasons, the woman did not expect to speak to the police at all until they tracked her down, and she subsequently opened up and confessed everything she knew.

The phone-call mystery was for the most part solved, but something else bothered officers deeply. When Novarro's body was found, they had discovered bizarre messages on the mirror, marks on the actor's neck and the word "Larry" scrawled on to the sheet next to his body. Nobody had any idea who the mysterious Larry was, but it was a big clue in the hunt for the killer and police were desperate to find him. After the phone-call information had implicated the Ferguson brothers, they began investigating any links they had to anyone called Larry, and quickly discovered that Paul Ferguson's estranged wife, Mary, had a brother with the very same name.

As the brothers were not particularly great fans of Larry and were aware that Novarro had known the man prior to the murder, police believed that the brothers scrawled the brother-in-law's name in an attempt to divert any suspicion away from themselves and on to the innocent man. It was also noted that the name had been written several times on a notepad next to the bed, and a pen had been placed in the dead man's hand to try and make it look as though he was attempting to leave a clue. However, the fact that his hands were tied tightly behind his back was a sure sign that the dying actor had not been the person to scrawl any of the words.

When the case went to court in 1969, it made headlines around the world. Because of his criminal past, Tommy Ferguson was put on trial as an adult despite his young age, though it was made clear that he would be spared the death sentence if found guilty. Elder brother Paul Ferguson's future did not look so bright, however, when Deputy District Attorney James M. Ideman indicated that he would certainly be seeking a death sentence for his part in the slaying.

The trial began with jurors being told that Ramón Novarro was killed with his own cane, after "wining and dining" the brothers at his home. Ideman described how the two men had tortured the aging actor in a bid to find out where he hid his money, reviving him in the shower when he began to pass out from his injuries. He went on to tell the court that the brothers later laid Novarro on the bed and tied his hands behind him with an electric extension, while they resumed the beatings in their quest for cash.

The emphasis was very much on the money aspect of the case – the idea that the Ferguson brothers thought the actor kept large amounts of cash around the house. But why the men presumed there was a lot of money in Novarro's possession was a mystery, particularly as they had only just met him that night and did not seem to know anything much about his life or career until that point. Had they been told by a third party that Novarro was wealthy and, if so, who? Did they go round to the house knowing for sure that there was money somewhere, or did they just presume that to be the case after he had told them of his fame in the days of silent movies?

Nobody seemed to have the answers to these questions, but one thing was clear – Ramón Novarro did not seem to be a man who kept bundles of cash lying around the house. Indeed, his secretary Edward Weber recalled that at the time of his death, the only money he knew the actor to have on his person was $45 in his wallet – and that was only because he had received payment from a cheque he had received a few days before.

When Brenda Metcalf took to the stand, she was nervous and near tears. Defence lawyers Richard Walton and Cletus Hanifin objected to her testifying against the brothers, although Superior Judge Mark Brandler swept their concerns aside and let the girl recall the conversation she'd had on the evening of the murder.

The girl repeated everything she had earlier told police: that Tommy Ferguson phoned her from the home and that Novarro was being beaten in a bid to find $5,000. The brunette's story stunned jurors, particularly when she described that during the call, her boyfriend had actually managed to ask her to marry him. She did not declare what her answer was, though; she declined to look anywhere near Ferguson in the courtroom, so it was pretty clear what she thought of him at that very moment.

Next on the stand came Victor Nichols, a friend of Paul Ferguson, who admitted to everyone that he had been the one to provide the brothers with Novarro's phone number. Not only that, but he had received a visit from them shortly after midnight on 31 October 1968, explaining that they were in trouble. When asked by Nichols what was wrong, Paul Ferguson replied, "Tom hit Ramón . . . Ramón is dead." They had been drinking, Nichols said, and as he served coffee, Tommy Ferguson had fallen asleep on the sofa. "You better wake him up," Nichols told Paul, before adding that he did not want to become involved with whatever had gone on that night.

When Tommy Ferguson woke up, a furious Nichols asked how he could possibly have done such a thing as kill the aging actor. "I hit him several times very hard and he is dead . . ." was all Tommy apparently had to say. Nichols had heard enough; as he had previously told Paul, he wanted nothing to do with their crimes, so he gave the brothers money for a taxi and sent them on their way. That, he hoped, would be the last he would see of the Ferguson brothers.

The testimony of both Metcalf and Nichols was confusing to say the least. One said it was Paul who had administered the beating, while the other said it was Tommy. It was very apparent early on, therefore, that this would be no easy case, and in the weeks that went by, things only became more and more bewildering.

On Friday, 22 August 1969, Dr Vernon J. Miller took to the stand to explain that Paul Ferguson suffered from a sociopathic disturbance and a chronic brain disease when drinking alcohol. The doctor said that while Novarro was attacked, Ferguson could have been mentally ill and a danger to both himself and others. He was able to come to this conclusion, he explained, because of an examination he had conducted where Ferguson was given twelve ounces of whisky and beer to drink. His "abnormalities" had come to light shortly afterwards. This excuse did not earn any sympathy from the Deputy District Attorney, however, who was placing the blame firmly at the door of Paul Ferguson, mentally ill or not.

On Monday, 25 August, came the moment for which everyone was waiting: Paul Ferguson took to the stand himself. From the moment he stood up, the gloves were off and he refused to take any blame for what had happened to Ramón Novarro. In his testimony he assured jurors that it was his brother Tommy, not himself, who had carried out the beating, and that he had been asleep the entire time. According to him, Tommy Ferguson had called his girlfriend on the house phone, before disappearing to the patio with Novarro, while Paul passed out after drinking vodka, tequila and beer.

He told the court that his brother had woken him up some time later with the words, "This guy's dead", and it was only then that he knew what had gone on. According to Paul he then walked into the bedroom to discover Novarro lying on the floor, covered with blood and his hands tied behind him. Then, according to the brother, he touched him on the shoulder and discovered his skin felt "starchy and tight like paper . . . I was sad," he said. When questioned further, Paul added that he had endured two previous weeks of bad luck and was appalled that he had now been thrown into the circumstances surrounding the death of a movie star. "I wanted to know why everything was happening to me," he told the astonished court.

Paul Ferguson went on to say how he had wanted to call the police, but that his brother put a stop to the plan by claiming they could cover everything up to look like a robbery. "Why did you join in this plan?" asked his attorney, to which Ferguson replied, "Stupidness." He then went on to deny that he had ever hit the actor with his cane, and claimed that the first time he had seen it was when it was brought into the courtroom. This information did not sit well with Tommy Ferguson, however, who sat glaring at him from across the room, shaking his head in frustration. It was obvious to all that he couldn't believe the words coming out of his brother's mouth that day.

The testimony turned to what Paul Ferguson had thought of the aging actor. "I thought he was a nice guy," he said, before explaining that Novarro had told him he could be a superstar like a young Burt Lancaster or Clint Eastwood. If the testimony was to be believed, it seemed that Ramón Novarro was so taken by Ferguson that he even called his agent to see about getting him into the movies. This little nugget of information was pounced on by the defence team, who presented it as a good reason why Paul Ferguson could not possibly be the murderer. "He would have no reason to kill a man who might have become his benefactor," they argued.

When cross-examined, it was put to the elder brother that he was just saying his brother murdered the actor to spare himself the death sentence. This was quickly denied by Paul, however, who once again told the court, "I didn't kill him, it was my brother," though nobody seemed to believe him. He then alleged that he had initially lied to police to protect Tommy, though had later broken down and confessed his brother's guilt after hours and hours of questioning.

In spite of being so adamant that Tommy had been the murderer, Paul did admit that he was continually haunted by the possibility that he had got so drunk he had murdered the man himself without realizing it. "If I killed Mr Novarro, I'd like to know that I did it," he said, before adding somewhat sincerely that deep down he knew he hadn't done it, because it had been Tommy who told him that Novarro was dead.

Several days later the court had a chance to hear another version of events when pale, nervous Tommy Ferguson took to the stand. It came as no surprise to anyone when he placed the blame for the death squarely on the shoulders not of himself, but on his brother, Paul. "I told a good many people I had done it because Paul told me to spread it around," he admitted, but explained his change of mind came after hearing that the actor had been bludgeoned by his own walking stick. "It turned my stomach against Paul," he said.

Explaining his version of events, Thomas told the court that they had both gone to Novarro's house to "hustle" him, and had no intention of murdering or robbing the actor at all. According to Tommy, after the killing happened, Paul Ferguson suggested to his younger brother that if he confessed to the crime, he would probably get only six months in a juvenile facility because of his age.

Tommy admitted that he did think he should confess to the slaying because he felt sorry for his brother. "He kept talking himself down," he said. He then started to speak about the visit they had made to their friend Victor Nichols's house, where Paul told him that his younger brother was the one who had killed the actor. But while Tommy told the court that had been a lie and denied ever undertaking the killing himself, he did admit to one cover up: that of making it appear to be a robbery. The motive of that, he admitted, was to try to divert suspicion away from the two of them.

It was soon time to talk about the now infamous telephone call between Tommy Ferguson and his girlfriend. The young man described how he had been talking to Metcalf but towards the end of the conversation had heard noises. Presuming there was a fight going on in the bedroom, he proceeded to hang up the phone, get two beers from the kitchen and then go to investigate what was going on. Once in the bedroom he was shocked to find Novarro lying on the bed with blood oozing from his face, nose and lips while his brother stood nearby. "Take him to the shower and clean him up," he reported his elder brother as saying to him.

When showering, the younger brother begged Novarro not to say anything to Paul Ferguson as he might become violent. Since it was apparent that there had already been more than a little violence in the house that night, this was a mute point, but nevertheless Tommy Ferguson told the jury that he was concerned enough for the man not to be even more hurt than he already was. "I have always been afraid of my brother," he told the courtroom.

Unfortunately, if testimony is to be believed, his warning did not save Ramón's life, as very soon afterwards Tommy found him lying in a pool of blood on the floor. When asked why he did not stop Paul beating him up, the younger brother strangely answered that he never saw him do anything. This was an odd answer, particularly as even if he wasn't in the room at the time of the beating, he would surely have heard something going on, just as he had done earlier. The fact that he was now saying that he had not been aware of his brother doing anything to the actor was confusing to say the least.

More bewildering testimony came when Tommy was asked who had tied Novarro's hands. He didn't appear to know and then told the court that while he had a memory of his brother doing the deed, he was confused as Paul "keeps telling me . . . trying to plant in my head . . . that I tied him". During cross-examination, however, his story changed, and he admitted that it was he, not Paul, who firstly had decided to tie the actor's hands together, and secondly actually proceeded to do the task.

The contradictory testimony continued with a discussion as

to why the brothers had written messages on the mirror and scratched marks into Novarro's neck. "We tried to make it look like some girls had committed the murder," Tommy said. Then, when the subject of money came up, the brother denied all knowledge of trying to find $5,000 in the apartment; they had gone there to hustle the actor, not burgle him, he claimed.

There then followed an angry scene when Tommy Ferguson told the court that when helping Novarro to the shower, the aging actor had muttered the words, "Hail Mary full of grace." Paul Ferguson, who had been listening to the testimony closely, suddenly launched an attack on his stunned younger brother, calling him a "punk liar" and a "son of a bitch". The brother's yell preceded him throwing a pen at Tommy, missing him by a mere fraction.

Spectators in the gallery, who had previously been nodding off with the sheer weight of the testimony, were suddenly awake and interested to know what would happen next. They were more enthralled than the judge was, however, and he immediately sent the jury out of the room and told Paul in no uncertain terms that he would be bound and gagged if he ever disrupted the court in that way again.

There was a surprise in court on 5 September with the arrival of Mrs Lorraine Smith, the mother of the Ferguson brothers. She managed to confuse proceedings even more than before by asserting that she had received five letters from her youngest son, telling her that both brothers had been responsible for the killing of Ramón Novarro. When asked where these letters were now, she infuriated everyone by stating, "I threw them away." She also denied rumours that she'd told Tommy to take full blame for the killing; saying "I meant I wanted him to tell the truth. I don't think either of them did it."

The long and disturbing testimony from both sides was finally at an end on 8 September, and on the 17th, the jury found both Ferguson brothers guilty of murder in the first degree. During the penalty trial a week later, a furious Paul

Ferguson stunned onlookers by apparently calling Ideman "a pig" and accusing him of falsifying evidence and lying. He also turned his attentions to the jury; "I didn't do it," he wept, though no one appeared to believe him.

Meanwhile, Tommy Ferguson surprisingly decided to "admit" to the crime once and for all, by announcing, "I caused his death. He died of a broken nose and I am the one who busted his nose." Why ever did you do such a thing? he was asked, to which he replied that he had considered Ramón Novarro to be "just an old punk".

This revelation could have been devastating, but Ideman wasted no time in announcing to the court that he believed the younger brother's "confession" was just a last-minute attempt to create doubts in their mind. Tommy retorted that he had decided to tell the truth because he didn't want it on his shoulders that his brother was sent to the gas chamber, while "I sit [in prison] like Mr Cool."

Ideman played along with the scenario and asked the younger brother straight out if he had murdered Ramón Novarro. "I caused his death . . . He caused his death . . . We both caused it. He was as much a part of it as I was," Tommy replied. Strangely, the "we" in question, according to Ferguson, was not his brother, but Ramón Novarro himself.

Ideman then asked Ferguson if it had bothered his conscience when he had previously blamed the killing on his brother. "Not a bit," he declared, before explaining that he had been told beforehand that Paul would likely get charged with manslaughter, while he would get off with the crime once and for all. "It's not our fault we got a dumb jury," he said.

But regardless of last-minute claims of guilt, in the end the two feuding brothers were sentenced to life in prison for their crimes, though by the time they were released, they had actually only served seven years. Tommy Ferguson later committed suicide, while at the time of writing, Paul Ferguson is currently in prison after committing another crime. He is said to spend his time writing books and stories.

35

The Bizarre Death of Albert Dekker

Albert Dekker was a character actor who was best known for his part in the 1940 film *Dr Cyclops* (1940), playing the role of Dr Alexander Thorkel. However, unfortunately for him, it is for his mysterious and weird death that he is most famous these days.

Born Albert Van Ecke on 20 December 1905, he grew up in New York with plans to attend Bowdoin College in order to become a psychiatrist. However, an introduction to Broadway actor Alfred Lunt put paid to any aspirations of being a doctor, and he instead made his stage debut in 1927 in a play called *Marco's Millions*. Albert then moved to Hollywood in 1937 to try his hand at movies, where he achieved some success, appearing in films such as *Strange Cargo* (1940) and the James Dean movie, *East of Eden* (1955).

Dekker's career was spent for the most part moving between the mediums of movies and theatre, and he achieved great success on Broadway in Arthur Miller's play, *Death of a Salesman*. In the movies he acquired a name for himself as a "barrel-chested character actor", and at one point in the 1940s he even tried his hand at politics, serving as the Democratic Assemblyman for the 57th district in California. However, this achievement got in the way of his acting career, so he stepped down at the end of his term, although he maintained a fairly outspoken interest in politics and at one point even found himself on Senator McCarthy's anti-communist "blacklist", much to his surprise.

In 1929 he married Esther Guernini and they had three children before later divorcing, though they kept in touch for the sake of their children. In April 1957, while Dekker was in Palm Beach, Florida, appearing in the Agatha Christie play, *Witness for the Prosecution*, their son Jan was found dead in the family home in Hastings-on-Hudson, New York. According to Dekker, the sixteen-year-old Jan had been experimenting with constructing a rifle silencer when the gun suddenly went off, piercing his right eye and killing him immediately. He was found in his bedroom by his mother, lying on a .22 calibre rifle and clutching a piece of cloth in his left hand. The tragic death was later pronounced as accidental by the coroner, though questions remained, mainly involving why he was in possession of a highly dangerous weapon in the first place.

After the tragedy, Albert Dekker's film career started to wind down somewhat, and as he got older he resigned himself to no longer trying to make it big in the movies. Instead, he was happy with the parts he was able to win and concentrated on making appearances on television shows such as *Bonanza* and *Mission: Impossible.*

In his personal life, the divorced Dekker eventually became involved with a woman called Geraldine Saunders, who later told reporters they were due to be married in summer 1968. However, this date never came for the couple, as death was about to come knocking on Dekker's door . . .

The actor had just returned from filming on location in Mexico, and on 2 May 1968 he and Saunders went to the Huntingdon Hartford Theatre, where they enjoyed their last evening together, at the opening of Zero Mostel's play *The Latent Heterosexual.* Dekker then made plans to see Saunders the next evening before returning to his apartment at 1731 North Normandie Avenue, Los Angeles. However, when he did not show up as planned, Saunders became worried and tried to reach him many times over the course of the next few days. Strangely, all calls went unanswered, so finally the woman decided to go round to Dekker's apartment to see for herself what had happened to her fiancé.

On 5 May, Geraldine arrived at Dekker's apartment where she was shocked to find his door covered in notes from concerned friends desperate to get hold of him. A sense of foreboding overcame her and she was so concerned that something awful had happened that she immediately ran down to alert the manager of the building, telling him that she had been unable to contact her partner for several days and was now worried that he was ill – or worse – inside his apartment.

The manager listened to her story and made the decision to use his pass key, opening the door to the actor's apartment and gingerly entering with Geraldine. They were both apprehensive about what they might find inside, but at first all looked to be okay. Certainly there was no sign of an intruder or a burglary, but there was also no sign of the actor either, which was rather concerning.

The two shouted his name over and over but to no avail, until finally the only room left to look in was the bathroom, which they were disturbed to discover was locked from the inside by a chain. By this point it was obvious that if Dekker was anywhere in the apartment, it had to be in this room, so the couple managed to break in and discovered a sight they would remember for the rest of their lives.

There was Albert Dekker, naked and kneeling in the bathtub with a noose tied one end around his neck and the other around the shower rod. The body was in "complicated knots" according to detective Daniel K. Stewart, who appeared on the scene shortly afterwards; his hands were cuffed; and hypodermic needles stuck out of his arms. Not only that but explicit words were scrawled over his body and on closer inspection the apartment contained a large number of women's clothes, whips and chains.

At first it looked as though the death was a suicide and was listed that way by the authorities. However, this was soon changed by the Deputy Coroner Herbert McRoy, who declared, "We have no information that this individual planned to take his own life, so it will be listed as an accidental death." But in spite of the ruling, everyone had to admit that the whole thing was bizarre: "This is certainly a strange death," McRoy told reporters. "But just because there was a rope around his neck does not mean that he committed suicide."

Still, an accidental death seemed a rather bizarre theory, given the way the man was found, and it was not long before rumours began to circulate that Albert Dekker had been murdered after a robbery gone wrong, as various items were discovered to be missing from his apartment. It could very well be the case that the man was killed after a bungled theft, but this would in no way explain the bizarre way Dekker was found. For a burglar to kill someone who has come home unexpectedly is not unheard of, but for him to then truss the victim up like a turkey and hang him from the shower rail calls for a little too much imagination.

Over the years it has become more and more likely that neither murder or suicide were the real reasons for the death of Albert Dekker, and instead it has been put forward that perhaps Dekker was a fan of autoerotic asphyxiation – cutting off the air supply to heighten orgasm. This would certainly account for the rope around his neck, but this theory has in turn presented further questions, such as was he alone when the deed happened?

It would seem possible that he was, given the fact that the bathroom was chained from the inside with no other way of gaining exit. However, it still doesn't explain how he managed to cuff his hands, stick needles into his body and then finally place a noose around his neck and over the shower rail. Unless, of course, this was a well-practised event – a way of releasing tension that the actor had performed on many occasions over the years.

In spite of all the rumours, stories and hearsay, it seems as though we will never know the full story of how and why Albert

Dekker passed away, and his death will always be something of a mystery. But one thing's for sure – his bizarre and unexplained death has ensured he will be remembered for many years to come, though unfortunately, mainly for the wrong reasons.

36

The Death of Pete Duel

It has long been reported that the Christmas and New Year period sees a shockingly high rate of people falling into depression and even committing suicide. This is easy to believe, with the cheer and goodwill experienced by many manifesting itself as deep sadness in others, but in actual fact the idea that suicide rates go up around the holidays is false. There are exceptions, of course, and certainly in the case of actor Pete Duel, Christmas 1971 was neither merry nor bright, and the sadness he had felt for many years came to an abrupt and tragic conclusion.

Born on 24 February 1940, Peter Ellstrom Deuel grew up in Penfield, New York, where he paid no real attention to his studies, but had a very keen interest in performing in school plays and taking part in sports. He was a scout, enjoyed counselling others, loved aeroplanes, and had a great fascination with nature and the countryside. Summer vacations at a log cabin in Canada were something both Peter and his siblings greatly looked forward to, especially since it was one of the only times they could have the full attention of their busy doctor father.

When he turned seventeen, Peter tried to join the Air Force but was rejected due to vision impairment. He took the news badly as it had been his dream to join up, though he eventually pulled himself together and headed off to college to study liberal arts. Unfortunately, what should have been a carefree time as a student turned to tragedy when his life was almost ended in a horrific car crash, which broke his pelvis and almost severed his tongue. The crash shook his entire world, but luckily he made a complete recovery, and ultimately it changed his life by forcing him to realize that what he really wanted to do was move to New York and study to be an actor. He did well and it wasn't long before his ambitions took him to Los Angeles to find fame and fortune under the name of Pete Duel.

Out in California, Duel managed to find regular work in television programmes such as *Channing* with Jason Evers and a comedy series entitled *Gidget*. Another sitcom followed in the shape of *Love on a Rooftop*, although when that was cancelled after just one series, Duel decided to expand his career by trying his hand at more serious roles and movies.

It was a good move and Duel became very successful in both television and movies, before also dabbling in politics in the late 1960s. However, his private life was not easy; he suffered from epilepsy which was made worse by drinking alcohol, and despite having various female admirers over the years, Duel never seemed to find the right person with whom to settle down. He once told a reporter, "Having a marriage when you're in show business and making it work is damn hard. It's damn hard for anybody. We weren't built to be with just one person all the time."

In spite of his pessimism in the area of love, Duel finally found love with Kim Darby, an actress he had met while working on the film *Generation*. However, despite introducing her to his parents and declaring that she was "the one", his world came crashing down in early 1970 when she broke the news that she was to marry a man she had only just met. Duel was extremely distraught, particularly when reporters started knocking on his door for a statement and then describing the spurned lover's failed relationship in all its glory in their newspapers.

For reasons known only to herself, Kim Darby had decided to marry the virtual stranger over Duel, but as one might expect, it did not work out the way she had thought. Just a short time after her wedding the relationship broke down and Darby immediately began contacting Pete Duel again. Her attempts at reconciliation were futile, however, as he had by now moved on to a relationship with a woman called Dianne Ray, and was said to be happily settled.

Around this time, Duel was offered the role of outlaw Hannibal Heyes, aka Joshua Smith, in *Alias Smith and Jones*. Unfortunately, the glow of winning another acting job quickly wore off when faced with the long and tiring hours involved in working on the series. Having no time for a social life was stifling and it wasn't long before Duel was complaining that he had no time for anything outside of work. Inevitably this meant that there was virtually no time for his love life either, and his relationship with Dianne Ray slowly became increasingly strained.

Then, as if that wasn't bad enough, devastation came when Duel crashed his car into another vehicle while intoxicated. Fortunately he had not been physically injured in the crash, but the people in the other car were hurt, and this knowledge played on his conscience for the rest of his days. He felt so bad, in fact, that during his subsequent trial, the actor sat down to write a long, heartfelt letter about his feelings regarding the tragedy, and presented it to the judge. The actor was then placed on two years' probation and his licence was understandably revoked.

Professionally things were becoming a nuisance for Pete Duel, and the long hours spent on the set of *Alias Smith and Jones* were increasingly getting him down. It wasn't so much the nature of the show that bothered him, but the regimented system of working on one programme one day, then another the day after. Duel wished he could have more time to prepare, but the schedule just would not allow it and the frustration took its toll. Added to his frustration was the fact that he now had to be driven to and from work, which made him feel as though he had no freedom in his life whatsoever; every day seemed to be controlled from morning until night by the studio.

In December 1971, he spoke to columnist Cecil Smith, and expressed his dislike for working on television: "Any series is a big fat drag to an actor who has any interest in his work," he said. "You slowly lose any artistic thing you may have. It's utterly destructive." When asked if he would be happier working on another series, he shrugged. "Exchange one kind of trash for another," he replied and complained that the whole thing made him weary.

Then as the year started to draw to a close, the actor became more and more tired and depressed over what he saw as the lack of fulfilment in his career. He had applied to become a member of the board of directors at the Screen Actors Guild, but shortly before Christmas received a telegram breaking the news that he had been unsuccessful. Distraught, he pulled out his .38 calibre revolver and took a shot at the unwelcome telegram.

The Christmas season was depressing; his health had been failing during the last year; and he had become despondent due to heavy drinking and flashbacks of the car accident earlier in the year. He expressed his concerns to both his brother, Geoffrey, and girlfriend, Dianne, both of whom were particularly concerned by his state of mind.

On 31 December 1971, Pete Duel spent the evening at his home, watching television with Dianne Ray. Both the day and the year came to an end, and Duel's girlfriend retired to the bedroom for what she hoped would be a good night's sleep. However, this was not to be, when Duel later entered the room himself. According to police reports, he walked over to some drawers and took out his pistol. "I'll see you later," he told Ray, before quietly leaving the room.

Not long after, Dianne Ray heard a gunshot coming from the living room, rushed in and found her boyfriend lying next to the Christmas tree, with the gun at his feet. He was dead.

The sudden death of Pete Duel was ruled a probable suicide, with the coroner concluding that the single gunshot wound to the head was consistent with a self-inflicted wound.

Unbelievably, just twelve hours later the cast and crew were back on the lot of *Alias Smith and Jones* at the instructions of ABC. The script was rewritten and a hurried announcement came that the actor would be replaced by Roger Davis for the remainder of the series.

The fact that the series was hurried back into production so soon after his death seems to prove that Duel was correct in his feelings about working on the television show, expressed just months before. "It's the ultimate trap," he said. It is unfortunate that, in the end, he felt that his only means of escape was by taking his own life.

37

The Dreadful Murder of Sal Mineo

At the end of the movie *Rebel Without a Cause*, Sal Mineo's troubled character Plato is fatally injured. Just over twenty years later the actor himself would sadly suffer the same fate, though in a very different way to the death he had acted out in *Rebel*.

Born on 10 January 1939 in New York City, Salvatore Mineo was the son of Italian parents, Josephine and Salvatore. From a very early age he developed an interest in the arts, after a talent scout came up to him on the street as he was playing with his sister, Sarina. After that he began taking part in dance lessons and drama, and learning his craft as a child actor while his siblings would watch him practise in the living room of their house. Once he had got a taste for acting, it wasn't long before he appeared on Broadway in the 1951 production of *The Rose Tattoo*, and he then achieved a great deal of recognition when he acted as the prince opposite Yul Brynner in the stage version of *The King and I*.

Sal dabbled with television as a teenager, before scoring his first film role in *Six Bridges to Cross*, a vehicle for Tony Curtis, which gave him the chance to play the younger version of Tony's character, Jerry Florea. It was a good role and a great opportunity for the young man, but it was his portrayal of Plato in the 1955 movie *Rebel Without a Cause* which really put him on the map as an actor. His performance was so deep and profound, in fact, that he was nominated for an Academy

Award for his role, though he ultimately lost out on the award to Jack Lemmon for his film *Mister Roberts*.

Still, this disappointment did not deter Sal for long, and he was inundated with fan mail from that moment on. He ventured into the music business for a while, which earned him more attention and fans, particularly when one of his songs, "Start Movin' (In My Direction)" reached number nine in the Billboard Hot 100. He also received another Academy Award nomination for his role in *Exodus* in 1960, and on this occasion he lost out to Peter Ustinov for his part in *Spartacus*. But despite his success on the screen, Mineo was still truly dedicated to his family, who remained in New York State. He bought his mother a home in Westchester County, which apparently cost the almost unheard-of amount of $200,000, and kept in close contact with his siblings and their families. He was very definitely a family man and while his film career was important to him, he always remained true to his roots.

By the early 1960s it was becoming apparent to everyone that Sal Mineo was being typecast in roles that always seemed to be some version of a troubled teenager. This was a problem by now as Sal was no longer a teenager himself, and he knew that it would not be long before acting those kinds of parts would be impossible. His popularity began to wane and soon nobody seemed to want him in their productions any more, which was a decision that baffled and troubled Sal Mineo. He still had his talent; he still had the ability to play roles; but sadly he became stuck in the rut frequented by so many former child actors – that of being too old to play a kid, and too young to play an adult.

It was a frustrating and difficult time for the man who had been acting his entire life, and when new parts began to open up, once again he would be typecast, only this time as a psychopathic bad guy. His personal life too was somewhat frustrating, as in spite of falling in love with his *Exodus* co-star, Jill Haworth, Sal was gay, something he fought against accepting for some years. This was a confusing time for the actor but in the end he decided publicly to admit his sexuality. He directed and starred in a somewhat controversial play entitled *Of Fortune and Men's Eyes*; the part included nudity and homosexuality, and from then on Sal became something of a trail-blazer, pioneer and hero for others struggling to be accepted as homosexual, particularly in the film business.

In the early 1970s, Sal worked on television in such programmes as *Columbo* and *Hawaii Five-O*, but his film career was practically over, his last appearance being in *Escape from the Planet of the Apes* in 1971, as Dr Milo the chimpanzee. In spite of the decline in film roles, by the mid-1970s his career was on the up when he appeared in the theatre production *PS Your Cat is Dead*. It received good notices in San Francisco, and when it transferred to Los Angeles, so did Sal, moving into an apartment he had used frequently in the past three years: 8563 Holloway Drive.

On the evening of 12 February 1976 Sal was heading home after attending rehearsals for the play, and drove into the garage space of the apartment building. Once he had exited the car, however, he was set upon by an assailant; a confrontation took place and the man knifed the actor in what was an apparently unmotivated and meaningless attack. As Sal lay bleeding on the road, the shady figure then fled quickly from the scene.

Inside the apartment building, a woman by the name of Mrs Mitchelson was going about her business when at approximately 9.15 p.m. she heard an almighty scream and a voice shouting, "My God! My God! Help me!" There then followed another scream before finally silence descended on the area and several neighbours came running out to see what was going on. One resident, Ray Evans, saw the actor lying on his side and noted that blood appeared to be coming from his head. It was not until he turned him over that he realized the blood was actually gushing from his chest and running towards the top of his body due to an incline on the ground where he lay.

As Sal gasped, Evans tried desperately to give him mouth-to-mouth resuscitation while others talked to him, telling him he'd be okay and that help was on its way. "I saw he was going into an ashen colour," Evans told reporters who arrived at the scene, "and I immediately started to give him mouth-to-mouth resuscitation. Everyone was yelling, 'Get the police. Get an ambulance.'"

Evans worked quickly and solidly on his neighbour and thought he was beginning to get a response, but it was not to be. Just as the police arrived, the actor gave his last breath at the age of thirty-seven, and was gone. The police at first decided it must have been a robbery gone wrong, but the discovery of Sal's personal belongings, including a small amount of cash in his clothing and his house keys lying beside him, dispelled that theory.

More confusion came when detectives interviewed nearby residents who all seemed to give differing accounts of what they had and hadn't seen during the course of the evening. Some said that there was no sign of the attacker at all, while others were adamant that he had been seen quite clearly running away from the building. His description, according to those who had seen him, was of a tall, white male with blond hair. This was a good lead until police interviewed other potential witnesses who gave their own descriptions; this time it was a five-foot seven-inch attacker, white with dark brown or black hair. Police were confused and after talking to as many people as possible, they were simply stumped as to who the attacker was and what could possibly be his motivation behind such a senseless assault.

Then several days after the murder, more intrigue came when mob boss Mickey Cohen stepped forward to claim Sal Mineo as a friend who had once frequented an ice-cream shop owned by Cohen's sister. "I don't think he was a close friend," Cohen told reporters, "but I just spoke to him seven or eight days ago." Describing the actor as a "fine young man", he then expressed his shock at the death and added that he doubted very much if Sal was having trouble with anyone in Hollywood.

"I think he'd have called me if there was any trouble," he said.

It seems that the mobster was correct, because Sal Mineo appears to have lived a very quiet and discreet private life, though his agent, Tom Korman, later explained to the makers of *Mysteries and Scandals* that he felt the actor let too many people into his life who shouldn't have been there. Rumours would surface that the murder was because of his lifestyle, and some thought it to be a crime of passion – a disgruntled lover who had come back for revenge. Others hinted at bizarre sexual practices and drug-taking, but this was incorrect; various attempts by the police to determine if these stories were true came to absolutely nothing. Instead, it would appear that the tales were an attempt by some to smear Sal Mineo's name for reasons known only to themselves.

Sal's body was flown back to New York several days after his death, accompanied by his friends and fellow actors Courtney Burr, Michael Mason and Elliot Mintz. His funeral took place at the Holy Trinity Catholic Church and was attended by co-stars and family, as well as Nicholas Ray, the director of *Rebel Without a Cause*. Sal's brother-in-law Charles Myers delivered the eulogy in the same spot that the actor himself had stood after his father had passed away just three years before. In the moving speech, Sal was described as a special person, "a gentle man whose sensitivity and understanding affected everyone he met". He went on to say that the actor had lived his life with courage, style and grace, and that no matter what, his body of work would always be remembered: "Nothing, not a person nor the passage of time, can take it away from him." He also ensured that everyone knew his brother-in-law was very different to the teenage, angst-ridden character he portrayed so often on the screen.

During the memorial, Sal's brother described him as being dedicated to his family, honest and sincere, while others wept openly in the front row, mourning the loss of their beloved friend. Sal's mother, Josephine, quietly let the tears fall from her face, unable to come to terms with the fact that she was burying her beloved son. Finally, after the service was over and everyone had said their goodbyes, Sal Mineo made his last journey and was buried next to his father in the family plot at the Gate of Heaven Cemetery, Hawthorne.

PS Your Cat Is Dead, the play in which Sal was appearing at the time of his death, went on without him, with Jeff Druce taking over his part. The director, Milton Katselas, told reporters that the whole thing had not been an easy task. "It's not a matter of just going on with the show," he said. "It's more a matter of overcoming." He then described the actor as a true gentleman who was always happy to tell a joke and take direction. "We loved him," he said, and it seems that everyone with whom the young man ever worked had exactly the same feelings. The play became a tribute to Sal, and his co-stars made positive and loving comments about him to the media. But still the question remained: "Who murdered Sal Mineo?"

Police remained baffled by the senseless crime for several years after the death, but then suddenly they had a lead. They arrested a man called Lionel Ray Williams who quite bizarrely was the complete opposite of the tall, white, blond man that many neighbours claimed to have seen. In fact, Williams was a short, black man with an afro haircut who was believed to have spoken to police a short time after Sal's death, apparently telling them that his death was the result of a drug deal gone wrong. There was no other information at that time to move that line of enquiry forward, so the police were unable to do anything more about it and Williams went on his way.

Then in October 1978 the man was in prison for another crime when he was rumoured to have told an inmate that he was the one who killed Sal Mineo as a result of an attempted robbery gone wrong. The conversation was heard by a prison warden who later told a colleague and an investigation began, resulting in the discovery that the man had apparently robbed someone just a mile away from where the murder had taken place, just thirty minutes after the event.

Williams was charged with the murder and the case went to

court in January 1979, where at first confusion reigned because of the initial impression that the attacker had been white. A twelve-year-old girl and her mother confused the court even more when they testified that the man the child had seen running away had dark curly hair that bounced as he ran, but she was sure his face was white. However, later a tape was played that showed this to be untrue, when the mother apparently admitted that her daughter had not actually seen his face or the colour of his skin – just the side of his head.

But one piece of testimony that did raise suspicions about the defendant was that of a neighbour who had seen the murderer run away from the scene and jump into a small, yellow car. As Williams was known to drive a rental car of the same distinct colour, this went some way in putting him at the scene of the crime that day. To this day, Lionel Ray Williams denies ever murdering Sal Mineo but the jury did not believe his plea and, after being described by Deputy District Attorney Michael Genelin as "a night marauder who would kill you if he had to – even if he didn't have to", the man was found guilty and sentenced to fifty-one years to life in prison. He actually only remained there for eleven years in the end, though he was soon back in prison after committing another crime shortly after his release.

The life and career of Sal Mineo was short; his death tragic and senseless. A gentle, kind man who always had a nice word for all whom he encountered, he will be best remembered for his part as Plato in 1955's *Rebel Without a Cause*. Sadly, no one could have possibly known at the time that Sal and those who acted beside him – James Dean and Natalie Wood (along with Nick Adams who played the minor role of Chick) – would all go on to have short lives with bitter endings. The film itself was a tragedy, their lives even more so, and yet the legacy of what Sal and his fellow young actors brought to the screen will live on forever. For that, at least, we can be grateful.

38

Elvis Presley, the King of Rock and Roll

Some deaths cause shock in Hollywood while others cause consternation across the entire United States. Occasionally, however, a death happens that seems to send quakes across the entire planet and it feels as if nothing is likely to be the same again. This was the case with Elvis Presley, whose death rocked the world to such an extent that he is still being mourned by his millions of fans even today, over thirty-five years after he left us.

Born on 8 January 1935 in Tupelo, Mississippi, Elvis Aron (spelt Aaron later in his life) Presley was the only child of Vernon Elvis and Gladys Love Presley following the death of his twin in childbirth. The child was shy but had a love of music that was so profound that his teachers encouraged him to enter a singing contest at the age of ten, and he learned to play the guitar shortly afterwards at the urging of his uncles. This love for music helped him to forget the fact that he was often bullied for being "shy" and "different", and it filled a gap brought on by the reputation forced on him as something of a loner. Still, he did not let his school years get him down and by the time he left, it was pretty clear what he was going to be in life: a musician, and a good one at that.

Anyone who watches shows such as *The X Factor* and *American Idol* can be forgiven for believing that it's relatively easy for a young person to get a recording contract in the present day. However, for Elvis and those from his era, it was anything but easy, and for some years after leaving school the young man played his brand of music in clubs and anywhere else just to get the exposure that would enable him to move up one step on the ladder and closer to his dream.

As with the pursuit of most ambitions, it wasn't an easy ride, and Elvis Presley faced disappointment and setbacks during his journey, but eventually his persistence paid off when in January 1956 he made his first recording for record label RCA. One of the songs recorded during that time was "Heartbreak Hotel" and shortly afterwards he made his first appearance on national television, when he appeared on *Stage Show* for CBS.

From here, Elvis's career went nowhere but up and over the next couple of years he released some of his most famous hits including "Don't Be Cruel", "Hound Dog", "Love Me Tender" and "Jailhouse Rock". Girls screamed his name wherever he went; riots erupted every time he appeared in public; and young men started copying his hairstyle and clothes. In short, within a few years of making it, Elvis Presley had become a legend of almighty proportions.

As well as being a tremendously successful recording artist, he was also sought after in Hollywood, where he was cast in a movie called "Love Me Tender", named after his hit of the same title. In the movie, Elvis plays a young man called Clint who stays home from the Civil War, while his brother Vance goes off to fight. Clint ends up marrying Vance's girlfriend while he is away, and the jilted man turns to crime, becoming involved with a train robbery.

The film was released in 1956 and it was the first of well over a dozen Elvis movies, which would all follow a similar pattern: some acting; some singing; and generally at least a little romancing. But while fans seemed to love his films and they are still frequently shown on television today, Elvis's work in Hollywood was not something with which he was particularly happy, as he wanted very much to be taken seriously both as a performer and an actor, something which this particular brand of movie did nothing to achieve. Unfortunately, the powers that be had other ideas; the films were money-makers and the ladies seemed to love them, so the movies would stick to the trusted format regardless of whether he liked it or not. He complained bitterly to his management team about being typecast, but in spite of any concerns the man had about this or any other aspect of his career, it seemed that nobody wanted to listen.

One film he worked on later in his career, the 1967 movie *Easy Come Easy Go*, showed Elvis attending a yoga class, where he is seen desperately trying to talk to one of the female members of the class. His actions during the session land him in hot water with the teacher, though when he attempts to leave the class, he finds he has unfortunately tied himself into a knot. This predicament then leads into a somewhat amusing – if not slightly corny – rendition of a song entitled "Yoga Is as Yoga Does".

What is interesting about this film is that while Elvis was a true rock and roller on the outside, on the inside he was actually a very spiritual man who took the philosophy of yoga very seriously indeed. His work in films was stressful; his career in music noisy; but in his private life he would forget it all by burying his head in a spiritual book, or losing himself in a karate class. In fact, so inspired was he by the martial art that he shared with friends his desire to be a teacher; something that was not about to happen while he was still the King of Rock and Roll.

Elvis married his long-term love, Priscilla, on 1 May 1967, after they had met while Elvis was serving in the US Army seven years before. By this time his problems with the movies he was being offered had become extreme, and when his next album – the soundtrack for *Clambake* – was something of a flop, the record company realized what Elvis had been trying to tell them for several years: his films were making him look like a joke to everyone who loved serious rock and roll music.

Elvis dealt with the disappointment of his album reviews by reading his spiritual texts and meditating according to the teachings of Paramahansa Yogananda, the author of *Autobiography of a Yogi*. His interest in the yoga guru was not a new thing, and in fact had become so intense during the making of the 1965 film *Harum Scarum* that he had decided to be initiated into Kriya Yoga, an advanced technique of meditation which had been mastered by Yogananda after learning it from his guru Sri Yukteswar.

However, before he could be initiated, Elvis first had to study a series of lessons from the Self-Realization Fellowship, which his spiritual adviser Larry Geller arranged with Sri Daya Mata, one of Yogananda's closest disciples. The meeting took place at the Monastic Center, atop Mount Washington in Los Angeles, and it was a great success. Daya Mata took an instant shine to Elvis, and after spending time alone with him in her living room and presenting him with two bound volumes containing lessons, she declared, "It's so heart-warming to see someone so famous take the time and interest to visit with us."

While Elvis's career was still not going the way he wanted it to, he returned to Mount Washington on many occasions, and began calling Mata – his new "spiritual mother" – "Ma". In return she encouraged the singer on his journey and gave him much-needed advice on his career, too, telling him to slow down, relax and take some time to enjoy the company of his family. But going further into his spiritual journey was taking its toll on his friends and family, and some associates worried about the amount of time he spent reading texts. Later, Priscilla recalled in her 1985 autobiography *Elvis and Me* that her husband would insist on reading metaphysical books together in bed, and wanted her to be interested in it too. This caused arguments between the couple, and as a result the relationship started to become fragile.

At one point during their marriage, the strain of balancing his life with Priscilla with his spiritual interests became so intense that Elvis decided to throw his precious library into an abandoned water well at Graceland. As if that wasn't enough, he then apparently set fire to them all in an effort to prove to

Priscilla that his spiritual books would not get in the way of their relationship again.

The marriage continued and despite still having some problems, the couple were both overjoyed when they managed to conceive a child: a little girl whom they called Lisa Marie. Elvis doted on his cherished daughter, and she felt exactly the same way about him, but sadly throughout Lisa Marie's early childhood, the relationship of her parents continued to unravel until it was barely hanging together at all.

Elvis threw himself back into his career and in 1969 began a series of shows at the International Hotel in Las Vegas. The concerts would become some of the most successful of his career, and photographs of him in the white, sequinned jumpsuit are perhaps the most famous images ever taken of the King of Rock and Roll. Indeed, even today there are numerous lookalikes who make their livelihoods specifically from this era of Elvis's life.

The Vegas shows received many positive reviews and his career surged into a definite upswing; but the same could not be said about his marriage. It had rumbled on for the past few years but Priscilla in particular was not happy, suspecting for some time that her husband was having affairs with some of his leading ladies. The intimacy of their relationship had all but ended, and she felt so lonely and abandoned that in the end Priscilla turned to a man called Mike Stone for the attention her husband was no longer giving her. Ironically, Stone was a karate teacher who had been introduced to Priscilla by Elvis some time before. The affair was short-lived but enough to tip the marriage over the edge, and after admitting the dalliance to her husband, the couple separated on 23 February 1972.

Despite trying to distance himself from his spiritual side at the urging of the people around him, it was to his guru, Daya Mata, that Elvis turned during this difficult time in his life. She gave him guidance and advice on how to deal with the situation, though in truth it is said that he never fully recovered from the marital separation. It is also clear to see in photographs that from this point on his health was beginning to suffer.

Presley had long been known for his love of food and after his divorce on 9 October 1973, his weight seemed to be fluctuating. He was also taking prescription drugs: he became addicted to Demerol and, shockingly, he was said to have overdosed on barbiturates twice, falling into a coma for three days during the first episode. Shortly afterwards he was admitted to hospital in a bid to rid himself of his addictions but his health was still most certainly causing concern to many people around him.

In spite of this, his management were still pushing him to do more work, and as a touring artist he was busier than ever. In truth, however, his body was breaking down and during one series of concerts he could barely function during rehearsals, standing in front of the microphone in silence, while his crew watched in shocked despair.

Elvis's health problems did not seem to ease throughout 1976 and he spent most of his time locked behind the gates of Graceland with his group of friends, the "Memphis Mafia", as they were known. His day-to-day life involved sitting in the house with the windows sealed, and no one from the outside world was allowed into his haven. His family were concerned by this behaviour and some colleagues believed that those surrounding him – hangers-on who were only pursuing their own ambitions – were sucking him dry. Still, Elvis seemed to appreciate their presence, particularly since he was no longer with Priscilla, and they would often be there when he became enraged and depressed over the fact that his once faithful wife had walked out on him.

The Memphis Mafia was around to see every part of Presley's daily life, but by this time the Graceland lifestyle was wearing thin for just about everyone. One of the bodyguards, Red West, had known Elvis since school and later said that he tried to get the singer to lay off prescription drugs, but he had refused. Then things came to a head when several staff members, including West, left Graceland for good; rumours began that they had been fired by Elvis's father Vernon after they had become too outspoken about his son's drug dependency.

By the end of 1976 Elvis was involved with a young woman called Ginger Alden, and two months later they became engaged. Things should have been looking up but this was an illusion; during several concerts the singer was so weak that he did not seem to know what was going on, slurring his words and unable to move in the way he used to do. Several concerts were cancelled, and the people around him became more concerned than ever.

Elvis Presley's final concert was held on 26 June 1977, and footage of the event is sad and painful to watch. His frame is bloated and beads of sweat cascade down his swollen face; everything looks to be an effort, and despite his size, in spirit he seemed to be a shadow of his former self. It is clear that he needed help, but alas no assistance seemed to be forthcoming and instead a massive series of concerts was planned for later that summer.

On 1 August 1977, Elvis learned that his former bodyguards were publishing a book about their years spent with him. He had tried desperately to halt the publication but it was no good; his health and drug problems were to be revealed for all to see, and he was devastated. But the shock of the book to fans and friends was quickly overshadowed when just over two weeks later, tragedy struck: Elvis Presley passed away, and the world of rock and roll came to a complete standstill.

Much has been written about how and why Elvis Presley died, and mysteries and whispers still surround the event over thirty-five years later. What we do know is that on the evening of 16 August 1977, the singer was scheduled to leave for his new tour. He was not looking forward to the tour, only agreeing to it because he was in need of the money. He was tired, weak and, what's more, knew that after the publication of his former employees' book, everyone would know precisely why he was no longer the star they had once known. He had no wish to depart Graceland. As things turned out, he was destined to leave, but not in the way anyone had imagined.

On the morning of 16 August he went into the bathroom of his Graceland home and – for whatever reason – collapsed. Several hours later, his fiancée knocked on the door of the bathroom, only to discover as she entered the room that Elvis was lying on the floor. The shocked woman slapped the singer several times in a bid to wake him before opening one of his eyelids to discover that his eye was blood red and unresponsive.

Panicking, Ginger called for Presley's road manager, Joe Esposito, to come to the room, which he did with several other staff members. From there an ambulance was called and the singer was taken to Baptist Hospital where he was pronounced dead at 3.30 p.m. An autopsy was performed and the official cause of death was given as "cardiac arrhythmia" – a severely irregular heartbeat – as well as a constriction in one of his arteries.

But what about the prescription drugs? Were they a contributing factor as to why the King of Rock and Roll's life slipped away that day? Some people seem to think so, though initial post-mortem examinations supposedly did not show any signs of drug abuse. This in itself is extremely odd, considering Elvis had been a long-term user of prescription medications and had been known to throw terrific tantrums if his staff tried to persuade him not to take them.

Elvis Presley's death continues to be a mystery and, as doctors said at the time, "the precise cause of death may never be discovered", though this has not stopped people discussing the matter from 1977 to the present day. Some people – including Elvis's stepbrother David Stanley – have put forward the idea that the star took his own life through a giant drug overdose, which was kept quiet from the media in favour of pushing forward the idea that he had died of a heart attack. The story behind the deliberate overdose is that Elvis had no intention of going on tour and had saved up his nightly drug dose until the morning he was supposed to leave, took the medication and passed away on the bathroom floor.

Other people dismiss this idea and claim that, as reported, Elvis's heart simply gave up when he was trying to gain some relief on the toilet. Of course, there are also those who believe that he did not die at all; that the whole thing was an elaborate hoax designed to put to rest Elvis the performer, and allow Elvis the man to live out the rest of his life in peace. This seems an elaborate story but a quick look on the internet gives an often entertaining insight into stories involving a wax body in the casket; supposed photographs of the King sitting in Graceland months after his death; and even a clip of an extra in the movie *Home Alone* who has been humorously labelled as an incognito Elvis enjoying a walk-on part.

The stories of whether or not the singer died of a heart attack, drug overdose or indeed if he is dead at all are countless, but in 1977 that was all irrelevant as fans from around the world wept and newspapers were full of headlines relating to his demise. The fans that lived in Memphis crowded round the gates of Graceland, and when Elvis Presley's body was returned from the hospital to his cherished home, the sound of crying could be heard all around. That evening cars came past the home with Elvis's music blaring from the speakers, while outside around 300 fans – old and young – spoke to each other about their love for the King of Rock and Roll, sharing their memories and stories of times gone by. But while they were upset, the real mourners were obviously Elvis's family, and in particular his young daughter Lisa Marie and ex-wife Priscilla, who had stayed friends with the singer until the end. Both took the death extremely hard, while Elvis's father Vernon was so upset he had to be placed under sedation.

Then devastation came just hours before the funeral, when a car seemed to lose control and headed towards a group of fans waiting outside Graceland. Most of the crowd managed to get away, but when the car swerved again it hit three teenagers, killing Juanita Joanne Johnson and Alice Marie

Hovatar instantly and critically injuring seventeen-year-old Tammy Baiter. Unbelievably, the car then careered off down the road, while a quick-thinking policeman managed to jump into his car and give chase, catching up and detaining the young man shortly afterwards.

Still, this awful incident did not stop thousands of spectators from lining the route to the church where the funeral was to take place, and by the time it was in full swing, women of all ages were seen fainting and shouting for the King. "God took my Elvis," cried one fan, while many more pulled at their hair, rocked back and forth, and threw flowers on to the hearse as it passed slowly by.

Elvis's copper coffin was taken to the family crypt, where his mother had been entombed some years before. However, while his family now hoped he could rest in peace with his loved ones, it was not to be, as shortly afterwards four men tried to break into the mausoleum in order – it is believed – to steal Presley's body. Thankfully the police had received a mysterious tip-off days before the event and immediately assigned several officers to the crypt, where they were able to give chase to the men the moment they were spotted. The incident was thwarted but it was more than enough to persuade the family that Elvis's body would not be safe lying in the public cemetery.

Arrangements were made and the bodies of both Presley and his mother were moved to Graceland, where they now lie in the Meditation Garden, a quiet spot favoured by Elvis during his lifetime as a place of reflection and peaceful retreat. It seems an appropriate place to be buried for the man who was once King of Rock and Roll and yet had a beautiful, quiet soul – who craved spirituality and encouraged others to do the same. His life may have been full of drama and personal upheaval, but in death it would seem that Elvis Presley has finally found the peace that he so desperately wanted, but perhaps was never able to find.

39

Mommie Dearest and My Mother's Keeper

Much has been said about the rivalry between movie superstars Joan Crawford and Bette Davis during the making of their film *Whatever Happened to Baby Jane?* Such is the extent of the public's interest in their relationship that whole books have been written about their problems, and a successful play based on the feud toured the United Kingdom in 2012. For their part, neither Bette nor Joan made any secret of their dislike for one another and made more than the odd snide comment over the years that followed the making of the film.

In the early 1970s, Bette was interviewed by Dick Cavett and told a story of being stung by a wasp during a trip to Scotland. Davis had suffered an allergic reaction after finding the insect in the sleeve of her dressing gown and jokingly Cavett asked if she thought Joan Crawford could have put it there. "No, that wouldn't be something she would do," replied Bette, and then a twinkle appeared in her eye. "Not a wasp," she continued. "A gun maybe, but not a wasp!" The audience laughed wildly, but jokes aside, both Joan and Bette most certainly did not appreciate each other and felt they had nothing whatsoever in common.

Unfortunately, it would later become apparent that they had at least one thing in common – daughters who felt the need to air their grievances with their mothers in the shape of a kiss-and-tell book. The first, a scathing account entitled *Mommie Dearest*, was published in 1978 and written by Crawford's daughter, Christina, who had been adopted by the divorced, single woman in 1940. The book was a biting – and often frightening – account of her life with Joan, and included stories of violent rages, abuse, humiliation and despair raged against not only Christina, but her adopted brother Christopher, too. The book told how the child was chastised for using wire hangers instead of padded ones; was spanked with a hairbrush so violently that it broke in half; and witnessed her brother being strapped to the bed in an effort to prevent him from sleepwalking.

Even Christmas – a time centred on loving and giving – was just another excuse for cruelty, according to the book, when Christina would be photographed surrounded by Christmas presents, only to find all but one of them promptly rewrapped and given away the moment the cameras were turned off. As if that wasn't enough, Christina says she was then forced to write thank you cards for all the presents she had been unable to keep, which could take days due to her mother's need for complete perfection in tone and grammar.

The childhood described by Christina was terrifying in every sense of the word and included being forced to eat portions of raw meat for dinner, which the child understandably hated. However, if she refused to swallow it, the meat would be wrapped up by her mother and kept for breakfast the next day. If that was pushed away also, out it would come for lunch until finally the child gave in and ate the putrid meal.

In the book, Christina also talked about the boyfriends her mother took over the years – all called "Uncle" by the child. From the age of nine she was mixing the gentlemen drinks, while her mother remained upstairs, readying herself for the evening ahead. Unfortunately, if the book is to be believed, while Crawford's look, style and appearance meant a lot to her, she didn't seem to care much about her daughter's clothes, as demonstrated by one particular episode.

The story went that during a childish adventure, a young Christina stripped some wallpaper from her bedroom wall, but on realizing the severity of what she had done, tried to paste it back on, which just caused even more destruction. Unfortunately, the patch was discovered by a furious Crawford, who took her revenge by heading straight to Christina's wardrobe, cutting her favourite yellow dress to shreds and forcing her to wear it for a week. If anyone asked why, she would have to tell them that it was because "I don't like pretty things."

After the abusive childhood described by Christina, she was shocked to discover that Crawford's last swipe was to write both her and her brother Christopher out of her will, "for reasons which are well known to them". Although they later successfully contested it, perhaps it was this final act that prompted Christina to write the book. However, while it may have brought her a sense of relief to get the story off her chest, with it came a great deal of letters and criticism from Joan's fans, who refused to believe that the star could have been such an abusive person. Christina was perhaps prepared for such a backlash, but thankfully for her, along with the hate mail came dozens of other letters from people who had suffered similar childhoods, and for those people at least, the book seemed to have helped them deal with their own abusive past.

Such a subject was always going to elicit discussion and outrage, and it is interesting to note that Christina's younger sisters, twins Cathy and Cindy, are both said to deny the claims against their mother, saying that she was firm, yes, but also loving and never abusive towards either of them. Her grandchildren (the twins' children) agree, describing her as a normal grandmother who would babysit and make lunch for them. However, as Christina has publicly stated, there was an eight-year age gap between the twins and herself, which made it impossible for them to have seen anything of her own younger years before she went to boarding school at the age of ten. "[Cathy] couldn't have known about my or Chris's experience. She wasn't there – she wasn't even born when I was adopted," she told the *Guardian* in 2008.

As well as the twins' denials, several friends of Joan Crawford (including first husband Douglas Fairbanks Jr) also came forward to say that they had been unaware of any abuse, but on the flip-side came claims by former staff members, who said that they themselves had witnessed wrongdoings in the Crawford household, though no one was apparently brave enough to say anything about it at the time. Along with those accounts came several similar ones from unnamed "friends" who claimed to have witnessed the cruelty at first hand, though once again they did not raise the subject with Crawford, claiming it would have been futile and could have resulted in the abuse becoming even more intense.

Crawford's son Christopher gave his own take on the situation in October 1978, during an interview with the *Los Angeles Times*. In the short feature he described how his adopted mother had once held his hand in the fireplace when she discovered he had been playing with matches, and revealed that he had been so unhappy that he had even run away from home on more than one occasion.

As if that was not bad enough, Christopher is reported to have said that he was sure Joan had never actually loved him, and that when he became a father, she held her granddaughter for just a few seconds before harshly handing her back. Then later, when his youngest daughter was born, the little girl needed urgent medical treatment for which he could not afford to pay. Apparently, Christopher phoned his mother for help, and during the call she told him that his daughter was not her granddaughter because "You were adopted." If this was indeed a true story, it is no wonder then that this was the end of any "relationship" Christopher ever had with Joan Crawford.

While some would argue that the validity of Christina Crawford's book cannot be 100 per cent confirmed, it also cannot be denied that Joan Crawford was a volatile woman who seemed to enjoy confrontation. Her public spats with Bette Davis were legendary, of course, but it did not stop there and she would often take swipes at other younger actresses such as Marilyn Monroe, for whom she seemed to have a particular distaste. But while there is every chance that the stories about Christina's childhood really could have happened, it is interesting to note that Crawford's many fans are still as adamant as ever that the woman they continue to adore was not the one portrayed in the book.

Of course by the time *Mommy Dearest* was published, the subject of the book was no longer living, which at least meant that Joan Crawford would not be personally affected by it. However, the next tell-all book came as a deep shock, particularly as the parent in question was Bette Davis, and she was still very much alive.

In 1985, while the star of *Dark Victory* and *All About Eve* was battling numerous health problems including recovering from a stroke, she was shocked to discover that her daughter, B. D. Hyman, had published a book about their fraught relationship. Many people assumed straight away that it would be written in the same tone as *Mommie Dearest*, but they were mistaken. While Christina Crawford's book was full of tales of childhood physical abuse, Hyman's volume, *My Mother's Keeper*, did not accuse Bette of being in any way an abuser. Instead, it blamed her for trying to control her adult daughter's life to such a degree that it was almost unbearable.

It cannot be disputed that Bette Davis was a force with which to be reckoned; she was a woman who had no fear of standing up to the studio or fellow actors and actresses at a time when it was relatively unknown to do so. Therefore, it is easy to imagine that she was a woman who liked to have a say in her daughter's life too. However, in fairness to Bette, this could be said for most mothers, and yet children who are not in the public eye tend to complain to friends and siblings, rather than put their thoughts into print.

As well as stories that accused Bette of trying to control her daughter's decisions, the book also detailed how Bette was a victim of assault by her then husband Gary Merrill, who had adopted B. D. as a child. It should be noted, however, that

Merrill later denied such stories, stating that the author had been motivated by "cruelty and greed".

My Mother's Keeper portrayed Davis as a drunken party animal who made a fool of herself at various public events, but the stories – seen through the eyes of B. D. – seemed to take many events out of context, seeing what many thought to be funny moments as something more sinister or contrived. In fact, so concerned were Bette's friends on reading these stories that they came forward to say that they had witnessed some of the parties and events described in the book, but they had seen things happening in a completely different way; that the events that were embarrassing to B. D. were actually entertaining to the rest of the guests at the party.

The book caused a sensation, and adding to the gossip was the fact that the memoir had a vast amount of conversational quotes supposedly between mother and daughter. This prompted many to question just how many of their conversations could possibly be remembered word for word after all these years. The conversations themselves were often grim and did not portray Bette in the best light, describing how she could not cope with B. D. having a successful marriage and almost willed it to fail in order for her daughter to go back to loving Bette and Bette alone. Even the cover of the book was a cruel blow, showing the aged actress with grey hair, wrinkles and bright red lipstick "bleeding" all around her mouth.

During the book tour, B. D. was asked if her work bore any comparison to that of Christina Crawford's memoir. She immediately denied that it did and went on to detail a story in which she had met Joan Crawford herself on the set of *Whatever Happened to Baby Jane*. According to B. D., the actress recoiled from her intended handshake, looked her up and down, and demanded she have no contact with her children, twins Cindy and Cathy, as B. D. would surely be a terrible influence on them. This, said Crawford, was due to Bette's daughter having an "unprotected childhood".

B. D.'s distaste for Crawford was clear to see, and she then described that while Christina was always looking for love from her mother as a child, B. D. herself had for the most part a very happy childhood, full of love and devotion from her actress mother. "There was no child abuse," B. D. said. "Mother never inflicted child abuse." This raised questions from readers, because if her relationship with Bette had been a good one, why did she feel the need to write such a scathing account of their life together?

"I love my mother very much," she said, before going on to explain that if she didn't, she would never have written the book, never mind publish it. She also described how the publication was an attempt to present her side of the relationship in a way Bette "cannot burn, throw away or ignore". According to B. D. her mother would frequently shut out everything she did not want to hear, and writing the book was the daughter's (perhaps somewhat naive) way of trying to make Bette change.

It soon became apparent that one of the things that had spurred on the writing of the memoir was Bette's relationship (or lack thereof) with B. D.'s husband Jeremy and their two sons Justin and Ashley. According to B. D., Davis was allegedly nasty and unpleasant to all members of her family, and even "terrorized" Justin and Ashley when they were small. This did not make sense to many people, particularly as B. D. was so quick to assure people that her own childhood was one of love and devotion.

What made her comments even more surprising was that Davis had worked on a movie (*Family Reunion*) with Ashley, during which time he had said some wonderful things about his grandmother. This, according to B. D., was as a result of having to say those things in order to keep her happy. Not so, said *People* magazine reader John Shea, who had worked with both Bette and Ashley on the set and found Davis to be very patient with her young grandson. According to Shea, each morning they would meet in Bette's dressing room to rehearse, and every day would involve the same thing – a great deal of love, support and coaching from grandmother to grandson.

B. D. Hyman never received a great deal of public support after the publication of the book and this can be seen clearly through internet forums and YouTube comments even today. Of course, Christina Crawford had her fair share of detractors, too, but whereas she could be seen as having a definite reason for wanting to come out against her abusive mother, readers felt that the same just could not be said for Hyman. With no actual physical abuse involved, for the most part B. D. just came across as a disgruntled woman, angry at her controlling mother and anxious to get her to listen to her side of the story.

Sadly, it seemed clear to friends of Bette Davis that her heart had been broken by the supposed disloyalty expressed by her daughter, and her health seemed to get worse over the next few years before her death in 1989. For her part, Davis responded to *My Mother's Keeper* in her own book, *This 'n That*, which was published in 1987. The book is a series of stories about Davis's life and career, though she left it to the very end before mentioning her daughter's work.

The last, untitled chapter is an open letter, which starts "Dear Hyman" and goes on to express a sheer disbelief at what had been written in her book. In the two-page note, Bette accuses her daughter of a lack of loyalty and appreciation for the life she was given, and says she believes her to be a great writer of fiction. The actress also states that she has no idea why the book was called *My Mother's Keeper* and says that financially she had been a keeper of her daughter for many years, and continued to be so through the selling of the book. She also added a postscript which included many letters of support for the actress, before promptly disinheriting her disloyal daughter.

After both Joan and Bette's deaths, public support has continued unabated and their films are still sold on DVD and watched on television. Both ladies are still legendary, and whether you love 'em or hate 'em, it is clear that they just don't make them like Davis and Crawford any more. Despite claims put forward by their daughters, their fans still think of them as two of the greats, and it is likely to remain that way for the foreseeable future.

Bette Davis's son Michael has continued to champion his mother's memory as both a loving parent and wonderful actress, running her estate and hearing from countless fans who tell him even now just how much the actress has inspired and entertained them over the years. The same can be said for Crawford's twins Cindy and Cathy, who have always denied their part in any awful childhood.

In spite of that, both B. D. Hyman and Christina Crawford have always stuck fast to the claims they made in their books, and B. D. actually went on to publish another volume, *Narrow is the Way*, in 1987. This book was not as popular, however, and she has since started her own church where she writes religious volumes and very rarely speaks publicly about her mother.

40

The Deaths of Charles Wagenheim and Victor Kilian

All suspicious deaths cause headlines in Hollywood, and there have been a great many over the years. But in 1979 two veteran actors were brutally murdered within days of each other and people began to wonder: Was there a serial killer on the loose, or were the deaths just a strange but tragic coincidence?

Charles Wagenheim was born on 21 February 1896 in New Jersey and suffered shyness for much of his childhood. His quiet nature was not something he particularly liked about himself so in an effort to gain some confidence, he decided he would try his hand at acting. The work was hard but rewarding; his shyness subsided somewhat and he became so enthralled with the idea of becoming a professional actor that he enrolled in an acting course at the American Academy of Dramatic Arts.

After graduating in 1923, Wagenheim went to Broadway where he was involved in several successful shows and ended up touring with a Shakespearean acting company. However, having most certainly developed a bug for the profession, he craved success not just on the stage, but in movies too, so in the late 1920s he moved to Hollywood to find his fame and fortune.

It was here that he received his first disappointment on the bumpy road to fame, when he discovered that work in Hollywood was very different to the New York theatre. While he had achieved a great deal of success on the East Coast stage, suddenly nobody seemed to want him in large roles in the movies. He therefore spent most of his time playing tramps, waiters, taxi drivers and anything else that came his way.

He did not complain, however, as the small roles he obtained helped to pay the bills, and after just over a decade of struggle, in 1940 he was given one of his best parts, as an assassin in Alfred Hitchcock's *Foreign Correspondent*. His career continued on a slow but steady path, and after playing a thief in the 1959 film *The Diary of Anne Frank* television came knocking at his door. It was there that, in the 1960s and 1970s, he found most of his roles, including a popular, regular role as Halligan in *Gunsmoke*.

In his later years, Charles Wagenheim lived quietly with his psychologist wife and earned money as landlord of a number of apartments that he had purchased in years gone by. Still, he continued to win the occasional acting job, too, and in 1979 took on a role on the TV show *All in the Family*, where he worked with fellow actor Victor Kilian.

Kilian was also born in New Jersey and had gone into acting as a teenager by joining a vaudeville company. His early career took an eerily similar path to that of Wagenheim, appearing on Broadway before trying his hand in the movies at the end of the 1920s. However, Kilian's career in films had been more successful than Wagenheim's, and he quickly became known as a stellar character actor, with roles in the likes of *The Adventures of Tom Sawyer* (1938) and 1939's *The Adventures of Huckleberry Finn*, in which he played Pap Finn.

Unfortunately his career was tragically marred during one film which saw him working with John Wayne. During a particular fight scene, things took a horrifying turn when he suffered an injury so bad that it led to the loss of an eye. Then in the 1950s things became bleak again when he was a victim of communist blacklisting in the McCarthy witch-hunts, which had hurt the careers of many actors and writers alike. Still, these setbacks did not deter the hard-working actor and he persevered with his career, appearing in various theatre shows and later making the successful switch to television, just as Wagenheim had done. It was while working on the small screen that he achieved a great deal of success and became a household name by starring as the Fernwood Flasher in *Mary Hartman, Mary Hartman*.

By the time Kilian worked with Charles Wagenheim in an episode of *All in the Family*, both actors were well into their eighties. The episode was entitled "The Return of Stephanie's Father" and revolved around the story of alcoholic Floyd Mills, who arrived at the home of main characters Archie and Edith to try and sell them his daughter, whom they had already been looking after.

Floyd is staying in a rundown, prostitute-filled hotel when Arthur and Edith arrive to negotiate with him over the care of the child. Before they meet him, however, they encounter the desk clerk played by Kilian, who asks the couple if they want to rent the room for an hour. Assuring him that they're not interested in sex as they're already married, they then move over to some chairs in the lobby, one of which is occupied by a tramp played by Wagenheim. At first he seems reluctant to leave, but eventually moves from his perch when Archie tells the tramp that there is an unconscious man in the alley who appears to have some money on him. "Oooh thank you," Wagenheim says, as he scuttles towards the door.

The two roles played by Kilian and Wagenheim may have been small, but they certainly raised a laugh or two during the filming. Unfortunately, just weeks later, before the episode was aired, the laughter stopped when tragedy struck both of the actors.

Charles Wagenheim's wife Lillian had previously suffered a stroke and a nurse, Stephanie Boone, was hired to help out at the couple's apartment at 8078 Fareholm Drive. Little did they know, however, that the woman apparently had a criminal record for armed robbery, and she now saw the Wagenheims as easy targets and allegedly began stealing items from their home.

Details of the last moments of Wagenheim's life are sketchy, but there are two theories as to what might have happened. The first is that the actor had become suspicious that his wife's nurse had been writing cheques and cashing them for her own gain. He had been keeping tabs on the woman, and after finding that he was right with his suspicions, had decided to have it out with her. She became so incensed at his bravado that their encounter inevitably led to Wagenheim's death.

The other theory is that the unsuspecting actor came back to the apartment after shopping and caught Boone rifling through his drawers and stealing items. Once again, he confronted her and demanded to know what she was up to, and the scenario ends with the same result as the first – she kills him after a heated argument.

Nobody is entirely clear on what exactly happened in the house that day but we do know this: on 6 March 1979 (which quite coincidentally was fellow-actor Victor Kilian's birthday) Charles Wagenheim was severely beaten around his head while in the bedroom of his apartment. The pounding he received was enough to knock him to the ground and ultimately kill him.

After the man had died, the nurse phoned the police and told them that she had briefly gone to the building's laundry room and returned to see the body of the elderly actor lying face down on the floor. His bedroom window was open, she said, and his wife was in the living room, oblivious to everything that had happened. Unfortunately for both Wagenheim and the police, the ailing woman was unable to help with any details after a stroke had left her unable to communicate.

At first the police said they had no idea who could have done such a thing to the innocent actor. However, just five days later, their suspicions were aroused when it was reported that Victor Kilian, who had acted with Wagenheim just a short time before, was also found beaten to death at his home at 6550 Yucca Street.

Kilian's son, Victor Jr, had been trying to get his father on the telephone but was unable to get through. Being concerned, the man travelled to his house and was devastated to discover his father was dead; the television was still switched on and a snack remained uneaten nearby. The police were called and an investigation revealed that the apartment doors looked as though they had been opened with a pass key. There was no definite motive for the killing, but it was decided that robbery was most certainly a possibility.

When they then discovered that Kilian and Wagenheim had recently worked together in *All in the Family*, the police were intrigued. Was it possible that the two men had been targeted because they had worked together? Was there a serial killer on the loose, going after old actors? It was hard to tell. However, there was no doubt that at first the two deaths did look as though they were somehow related, and police began intensively investigating the Wagenheims' nurse over the course of the next three months to see if she was responsible for one or both murders.

After looking at the case for some time, the police came to the conclusion that while it was likely that the care-worker was at the very heart of the Wagenheim mystery, it just did not make sense that she would have had the inclination or opportunity to be at Kilian's house too. So in the end, their suspicions came to nothing and, to this very day, the savage killer of the elderly actor Victor Kilian has never been found or brought to justice.

The same could not be said in the Wagenheim case, however. After the police discovered the nurse's past armed robbery and escape convictions, things started to make more sense. On Friday, 25 May, the police travelled to the Los Angeles County Animal Shelter, where the nurse was now working as a kennel attendant. There they arrested and charged the woman for the murder of Charles Wagenheim, and for good measure added on a charge of grand theft too. She eventually pleaded guilty to voluntary manslaughter and in January 1980 was sentenced to eight years in prison.

No other details were ever revealed about why the nurse had any motive or wish to kill Charles Wagenheim, and to this day people still take to the internet to discuss what really happened during the course of that week in March 1979. Many still believe that somehow the two killings are related, though after studying what we know of the events, it seems unlikely. The two actors had worked together, certainly, but it appears just a tragic coincidence that they were both taken from life within a week of each other, and in such a violent and undignified way.

41

Natalie Wood Drowns Mysteriously

There have been many, many mysterious deaths in Hollywood. Some involve hotels, some involve mansions, a few involve gardens or driveways, but ask anyone for the name of someone who suffered a strange death involving a boat, and most – if not all – will say just one person: Natalie Wood.

Born on 20 July 1938, Natalia Nikolaevna Zahkarenko was the daughter of Russian parents, though she herself was born in San Francisco. Natalie loved the movies and her mother would take her to the cinema at every opportunity, where she would sit on her lap and watch the great stars sparkle on the silver screen. Her mother saw a certain something in her child, and after Natalie gained a few small roles, she decided to move the family to Los Angeles, where she actively pursued a career as a showbiz mother to her young daughter. Once in California, things looked bright for Natalie and she was cast – aged just seven – as a German orphan in the movie *Tomorrow Is Forever* (1946). Not only that, but the film was a vehicle for Claudette Colbert and Orson Welles, meaning that Wood was introduced to Hollywood royalty from a very early age.

But while *Tomorrow Is Forever* was a success, it was her appearance in the 1947 Christmas movie *Miracle on 34th Street* that propelled the young child to superstardom. The film tells the story of a department store Santa who insists he is the real thing, and Natalie plays a young girl who had been prompted by her mother to reject all notions of Santa Claus, magic and fantasy. Of course, everything works out well in the end and as a result the film has gone on to become one of the all-time Christmas favourites, still being shown on television each year over sixty-five years since its first release.

Natalie's star continued to climb and she made a successful transition from child star to young actress, starring opposite James Dean and Sal Mineo in the 1955 film *Rebel Without a Cause*. But in spite of the fact that she was a hard-working actress, she still managed to keep up with her studies and graduated successfully from high school, much to the delight of herself and her family. Then six years after *Rebel Without a Cause* came *West Side Story*, which was undoubtedly one of her most – if not *the* most – famous and successful movies as an adult actress.

But away from a movie career, the young woman craved a happy and peaceful personal life, and in the mid-1950s, while still a teenage actress, Natalie was introduced to actor Robert Wagner, who was eight years her senior. The two travelled in different circles, so they did not have the chance to get to know each other well at that time, and it was not until 1956 when Wagner saw her again at a fashion show that he began to take a real interest in her. Natalie had long since had a crush on the famous movie star (although she had chosen not to advertise the fact), so when Wagner asked her to accompany him to a film premiere – which also happened to be on her eighteenth birthday – she was absolutely delighted.

The couple began dating seriously from that moment on, though Natalie's family – and in particular her mother Maria – were very much against the idea of the young actress dating an older man. Still, the relationship continued and on 28 December 1957 they were married in a quiet ceremony in Scottsdale, Arizona, away from the glare of Hollywood glitz and glamour.

Natalie Wood and Robert Wagner were classed as Hollywood's golden couple – the happiest romance in the whole of California. It was, as these perfect marriages often are, just an illusion though, and in reality the marriage began to crumble quite quickly, with Wood later complaining that her husband would criticize her friends and the way she kept house. He was also reported to have left her alone while she was ill with flu and had also been rude to her mother, which did not go down too well at all, considering her mother was against the marriage in the first place.

Things were tested even more when Natalie got herself into a dispute with Warner Brothers, which saw the studio taking offence at the actress asking for more money and retaliating by suspending her for eighteen months, the longest suspension in Hollywood history. With no work to do, Wood was often seen sitting on Robert Wagner's sets, watching him film his latest movie, but this too caused problems and on one particular occasion a director put his foot down and ordered her off the set.

The problems were further intensified when rumours came of a romance between Natalie and actor Warren Beatty, which columnist Hedda Hopper decided to ask Natalie about in the midst of her marriage problems. "You may or may not know that I haven't been discussing anything that personal," she told the reporter, and when Hopper mentioned that it had always appeared that she and Wagner shared an idyllic marriage over the years, she replied, "Lots of things can happen in that time – and did."

When the couple announced a separation in June 1961, their representatives told reporters that there were no plans for divorce and the couple hoped that they would be able to work their problems out. This was not to be, however, and in April 1962 the couple were granted a divorce in just eleven minutes after Wood told the judge that during the last year of their marriage, Wagner preferred going out by himself to staying in with her. "He was always telling me he was going out to play golf and didn't have time to discuss our problems," she said.

On 30 May 1969 Natalie married Richard Gregson, a British producer whom she had been dating for a couple of years. The marriage did not last and they separated in 1971, though the relationship did give Natalie a much-loved daughter called Natasha. Shortly before the divorce was finalized, Wood and Wagner ran into each other in a restaurant and, much to the surprise of everyone, rekindled their romance. It was a fast-paced affair and just months after the divorce from Gregson, the two tied the knot again in a quiet ceremony aboard their boat, *The Splendour*, in the presence of just a few of their closest friends.

"It's wonderful," Natalie told reporters at the time. "We're starting again. We're starting new." Wagner got in on the act, too, by declaring that their new life was beginning aboard the boat, which as it turned out would become a highly ironic comment.

It would seem that this second attempt at marriage was a lot more successful than the first, possibly as a result of both Wagner and Wood being older and more settled, and also because by this time the actress had decided to tone down her acting career and go into semi-retirement. She gave birth in March 1974 to their daughter, Courtney, and while she did still enjoy the occasional film role, she spent most of the time at home, raising her children.

In late November 1981, Natalie was making a movie entitled *Brainstorm* with actor Christopher Walken. Despite being scared of water – and particularly dark water – Natalie loved sailing in their yacht and that Thanksgiving weekend, she and Wagner invited her co-star to join them on their boat. The friends, together with the ship's captain Dennis Davern, sailed the boat out to Catalina, stopping first in Avalon, and then continuing to Isthmus Cove where they went ashore for dinner and drinks. The official statement from Wagner's representative stated that after the trip to the restaurant, they all returned to the boat, where Robert went to his cabin and Wood to the stateroom. By the time the actor went to the room to join his wife, however, she was apparently nowhere to be found, and an inflatable boat that had been tied to the yacht had disappeared.

"Since Mrs Wagner often took the dinghy out alone, Mr Wagner was not immediately concerned," said the representative, adding, though, that after ten or fifteen minutes Wagner was worried enough by the disappearance to take a small boat out to look for Wood himself, only to come up with nothing. Help was called and by 7.45 a.m. on 29 November 1981 the body of Natalie Wood was found tragically floating face down in the ocean, her inflatable boat close by.

After formally identifying the body of his late wife, a distraught Robert Wagner returned to Beverly Hills where his family were waiting for him. He then had the unenviable task of breaking the news about Natalie's death to her daughters Courtney and Natasha, who took it very hard. Natasha was told first, and it was the sound of her screams that woke Courtney. She later told *Fox News* that she was very lucky to have her nanny by her side when her father announced the news that she wouldn't be able to see her beloved mummy again.

Meanwhile, the body of the beautiful forty-three-year-old actress was taken back to Los Angeles for an autopsy to be performed. It was announced shortly afterwards that a blood alcohol level of .14 was found, as well as caffeine and "very small amounts" of two medications, though this was said to be in no way related to her death. Coroner Richard Wilson released a statement that said it looked as though the actress had taken a headache tablet, a seasickness pill and had drunk a cup of coffee, hence the traces of medications and caffeine found during the autopsy.

It was determined that Natalie Wood, wearing just a nightdress and parka coat, must have untied the dinghy boat and tried to climb aboard, only to lose her footing, slip and consequently drown in the water below. This was further shown to be a possibility when it was revealed that the actress had slipped while trying to board the same boat in order to go to dinner that evening. On that occasion she did not fall into the water, but she was not so lucky, it would seem, later that night. Bringing all the evidence together, a verdict of accidental drowning was reported although even at this early stage there were rumblings and rumours that not everything had been as simple as had previously been thought.

Coroner Thomas Noguchi – who was famous for performing the autopsies on the likes of Marilyn Monroe and Robert Kennedy – claimed that while on the yacht, there had been a heated argument between actors Robert Wagner and Christopher Walken. Conclusions were formed that the argument may not have been about Natalie Wood, nor involved her in any way, but had annoyed her to such a degree that she decided to seek solace on board the inflatable boat. She then slipped and fell into the water in the process.

This idea of a heated argument was brushed aside somewhat by investigator Roy Hamilton, however, who told reporters, "I don't know where the coroner got that information. I think he was juicing it up a little bit." It would seem that Noguchi's love of talking freely to the press and "juicing things up" led him to be reprimanded shortly after the investigation, and he would ultimately step down from his position as a result. Meanwhile, Assistant Coroner Richard Wilson came into the debate by adding that argument may be too strong a word, and instead there may have been an "animated conversation . . . a heated conversation . . . a lot of conversation over a number of hours".

The idea of the argument was presented to Robert Wagner's representative, lawyer Paul Ziffren, who gave a statement saying that he could not possibly elaborate on any disagreement between Wagner and Walken as he had not yet talked to him. "He's still in a total state of shock," said Ziffren. He then added that it was an important matter that Noguchi had concluded death by accidental drowning, "and frankly, I don't see the relevance of some of the other things".

Many others didn't see the relevance either, except for Noguchi's supposed love for juicy details, but still he did manage to bring things back down to earth when he told reporters that there was "no evidence of foul play" on Natalie's body, and bruises – including one that had been found on her left cheek – were caused by her falling against the yacht as she fell. "It was not a homicide," he said, before adding, "It was not a suicide, it was an accident." However, he did add that the woman could quite possibly have yelled for assistance while in the water, "but no one heard".

The fact that the coroner brought up the idea that Natalie could have tried to get help ties in with what a woman by the name of Marilyn Wayne told police on the morning after the body had been found. She and a friend had been on a boat in the same cove as the Wagners when the tragedy happened, and Wayne had been asleep before being woken up by her friend. According to her, her friend frantically shook her awake to ask if she could hear a woman crying for help. Wayne listened quietly and sure enough, there was a voice shouting, "Help me, somebody help me", from the water.

The friends looked into the dark sea but could not determine where the voice was coming from. Added to that, there was a party on another boat near to them and several times they heard people shout, "We're coming to get you." Presuming that the shouts for help were related to fun at the party, they did not feel they should interfere. "Boats are funny," Wayne told reporters. "People don't want you interfering on their boats. You never know what the reaction will be." Other boat owners in the vicinity later claimed not to have heard anything at all though the two friends remained adamant that the woman's voice was clear and coming from somewhere in the water. Shortly after midnight, however, the sound stopped altogether, and silence fell on the water once more.

While people were arguing over whether or not there was any kind of mysterious circumstance that led to the death of Natalie Wood the actress, Natalie the wife and mother was buried beneath a tree in Westwood Memorial Park – the same cemetery where Marilyn Monroe and a host of other stars were laid to rest over the years. Friends including Frank Sinatra, Rock Hudson and Gene Kelly attended the proceedings, while Roddy McDowall paid tribute to the star, saying that she was "capable of truly giving with adult delight and childlike naughtiness". Robert Wagner, his daughter Courtney and Natalie's daughter Natasha then took a flower each as a memento, before the grieving man finally leant over the coffin and said a brief goodbye, kissing the closed casket just one last time.

Friends and co-stars then gave their tributes to the world's press with Michael Caine describing Natalie as a "great family woman, which I've noticed is quite rare in America. She was devoted to her husband and her children." James Stewart, who acted with Natalie when she was just a child, declared, "we were just sure she would develop into a very fine actress – and she did", while Fred MacMurray, who had also worked alongside the child actress, described her as a "lovely little girl".

The tributes were warm and heartfelt but, once given, the friends of Natalie Wood then went back to work and on with their lives. The Wagner family, however, were left to try and pick up the pieces, but this need for quiet reflection did not stop the many rumours and stories springing up over the years, with many discussions and even whole documentaries being dedicated to what could – or could not – have happened during that dark night in 1981.

In November 2011 the case of Natalie Wood's death was reopened after lobbying from the actress's sister Lana, Natalie's biographer, Marti Rulli, and the captain of the boat, Dennis Davern. It had taken the Los Angeles County Sheriff's Department a year to reopen the case, but after claiming that new information had been presented, a new investigation was sought and the press went frantic.

According to reports at the time, some of the new information came when an audio emerged of Lana Wood discussing her sister's death. In the tape the woman apparently discloses that the boat's captain Dennis Davern told her that when Natalie fell overboard, Robert Wagner had insisted she be left in the water to "teach her a lesson". Unfortunately – if the story is to be believed – the lesson went too far and the woman ultimately drowned.

Another piece of new evidence was that the captain had apparently admitted to lying during a previous enquiry, and later claimed that a fight between Wood and Wagner had taken place prior to the actress's death. These two pieces of information were enough to reopen the case and the press went wild about the possibility of more mud-raking and mystery. Of course, the first person they contacted was Robert Wagner, though it has to be said that it was made very clear from the start that he was not a suspect in the death of his wife. Through a spokesperson the actor and his family declared that they were in full support of the department's work, though added that they sincerely hoped the new information was from a credible source, rather than someone simply trying to profit from Wood's death, thirty years afterwards.

Although Christopher Walken was not considered to be a suspect in the inquiry either, newspaper reporters still banged on his door for a comment. None came, however, and instead he hired a lawyer to represent his interests in the case. A year later the actor appeared on CBS *This Morning* and declined once again to talk, stating that there was so much information on the internet that anything the interviewer wanted to know could be easily looked up.

Not much is known about the reinvestigation, as much of the information was kept under wraps. However, one interesting thing surfaced, and that was the whereabouts of the boat, *The Splendour*, which had been the biggest dumb witness in the Natalie Wood case. Its owner, Ron Nelson, had bought the boat in 1986, and had known about the investigation for a few weeks before it became public knowledge. However, whether or not the police found anything of any interest in the boat itself is unlikely, as after thirty years and some time being used as a charter boat, any remaining evidence was going to be long gone.

Eventually, after nine months of investigation, Natalie

Wood's death certificate was amended from accidental drowning to "drowning and other undetermined factors" and stated that the circumstances surrounding the death were "not clearly established". Then in early 2013 more information was released when it was claimed that the bruises found on Natalie Wood's body had been sustained before she went overboard, and not after. The marks, it was stated in the report, could have been "non-accidental", according to the medical examiner, and investigations are said to continue quietly though it is not known how long they will remain active. In the meantime, the coroner's office is not willing to openly discuss the case, preferring to leave the majority of its enquiry private for as long as possible.

After two investigations and thirty years of speculation and rumour, Natalie Wood's death still remains a mystery and unless something substantial is brought to the table, it seems that it will forever remain that way.

42

John Belushi Dies at the Chateau Marmont

The Chateau Marmont Hotel in the heart of Hollywood is as luxurious a hotel as you could possibly hope to stay in. Its guest book reads like a who's who of the entertainment business, and former guests include the likes of Marilyn Monroe, Jean Harlow, Clark Gable and Elizabeth Taylor. The hotel prides itself on being the place to be whoever you want to be, and it is said that Columbia Pictures executive Harry Cohn once said that if you had to get in trouble, you might as well do it at the Chateau Marmont. But while the hotel is everything you could possibly want in terms of glamour and sophistication, it also received unwanted attention in 1982, when *The Blues Brothers* star John Belushi passed away in bungalow number three.

Born in Chicago on 24 January 1949, John was one of four children born to Agnes and Adam Belushi. Always a joker, he had an interest in comedy from an early age, and his high jinks in school caused chaos in more than one classroom. In short, he was the class clown who loved to laugh, but it was love of another kind that he found as a teenager, when he attended Wheaton Central High School and fell for his future wife, Judy Jacklin. The two teenagers dated and Belushi developed an interest in sports and theatre, appearing in several stage productions in Chicago and then dabbling quite successfully in improvised comedy.

It was his interest in making people laugh that led to John's first real break, when he appeared with a Chicago comedy troupe and performed with them eight times a week. Belushi later said that the audience expected the comedians to fail a third of the time and "you learned to write on your feet". Rather than expecting him to fail, in actual fact the audience loved the comedian and he succeeded in unwittingly upstaging the other performers just by being on the stage.

As he grew into his twenties, the young man was drawn more and more into the comedy profession, and by 1972 he was appearing off-Broadway in *National Lampoon's Lemmings*. Having got a taste for the bright lights of New York, it wasn't long before both Belushi and Jacklin were living full-time in the Big Apple where the couple gained work on *The National Lampoon Radio Hour* – him as a player and her as producer. The programme was a hit and gave them enough security finally to settle down and marry, which they did on New Year's Eve, 1976.

John's popularity began to increase and he became one of the original cast members of *Saturday Night Live*. The show is now famous for spawning the careers of such greats as Dan Aykroyd and Chevy Chase, and it was a fabulous outlet for Belushi's comic magic. In the show he entertained viewers with his version of a Greek restaurant owner who served every customer with cheeseburger, chips and Pepsi no matter what they originally ordered. Then there was his version of a samurai warrior who howled in mock Japanese all the while slashing his sword. He was a huge success, something he put down to his ability to make fun of himself: "Most movies today make people feel inadequate. I don't do that," he said in an interview shortly before he passed away.

Thanks to *Saturday Night Live*, John developed a deep friendship with Dan Aykroyd, who later explained how they developed their most successful act, "The Blues Brothers". Apparently on the very first day the two met, they went out for a late-night drink and got speaking about music. John was into punk and heavy metal, while Dan was very much interested in the blues. Insisting that John should at least listen to some blues music he put some on and from there the idea of "The Blue Brothers" was born. After that night, the Blues Brothers sketch became a regular part of *Saturday Night Live*, and was an instant hit with viewers and producers alike.

The sketch grew into something of a phenomenon, and Belushi and Aykroyd released an album of their hits, before making *The Blues Brothers* movie, which was released in 1980. The film was not such a huge hit at the box office, though over the past thirty-plus years it has gone on to be considered a cult movie and has inspired countless tribute acts, impersonations and even a popular London theatre show. Not only that, but the Blues Brothers as a band has gone on, long after the passing of Belushi, with a string of guest singers, a world tour, festival appearances and another movie called *Blues Brothers 2000*. There is even talk of a TV series being made, such is the continued success and inspiration of the Blues Brothers.

On stage it seemed that Belushi was a carefree soul who never had a problem in his life, but as is the case with many comedians, behind his fun-loving persona lay a somewhat troubled man. He was admired by many for the fact that he was a little overweight and average-looking, and yet still a huge star, though while these things inspired others, sadly they were the very things that Belushi worried himself about to the point of despair. He hated the pressure of his career and the way people were constantly telling him to watch what he said and did in public. He was a relatively free spirit and the idea of being restricted was certainly taking its toll.

In order to take the edge off his anxieties, Belushi unfortunately began using large amounts of cocaine; a habit which was not made any easier given the industry he was in. Drug-dealers and hangers-on found it easy to offer Belushi everything he wanted in terms of narcotics, and it got to be such a problem that the actor himself even employed people to stop the dealers approaching him in elevators and other public places.

His drug-taking was so extreme it seems, that when making the movie *Animal House*, director John Landis observed that he abused his body "in ways that would kill bulls", and worried constantly that the actor was going to burn himself out. Friends also became concerned, especially when Belushi claimed that he disliked himself so much that he didn't like anybody who liked him.

John spent the summer of 1981 at Martha's Vineyard where he owned a property. Encouraged by his wife Judy and his friend Dan Aykroyd, the comedian cleaned up his act somewhat, relaxed in the hot tub and took life easy for once. Both Aykroyd and Judy also kept away the unscrupulous people who had been hanging around the star, and together they all had – as Aykroyd later described to *Guardian* writer Sean O'Hagan – "a beautiful summer".

But it wasn't long before John's demons returned, when he moved back out to Hollywood in order to work with writer Don Novello on a screenplay entitled "Noble Rot". The pair had a lot of work to do and Belushi would often stay awake all night in order to keep up with his deadlines. So obsessed was Belushi with getting the job done that the actor even ate in his room at the Chateau Marmont hotel, preferring to work as many hours as possible rather than go to a restaurant. However, even after undertaking a huge amount of work in relation to the prospective movie, it would seem that the studio bosses were still not quite happy with the script, and Belushi was furious. Added to that, he had been offered a role in a movie called *Joy of Sex*, which would have involved a huge fee, but the character was not entirely likeable, therefore leaving him feeling conflicted. In short, Belushi found the entire experience of negotiating his future exhausting, and he seems to have taken solace in using and abusing drugs in a big way during this time.

In order to get some distance from himself and the troubles in Hollywood, Belushi travelled back to New York to visit his wife Judy, but because of the troubles he had left behind in

Hollywood, he was not the best of company. The visit was stressful and after about a week he returned to California to try and sort things out with the screenplay and the movie, once and for all.

Arriving back at the Chateau Marmont hotel, Belushi seemed stressed and hotel staff noticed that there were times when he seemed so tired he would avoid talking to people. He also seemed unhappy and acutely lonely, something which had plagued the actor for some time as he had always hated to be alone. Other times, however, he would seem to be back to his old self, joking and happy, though his mood swings were undoubtedly giving people around the hotel further cause for worry. The hotel manager, Suzanne Jierjian, later told the *Los Angeles Times* that the actor seemed to be driving himself incredibly hard. "He seemed like he was very, very tired," she said.

It would appear that while Belushi's previous visit to the hotel was a low-key, work-heavy affair, this time, however, he was determined to party. He telephoned Cathy Evelyn Smith, a woman he had been friends with for several years and who was known as a backing singer and "groupie". She was also – unfortunately – rumoured to be a drug dealer. From the moment Belushi arrived in Los Angeles, the two hung out together, and according to the woman, they spent at least one evening together – platonically she claimed – drinking California wine and "inhaling cocaine through the nasal passages". She also claimed that they had been injecting too.

On 4 March 1982, Belushi rang his wife Judy from his room at the Chateau Marmont to give her news about his work, and from his tone during the call she sensed that he was not at all happy with the way things were going. Still, there was nothing she could do to make him feel any better with the situation, so she just listened to her husband's worries as he apologized for his behaviour during their last visit and told her that he loved her. That was the last time Judy ever spoke to her husband.

That evening John went out to a restaurant with Cathy

Smith before ending up in the VIP section of the Roxy nightclub. There he became extremely intoxicated and felt so ill that Smith drove him home and helped him into his bungalow at the Chateau Marmont. Once there he vomited in the bathroom, before proceeding to drink wine and snort cocaine, despite still feeling unwell and in no fit state to carry on partying.

The drug-taking continued well into the early hours of the morning and Smith later reported that the actor became pale and sweaty. Still, the night did not end there and at some time before 3 a.m. Belushi welcomed two friends to the bungalow – actors Robert De Niro and Robin Williams. They both arrived separately but neither stayed for long after becoming disturbed by what they had found to be going on in the room.

Williams in particular was said to have thought of Cathy Smith as "creepy" and wondered what on earth Belushi was doing hanging around with her. He had been battling his own demons for some years and knew enough about Hollywood to be concerned for his friend's welfare. Before he left the hotel, he told Belushi to call him if he ever got out of bed again, and what happened later disturbed him so much that he is said to have gone "cold turkey" in order to wean himself off drugs. In 1988 the evening was still playing on his mind and, during an interview with *People* magazine, he described the tragedy as "frightening" and a wake-up call for "a whole group of show-business people".

After both Williams and De Niro had left the bungalow, the drug-taking between Smith and Belushi continued in a rampant fashion, and at 6.30 a.m. the actor took a shower and complained that he felt cold. He turned up the heat but still felt decidedly unwell – not really surprising considering the amount of drugs he had ingested that evening. Then at around 8 a.m., the couple ordered room service, but Belushi fell asleep on his bed before it arrived. Cathy Smith – still awake – took delivery of the order, and later said that at this point she noticed that her sleeping friend was breathing in a very erratic way, wheezing and visibly shaking.

She was concerned enough to wake him up, and later described that he was not pleased to be woken and assured her that everything was okay. He then drank a glass of water, took some more drugs and fell back to sleep, but not before asking Smith to stay with him as he did not want to be alone. She stayed for a while but had personal business to attend to away from the hotel, so after looking in on him one last time, the woman took Belushi's Mercedes and left for the morning.

What happened next is something of a mystery and it is unclear as to whether or not the actor ever regained consciousness. However, what we do know for sure is that his personal trainer, William Wallace, tried several times to contact Belushi by telephone and could not get through. He arrived at the hotel at 12.15 p.m. and on entering the room discovered the actor lying on the bed, having obviously passed away. He summoned the hotel security man, Bruce Beckler, and together they took the actor's body from the bed and tried desperately to revive him but it was no good. Paramedics later commented that Belushi was probably dead by 10 a.m. that morning, a good two hours before being discovered by Wallace.

By the time Cathy Smith arrived back at the hotel, the police had surrounded the building and, as she had made the mistake of driving up a one-way street in the wrong direction, she was stopped by the police, who pointed out what she had done wrong. On mentioning that this was the route John Belushi told her to take, the officers immediately seized the woman and took her away for questioning, apparently not informing her until hours later that the actor had passed away.

It was during this police interview that the coroner later said Smith presented officers with a blackened spoon and syringe, which she had taken from the room in an effort to keep the drug-taking secret from the hotel's cleaning service. She had not cleaned the room as much as she had believed, however, when officers on the scene found not only a "green leafy substance" in a container, but also hand-rolled cigarettes, papers and – most revealingly – traces of white powder on a dresser.

Smith was released after questioning, but quite surprisingly, rather than just choosing to fade into the background, she actually consented to an interview with *ABC News* to talk about Belushi's last days. The interview was not particularly revealing and while she freely admitted that it wasn't totally out of the question that Belushi had overdosed, she chose not to admit witnessing the actor taking drugs that evening. Added to that, her lawyer stopped the interviewer from asking about the rumours of her drug-dealing, before finally jumping to his feet and calling a halt to the programme altogether when Smith was asked about the rumours of drug-taking among Belushi and his friends.

Los Angeles County Coroner Thomas Noguchi – who had also investigated the deaths of Marilyn Monroe and Natalie Wood – was assigned to the case and, on performing an autopsy, he declared that the procedure had not yet established a cause of death. Further tests were ordered and at that point police attested that they could see no foul play involved in the death.

By this time the news had been wired around the world and Belushi's friend and co-star Dan Aykroyd travelled to John's home in order to break the sad news to John's wife, Judy. She was understandably upset and confused, and immediately tried to get answers from the police as to why and how her husband had died. However, during an interview with *People* magazine some years later, she recalled that the police were not helpful and that one officer actually asked her what she expected, as "the guy was a junkie". Considering this was a young widow grieving the loss of her husband, it was not the most compassionate way to behave, but it seems this was only the tip of the iceberg. Over the next few weeks she would be told all kinds of rumours, including how Belushi had drug marks over his entire body, which made her feel awful and ultimately turned out to be false.

Meanwhile, fans began to gather in Chicago bars and at comedy clubs in a desperate attempt to get "closer" to their lost idol, talking about the laughs he had brought them and the tragedy that had unfolded in a lonely hotel room just days before. Tributes began to pour in from friends, though some – including Robin Williams – were too upset to talk. Dan Aykroyd was described as having "submerged in New York", completely overwhelmed at the loss of his friend, while John's siblings, Marian and Jim, were beside themselves with grief. Jim struggled through a stage production of *The Pirates of Penzance* on – according to him – "Valium and alcohol", while friends desperately tried to provide comfort to them. It was well meant but unfortunately unsuccessful: "Nothing can help now," Marian told the *Los Angeles Times*.

On 8 March 1982 sources at the Los Angeles County Coroner's Office revealed that it was believed that the actor had died after a drugs overdose. Rumours surfaced that his arms had needle marks and prominent veins, and one unnamed source disclosed that it had been free-based cocaine (the purest and most potent form of the drug) that Belushi had been injecting that evening.

Although no official word could be obtained from Noguchi and police were denying all knowledge of any official results, the stories did actually turn out to be true. On 10 March the coroner's office finally revealed that the death had been caused by a mixture of heroin and cocaine being injected into his veins, and that samples taken from his room at the Chateau Marmont Hotel had been found to be drugs. The levels of narcotics in Belushi's body were described as "extremely large" and "substantial", while on the death certificate it listed "Acute Cocaine and Heroin Intoxication" as the cause of his death, which was registered as an "accident".

Friends and colleagues of the actor were not surprised to hear of the death verdict, though several did declare that they had never witnessed him taking drugs in front of them in the past. One unnamed friend assured reporters that while working on films, Belushi never touched drugs, though in between projects he had been known to inject heroin and snort cocaine for at least the past two years. However, while the reports of drug-taking were shocking, friends did point out that John had expressed a recent desire to straighten himself out and get off heroin once and for all.

His wife Judy later said that she had believed that Belushi was turning a corner, while friends at the time gave their opinion that if he had been with his wife – who disliked his drug-taking immensely – he never would have lost his life. "If she had been with him, he'd still be alive today," one told the *Los Angeles Times*, and this was something that played on Judy's mind for a long time afterwards, before she eventually allowed herself to realize that her presence might not have saved him; that there were no guarantees either way.

All the "ifs and buts" were no use in bringing back John Belushi; he had gone and everyone was faced with the inevitable loss. The body of the once vibrant comedian was taken back east to Martha's Vineyard where he owned his holiday house, in order for his friends and family to say their last goodbyes; 150 mourners gathered at the West Tisbury Congregational Church, while hundreds of fans, neighbours and the curious stood on the street to pay their respects. The ceremony was solemn but included the odd hint of humour and comedy, just as John would have wanted, with the reverend at one point quoting the comedian's catchphrase, "Wise Up!" to the amused congregation.

The funeral may have been a small, conservative affair, but there was a chance to remember the star in a grander way several days later when a thousand of Belushi's friends and family met at the St John the Divine Cathedral in New York. There John's brother Jim told the congregation that he was sure his sibling would have enjoyed cartwheeling down the aisle of the cathedral, while co-star Dan Aykroyd promised that he would always remain Belushi's "number one fan". He then held up a cassette player and played a song entitled "Two

Thousand Pound Bee", which he told the congregation that he and Belushi had always said would be played at their funerals.

In the days and months ahead, a full investigation was conducted into the death of John Belushi, but it was felt that his passing was just another Hollywood tragedy with no one to blame but the actor himself. However, all this changed when Cathy Smith – who was by now living in Canada but still apparently not willing to fade into the background – gave an interview to the *National Enquirer*. In the damning article, the woman apparently gave the shocking announcement that she had injected Belushi with a "speedball" – a mixture of heroin and cocaine – shortly before he had died.

This news caused a firestorm and the Deputy District Attorney Michael Genelin immediately urged police to reopen the case, saying that if the quotes were true, Smith had in effect confessed to second-degree murder. Officers headed to Canada to interview the woman, but by then she was denying saying such a thing and threatening to sue the *National Enquirer* for damages. In a statement released through her lawyer, Smith said that she was anxious to clear up misunderstandings caused by her words being taken out of context, and that she was willing to be interviewed, after "certain documents" had been reviewed.

Unfortunately for Smith, the *National Enquirer* refused to revoke the comments and told reporters that they would be standing behind their story "fully", revealing that they had reportedly paid the woman $15,000 for her interview. Smith's lawyer immediately issued a statement which said that the sometime singer was drunk and on drugs when she had spoken to the magazine, and even more controversially, claimed that the alcohol had been provided by the reporters themselves. He denied that she had ever said anything to them about giving Belushi a final – and fatal – drug hit, and declared that the article Smith had approved was not the one that had ended up on the news-stand. Finally, he tried to assure everyone that the whole episode had left his client very "distressed and dismayed".

The *National Enquirer* released a statement of their own, not only denying that their reporters had plied Smith with drink but also confirming once again that they would stand by their story. Why? Because Smith had apparently been taped during the interview and the audio had confirmed that what was printed in the magazine were indeed her words. Meanwhile, officers were also not convinced by Smith's denial and spent an hour with her, asking about the alleged comments and trying to get to the bottom of what happened, once and for all.

By this time Police Chief Daryl Gates was getting more and more frustrated with the entire episode, angry that Smith had sold an interview and anxious that their new leads might in fact be "a wild goose chase". Reported to want to get the case wrapped up for good, he was then quoted as describing John as "a horrible person", which provided fodder for the newspapers and caused outrage among his friends. Ten of his closest colleagues teamed up and released their own statement to the newspapers, saying that they had known Belushi well, while Gates had never even met him. Describing him as a "sweet and wonderful person who obviously made some tragic choices", the friends then described the statement by Gates as a "callous and simplistic attack" against their friend.

The investigation continued, with police examining new evidence and re-interviewing friends and those who could possibly provide a substantial lead. Finally they decided that Cathy Smith should be charged with the murder of John Belushi, and went in search of the elusive woman. Still in Canada and refusing to return to the United States, she then gave another interview – this time to the *Toronto Sun* – where she expressed her opinion that the police were trying to find a scapegoat for the death and that the murder indictment was "no big deal".

But a big deal it was, and on realizing that the matter would not be dropped, Smith surrendered to the authorities and was held in a Toronto prison before finally being extradited to the United States. A trial was ordered and Smith was charged not only with second-degree murder, but also thirteen felony charges related to providing and giving heroin and cocaine to Belushi. Smith was devastated at the judge's decision, while her lawyer spoke to reporters outside the court and described the entire episode as "an absolute tragedy", adding that he had no idea why people could not just let John Belushi rest in peace.

While Smith was initially to be put on trial for second-degree murder, by the time it all came to a head she had accepted a plea-bargain and the charge had been downgraded to involuntary manslaughter with three additional counts of providing drugs to Belushi in the days before his death. It was looking slightly better for Smith than it had before, but she still wasn't out of the woods. By this time portions of the now infamous *National Enquirer* tape had been presented to the court, and various witnesses had spoken of her association with the actor. It was also pointed out that in spite of attending numerous drug rehabilitation programmes, Smith still had a big drug problem, which prompted her lawyer to say that he hoped his client would not end up in prison.

The Deputy District Attorney Elden S. Fox had other ideas, however, and announced that probation was not a possibility because Smith had not yet understood the gravity of what she had done. Besides, he said, the woman might run to Canada in a bid to avoid the authorities, so in the end it was decided that Cathy Smith should serve fifteen months in prison beginning in December 1986, almost five years after the death of the Blues Brothers' actor.

The death of John Belushi is just one example of how the extremes of fast living in Hollywood can lead to pain, tragedy and destruction. Still, in spite of the terrible nature of his death, Belushi left a body of work that inspired millions and he will never be forgotten. Indeed his brother Jim and best friend Dan Aykroyd have both described how they still feel "haunted" by the actor to this very day. Aykroyd told the British newspaper, the *Guardian*, that he thinks of his friend every time he visits a blues club. Then in 2008, Jim Belushi told an interviewer that he is constantly reminded of his brother every day, particularly when people approach him in the street: "People just say, 'I loved your brother,' and I always go, 'I loved him too.' You just can't hide from it," he said.

43

Madonna's Nude Scandals

When Madonna Louise Veronica Ciccone was not the global superstar she is now, she supplemented her income as a dancer in New York by taking odd jobs as a hat-check girl at the Russian Tea Room and a "jelly squirter" at Dunkin' Donuts. Neither job paid well and she was quickly fired from Dunkin' Donuts for squirting the jelly too liberally – mainly all over the equipment rather than the doughnuts.

However, her luck changed when she discovered that she could model nude for art and photography students at the New School for a lot more money than she ever could working odd jobs. When not dancing, the twenty-year-old Madonna would head to the school and pose for three hours to earn enough to buy food, which – when struggling – would often be yoghurt, nuts and occasionally popcorn.

While working at the New School, the young model would often meet budding photographers who would ask her to pose privately for them at their "studio". Of course, these studios were mainly apartments or dingy rooms, but as long as it was above board and she got paid, she didn't mind too much. "It was really good money and very flexible hours which is why I chose to do it – it wasn't because I enjoyed taking my clothes off," she told Rupert Everett during the 1998 television special, *Madonna Rising*.

But take her clothes off she did, and it went further in 1979 when Madonna saw an advert that required an actress to dance and act in a student movie being made nearby. There was no way she would ever get rich from such a role – and in fact it turned out the job was a non-paying one anyway – but hoping for a boost up the career ladder, Madonna auditioned for and won the role of Bruna, a passionate woman in a group of sex-slaves who falls in love with a young, "normal" man. Even the most liberal of critics would describe the film as pretty dire, with stilted dialogue and forced performances from almost every member of the cast.

The story was not exactly pleasant viewing either and at one point the film includes some rather disturbing scenes when Bruna is raped by a man in a restaurant toilet. She decides afterwards to take her revenge and together with her group of slaves drives around New York in order to find the attacker. Eventually she tracks him down and ends up carrying out a sacrifice, complete with tomato-ketchup blood, which is smeared all around the end of the movie.

Just like her modelling career, *A Certain Sacrifice* required Madonna to disrobe and take part in scenes that at the time were described as "soft porn". By today's standards it is very tame, but nevertheless, the film and her modelling career were not the sort of thing she wanted her strict Italian father to know about. He had been against her moving to New York in the first place, and had begged her to come home on discovering she was sleeping in a rat-infested apartment. What he would think of this new career was anyone's guess, but Madonna decided to keep it from him, in the hope that he would never be in the position to find out.

However, not even Madonna could have predicted the huge amount of global publicity and stardom she was to achieve in the mid-1980s, and after hitting the big time it was not long before the associates of her past were crawling out of the woodwork. The first came in 1985 when two of the photographers she posed for – Martin Schreiber and Lee Friedlander – decided to cash in on Madonna's fame and sell their photographs to *Playboy*.

Much to Madonna's dismay, the photos were snapped up and the offending issue went to print on 10 July 1985. Then just three days later, *Penthouse* got in on the act by publishing seventeen pages of nudes by photographer Bill Stone. As if that wasn't bad enough, along came a video version of *A Certain Sacrifice*, and while Madonna tried desperately to stop the release, she lost the fight and the film was seen by millions around the world. Madonna tried to play it down by joking that she didn't want *A Certain Sacrifice* to be released because of the quality of her acting, not the nude scenes, but in private she was absolutely furious that her past was coming back to haunt her.

The nude scandal embarrassed and upset her family in Michigan; her father was furious and her grandmother apparently burst into tears on hearing the news. However, the show had to go on, and at exactly the same time as the photos were released, Madonna was scheduled to perform at the Philadelphia concert for Bob Geldolf's "Live Aid".

Many predicted that the star would not perform; that she would cancel because of the embarrassment of her nude pictures going public. However, in true Madonna style, she declared she was not ashamed, and travelled to the gig with her then fiancé, Sean Penn. Describing her as "The woman who has pulled herself up by her bra straps, and has been known to let them down occasionally", Bette Midler introduced Madonna and she danced on to the stage as if she didn't have a care in the world.

However, while Madonna had previously been known to wear her lacy underwear in public and little else, on the occasion of Live Aid the singer chose to cover up completely. Wearing flowery trousers, a cut-off shirt and a long jacket, she laughed when chants of "Take off your coat" were heard from the audience. "I ain't taking shit off today," she squealed. "You might hold it against me ten years from now."

Madonna's good humour and wit during the entire nude episode won fans over, and in the end nobody seemed to care what she had done before fame had come her way. However, people were not quite so forgiving seven years later when she decided to go one step further and release a book entitled *Sex*, which was full of pictures of the singer in all kinds of provocative positions – most of which were nude or semi-nude. Then in the same year she also released an S&M-inspired video for the song "Erotica", an album with the same name, and finally landed the lead role in *Body of Evidence*, an erotic thriller which required her not only to disrobe, but also to perform in various revealing sex scenes.

While fans had been quick to forgive the nude scandal, many people decided they had had enough of the sex being pushed down their throats by Madonna and her overexposed body. Her album sales plummeted and reviews for *Body of Evidence* were dire, though in truth many people still went to watch the movie, just to see for themselves how far the superstar had gone this time. Though still hugely famous, for several years after the *Sex* book her career floundered and many began writing her off as a has-been. She wasn't, of course, and her re-emergence in 1996 as both Evita (in the film of that name) and mother to baby Lourdes ensured her life and career were both back on track.

Madonna declared that the *Sex* period was a rebellion, "a statement on the hypocrisy of the world that we live in". She had no regrets about doing it, but by the time she reached her fifties, it was thought that her desire to express her art through her own nudity had come an end. Little did anyone know that in 2012, just a week into her successful MDNA tour, the almost fifty-four-year-old singer would do it again when she was performing her 1995 hit, "Human Nature".

While standing close to fans at the front of the stage in Turkey, Madonna stripped off her costume right down to an elaborate bra made up of two layers. The outer layer was taken off, and then out of the blue, the singer suddenly pulled down the cup of her remaining bra, exposing her right breast fully to the amateur cameras in the front row. Then, as fans applauded loudly, she turned her back to the audience, unzipped her trousers and thrust her hand into her groin, where it stayed for a number of seconds before order – and clothes – were finally resumed.

Whether or not this was a premeditated action remains to be seen, but one thing is for sure: the episode was beamed worldwide on YouTube, where it was picked up and repeated in newspapers around the globe. Unfortunately the comments were not positive and at times downright insulting, but Madonna had achieved what she may have wanted: publicity not only for her tour but her also new album. By the time the show hit the next stop, Rome, people crowded into the auditorium, wondering if the last show would be repeated. It wasn't; "Human Nature" started up but no breast was revealed. However, the crowds did get a little peep-show moment when the star turned her back to them and took down her trousers, revealing her lacy panties underneath. Once again it hit the headlines; once again it gained publicity for the tour.

The tour carried on in such a fashion for the rest of 2012, with every night being a moment of will she/won't she? Some days she did flash her body to the waiting fans, and others she didn't, but whenever a breast was revealed, it was certain that someone would take a picture that would be transmitted around the world.

The tour ended in December 2012, and was quickly named the biggest grossing tour of the year, beating Bruce Springsteen into second place. Some cynics claim that it was only because of the nudity that the tour sold so well, but this is not so, as most of the concerts were sold out long before the tour hit Turkey and no doubt long before the idea of flashing her breast came into the singer's mind.

In spite of what the doubters and cynics say, it would seem that Madonna's continued success is as a result of her body of work, not her physical body. Yes, her love of nudity has caused controversy from the very beginning of her career and has brought her many headlines along the way, but the notoriety of such acts can only go so far on the journey to continued longevity. Once at the peak of a career, only a mixture of ambition, talent and determination can keep you there, and no matter what anyone says, it is clear that Queen of Pop Madonna has all three in spades. Long may she reign.

44

Rock Hudson Dies of AIDS

In the mid-1980s, AIDS was still a mysterious disease that caused a great deal of confusion, with misinformation rife in terms of how it could be transmitted and prevented. It was a condition that was talked about in hushed voices; a secretive illness that nobody wanted to discuss openly; and many people stuck their heads in the sand in the hope that ignorance was bliss. However, things have a habit of being found out, and in 1985 the world was rocked by the discovery that Hollywood star Rock Hudson was dying as a result of AIDS, and no one could deny its existence any more.

Born in Illinois as Roy Harold Scherer Jr on 17 November 1925, Rock had an unsettled early life after his father left the family home during the days of the Great Depression. Fortunately for him, he acquired a new father when his mother remarried and he went on to have a decent life as a teenager, singing at high school, taking part in school plays and working as a newspaper boy to earn pocket money.

Rock had a keen interest in acting and after serving in the Philippines during World War II, he moved to Los Angeles to make it big. Success came slowly, however, and he spent some of his time working as a truck driver to pay the rent, before finally earning a small part in the 1948 movie, *Fighter Squadron*. The part was a success and he was featured heavily in magazines of the day, where women began to sit up and take notice thanks, for the most part, to his smouldering good looks.

By the mid-1950s Hudson's popularity was ensured when he was cast alongside Jane Wyman in *Magnificent Obsession* (1954). Then his dreams came true when he was nominated for an Academy Award after co-starring in *Giant* with Elizabeth Taylor and James Dean.

In spite of Rock's huge appeal to women as a romantic figure, he was harbouring a secret – he was gay. It was a fairly well-known "secret" in Hollywood, with Doris Day and Elizabeth Taylor both later saying that they had known of his sexual orientation. However, to everyone else Hudson was most certainly a straight man and, after a near miss in the mid-1950s when *Confidential* magazine threatened to "out" him, the actor married a secretary called Phyllis Gates, which reinforced the public's belief that he was, in fact, heterosexual.

Strangely, Ms Gates later claimed that she married Hudson out of love, not as a favour made to keep his sex life out of the newspapers, but sadly it would seem that the actor did not feel the same way. After several years they were divorced, with Phyllis citing mental cruelty as the reason for separation. She came away with a hefty alimony and Rock was able to continue projecting an untarnished romantic image, which did him no harm at all when in the late 1950s and into the 1960s he starred in a string of romantic comedies with Doris Day, including the hugely successful *Pillow Talk* (1959) and *Lover Come Back* (1961).

The 1970s saw Hudson making a successful move to television in the long-running TV show *McMillan & Wife*, though by this time it did seem quite apparent that his career was slowly but surely winding down. He was a big drinker and heavy smoker, and this resulted in a series of health scares including a heart attack in 1981 and then heart-bypass surgery. But in spite of this, he did continue to work, and was cast as Linda Evans's love-interest in the highly successful drama series *Dynasty*. However, by this time his good looks were quite obviously ravished and his speech was becoming slow and somewhat slurred. This raised more than a few eyebrows, particularly when he was photographed with former co-star Doris Day, looking extremely thin and drawn, clearly weighing several stone less than just a short time before.

The reason for Rock's haggard looks was – of course – because he was suffering from HIV. However, knowing the stigma that was attached to the fledgling disease, neither he nor his publicity staff wanted to admit that this was what was causing him to be so gaunt. Added to that, it was still not public knowledge that the actor was even gay, so to suddenly announce that he had HIV would have led to more gossip and questions than anyone was prepared to handle.

But being able to keep the news a secret was getting to be an impossible task, and on 23 July 1985 – after the actor had collapsed in a Paris hotel and was rushed to hospital – it was reported that he was in the city in order to receive treatment for an undisclosed illness. The gossip mills went into overdrive and it was clear from the start that the media were never going to just let the story go without a solid answer to their questions.

Finally Hudson's press people stepped up to make a statement, though it was not quite what everyone was expecting . . . At first they announced that he was suffering from inoperable liver cancer, but then this backfired when it was discovered that the hospital where he was staying was a leading facility in AIDS research. The newspapers went into overdrive again and a great deal of speculation ensued, which led to the disclosure that the actor was actually in hospital for tests. What kind of tests? asked the newspapers. "Everything" was the reply.

But still, neither the public nor the media were satisfied with the answers being given, especially when it was found that this was actually the actor's second visit to Paris for treatment. Everyone pressed for a true comment but none was immediately forthcoming, and instead his representatives tried desperately to dampen down the rumours. They told newspapers that it had definitely been confirmed that his condition was inoperable liver cancer, then when the questions became too much, suddenly no one was available for comment and the whole camp went silent.

Finally, everyone involved with Rock Hudson knew that they were fighting a losing battle to keep his illness out of the newspapers, and it was decided to admit the truth once and for all. This grisly task was given to his spokeswoman, Yanou Collart, who told waiting reporters that, yes, the actor did have AIDS and that he had actually been diagnosed over a year before.

Strangely, though, instead of answering the queries asked by the media and public over the course of the past few weeks, the statement actually caused more questions when Collart added the bizarre "fact" that recent tests had shown that Hudson was now free of the disease and he was, in fact, cured. Since there was no known cure for AIDS then – or now – this comment was confusing to say the least. Did they really believe the actor was now cured, or were they still trying to cover up the truth? Nobody seemed to have a clue.

The news that Hudson had recovered from AIDS was soon disputed by doctors throughout the United States who stepped in to say that no treatment could currently cure the disease and that if the actor had been suffering from AIDS at some point, then he would still have it now. More confusion came when it was revealed that Hudson had been first treated in the Paris hospital without any of the doctors knowing that he had previously been diagnosed with AIDS. Without being aware of this important information, they had surmised that his liver was suffering abnormalities and that it was – quite tragically – an inoperable condition.

The media reports into Rock Hudson's illness were littered with untruths and speculation. Hudson was receiving an experimental drug which would block the disease, said one statement. No, it was far too late for him to receive any treatment like that, said another. Rock had flown to France in order to seek help with his AIDS treatment was another comment. No, he had only ended up in hospital after collapsing in his hotel, said another. With the stories getting more and more out of hand, at last Rock's spokeswoman had to confirm the real situation once and for all. Yes, the actor still had AIDS, she confirmed, but no, none of his people knew how he had actually become infected. "I have no idea if he knows how he got it," the spokesperson told the *Los Angeles Times*.

Of course, this brought up the question of whether or not Rock Hudson could possibly be gay, and it was not long before newspapers were quoting columnist Armistead Maupin as saying that nine years earlier, he had asked the actor about his sexuality. Apparently Maupin was of the opinion that Hudson was gay and had enquired as to whether or not he would ever discuss it. "Rock seemed to take to the idea," Maupin told the *San Francisco Chronicle*, before adding that Hudson had told him one of these days he would have a lot to tell, and that he had learned the Hollywood lesson very well: keeping quiet about his real love affairs and being happy to allow various gossip columnists to make up imaginary girlfriends for him.

Despite the rumours and comments, no official statement on the star's love life was forthcoming and his representatives announced – rather questionably – that they knew absolutely nothing about his sexuality at all. Still, while the press attention that centred on the actor's illness was most unwelcome in the Hudson camp, something quite extraordinary was bubbling away behind the scenes. Instead of people immediately lambasting the actor for having the dreaded and mysterious AIDS virus, many were responding to the news reports by raising their own awareness of the disease and coming forward to get themselves tested.

Information about the illness was no longer being swept under the carpet; now everyone seemed to know what AIDS was, and even President Ronald Reagan gave his support to the ailing actor by telephoning him in the hospital. Furthermore, donations were beginning to trickle in to AIDS charities and a walkathon was held in Hollywood which attracted twice as many people as it had the year before, raising $630,000 for those suffering from the syndrome. The executive director of AIDS Project/Los Angeles said that the announcement that Rock Hudson had the disease was the most important thing that had ever happened in the fight against the illness, and this most certainly seems to be the case. Whether he knew it or not, Rock Hudson was now a strong force within the AIDS community and he was doing more to spread awareness than any person or campaign had ever done before.

Sadly, while the actor's plight was bringing attention to the disease as a whole, it was also the subject of yet more gossip and misunderstanding from those who refused to educate themselves. Various individuals began asking if Hudson could have given AIDS to his *Dynasty* co-star Linda Evans, as the two had shared kissing scenes in the television show before it was announced he was ill. This was such a topic of concern and intrigue that it even appeared on news programmes; rumours began that producers would now insist on AIDS tests for all actors before shooting intimate scenes, and that actresses would most likely refuse to kiss gay actors on camera.

Doctors were brought in to dispute the tale that you could contract AIDS from kissing or touching someone, but many people still did not believe it. In fact, when Princess Diana was later seen shaking the hand of an AIDS patient in a UK hospital, there was outrage that the future Queen of England could possibly have exposed herself to the disease. It was a ridiculous concept, of course, but one that was very much on the minds of misinformed people during the mid-1980s.

Meanwhile, on a personal level, Rock Hudson was discharged from the Paris hospital where he had been staying since his collapse, and flew back to California. He was immediately admitted to the UCLA hospital where his condition was reported as fair, and from which a statement was made to say that he had approved the idea of a Rock Hudson Foundation to be set up to raise money for AIDS. Then on 25 August 1985 came the news that he had been released from hospital in order to rest at his home, though it was made clear that he would still need continuous care.

A surprise announcement came when it was said that despite his illness, Rock Hudson was preparing to write his autobiography with an author called Sara Davidson. All proceeds were to go to AIDS research and the book would be written using interviews given from Rock's bedside. The fact that he was strong enough to attempt to do such a thing was a positive sign and the future began to look rather more hopeful. He also sent a statement to be read out at an AIDS project event, where he thanked Elizabeth Taylor for her friendship and said that while he did not wish to be sick, he was glad that his illness was at least having some positive effect on others who needed help.

Unfortunately, while Hudson's comments showed some kind of lucidity on his part, any concept of a return to health was sadly something of an illusion. At 9 a.m. on 2 October 1985, Rock breathed his last; surrounded by members of his staff, he slipped quietly away at his home in Beverly Hills. Fans wept when the death was announced and funeral plans were quickly drawn up, which saw his body cremated and the ashes scattered into the Pacific Ocean. Then a hundred of his closest friends gathered in the garden of Hudson's home to pay tribute to the man who had soared to the very top of the Hollywood list, only to come crashing back down due to ill health. Mexican food was served; a mariachi band played; and friends including Elizabeth Taylor and Carol Burnett remembered their pal in his heyday when the world of showbiz had been at his feet.

Along with the tributes from co-stars and friends, a strange undercurrent of anger and suspicion began bubbling away in the newspapers over the authenticity of many of the statements Rock Hudson was supposed to have made over the course of his illness. Some friends told reporters that the actor had not even known his disease had become public knowledge, while one of his associates, Ross Hunter, told columnist Marilyn Beck that for the most part the actor was not lucid when he had gone to visit him. Hunter later added that of course he hadn't been with him all the time, which prompted other friends and staff members to recall that when they had visited the actor in the final months, he had always been perfectly coherent with them.

However, this revelation of whether or not Hudson knew his disease was public forced his spokesman, Dale Olson, to admit that it had been himself, not the actor, who had written the statement which was read out at the September AIDS event. However, he made it clear that Rock had approved every word and very much understood what he was reading.

In the end, away from the controversy surrounding the secret of his illness and the questions raised after his passing, the death of Rock Hudson was a tragic and sad affair but with it came a ray of hope that people could stop whispering about AIDS and begin to educate themselves and others regarding the actual facts. His death – like so many before and after – left the world a darker place, though it was not in vain. His fight helped pave the way for celebrities including Elizabeth Taylor, Joan Rivers, Madonna and Princess Diana to give compassionate support to those who were suffering; it went a long way to reduce stigma, and for that alone, Hudson's passing has helped many people over the course of almost thirty years. Perhaps without even knowing it, the man who hid his illness and sexuality from the world for such a long time managed to open the floodgates and let education about AIDS, and the acceptance of those who were suffering, finally begin.

45

The Tumultuous Marriage of Madonna and Sean Penn

There are some Hollywood marriages that are over in a flash; others that surprise everyone by lasting a lifetime. There are quiet marriages, loud marriages, violent and tempestuous marriages . . . and then there is the marriage of Madonna and Sean Penn.

By the time Madonna Louise Veronica Ciccone met actor Sean Penn, she was already on her way to becoming a major superstar, while he was an intense actor and aspiring director. The pair met on the set of Madonna's 1985 video for "Material Girl" and although she wasn't overly impressed with him at first, they soon began seeing each other regularly, and were photographed backstage at Live Aid, huddled in each other's arms.

Madonna had never appeared to be the marrying kind, but Penn eventually won her over and proposed one morning as the singer was jumping up and down on her bed. According to the singer, Sean suddenly got a particular look in his eye and she had been completely certain that he was about to pop the question. She told the actor that whatever he was thinking she was definitely going to say yes, so he took the opportunity to ask for her hand in marriage, and of course she accepted.

The much ballyhooed wedding took place on 16 August 1985 in the mountain-top garden of 6970 Wildlife Road, Malibu, the home of Penn's friend Dan Unger, and it was a noisy affair. Although the pair tried to assure the media that the only thing happening that day was a joint birthday party (their birthdays are a day apart), they failed to convince anyone, particularly when guests started showing up wearing wedding outfits, complete with presents.

Reporters and photographers went wild, hiding in the bushes and trying to bluff their way into the house. When that failed, they finally hired helicopters and by the time the bride appeared in the garden dressed in a huge white dress with a black bowler hat and veil, there were over a dozen copters flying above her head.

"That whole time was almost too much," she later said. She had never expected in her wildest dreams to be married with helicopters buzzing around, and declared the entire affair "a circus". Still, she was determined not to let it ruin her day and while it is fair to say that the noise could have stressed out the calmest of brides, for Madonna it was all just too hilarious for words. "In the end I was laughing," she said in an interview. "At first I was outraged and then I was laughing."

But while Madonna might have seen the funny side, her groom most certainly did not, and at one point he was apparently seen on the sand, spelling the words "Fuck Off" in giant letters and waving a gun at the passing helicopters. It was not a good start, and Sean and Madonna's life together did not get much better.

From the very beginning their marriage was one of arguments and controversy. As with many newlywed showbiz couples, Madonna and Sean thought that it would be a good experience to make a film together, but this turned out to be one of the worst decisions they could have made. During the making of the film, *Shanghai Surprise*, they fought constantly and became so aloof with other cast members that when the cast and crew landed in England, the newspapers christened them "The Poison Penns". The film's producer, George Harrison, was highly disappointed by the bad press and encouraged Madonna to accompany him to a conference to thwart the rumours and stories quickly spreading about the couple.

Despite the good intentions, the event did not go particularly well, especially when one reporter repeated a rumour that Madonna's management contract was up for sale. "Did you know that, and George, would you like to buy it?" he enquired. George Harrison chewed on gum uncomfortably while Madonna tried to avoid the question.

"You're a little troublemaker, aren't you?" she quipped.

"I'm not the only one, there's a room full of them," retorted the reporter.

He was right, and the conference lurched from one uncomfortable moment to the next, with Madonna complaining afterwards that the press had been unbelievably vicious and rude. Her comments may have been fair but unfortunately for her they only fuelled the fire of negativity surrounding the film. This in turn seemed to send Madonna and Sean Penn into even more explosive bust-ups between themselves and others, on and off set.

Once the movie was released, the reviews were poor (and even today it only claims a rating of less than three out of ten stars on the Internet Movie Database), but Madonna did not seem to be willing to place the blame at her own door, and instead stated that while she liked the script, by the time they got on set, it was clear to her that the man at the helm of the film was a TV director who was in over his head when it came to directing a movie. "It was downhill from the second day," she told reporters. She also complained that her scenes were cut so much that it made her "look like an airhead girl, without a character".

Whoever's fault it was, *Shanghai Surprise* was a box-office disaster, but Madonna pressed on with her film career regardless and went on to work on a project initially called "Slammer", a comedy about a young woman called Nikki Finn who is trying to clear her name of a crime she didn't commit. Even before it was released, rumours were abounding that it would be a stinker. The critics didn't disappoint: even Madonna's co-star, a cougar called Murray, got better reviews than she did.

To add to the frustration, the title "Slammer" became a hilarious twist for the media, as by the time it was scheduled to come out, Sean Penn was in the slammer himself after an incident on the set of his movie, *Colors*. The film was renamed out of respect for him, and it ultimately went on to be called *Who's That Girl*, which just happened to tie in with both the soundtrack song and Madonna's upcoming world tour.

Luckily, while her films most certainly were not burning brightly at the box office, the world tour was a big success and Madonna played for the first time to stadium audiences on many continents. Unfortunately, being away from the States for so long, combined with the time spent apart from Penn during his prison stay, put tremendous strain on the already volatile marriage. When interviewed by Simon Bates for BBC Radio One, Madonna lamented, "Love feels like a huge hand that comes around my whole body and sometimes it's all furry and warm and it feels good, then other times it's all scratchy and it hurts."

Once the jail term and world tour had ended, Mr and Mrs Penn settled down to what they hoped would be a quiet life. However, wherever they went the couple were followed by fans and paparazzi, all throwing questions, flashbulbs and comments in their direction. Things grew worse when fans started ringing the couple's doorbell every day, which infuriated Penn no end. "What do they expect, for us to invite them up for a cup of coffee?" Madonna later pondered.

Of course, the press loved Sean's reaction to being followed, and it became a common occurrence to see photographs of the actor shouting in the street, while his wife tried to hide her face with her handbag. By the end of 1987, however, things had come to a head and Madonna filed for divorce on 4 December 1987, though it was ultimately called off when Sean managed to convince her that they could make it work. She withdrew the application on 16 December and the two were soon photographed reportedly renewing their wedding vows in an attempt to hold their marriage together.

In 1988 Madonna returned to New York in order to appear on Broadway in David Mamet's play, *Speed the Plow*. She seemed to hate the experience of working on stage every night, but was buoyed when she began a friendship with comedienne Sandra Bernhard. The two began hanging out together after the show, frequenting nightclubs and being photographed intensively – mainly by newspapers eager to see if the two women were more than just good friends.

The two managed to cause headlines during a colourful rendition of *I've Got You Babe* at a charity concert, and then provoked a huge amount of scandal when they appeared together on the *Late Show with David Letterman*. Dressed identically in white T-shirts, denim shorts and white socks, their "performance" raised many eyebrows as they hinted at being intimate together and then joked that Sandra had slept with Sean Penn. "She's using me to get to Sean," Madonna laughed, though few in the audience thought it was funny.

Of course, the person who was the least thrilled was Sean himself, who was said to be furious about the entire episode. It was common knowledge that he disliked Sandra Bernhard intensely and the feeling was apparently mutual. By the time Madonna arrived back in Los Angeles in autumn 1988, the marriage was more fractured than ever.

The couple struggled on for a few more weeks but it was clear to both Madonna and Sean that any relationship they may have had in the past was more than over now. However, it would take a violent episode in December of that year to finally bring an end to the marriage once and for all.

Stories vary on what really happened that night, but most agree that on the evening of 28 December 1988, Sean entered the family home and began abusing and threatening his terrified wife. According to media at the time, he "bound and gagged Madonna for 9 hours" before she finally escaped and headed to the sheriff's office where she filed charges of "corporal injury and traumatic conditions" and "battery".

Neither Sean nor Madonna ever spoke publicly about what

really happened on that evening, so we must rely on the thoughts and observations of "friends", but whatever events unfolded within the mansion, they were most certainly enough for Madonna to go through with a divorce, though she did eventually drop the charges against her ex. Just months later, she laid her heart bare on the failure of her marriage in the highly personal album *Like a Prayer*, which included song titles such as "Till Death Us Do Part", while the video for a song called "Oh Father" showed the star being slapped by someone presumed to be her husband.

In spite of dealing with the break-up through her work, Madonna has never publicly slammed Sean Penn in interviews or comments, and in fact her quotes on the subject have always been the complete reverse. Shortly after the marriage break-up she told an interviewer that while she might have twinges of regret, she felt sad more than anything. She had learned a great deal about herself during the years with Sean, and chose to concentrate on that rather than the bad feeling that had ultimately erupted. She even addressed her broken marriage in the 1991 documentary *Madonna: Truth or Dare* (also known as *In Bed with Madonna*), when backing singer Donna DeLory asked, "Who has been the love of your life, your whole life?" Madonna immediately replied, "Sean . . . Sean."

It would take Madonna another eleven years to dive into matrimony again, this time with director Guy Ritchie. The marriage brought two children – Rocco and David (in addition to Madonna's daughter Lourdes by ex-boyfriend Carlos Leon) – and while it eventually ended in divorce, it was clear to see by this time that the singer was calmer, quieter and far more open to sharing her life with another person.

Sean Penn, meanwhile, began a relationship with actress Robin Wright who bore him two children before going on to marry the actor in April 1996, days after Madonna had announced that she was pregnant with Lourdes. The Penn – Wright marriage was ultimately not a successful one, though the couple did stay together for fourteen years – on and off – before finally agreeing to divorce.

As for Madonna and Sean, unbelievably there are still fans and supporters who wonder if they will one day reunite. They have been seen together on several occasions, and when Madonna won the Most Fashionable Artist 1995 at the VH1 Fashion Awards, it was Sean who unexpectedly presented her with the trophy. During her speech she exclaimed, "That was really dirty!" but the affection they still had for each other was clear when they hugged tightly for several seconds before Sean finally left the stage.

In October 2012 the rumours of reconciliation began again when Penn was spotted outside the Los Angeles Staples Center, while Madonna was due to perform on stage as part of her *MDNA* tour. Sean apparently watched the concert and afterwards was said to tell fans that he thought it was "okay". Did he meet up with Madonna while he was there? Who knows, but one thing's for sure, while they are both still around, the rumours of reconciliation will always swirl, and hope will never fade in some camps that "The Poison Penns" may one day get back together.

46

Zsa Zsa Gabor Slaps a Policeman

Zsa Zsa Gabor has been the subject of numerous headlines and scandals over the years, including her many very public marriages (and even more public divorces.) Over the years newspapers have loved her for her outspoken views on a variety of different topics, but unfortunately in recent years her appearances in the newspaper headlines have been of a sad nature due to her ever-increasing illnesses and poor health.

Who can forget the photographs of the once glamorous star, confined to bed while trying to celebrate her ninety-fifth birthday? Then there were the rumours that her husband was the secret father of Anna Nicole Smith's daughter. He wasn't, of course, but headlines such as these have not been the kind of articles Zsa Zsa would surely ever want to see. However, back in 1989 Zsa Zsa was at the peak of her scandal-making ways when she made headlines around the world after a highly publicized encounter with a traffic policeman . . .

Born Sári Gabor in Budapest on 6 February 1917, the girl who would grow up to be Zsa Zsa began her career aged fifteen, when she took her first stage job in Vienna. Moving on to become Miss Hungary, it wasn't long before she moved to the United States, where she hoped to carve out a career for herself in the movies. She was successful and, after appearing in her first movie, *Lovely to Look At* (1952), she went on to star in dozens more including *We're Not Married,* a vehicle which saw her appear on the same bill as Marilyn Monroe, though the two did not actually share any screen time.

Zsa Zsa's luck in the movies was better than her luck with men, however, and between 1937 and the present day she has been married a staggering nine times, with seven ending in divorce, one annulled after a day, and the final one – to Frédéric Prinz von Anhalt – being the longest, continuing from 1986 to the present day. However, it seems she has never taken her marriage problems seriously, and has often injected her own humour when interviewers have insisted on asking her about them.

"How many husbands have you had?" one is reported to have asked.

"You mean apart from my own?" came the actress's reply.

By the time 1989 rolled around, Zsa Zsa was seventy-two years old and had been a talk-show and media favourite for many years. She was still in good health, but in spite of that, the year had not started well when she was spotted on a Delta Airlines plane removing her two beloved shih-tzu dogs from their travel compartments so they could sit with her in the cabin. Passengers quickly complained at seeing the dogs free from their cages, and cabin crew asked the actress to return the dogs to their crates.

She refused point blank to do as she was told, which forced the now impatient crew to drag the captain into the proceedings in a bid to get her to obey the rules. When even he could not persuade the actress to re-crate the dogs, a Delta agent came on board but was apparently met by a stream of insults and a firm refusal. This turned out to be the last straw for the crew on board and they called in the police, who quickly escorted Zsa Zsa from the aircraft, dogs in tow.

"He screamed at me like I was some criminal," Zsa Zsa later complained about the Delta agent before adding that even if she lived to be 100, she would never understand why five policemen had been sent to take her off the plane. But while Zsa Zsa was appalled at her treatment by both the crew and the police, this would not be her last brush with the law during 1989.

It all started on 14 July when the actress was driving on Los Angeles's La Cienega Boulevard in a Rolls-Royce belonging to her husband, Frédéric Prinz von Anhalt. She was trying to run an urgent errand, but instead found herself pulled over by Officer Paul Kramer, who told her the registration plate on her car had expired. The actress explained that she believed it had been renewed earlier that year, so the policeman asked her to present her driver's licence. Unfortunately, she soon realized that her new licence was at home in her handbag, so instead Zsa Zsa showed him an old one she kept in the glove compartment. This, of course, had also expired. The officer's patience was beginning to wear thin and he went to his car to check out the situation with the Department of Motor Vehicles.

Zsa Zsa later told television interviewer Arsenio Hall that she sat in the car for some time, boiling in the heat and unable to turn on the air conditioning for fear of overheating the engine. She then decided to exit the car and make her way to the policeman, who was still on the telephone. According to Zsa Zsa, the following alleged conversation then transpired:

"Officer, can I go?" asked the actress.

"F-off," replied the officer.

The confused Zsa Zsa took that to mean she could now leave the scene, started the Rolls-Royce and headed off down the road. Meanwhile, Officer Kramer was shocked to discover Ms Gabor taking off in the Rolls-Royce, and quickly drove after her.

The policeman finally caught up with her at the corner of Olympic Boulevard and Le Doux Road, where he ordered the actress out of the car. She did not understand what she had done wrong, apparently, and according to Zsa Zsa, Kramer then allegedly grabbed her and pulled her out of the car, causing her to bruise her arm in the process. "I used to like men who spanked me but not like this!" she later joked to Arsenio Hall.

The actress responded to this abrupt exit by slapping Officer Kramer in the face. The Beverly Hills policeman was understandably shocked by the outburst, cuffed Zsa Zsa's hands behind her back, and then sprawled her on to the bonnet of her car. At this point, according to later comments by the actress, her main concern was the fact that her short dress was rising higher and higher up her legs.

Still handcuffed, she was then ordered to sit down at the side of the road to await the arrival of more officers. The actress later laughed at the incident by exclaiming, "The things on my wrists hurt like hell, and they were ugly things – not handsome like diamonds!" Zsa Zsa started to cry for help and people began to notice the furore going on around them. One man – a tourist from Israel – even came over to help her retrieve her sunglasses, which had fallen off during the developments.

When back-up arrived a short time later, the Rolls-Royce was impounded, and the furious actress was arrested and taken to the police station. There she was searched (and allegedly told by a female police officer that she needed to lose weight), and fingerprints and her mug shot were taken. She was then booked for battery of a policeman, evading a policeman, being an unlicensed driver and driving an unlicensed vehicle. To top it all off, they also slapped her with another accusation: that of having an open bottle of alcohol in her car – something to which she took great offence, declaring that it had been in the glove compartment for years.

The police were unfazed, however, and the actress was told to appear at the Beverly Hills Municipal Court on 12 July to answer the charges. She repaid the favour by declaring, "They are stupid . . . uneducated. How can they do that to a lady like me?" She also denied slapping the policeman on purpose, stating that she only hit "this gorgeous, tall policeman" because she felt he was about to break her arm as he pulled her out of the car. Added to that, she also alleged that when the officer had thrown her over the bonnet of the car, he had called her a "whore".

The day after the episode, Zsa Zsa gave a news conference,

during which she showed off bruises on her arm and demanded the return of the car and a brooch, which she stated must have fallen off during the episode. "I want that gorgeous policeman to know that he can't manhandle women," she told reporters. "I'm standing up for the battered women of America."

When Gabor was arraigned on 12 July, she arrived in a large, silver limousine, which set the tone for the entire trial. This was not going to be just any "driving without a licence" trial, and by the time the case properly began in September 1989, the press were on tenterhooks, ready to report every eccentric move Zsa Zsa made. Luckily for them, she did not disappoint.

Arriving with an entourage that included two hairdressers, the actress sauntered past the hundred waiting reporters, with a bright, "Hello darlings!" When she refused to answer media questions, the paparazzi descended on one of her hairdressers for an exclusive interview, reporting afterwards that Zsa Zsa's hair was styled that morning in its normal way, and that while her hair was being worked on, she had apparently looked innocent enough. It wasn't exactly tantalizing, but it was all the reporters could get before the entourage crowded its way into the courtroom.

Once there, Zsa Zsa wasted no time in pleading innocent to all charges filed against her: battery of a police officer; disobeying a policeman's orders; driving with an expired licence; having an expired car registration; and driving with open alcohol in the vehicle. Luckily for Zsa Zsa, one of the said charges – that she was driving with an expired registration – was dropped by Judge Charles G. Rubin when it was found that the car was indeed legally registered.

The day was long and perhaps not as exciting as the press hoped it would be, though on leaving the court Zsa Zsa did say a few words, describing the jury as "charming, every one of them". This, unfortunately, was all the journalists would get from the actress that day, though they were able to soothe themselves by speaking to a woman who was more than a little annoyed with events going on inside the court house.

Joelle Nelson had won a competition to travel to Los Angeles for the trial, and wearing her "Free Zsa Zsa" badge, she had been ecstatic to find herself riding in the same elevator as the actress herself. Unfortunately for Nelson, however, her handbag was in Zsa Zsa's way, and the poor woman found herself on the receiving end of a stern word from the impatient actress. "She was very rude," Nelson said, much to the amusement of the waiting reporters.

The next day Zsa Zsa arrived at the courthouse wearing a leopard-print dress and declaring that she had more than enough clothes to keep her going, regardless of how long the trial continued. Because of a gagging order, however, the number of reporters and fans had fallen considerably from what it had been just a day before, and the most anyone could get out of the actress was how well she had slept the night before, and the tantalizing fact that she believed leopard print was back in fashion.

The entire day was again drawn out and the reporters complained that all that seemed to be going on was the selection of the jury. Fans began to fidget and reporters yawned, but a moment of light relief was served when one admirer suddenly got up and declared, "Sorry, I have to leave to catch a spaceship", much to the amusement of everyone around him.

Day three proved to be more exciting, especially when Zsa Zsa entered the building. At the door of the courthouse, she was inundated with questions. "How are you feeling?" shouted one reporter, to which the actress replied that her mother was deathly worried about her; that she had telephoned that morning to see if she was going to be sent to prison.

"I told her I hoped not," Gabor was reported to say. "I have claustrophobia and would be very unhappy in jail, and besides, they are all lesbians in jail and I'm so scared of lesbians. Can you imagine being in jail with all those women?" This alleged comment was so astonishing that it would later earn her a letter of complaint from an unnamed gay organization. She told reporters that the letter had been sent to tell her what "lovely people" they were. "But I already know it," she replied.

Outburst over for one day, Zsa Zsa then entered the courtroom in time to hear Officer Paul Kramer describe how she had slapped him so hard it had bent his sunglasses. "I was very surprised," he told the jury. An enlarged copy of her driver's licence was then given to the court, which seemed to show that despite being born in 1917, the actual licence appeared to have been altered to 6 February 1928.

In spite of the fact that she was not supposed to talk to waiting reporters, Zsa Zsa did not do as she was told, and instead seemed happy to respond to at least some of their questions. Outside the courtroom the actress said that she had not noticed before how gorgeous her arresting officer was, though she made it clear that she felt he had lied during proceedings. She then gave a quick plug for her own brand of face cream by telling reporters that the only good thing to come from all this was the fact that the line was now, "selling like hot cakes".

But the plug came at a price, and the next day the actress found herself reprimanded by the frustrated judge for giving out information to reporters, both on her way to and from the courtroom. "This is my first and last warning," he told her. "I'm going to ask you to comply and not make any comments to the media. Just say, 'No comment.'"

"Yes sir," replied the bemused actress, and then continued to comment to reporters during a break in proceedings.

The case very quickly turned into a circus, and newspaper headlines were dominated by Zsa Zsa's outbursts in court. One day she burst into tears and tried to run from the room, only to find herself stopped and ordered to return to her seat by the judge. Then on another day during questioning, the actress described the officer as "the toughest, nastiest, rudest person I ever saw in my life. He was like a wild animal."

When asked how often she is generally pulled over by policemen, she replied, "Very seldom. Usually they want to marry me." This raised a laugh from the courtroom, but she then went on to confuse everyone by forgetting the exact derogatory names the officer was supposed to have called her and how long she had waited for him to check her licence.

The actress then infuriated just about everyone when she accused the officer, Paul Kramer, of faking a recent motorcycle accident to win sympathy. She even decided that because the officer had not been kind to her, he must clearly be gay. With that in mind she then attempted to "out" him and reportedly told the court, "Don't you know, a gay man would not like a woman like Zsa Zsa Gabor. Why would he? I marry all the men he would want to have." Fearing being sued, this comment forced her lawyer, William Grayson, to tell reporters that neither Gabor – nor himself – knew anything about the personal life of Officer Kramer.

Despite being told to never talk to reporters herself, Zsa Zsa continued to entertain them, claiming that she had just received a supportive message from former President Ronald Reagan, telling her to telephone him. Reporters were sceptical so called the Reagan offices themselves, only to be told by a spokesman that he had absolutely not telephoned the woman, and was unlikely to do so in the future.

On day twelve she turned up late, after the policeman at the centre of the slapping incident was slowing down traffic on his speed patrol. "Officer Kramer made me late," she told waiting reporters. "He stopped the traffic with a radar gun. There he was, looking his gorgeous self, with a radar."

Despite bringing in witnesses to back up her claims against the policeman, questioning the authenticity of video evidence and weeping on several occasions, by the end of the trial Zsa Zsa Gabor was found guilty of slapping a police officer; possessing alcohol in her car; and driving without a licence. She was, however, acquitted of driving away from the officer, as jurors believed it might have been a result of a miscommunication, rather than a deliberate attempt to "escape".

Once again speaking to reporters afterwards, the actress

declared jail would give her time to write a book, and that a famous restaurant had promised to deliver food to her three times a day. She then told everyone she was heading home to swim in her pool, and zoomed away from the court in her flashy Rolls-Royce.

In the end, Zsa Zsa Gabor was sentenced to three days in prison and 120 days community service. However, even that caused controversy when the actress was accused of not doing enough hours during her service. Thankfully for her, however, the community service boss came forward to stick up for the actress, surprising everyone by stating that instead of the 120 hours initially demanded, she had actually done eighteen hours over what she was supposed to do.

As for the jail term, Zsa Zsa and her team of lawyers appealed it for many months until finally they gave in. The actress went to the El Segundo Jail for three whole days, where she was said to have a room all to herself, and enjoyed daily visits from her husband.

When it was time for her to leave prison and head home, Zsa Zsa was met at the gate by the ever-present reporters. They all crowded round, shouting questions from every corner.

"What do you intend to do next?" asked one reporter.

"Go home for a hot bath." she replied.

"And how was the food in prison?" asked another.

Zsa Zsa screwed up her face, took a breath and exclaimed, "It was terrible! I wouldn't give it to my dog."

And with that, she climbed into her waiting car, and was gone, her criminal days behind her.

47

River Phoenix Dies Outside the Viper Room

The Viper Room nightclub is famous for its all-black exterior, the notorious celebrities who have walked through its doors and the fact that film star Johnny Depp was once a co-owner. However, on Halloween 1993, it became infamous as the scene where up-and-coming actor River Phoenix met his end, on the pavement right outside the front doors of the club.

Born on 23 August 1970, River Jude Phoenix grew up with his four siblings – Rain, Joaquin, Liberty and Summer – in what River himself described as a "hippieish" lifestyle. He wasn't wrong; his family were extremely unconventional and at one point were part of a religious cult, which left them living in poverty to such a degree that Phoenix began playing guitar on the street just to earn enough money to support his hard-up family.

They were essentially nomads and enjoyed moving around a lot, settling in Venezuela for a time, as well as Puerto Rico, Oregon (where River was born) and Florida. However, it was while living in Los Angeles that the family's fortunes were turned around, when an entertainment agent decided to sign all of the children to a management contract.

Aged ten, River Phoenix became a child actor, working on the TV show *Seven Brides for Seven Brothers* before going on to TV movies such as *Surviving: A Family in Crisis* and *Circle of Violence: A Family Drama*. But it was in 1986 that the actor was really brought to the attention of the public, when he was cast as Chris Chambers in *Stand By Me*, a Rob Reiner movie based on a story by horror writer Stephen King. The film is a coming-of-age drama, telling the tale of four young boys who go on an adventure to find a dead body. It ends with the main character, Gordie, updating viewers on what happened to his friends as they grew up, revealing that the character played by River was stabbed and killed when trying to break up a fight in a fast-food restaurant. This revelation made a sad ending to the movie, but became even more poignant after the premature death of Phoenix just seven years later.

After *Stand By Me* was released, River's career went from strength to strength and he was nominated for a Golden Globe and an Academy Award for his role in *Running on Empty* (1988). He also became quite involved in the Los Angeles music scene, as well as going on to win the role as the young Indiana Jones in *Indiana Jones and the Last Crusade* (1989). It was this small but important role that would ensure that children of future generations would be aware of River Phoenix's life and work.

But the actor's successful career came crashing down in a tragic way at the end of October 1993, when River was partying at the new Sunset Boulevard club, the Viper Room. The establishment played host to many of Hollywood's elite, including Johnny Depp himself, who could often be seen playing there with his band, "P".

On the evening of 30 October, P were performing in the club when River Phoenix entered with his sister Rain, brother Joaquin and girlfriend Samantha Mathis. River had been making a movie, *Dark Blood*, and was in Los Angeles to film the last interior shots. Taking a night off, he had decided to party at the Viper Room, where shortly before 1 a.m., he entered the club bathroom. There, a dealer apparently offered the actor some kind of drug, the ingredients of which are still up for debate, though it is widely believed to have been a "speedball", a combination of heroin and cocaine. River had already taken drugs that evening, but regardless of that he took what was offered to him and immediately became acutely unwell.

Staggering back into the club, the ailing actor told his friends he could not breathe, and the story goes that he then passed out in the club, before being dragged outside for some fresh air. Once there River Phoenix collapsed again and started to suffer seizures, while his friends tried to revive him and an ambulance was called. Paramedics arrived and later described that by the time they were able to work on the actor, he had already flatlined, right there on the pavement outside the Viper Room. At least one paramedic later said that he believed the actor was most likely dead or almost dead by the time he had managed to reach the exterior of the club.

The paramedics did all they could to save River, while at the same time rushing him by ambulance to Cedars-Sinai Medical Center. They arrived at 1.34 a.m., and doctors continued the attempts to revive him, but ultimately were unable to do anything at all to save the actor's life. At 1.51 a.m. on 31 October 1993 River Phoenix was pronounced dead. An autopsy was performed on the young star and it was revealed that the cause of death came as a result of lethal doses of cocaine and morphine, with his blood also containing ephedrine, marijuana and diazepam.

Back at the club, Johnny Depp and the other patrons were absolutely horrified that River Phoenix had died as a result of taking drugs in the club. The venue immediately closed and a sign was displayed outside which read: "With much respect and love to River and his family, the Viper Room is temporarily closed. Our heartfelt condolences to all his family, friends and loved ones. He will be missed. – All of us at the Viper Room."

From all over Los Angeles, fans and the curious travelled to the nightclub in order to scribble graffiti on the wall near to the scene of River's death, and proceeded to lay flowers, cards and other tributes. After that fateful evening, on the anniversary of River's death the club would close on the orders of Johnny Depp. The sign "Gone Fishing" was placed on the door one year, and "Closed for Remodelling" the next. However, the crowds kept coming to the Viper Room to seek out the location of River's death, and eventually the morbid curiosity took its toll. Co-owner Johnny Depp took the decision to sell his share of the club in 2004, after sources claimed he was "disgusted" at the endless stream of macabre passers-by.

Ironically, River Phoenix was known throughout the world as a clean-living vegan who was extremely anti-drugs and often appeared on chat shows to talk about the environmentally friendly politics he believed in. How long he had been taking drugs is not known, but apparently his father had been worried about his children's involvement in the movie business for quite some time, and had asked all of them to give up their careers in order to help him with the family restaurant he had established in Florida. River assured his father that he would do just that, as soon as he had finished the films to which he was contracted.

Unfortunately for both of them, when River did indeed come back to his family, it was not in the way they had hoped. After his cremation, his ashes were taken back to the family ranch, where they were said to have been scattered around a tree; an apt place for the environmentally conscious young actor, who had always tried to remain close to his hippieish roots.

48

Madonna's Hollywood Stalker

Madonna has never been shy of controversy and has courted many scandalous headlines over the years, but in 1995 there was one headline she most certainly did not want to see – the news that she was being stalked by a deranged fan.

Robert Dewey Hoskins was a homeless drifter when he developed an interest in the singer. However, his curiosity went far beyond buying her albums and seeing her on tour. For Hoskins, there was nothing he wanted more than to meet Madonna, and it didn't take long for his obsession to enter dangerous territory when he decided that one day he would not only meet her, but make her his wife.

On 7 April 1995, Hoskins travelled to Madonna's Hollywood home and scaled the forty-foot wall, intent on seeing the star for himself. He was out of luck, however, as she was not in, and he was quickly chased away by her bodyguard, Basil Stephens.

The very next day he returned with a deranged note. Ringing the gate until Madonna's assistant, Caresse Henry Norman, finally answered, Hoskins demanded to speak to the singer. He was not pleased when told that she was out, and then proceeded to threatened to "slice Madonna from ear to ear", and kill Norman along with everyone else in the house.

Minutes later, bodyguard Stephens arrived and was handed a religious leaflet on to which Hoskins had scrawled the words "defiled", "I love you", "You will be my wife for keeps" and "kiss kiss kiss kiss kiss".

"It's irrational," Madonna later said in court. "It's not based on reality. The person who wrote it was very sick."

When Stephens refused Hoskins's demands to give Madonna the paper, the man blew his top and threatened to kill the bodyguard. Things almost got very ugly when Madonna arrived home just minutes later on her bike, though thankfully Hoskins only managed to glare at her as she was quickly taken into the house.

"He had a really crazy look in his eyes and he was staring at me in a very strange way," the star later testified. "I was actually very disturbed about the look in his eye."

During later testimony, Madonna stated her belief that Hoskins did not try to harm her only because he didn't recognize her, as she was wearing a cap, sunglasses and baggy clothing. The singer no doubt hoped that he would disappear from her life as quickly as he arrived, but she was wrong.

On 29 May 1995, Hoskins returned to the house once more. This time he threw several bags over the wall and then scaled it himself, landing roughly in the grounds of the house. He couldn't believe his luck that he had actually got inside and began to trudge towards the front of the house, peering through the front door when he reached it. Of course, he didn't count on being spotted by bodyguard Basil Stephens, who later testified that it "looked like he was bringing his bags and he was moving in".

When Madonna's bodyguards confronted Hoskins, he boldly announced that he lived on the property and he would see to it that they were fired for disturbing him. He was thrown out, but a short time later he was back, spotted next to the pool, dripping wet and wearing a pair of shorts. By this time the bodyguards had endured enough and demanded that Hoskins lie down on the ground. He didn't and instead began to take clothes out of his bags and get dressed as though he were completely oblivious to the bodyguards being there.

Finally, as Stephens stood guard while his colleague went to check if the police had arrived, Hoskins made a sudden leap at the bodyguard, trying to choke him and get his gun from its holster. The incident ended badly when Hoskins was shot twice by Stephens, who believed he had killed him and ran to get help. Several minutes later he returned, only to find the stalker sitting near the pool with wounds to his stomach and arm. The bodyguard apologized for shooting Hoskins, to which he apparently replied, "No problem", and was then taken to hospital by ambulance.

The case went to court in January 1996, after being stalled due to Madonna's reluctance to face her stalker in court. Eventually she succumbed after being threatened with jail and a $5 million bail, though she did make a last-ditch request to be allowed to testify via video link, though this too was turned down.

Finally, the star entered the courtroom to give her version of events. Madonna looked terrified, and when asked how she felt, she took a deep breath. "I feel sick to my stomach," she said, before going on to explain that she was incredibly disturbed to be sitting across the room from someone who had threatened her life not once, but repeatedly. "I feel we are making his fantasies come true," she said, and then told the court that since the ordeal she had been absolutely terrified and had suffered nightmares as a result of the unwanted attention.

Things were made no better when Hoskins's lawyer, John Myers, described his client as harmless and claimed that prosecutors should have only filed trespassing charges against Hoskins, since he had never tried actually to harm Madonna. He also upset the singer by calling her a "prima donna"; "she comes in here and she's acting. She can't stop acting," he said.

The jurors did not agree, and it took them no time at all to find Hoskins guilty of one count of felony stalking, one of misdemeanour assault and three of making terrorist threats. A smiling Hoskins was eventually sentenced to ten years in prison, which led Madonna to release a statement saying, "I hope the outcome of this case lets other stalking victims know that the system can, and does, work."

Apparently because of the "negative energy" that she felt the house had attracted, Madonna left her home, but it was not the end of her problems with Robert Dewey Hoskins. He was released from prison after serving his time, and since he was so deeply disturbed, he was eventually taken to a psychiatric hospital in Norwalk, California. Quite astonishingly, however, he was able to escape on 3 February 2012 and the Los Angeles Police Department issued a statement declaring that "Hoskins is highly psychotic when not taking his medication." He was also described as having "very violent tendencies".

For Madonna, who was by then living in New York with her family of four children, this must surely have been a worrying development. Fortunately Hoskins was found a week later, not far from the facility from which he had escaped. However, his name was in the headlines again just weeks later when it was discovered that he had once leased a locker, the contents of which had been sold to a new owner after Hoskins had failed to keep up with the lease payments.

The new owners were not aware that the previous owner was the man made notorious through his Madonna obsession. On opening a box, they were in for a shock. There inside were countless items of Madonna memorabilia, along with box cutters, condoms and a creepy mask. The stash confirmed that Hoskins was surely not the harmless, homeless man he had claimed to be in court, and that, very possibly, his threats to "slice Madonna from ear to ear" were not far from the truth.

49

Hugh Grant's Hollywood Scandal

Born on 9 September 1960, Hugh Grant is known for his roles in hit films such as *Four Weddings and a Funeral*, *Notting Hill* and *Bridget Jones's Diary*. However, while most actors long for the attention that only a hit movie can bring, Hugh's role in a real-life arrest gave him the kind of notice that almost every actor dreads: the Hollywood scandal.

Hugh Grant and Elizabeth Hurley were the UK's golden couple, frequently photographed together at film premieres and red-carpet events. During the 1994 premiere of *Four Weddings and a Funeral*, Hurley wowed everyone by wearing a Versace gown held together only by safety pins. She had been lent the dress by the fashion house, and it turned out to be a highly lucrative loan, with her appearance in the gown raising her profile and leading to modelling jobs and a contract with Estée Lauder.

After that it became a trend that at every premiere they attended, Hurley would be dressed ever more elaborate gowns; fans waited impatiently to see what she would wear next, and she never disappointed. The couple could do no wrong, and their stars continued to rise when they created their own film company, Simian Films, which the actors intended to use to develop film projects.

However, the couple's relationship changed forever in June 1995 when Hugh Grant travelled to Los Angeles to publicize his first major studio film, *Nine Months*, co-starring Julianne

Moore. Hurley did not travel with him; instead, she stayed behind in London to work on her own projects and await his return.

On the evening of 27 June, a bored Grant decided to leave his Los Angeles hotel and drive his BMW down Sunset Boulevard. Eventually he arrived at the red-light district, where he encountered a lady of the night by the name of Divine Brown. At first she avoided him, thinking he might be a policeman, but eventually he stopped the car and proceeded to introduce himself as "Lewis". Brown later said that she thought he sounded like Prince Charles, but had no idea that the baseball-cap-wearing man was the British actor Hugh Grant. To her he was just another job, and to that end they retired to a quiet side street, where after some small talk, they proceeded to get to know each other a little better.

However, it wasn't long before two policemen were drawn to the car because the brake lights kept turning off and on, apparently as a result of Grant's foot tapping on the car's peddal. The policemen were said to be slightly amused but decided to put an end to the events unfolding inside by knocking on the window and shining a light inside the vehicle. Understandably the couple's shenanigans were interrupted and before they opened the door to the officers outside, Brown quickly told Grant to tell them no money was exchanged. The couple then greeted the officers who took both of them into custody.

Hugh was arrested for the misdemeanour of lewd conduct in a public place, pleaded no contest and was fined $1,180. He was also placed on two years' summary probation and had to undertake an AIDS awareness programme. Brown was released and it was only after she got home and saw the mug shots of both herself and Grant on the news that she realized exactly who she had encountered that night; she was quite surprised, to say the least.

Within hours the news of Hugh's arrest and accompanying photographs were making headlines around the world, much to the entertainment of just about everyone. Reporters flocked not only to catch a glimpse of Grant himself, but also his girlfriend Elizabeth Hurley, who was so besieged that she had to hide in her house with the curtains drawn and the doors firmly locked. For days photographers camped outside, while she stayed inside, furious about the drama created by her boyfriend on the other side of the world.

Unfortunately for Grant, while he may have wanted to rush back home to flee the spotlight, instead he had to go ahead with his promotional tour for *Nine Months*. However, he managed to get through it with his humour intact. He decided not to ignore the questions that came his way and, instead of skirting around the issue, he actually made no bones about his arrest when interviewed by Jay Leno. "I did a bad thing," he said. "And there you have it."

Meanwhile, the media could not believe their luck at the scandal erupting around them, and neither could Divine Brown. The *News of the World* bought her a gown similar to the one Elizabeth Hurley had worn to the *Four Weddings* premiere, dressed her in it and splashed her all over the front pages of the UK newspaper. She was invited on to chat shows such as *Jerry Springer*, appeared on *Judge Judy* and gave newspaper interviews around the world, gaining quite a following in the process.

The scandal not only brought her attention, but ultimately made her a millionaire; her children went through private school; she bought her own house and shopped for jewels and clothes on Rodeo Drive. She started her own record company; gave up prostitution for good; and moved to Atlanta for a quieter life. Even today, nearly twenty years later, Brown still appears in documentaries and on television, talking about the night her life changed forever.

But what of Hugh Grant? He eventually returned home to his girlfriend, and although we can only guess at what was said, the chances are that it was nothing of a positive nature. The relationship floundered and a grim-faced Hurley was photographed at the Los Angeles premiere of *Nine Months* in a subdued white dress, no smile to be seen. The couple were golden no more, and although their relationship continued for another five years, they eventually called it quits in 2000.

Quite surprisingly, however, Hugh Grant and Elizabeth Hurley have since put aside their differences and have remained good friends. They have amazed everyone by being godparents to each other's children and have frequently enjoyed family holidays together. Hugh's career was not tainted by the experience and, in fact, initially went from strength to strength; he became a huge star in the States, and appeared in movies such as *Bridget Jones's Diary* (2001) and its sequel, as well as *Two Weeks Notice* (2002) with Sandra Bullock.

One person who believes that the incident did Grant a favour is former prostitute Divine Brown. Speaking to the *Daily Mail* in 2010, she said that she believed Grant was not very famous in the States at the time of his arrest. "It was me that helped his career," she said. "I know he helped me upgrade my future and my family, but I upgraded his, too."

50

John Denver Leaves on a Jet Plane

At first glance, John Denver, the popular country singer and conservationist, may seem to have more to do with his beloved Colorado than Hollywood. In actual fact, having made countless movies and TV appearances, he can certainly be included among the stars who have walked the Los Angeles boulevards in search of fame and fortune.

Born Henry John Deutschendorf Jr on New Year's Eve, 1943, John was a military forces' child, moving around the country with his parents as a result of his father's job. The child was shy and retiring, and he had very few friends due to the fact that the family were never in one place for more than a little while. So instead of putting his energies into making friends with people to whom he would soon be saying goodbye, the boy decided to spend time concentrating on his love for music, learning to play the guitar and singing a great deal.

His love for music resulted in Denver being a member of the Tucson Arizona Boys Chorus for several years, though another school move put paid to that. He then harboured dreams of becoming a successful singer, and during high school decided to take himself off to Hollywood in order to begin his career. This was news to his family, however, who immediately ordered him back from the city in order to finish his high-school education, much to his dismay.

After joining and leaving several bands in Texas during the 1960s, the young man took off once again to Hollywood, this time ignoring his family's pleas to come back home. He changed his last name to Denver after the capital city of his favourite state and set about making a living by singing in Los Angeles folk clubs. He then won a place with the Mitchell Trio, which was a real turning point in his life and enabled him not only to record albums but also to write songs and practise his craft while being paid for what he loved to do best. By the time the band split, several years later, John Denver had acquired a huge amount of experience; he had also seen his song "Leaving on a Jet Plane" recorded by music heavyweights Peter, Paul and Mary, and was beginning to receive a great deal of acclaim for his solo work. However, there was still much more to do and Denver embarked on a tour which saw him play free concerts in schools, cafés and anywhere that would let him play.

Perhaps the most interesting thing about this part of John Denver's career was the fact that nobody had suggested that he should go on tour; he had done it on his own initiative, seemingly just for the love of playing and meeting new fans. He often turned up at radio stations in order to play and talk, and he would also sell his albums before and after other artists' gigs. It was a gamble that paid off, and the tour was so successful that his record company, RCA, then decided to invest more money in his album, *Rhymes & Reasons*, which then led to an extension of his recording contract.

John Denver's peak was in the 1970s and it was during this period that he wrote some of his most famous songs, including "Annie's Song", which went to number one in the USA during 1974. This song has remained one of the quintessential Denver records, and was featured on a television commercial in the UK in late 2012, leading the single to appear once again in the charts, almost forty years since its first release. What is astonishing is that the track was actually written by Denver in about ten minutes while on a ski-lift in 1973. He later explained that he was caught up in the moment, enjoying the nature around him when inspiration suddenly took over. As soon as he had finished skiing he headed straight home and wrote the song down, dedicating it to his wife, Annie.

Annie and John had married in late 1967 but the marriage had been thwarted by problems, particularly insecurities from both sides which were related to John's burgeoning career and travel commitments. When they had first met, the singer was a nobody; a fledgling singer with a band that was not huge in any way. However, by the 1970s he had become almost legendary and Annie just did not know how to handle the sudden fame and everything that went with it. She later complained that she had no idea who she was at this time, which is understandable given the sudden brush with fame she had encountered.

As a result of their problems, the pair had recently separated and the singer moved out of their new home in Aspen to get his head together. Soon, however, the couple decided they really were deeply in love with each other and it was after this reconciliation that "Annie's Song" was born. The 1970s also saw John and Annie becoming parents to Zach and Anna Kate whom they adopted when it was thought that John was sterile. A nomad at heart, Denver was given a stability by the children he had rarely known and also awakened a side of him that he had not explored very often – being happy.

The movie industry called on Denver when they were in need of a good song, and his music has been featured in many films and series including *The Simpsons* (1994). As an actor John's work in Hollywood saw him star in television shows such as *McCloud* in 1974 and *The Muppet Show* in 1979. His appearance in the TV movie *The Christmas Gift* (1986) allowed him to play a slightly more serious role as a widowed father of one, but perhaps his most famous part came nine years earlier, when he starred alongside George Burns in *Oh, God!*

John often portrayed hippieish, laid-back and happy-go-lucky characters. This reflected the man in some ways, as he had a deep affinity with nature and never ceased promoting conservation and humanitarianism until the day he died. However, deep inside, in the privacy of his own soul, he was an insecure person who often wondered what he was doing and where he was going with his life. He freely admitted to having "incredible lows", and once said that when he got depressed, "I question whether life is worth living." This surprising negativity often presented itself in drug-taking, infidelity and even suicidal tendencies, but fatherhood balanced him somewhat – at least for a while.

During the late 1970s John Denver became known for his many television appearances, which included acting as a host for the Grammy's in 1978 and 1979. However, while things had appeared rosy with Annie for a time, their troubles began once again, partly because of his touring schedule but also his inability to completely turn off from work. John later told an interviewer that he would often be at home physically, but his mind would still be on the road. This was understandable given the amount of time he was away, but it didn't help matters, particularly when he arrived back at the house in the hope of being lavished with attention from his family, only to find that Annie needed to look after the children instead of him.

As the 1970s turned into the 1980s things only got worse, and the couple separated and later divorced. The separation threw the singer into a deep depression. After discovering that his ex-wife had cut down his favourite trees at their home, he lost his temper, picked up a chainsaw and proceeded to saw through the kitchen table and the former marital bed. He apparently only stopped when the blades got jammed by the sheets, which forced him to cease his destructive endeavour.

It would seem that the divorce from Annie was the beginning of a particularly sad downturn for John Denver, during which time he lost his father and wondered where he was going in his life. It was also during this time that he wanted to fulfil a dream of being the first civilian in space, and after taking and passing examinations at NASA, it looked certain that he would be included in the mission. In the end, however, John was not part of the programme and he did not get his wish to head off into the solar system. This would turn out to be a bittersweet development, as the shuttle intended for John's trip was *Challenger*, which exploded during take-off in 1986, shocking the world. John was devastated by the tragic events and wrote a song entitled "Flying for Me" about the ill-fated shuttle and the astronauts who lost their lives.

Still, in spite of the sadness recently experienced in his life, John did manage to find temporary happiness when he went to Australia and fell in love with a young singer called Cassandra, who was almost twenty years his junior. She travelled back to the United States with him and became one of his backing singers, going on the road and even writing songs with him. Two and a half years later they married, and despite a previous diagnosis of being unable to have children, John shortly after became a father to a baby girl, Jesse Belle.

The three settled down to a peaceful family life together; for a while at least, until – as had happened with Annie before – John and Cassandra started rowing regularly, which resulted in them eventually separating. Describing divorce as "just the most awful thing in the world", he told a British newspaper that he wasn't sure he'd ever get over it and couldn't imagine getting married again. There then followed a period of great sadness for Denver, as his record sales plummeted, he lost his recording contract and entered a period of psychoanalysis in order to figure out, once and for all, who he really was. Unfortunately, while he seemed determined to settle down and still remain a good father to his little girl, scandal dogged him from many corners. His ex-wife Cassy once told an interviewer that John Denver was a bully who drank every night, threatened her and was determined to take their little girl away.

The two fought for custody, and though Cassy ultimately won, it cost millions of dollars finally to get the situation under control. Denver retaliated to Cassy's claims by saying that during the marriage she had managed to "make a fool of me from one end of the valley to the other". There was no going back romantically for either of them, but by the time John died in 1997, they were apparently back on speaking terms, with

John buying a home close to hers and seeing his daughter as often as his touring schedule would allow.

In 1993 John hit the headlines when he was pulled over after his 1963 Porsche was seen weaving across the road. He was breathalyzed and found to be over the limit, later pleading guilty to a drink-driving charge which shocked his fans around the world. Until that moment in time, John Denver had always been known as something of a peace-loving hippy who had never been in trouble in his life. It was only after the publication of his autobiography, *Take Me Home* (1994), that fans got to find out that he had dabbled with drugs during his early days.

As a result of the charge he undertook community service and saw his driving licence suspended, but this was nothing compared to a year later, on 21 August 1994, when he was once again charged with driving under the influence after he accidentally crashed his car into a tree. Witnesses claimed that the singer had been drinking whisky in a bar as if it were lemonade, and while the physical injuries were minor, the whole incident was enough to send the singer into rehab. "I wasn't really an alcoholic," he later told a British newspaper, "but I was losing control." The trial for this particular misdemeanour resulted in a hung jury in 1996 and was still being sorted out by the time he passed away a year later.

John Denver was a keen pilot and his father taught him how to fly in the mid-1970s. For both men this had been a cathartic experience, something they could finally relate to and understand. The singer became known for flying himself to concerts and investing in a series of planes which included a Christen Eagle aerobatic model, and two Cessna 210s. However, it would be this love for planes that ultimately cost Denver his life, when on 12 October 1997 he crashed into the water at Monterey Bay, California.

That morning the singer told friends he was in for a great day, as he would be firstly putting in a few rounds of golf, and secondly taking out his new experimental Rutan Long-EZ plane in order to fly up and down the California coast. He was excited to pick up the plane and, after practising a few take-offs and landings, he then headed off at 5.12 p.m. for what he planned to be a one-hour flight. Not long afterwards, however, the airport control tower told the singer they could not track him very well and suggested he change to a different radio frequency. He did as he was told and asked the operator, "Do you have it now?" These would be the last words ever spoken by John Denver.

After it had been flying for a short while, witnesses saw the plane doing manoeuvres that they took to be some kind of aerobatic display. The plane also made noises as if it were back-firing, and then suddenly it began going up and down, then side to side, before finally nose-diving, crashing into the sea with a tremendous noise. Pieces of the plane shattered around the once calm water, and witnesses froze in terror at what they had just seen before rushing to their homes to telephone for medical assistance. Sadly, it was not only impossible to save Denver's life but also, because of the nature of the accident, it was initially difficult even to ascertain that he was the pilot. However, after a brief investigation by police, identification was made and an official announcement came that the singer had, indeed, sadly died.

Over the days, weeks and months ahead, there would be many rumours as to how or why John Denver's plane crashed. Some cited pilot error; others said that he should not have been in the air in the first place as he no longer had the medical certificate that was required for such flights. Then others said there must have been something technically wrong with the plane for it to have crashed so suddenly; and when a gun was said to have been found in John's car, others wondered if the accident had been a deliberate attempt to kill himself.

However, putting aside the wilder rumours and conspiracy theories, it would seem that it is possible that the accident could be linked to John Denver's inexperience of flying this particular style of plane. The craft was said to have been built with the critical fuel control valve behind the pilot, rather than in the more common position in front. According to one theory, it is possible that at some point the plane started to splutter as if it were running out of gas and Denver tried to reach behind to get to the fuel control valve, which he was apparently unable to see without looking over his shoulder. While the details of his last moments can only be guessed at, it would make sense that in order to get to the valve, Denver may have released the plane controls for a moment as he turned around to reach over his shoulder, losing control of the aircraft as he did so.

The aftermath of John Denver's death showed the same effect as the deaths of other musicians: an increase in his record sales and various tributes paid, listing his accomplishments and the positive impact he had on the music industry as a whole. Just a few years before, John had spoken candidly about his lack of a record deal and his soured relationship with the industry; of the sadness felt when DJs refused to play his records. After his passing, some of the same people who had treated him as a has-been such a short time before were proclaiming their admiration for his talents now; it took his death for some people to realize just how much John Denver had given to the world of music.

Throughout the course of Denver's life, a strong theme of flying, nature, water and adventure was always present. He sang of leaving on a jet plane; of sunshine, eagles, mountains, and sky; he wanted peace in his life by living in the country and being at one with nature. Perhaps it is fitting that the man who always wanted to fly and experience the natural world to the full passed away doing exactly what he loved. It may have been untimely; it may have been tragic; but it was a strangely prophetic way to go and, for some, this makes his music even more meaningful.

51

The Ups and Downs in the Life of George Michael

In the 1980s there was no bigger "boy band" than Wham! George Michael and Andrew Ridgeley were the imaginary boyfriends of millions of teenage girls who would sing along to songs such as "Wake Me Up Before You Go-Go", "I'm Your Man" and "Freedom". As Wham! the two men toured the world, becoming big not only in the UK but the lucrative United States too, and even made history by playing a concert in China, back then an honour bestowed on very few Western groups. By the time they decided to break up, they were so popular that their final concert was held at a packed-out Wembley Stadium and women wept in the audience as it became apparent that this was indeed goodbye.

However, while George Michael was desired by legions of female fans, in reality he was only ever publicly attached to three women: actress Brooke Shields, model Pat Fernandez and make-up artist Kathy Jeung. The reason for this is now clear. George was keeping a secret from the world: he is gay.

After the members of Wham! had gone their separate ways, George Michael went on to enjoy huge success as a solo artist; and his "I Want Your Sex" video, co-starring then girlfriend Kathy Jeung, became one of the most controversial clips ever made. Naked under discreetly placed sheets, the singer is seen blindfolding his partner and later writing the words "Explore" and "Monogamy" on her back.

The video made it look as though George was happily

heterosexual, but in real life he knew he was attracted to men and often wondered if it was possible he could be bisexual. This theory was put to the test after meeting the man who became one of the biggest loves of Michael's life, the fashion designer Anselmo Feleppa, and a deep friendship endured for two years until Anselmo sadly died in 1993, leaving a large gap in Michael's life, which some say has never been filled.

Rumours started to circulate that George had been romantically involved with Feleppa during their friendship, though he refused to confirm it in public, but he did "come out" to his parents in a letter written shortly after his close friend's death. For the next five years George publicly kept a low profile on the dating front. He had owned a house in Beverly Hills for some time and it was a well-known secret in Hollywood that he was gay, but to the world at large he was still very much heterosexual. That is until 7 April 1998 when he visited the Will Rogers Memorial Park in Beverly Hills and his life changed forever.

Entering the public toilets, Michael was followed by an undercover policeman called Marcelo Rodriguez, who – unknown to George – was taking part in a sting operation. According to the singer in an MTV interview, "He started playing this game, which I think is called, 'I'll show you mine, you show me yours, and then when you show me yours, I'm going to nick you!'"

Within minutes of beginning the game of peep show in the toilet, George Michael was arrested for engaging in a lewd act and was eventually fined $810 and sentenced to eighty hours of community service. He had been well and truly outed to the world, and his arrest and true sexuality were now open for all to see. George was mortified but ultimately the incident was a freeing experience, enabling the singer to be himself for the first time in his adult life. Indeed, he took the entire event in good spirit and, instead of hiding, actually made fun of it in his video for the song "Outside", which featured men dressed as policemen, kissing in public.

The video amused fans but outraged arresting officer Rodriguez, who claimed the video had mocked him. He also insisted that George Michael had slandered him in interviews, and was so upset that the matter went to court, only ending when it was determined that as a public official, Rodriguez was not entitled to recover damages for the distress he had suffered.

The public toilet incident was the end of George Michael's days as a secret homosexual and he was now free to enjoy life as the partner of Kenny Goss, his long-time boyfriend. Unfortunately, the pair broke up after a series of other scandals hit the headlines during the latter part of the 2000s . . .

In 2006 George Michael caused a hold-up in a London street when he reportedly fell asleep in his vehicle at some traffic lights. He was arrested for possession of class C drugs, and then, later in the year, he was accused of engaging in public sex, this time on Hampstead Heath in London. His troubles did not stop there, however, as in 2010 he accidentally drove his car into the front of a Snappy Snaps photography shop in North London and was charged with possession of cannabis and driving while unfit. After pleading guilty he was sent to prison on 14 September for eight weeks (although he eventually only served four). He also had to pay a fine and was slapped with a five-year ban from driving.

In early 2011 George Michael spoke about his prison sentence on Chris Evan's BBC Radio 2 breakfast show. Explaining that he believed it was karma, he admitted that he felt he did deserve to be punished: "It's so much easier to take any form of punishment if you believe you actually deserve it, and I did," he candidly said.

Although initially sent to the notorious Pentonville Prison in London, Michael was eventually transferred to Highpoint open jail in Suffolk, where he is said to have given his autograph to every prisoner and staff member who asked for it. He also signed a guitar for an inmate and when he realized that he was signing on the tenth day of the tenth month of the tenth year of the new millennium, it became a poignant moment. "It's like the clock rolling round to the end of something," he said. "Tomorrow I start again."

After his experience of prison, George Michael kept a pretty low profile, working on new music and planning his "Symphonica" tour. Unfortunately his world was rocked once again towards the end of 2011 when he was rushed to hospital in Vienna while suffering from pneumonia. A tracheotomy had to be performed and although his illness was played down to the public, he was on the brink of death for several weeks.

Family and friends kept a vigil at the hospital, while fans around the world prayed for his recovery. Their prayers were finally answered just days before Christmas 2011, when he was well enough to be released from hospital and travel back to London, where he gave a press conference.

Fighting back tears, George told reporters that doctors "spent three weeks keeping me alive basically . . . It was basically by far the worst month of my life." Poignantly he added how incredibly fortunate it had been that he had fallen ill where he did, as "the hospital in Austria that they rushed me to was absolutely the best place in the world I could have been to deal with pneumonia. So I have to believe that somebody thinks I've still got some work to do here."

He was right; he still had concerts to perform and he made a pledge on that cold winter's day that he would "play to every single person who had a ticket" for the cancelled performances on his tour. His eyes watering, he then added that he intended to play a show for the doctors and staff in the Austrian hospital that had treated him during his illness. "I spent the last ten days since I woke up literally thanking people for saving my life, which is something I've never had to do before, and I don't want to have to do it again," he said.

He made good his word; and after giving a memorable performance at the closing ceremony of the London Olympic games, George Michael went back on the road in September 2012, choosing first to stop in Vienna to perform for those who had saved his life almost a year before. "This is one of the greatest honours of my life," he told them, before singing the classic song, "Feelin' Good".

However, while performing the concerts did make George Michael feel good on the outside, inside he was very much trying to get himself back together after the trauma of his near-death experience. He had believed that pressing on with his projects and going back on the road would enable him to recover emotionally from what had happened, but sadly he was wrong. On 29 September, after playing eleven concerts, and with many more to go, George announced that he was going to honour the remainder of the UK shows, but would have to cancel the Australian leg of his tour. In a statement on his official website he said that the cancellation "breaks my heart".

"I have tried in vain to work my way through the trauma that the doctors who saved my life warned me I would experience," he said, before going on to explain that the medical specialists had recommended complete rest and post-traumatic counselling, which he had previously thought he didn't need. "I believed (wrongly) that making music and getting out there to perform would be therapy enough . . ."

Sadly it would seem that while George Michael was more than willing to go back on the road, he had completely underestimated just how much he had been through, and how difficult it would be to recover. He ended the statement by apologizing to his Australian fans and declaring that after the UK leg of the tour ended in mid-October 2012, he would "receive the treatment which is so long overdue".

He did as he promised, and at the time of writing the singer seems to be doing well in his recovery; a new song "White Light" was nominated for awards and he has continued to look to the future. At the beginning of 2013 the future looked bright, and he tweeted to fans that he was looking forward to the New Year which he promised would be filled with great new music.

52

Winona Ryder Is Arrested for Shoplifting

Winona Ryder may have had some wonderful movie roles over the years, but it was her part in a real-life drama that brought her unwanted headlines around the world and the biggest courtroom drama she had ever seen.

Born on 29 October 1971 as Winona Laura Horowitz, Ryder grew up in and around California, and at one point lived on a 300-acre commune. This living space ensured she became a big fan of books, thanks to the fact that their home had no electricity and therefore no television. But this lifestyle was not going to entertain the youngster for long, and by the time she was twelve, Winona was showing great interest in a career in acting. With that in mind, she began taking lessons in her spare time and in 1986 was ecstatic to discover that her first professional film role would be in *Lucas* alongside actor Charlie Sheen.

More movies followed, including *Beetlejuice* in 1988 and *Edward Scissorhands* in 1990, the latter also featuring her then boyfriend Johnny Depp. However, it was her role in the 1990 film *Mermaids* which won her not only critical acclaim but a Golden Globe nomination for Best Actress in a Supporting Role. She missed out on winning the award, but this was rectified several years later when she won the Golden Globe Award for Best Supporting Actress, and then an Academy Award nomination for her role in *The Age of Innocence* (1993) with Michelle Pfeiffer.

Her career went from strength to strength during the 1990s, with another Oscar nomination coming for her role as Jo in *Little Women* (1994). By the time the new millennium arrived, she was presented with a coveted star on the celebrated Hollywood Walk of Fame, but unfortunately for Winona, the glory of her glittering career came to an abrupt halt in December 2001 when she decided to visit the Saks Fifth Avenue store in Beverly Hills.

Two months before her shopping trip, the actress had broken her arm and was prescribed Oxycodone to relieve the pain. However, instead of just taking the pills while going through the healing process, the actress found herself continuing with the prescription even after her arm was better. The pills left her confused and this soon became apparent during her trip to the Saks Fifth Avenue store.

On CCTV footage later shown in court (some of which is now freely available on the internet) Winona is seen walking around the store in a large, cream-coloured coat, her arms full of designer clothes. She stops periodically, hoisting the garments up into her arms, and generally looking more than a little conspicuous. The actress is seen trying on hats and even wearing one which still has a tag attached as she saunters around the different departments. Coming in and out of the store's dressing room, Ryder is at times helped by various sales assistants, one of whom appears to come to the dressing room with a credit card receipt.

Finally, after about ninety minutes, Winona Ryder is observed with her arms full of items, while she boldly walks out of the store. Two security guards are then seen rushing after her; they unburden her of the items, and march her back into the store. The footage then shows the actress looking at the guards in what can only be described as a very shocked, confused state.

Once Winona Ryder was brought back into the store, she was immediately taken to the security room, where she was thoroughly searched. During this examination the store's guards allegedly found a number of items that the actress had indeed paid for, but among them were a number of other – unpaid for – garments, such as two black hats, various pairs of socks, a blouse, hair accessories and handbags. The actress was later charged with second-degree commercial burglary, grand theft of personal property, vandalism and, as her prescription pills were also on her person, possession of a controlled substance.

Once the world was informed of Winona's misdemeanour, her lawyer, Mark Geragos, stepped forward to describe the charges as "out of whack". He also claimed that his client had prescriptions for the drugs and receipts for the clothes, and would prove it in court. Winona, meanwhile, was understandably mortified by the entire episode and deeply embarrassed. She decided not to say anything personally to the press, and instead endeavoured to just ride the storm and wait for it all to be over. However, her publicist, Mara Buxbaum, did release a statement on her behalf, which read: "We are shocked at what appear to be grossly exaggerated charges. We look forward to the opportunity to explain and resolve these allegations."

When the trial began in June 2002, Winona suffered a setback to the recovery of her broken arm, when she was met by a huge throng of reporters and cameras on her entrance into court. She was jostled so much, in fact, that her healing arm was fractured by a television camera, which resulted in the actress having to see a doctor and wear her arm in a sling.

Things were made no better when the Saks's security manager took to the stand to testify that he had seen Ryder walking round the store just after 4 p.m. on the day of her arrest, visiting departments such as Yves St Laurent and Donna Karan. The actress was pulling blouses and bags from racks, he said, tried on a black hat without replacing it on the shelf, and concealed a handbag in another bag she was carrying. He also claimed that although there were three cash registers open on her way out of the store, Ryder had walked past every one of them.

A few days later – after a break so that Winona could rest her arm – the security investigator took to the stand and claimed that on first sight, she believed Ryder was a homeless lady, until she finally recognized her as an actress. She then said that she was asked by her manager to keep a close eye on Winona, and even admitted to spying on her through slats in the dressing-room door.

What she allegedly saw was Winona Ryder sitting on the floor, taking security tags from various items, one of which left a bloodstain on a bag after she accidentally cut herself with scissors (although it was discovered in later testimony that the security woman had not actually seen the actress cut herself). She then explained that she saw the actress wrapping up various small items such as socks and hair accessories, and bundling them into a bag. This testimony was bad news for Winona, but there was one bright spot to the day, when it was accepted by the court that Winona did in fact pay for $3,700 worth of goods, though the socks, hair accessories and some other items did not appear to be listed on the receipts.

Once proceedings were finished for the day, Winona and her lawyer left the courtroom and were besieged by reporters, though unfortunately for them, they were ordered to keep a distance of at least ten feet to protect the actress's arm. The press all shouted questions, and while Winona chose to stay quiet, lawyer Mark Geragos had a few things to say about what he had heard on the stand that day.

"That testimony was as close to full-blown perjury as I've ever seen in a courtroom," he said, before adding, "I have evidence that Saks targeted [Ryder] as a celebrity. They found a more-than-willing partner in a district attorney."

Because of delays caused by accusations of an unfair trial, the shoplifting case plodded along for months, inspiring "Free Winona" T-shirts and a variety of television skits. Finally, however, the trial resumed in October 2002 after any chance of an out-of-court settlement fell through, though thankfully for Winona, the drug charge had by that point been dropped.

The reason for this, it seemed, was that she quite obviously had prescriptions for the pills in her possession and nobody had any chance of proving that they had been obtained illegally.

Still, the other charges stood and Winona was forced to sit through the testimony of Saks's security manager, Kenneth Evans, who told the court that the actress had confessed that she had shoplifted in order to research an upcoming film role. He told jurors, "She just said she was doing what her director told her to do in preparation for her role as a shoplifter." This was a line which brought much surprise to the defence team, and looks of confusion all round.

The defence then retorted by declaring that Winona Ryder had never stolen anything, and instead was set up by the Saks security staff, who were concerned that their CCTV footage did not show the actress doing any of the things of which they had initially accused her. "Their testimony is bald-faced lies," defence lawyer Mark Geragos told the jury. Meanwhile, Winona's publicist Mara Buxbaum told reporters that while it was true her client did talk to the security staff about future film roles, it was "utterly ridiculous" to suggest that she had told them she had been shoplifting as research.

The court was shown the by now famous security footage, which detailed Winona Ryder walking around the store, and although no footage was seen of security tags being taken off the clothes, security manager Evans was quick to tell the court that he had found a selection of the tags in the pocket of a jacket in the Chanel department. Material on these tags matched material from the stolen garments, he said. The matter of the actress cutting herself was brought back up when it was pointed out that Winona had been seen accepting a sticking plaster from a member of staff.

Jurors were told by the prosecution that Ryder had gone to the store equipped to shoplift, with scissors to cut off the tags and a large bag to hide the goods inside. "You will begin to watch that shopping bag grow and grow," Deputy District Attorney Ann Rundle told them, as she assured everyone that the entire episode added up to a simple case of theft, "Nothing more, nothing less."

Much of the trial was taken up by going over the "shoplifting" story again and again, with cross-examination adding some elements to the tale while correcting others. Disgruntled ex-employees were called to the stand; lawyers were chastised for making unnecessary remarks about the truth of testimony; and so it went on and on. Everything was discussed from the dressing room the actress had specifically requested; to the number of security tags found in the store; to the revelation that while Ryder had bought various items by credit card, she had apparently never asked the sales assistant to keep her account open. It all became a little like *Groundhog Day*, and as Winona sat in the courtroom, the frustration on her face was clear to see as she made detailed notes and shook her head on numerous occasions.

Finally, in early November 2002, Winona Ryder was convicted of felony grand theft and vandalism, though she was acquitted on the burglary charge. The actress showed great shock during the verdict but remained quiet, though she just about managed to find a few words outside the court for waiting newspaper reporters. "I'm sorry," she said. "Thanks for asking [but] I just can't talk right now."

Deputy District Attorney Ann Rundle found more to say, however, when she left the court and was besieged by the press. "We are simply asking for Ms Ryder to take responsibility for her conduct, and that's what this trial has been about," she said. She added that she planned to ask the judge to place the actress on probation, pay the department store for the items and take part in community service.

Jumping to Ryder's defence was her publicist Mara Buxbaum, who told reporters, "Winona is grateful to her family, friends and those who have supported her. She was preparing for the worst and hoping for the best."

When it was time for sentencing, the actress arrived in the court dressed soberly in black, and sat in a chair, awaiting the judge's decision. However, things threatened to become heated when her lawyer told the court of the reward she had put up for the safe return of a missing schoolgirl some years before. Ann Rundle took great offence to this story being brought up and attacked the actress during her speech.

"For someone to trot out the body of a dead child and in some way say because she supported—"

Rundle was unable to finish the sentence when Winona's counsel angrily interrupted the attack and Ryder herself jumped to her feet, her mouth wide open in utter shock and disbelief.

After the outburst, Superior Court Judge Elden S. Fox passed down 480 hours of community service, three years' probation and mental health counselling, before lecturing Winona Ryder about her conduct.

"You have disappointed many people inspired and entertained by your talents," he said, before then going on to tell the actress that he felt she had refused to accept any personal responsibility for what happened in the store, and that while he had no intention of making an example of her, he most certainly wanted to hold her accountable for her actions. "If you steal again you will go to jail," he warned.

Outside the court, a disgruntled Ann Rundle told reporters that she believed the only remaining issue was "whether or not Miss Ryder will stop pointing fingers at others and start examining her own behaviour". Meanwhile, defence lawyer Mark Geragos commented on the outcome by saying that he believed the sentencing was reasonable, "given what the convictions were".

Once the trial was over, Winona Ryder tried desperately to get on with her life in a quiet manner. She did the community service, dealt with her issues concerning painkillers and made a conscious decision to take time off from her film career. She moved to San Francisco to be near her parents, who had been a great support during the trial.

While many people (and possibly even Ryder herself) believed her career to be over, once the scandal had died down the actress went on to play a variety of parts in films such as *The Private Lives of Pippa Lee* (2009) and *Star Trek* (2009). Her career was back on track, but her biggest comeback was yet to come, when she played the small but important role of Beth in the 2010 film, *Black Swan.* Winona acted as a former prima-ballerina whose career is coming to an end, much to her horror, and while the part may have been small, it succeeding in winning her new fans and a great deal of critical acclaim.

As for the shoplifting scandal, Winona Ryder remained tight-lipped about it until 2007, when she eventually opened up ever so slightly in an interview with *Vogue* magazine. In the piece she stated that she didn't feel a tremendous sense of guilt over the episode, because her actions had not hurt anybody. If she had, she admitted, "It would have been an entirely different experience."

53

The Brad Pitt, Jennifer Aniston and Angelina Jolie Love Triangle

There have been many love triangles during the history of time; probably the most famous being the one between Princess Diana, Prince Charles and Camilla Parker Bowles. This particular triangle spawned the phrase "There were three people in this marriage; so it was a bit crowded," which has been used time and time again ever since. However, our next scandal spawned the phrases "Team Jolie" and "Team Aniston", and would encourage discussions and debate around the water-cooler for many years to come.

As Rachel Green in the hit show *Friends*, Jennifer Aniston was the darling of television when she met Brad Pitt, the star of *Se7en* (1995) and *Interview with the Vampire* (1994). The two started dating in 1998 and quickly became the talk of the world, especially when they decided to marry in July 2000 in a private Malibu ceremony. The ecstatic couple spurned lucrative offers from magazines, and instead released a black-and-white photo of themselves in aid of charity. The couple were photographed looking happy on their big day, with Jen wearing a white dress, veil and her hair hanging loose, while Brad dressed in a smart suit and tie.

Mr and Mrs Pitt were the perfect Hollywood couple and even appeared in an episode of *Friends* together, which saw them going head-to-head in a showdown over old high-school grievances including Pitt's "I hate Rachel" club and made-up rumours of Rachel being an hermaphrodite cheerleader from

Long Island. The episode was a huge hit with fans and cemented their status as one of the happiest couples in show business.

Unfortunately, their marriage seemed to come to an abrupt halt after Pitt was contracted to work with Angelina Jolie on the film *Mr & Mrs Smith* (2005). The two actors fell for each other, and while both still deny having a full fling on set, there can be no doubt that there was a huge attraction there. Of course, stories from the set were quick to leak out into "real life" and rumours swirled around for quite some time about whether or not Pitt was going to leave his wife. The curious public didn't have to wait long, however, as while the two tried to hold things together for a time, it soon became clear that the marriage was just not working and their separation was announced on 6 January 2005.

Very quickly stories started to circulate that Pitt was in love with Angelina Jolie and the whole world seemed to be on either Team Jolie or Team Aniston; there was simply no room for being "on the fence". To some, Angelina was seen as the brazen woman in the middle, the home-wrecker who had torn the couple apart. In reality, however, while the relationship with Jolie was certainly a symptom that something was wrong in the Aniston/Pitt partnership, she doesn't seem to have been the cause of the split. Instead, there may have been problems for some time before she came on the scene, with Pitt's friends declaring that it was actually Aniston's apprehension about having children that had caused the break-up. For her part, Jennifer herself later claimed that there was a "sensitivity chip" missing from her estranged husband.

The pair eventually divorced on 2 October 2005 and Jennifer went on to make *The Break-up* with actor Vince Vaughn. The film centred on a couple who were – as the title indicates – breaking up. Producers were loath to offer Jennifer the part, knowing what she had just been through, but she pressed ahead anyway. "What a great way to exorcise [the divorce]" she later declared.

During the filming, Jennifer developed a close friendship

and rumoured romance with co-star Vince Vaughn, while Pitt was finally free to enter into an intense relationship with Angelina Jolie. Jolie had previously adopted a son, Maddox, and was in the process of adopting a daughter, Zahara, at the time, and very quietly Pitt went on to adopt the children, too. Then although the pair continued to remain silent about their relationship, it soon became impossible to deny they were anything but good friends when in May 2006, Jolie gave birth to their first biological child, a daughter they called Shiloh.

By now any hopes of Jennifer Aniston and Brad Pitt reconciling were firmly out of the window, but the media were still obsessed with what the two thought of each other, and why the marriage had gone disastrously wrong. For their part, the couple have always remained largely tight-lipped about each other, and still claim to be on a relatively friendly basis. So cordial, in fact, that rumours have developed over the years of secret meetings, letters and phone calls – none of which have ever been proved, although in the February 2009 issue of *W Magazine*, Pitt did admit that the two check in with each other occasionally. "She was a big part of my life, and me hers," he said.

After the initial adoption of Maddox and Zahara, and then the later birth of Shiloh, Brad Pitt and Angelina Jolie went on to have three more children: Pax was adopted in 2007 and then biological twins Knox and Vivienne were born in 2008. No children have appeared since then, though the couple have not ruled out the possibility. Pitt relayed his feelings on fatherhood at the Venice Film Festival by describing it as the most fun and the "biggest pain in the ass" that he had ever experienced in his life. "I love it and can't recommend it highly enough," he told reporters shortly before the arrival of his last two children.

Both Jolie and Pitt have admitted that their children are desperate for them to marry, and in the summer of 2012 it was rumoured that they were about to tie the knot in a French chateau. That never happened – or if it did, it remains the best-kept secret in show business. Then in December of the same year it was once again claimed that they had secretly married over the Christmas period. But in the face of rumours and hearsay, as of March 2013 the two remain happily unmarried, although some sources predict they won't remain that way for long.

As for Jennifer Aniston, she has enjoyed a great deal of film success with hits such as the real-life story of *Marley and Me*, in which she played a wife juggling three children and a disobedient canine. She may soon be able to play this role in her personal life, too, as in August 2012 it was announced that she was engaged to actor Justin Theroux, who she had been dating for the past year. Aniston has said she is extremely happy with her new fiancé and is very much looking forward to the future. It is not yet known when the wedding will take place, but you can be sure that if it is anywhere near the time when her former husband gets married, the comparisons will be set to run and run.

54

The Tragic Life and Death of Anna Nicole Smith

The life of Anna Nicole Smith reads like a Jackie Collins novel, but unlike a Collins novel, where the good characters usually have a chance of living happily ever after, the last years of Smith's life led not only to mystery and scandal, but to tragedy too.

Born Vickie Lynn Hogan on 28 November 1967, Anna Nicole Smith had a tumultuous relationship with her mother and for the most part was raised by her aunt in Mexia, Texas. By the time she was seventeen the young girl was married to Billy Wayne Smith, and gave birth to their son, Daniel Wayne, just nine months later on 22 January 1986. The marriage didn't work out, however; Anna had ambitions to be famous and just a year after Daniel's birth she packed her bags and moved to Houston in a bid to make her dreams come true.

In 1991, while working in a strip club, Anna met eighty-six year-old oil tycoon J. Howard Marshall and the two embarked on a highly scandalous relationship, much to the obvious dismay of his worried family. Marshall was richer than any man Anna had ever known, and though she tried to reassure everyone that her intentions were honourable, it came as no surprise when she was labelled a gold-digger who was dating Marshall not for love but for what he could buy her.

While we will never know the true feelings between the couple, another older man entered Anna's life during this time. She was discovered by Hugh Heffner, who placed her on the cover of the March 1992 issue of his magazine, *Playboy*. The cover was a success; Anna was a huge hit with readers; and in 1993 she was voted Playmate of the Year. Lots of publicity followed and Smith, a huge Marilyn Monroe fan, decided she was going to be just like her, revelling in dressing up in a replica of the famous *Seven Year Itch* dress and channelling her inner Marilyn at photo shoots.

Many modelling jobs followed, including shoots for Guess Jeans and H & M, and she even won an appearance in 1994's *Naked Gun 33 and a third*, playing Tanya Peters, the villain's entertaining girlfriend. She gave a fun performance and won much praise, though the same cannot be said for her next "performance" on 27 June 1994 when the twenty-six-year-old Smith walked down the aisle to marry her by now eighty-nine-year-old boyfriend, J. Howard Marshall. They both raised eyebrows in the congregation by wearing matching white outfits, and guests could not help but notice that the groom was much less mobile than his bride, sitting in a wheelchair during the ceremony and then afterwards being wheeled up the aisle with his beaming bride walking in front.

The marriage caused a huge media uproar and J. Howard Marshall's family were incensed, convinced that the young blonde was only after the ailing billionaire's money. Their feelings seemed justified when it was discovered that, just hours after the marriage, Marshall was apparently left alone and in despair when Anna preferred to take off for Greece on a modelling assignment rather than spend time alone with him on their honeymoon.

Needless to say, her $50,000 monthly allowance did nothing to quell their fears, and to add to their worries, rumours surfaced that the model refused to live in the marital home, conducted extra-marital affairs and tormented her husband by exposing her naked breasts to others while in his presence. Of course, if any of this was true, Anna was not about to admit it and denied any wrongdoing during several interviews: "I know people think I married Howard for his money, but it's not true.

I love him," she said. She also declared that she was actively looking after her husband while he was unwell, though her lawyer later revealed that at one point during the marriage, Smith was banned from seeing her husband for more than an hour a day on the orders of Marshall's lawyers and doctors. The restrictions were finally lifted, though according to Smith's lawyer, Diana Marshall, "They lost a lot of precious time they could have spent together."

Eventually, on 4 August 1995, just thirteen months after the wedding, J. Howard Marshall passed away and his son, E. Pierce Marshall, took it upon himself to arrange a private family funeral on 13 August. Unfortunately for him, however, Anna did not agree to this arrangement and after talking it through with friends of her own, arranged a memorial to end all memorial services, in Houston on 7 August.

The grieving widow turned up wearing a low-cut white dress and veil, which some mistakenly took to be her own wedding dress from the year before. It wasn't, but still, it looked in remarkably bad taste to wear such a plunging gown to the funeral of her dead husband. Added to that, Anna also carried her little black dog under her arm and was accompanied by her young son, also adorned in white.

The event turned out to be quite a spectacle and Smith tried to recite a eulogy but could only manage to say a few words before breaking down. Then several of Anna's friends – who had only known Marshall very briefly – got up to speak about the couple's love. Harps played; the minister read from the Bible; and – quite astonishingly – Smith and her son Daniel then sang the Bette Midler song "Wind Beneath My Wings" before running dramatically from the room.

Not surprisingly, Marshall's family was not in attendance and remained absolutely furious that the model had played such a significant part in their father's life and his funeral. Almost immediately a battle commenced between Anna and Marshall's son, Pierce, over who should be entitled to the oil man's $1.6 billion estate, with both sides arguing that they were the ones entitled to the money. Whole books could be written about the much ballyhooed case, with decisions and appeals going back and forth between the two parties for so long that in 2011 the case was still rattling on – years after the death of both Anna Nicole and E. Pierce Marshall.

In 1996, Smith hit the headlines once again when she was forced to file for bankruptcy after an employee sued her for sexual harassment. She later told *Extra* what she was going through at the time, saying that she was totally overwhelmed due to the number of people who seemed to be suing her and adding: "I'm this one little girl; I'm this one little person. And I've got 50 things thrown at me, and I'm like what did I ever do? I've never hurt anybody . . . I couldn't handle it." Anna became exceptionally depressed with the situation she was in, and took solace in prescription pills, food and alcohol.

Through the stress of the court case and her day-to-day life, Anna began to pile on weight and soon became addicted to the tablets she was continuously taking. Unfortunately this all backfired when she became so dependent on her medication that she had no knowledge of particular jobs she had done or people to whom she had spoken. Then one evening she accidentally overdosed and was rushed to hospital. She fell into a coma and, by the time she woke, she had developed pneumonia and was given a fifty-fifty chance of survival. It was hit or miss for some time, but somehow Anna managed to pull through, and later told reporters that she had needed to learn to walk and talk all over again. "It was bad," she confessed. She also assured an interviewer on the *Extra* programme that she would never take pills again. When asked if she worried she'd ever go back to drugs, she replied, "Oh absolutely not. That will never happen again I promise. No!"

But while it seemed for a time that Anna's demons had been silenced, it was all an illusion. By the time she started making her reality show, *The Anna Nicole Show*, in 2002, it was clear that she still had a problem. Panned by the critics for her outrageous behaviour on screen, the programme showed Anna arguing with her staff, including lawyer Howard K. Stern, trying to avoid her toothless cousin who had suddenly shown up on her doorstep, and embarking on a pizza-eating contest with her son and personal assistant.

The entire show became a source of gossip at water-coolers everywhere, particularly when a clearly drunk and overweight Smith was seen gyrating with lap dancers in Las Vegas, and simulating sex (fully clothed, thankfully) with her lawyer. The show was so bad that it became something of a train wreck, but there was a sadder side to it, too, as even the most hard-hearted of people could see that here was a woman in obvious pain and distress. Anna was frequently taped slurring her words, as though back on medication, and while she was most certainly larger than life during most of it, there were certainly times during the show when she seemed like a little girl lost, surrounded by paid friends, when all she really needed was a hug from a loving parent.

Eventually – and predictably – the show was cancelled, and perhaps after seeing herself on screen, Anna took the opportunity to embark on another quest to slim down and clean up her act. She seemed to succeed and began dating photographer Larry Birkhead, conceiving his child in late 2005. Fans would have to wait until June 2006 for an official statement, however, which came – quite predictably – in a video posted on her website.

Floating on an inflatable bed on her swimming pool, Anna announced that she had been reading a lot of gossip about herself in the newspapers and wanted to stop the rumours that had been circulating. "Yes, I am pregnant. I'm happy, I'm very, very happy about it," she said, before adding that everything was going very well with the pregnancy and she promised to let fans share her excitement through her website in the months to come.

This revelation intrigued both fans and the media, who wondered who was responsible for the pregnancy, but Anna remained tight-lipped and refused to name the father of the child. This decision only succeeded in making the reporters even more intrigued and they began camping out on her doorstep in order to try and catch the future father coming or going from the house. This media attention did not sit well with the pregnant Anna, so she surprised everyone by moving to the Bahamas, where she hoped to live a quieter and more fulfilled life.

By this point it seemed that everything in Anna's life was going much better and everyone hoped that she had turned her life around – that she was off prescription drugs and happily waiting for the birth. Unfortunately, while on the outside everything did indeed seem to be positive and moving forward nicely, inside all was not as it seemed, though somehow she managed to keep this side of her life very much hidden from fans and reporters.

After her death, the Los Angeles Superior Court acquired a disturbing video of a heavily pregnant Anna Nicole being painted as a clown by a friend's young daughter. The footage shows the model denying that she is pregnant, and instead she assures the camera that she is only suffering from gas, and that her real baby is lying next to the pool. The camera, controlled by lawyer Howard K. Stern, pans towards the "baby", which is really a plastic doll. "[Anna] has major brain trouble," observes the little girl, who seems to be the only sensible person in the house.

The video gets even more bizarre when Anna Nicole is seen changing and caring for the doll in the nursery at her home, cooing and later wheeling it around in a pram. "This footage is worth money!" laughs Howard K. Stern, as a clearly disturbed Anna looks fuzzily into the camera. Bizarrely, it was later denied that Anna was on drugs at all during the episode, but if she wasn't she must surely have been a much better actress than originally thought.

On 7 September 2006 Dannielynn Hope Marshall Stern was born, and Howard K. Stern was listed as the father on the birth certificate. This was at best a mistake and at worst a lie, as in reality the baby was most definitely the result of Anna's romance with Larry Birkhead. On the evening of 9 September 2006, while recovering in a Bahamas hospital after the birth, Anna was thrilled to receive a visit from her son, Daniel. Unfortunately, while sitting at her bedside the next morning, the twenty-year-old passed away suddenly, much to the shock and distress of his mother who lay just feet away from his chair.

The autopsy revealed that Daniel had a combination of the drugs Zoloft, Lexapro and Methadone in his body, and the death sent the distraught Anna Nicole into a downward spiral. For many years Daniel had been the only light in the model's life, and now her little boy was gone, for reasons that remained too unexplained and confusing for the young woman to bear. During the funeral Anna demanded they open the casket and when her wishes were fulfilled, she shocked everyone by trying desperately to climb inside, insisting she wanted to go with her son to the afterlife. Unfortunately this was an episode from which Anna would never recover, and from then on her life seemed to be even more of a tragic roller-coaster than ever before.

On 28 September, just eighteen days after the death of Daniel, Anna Nicole and Howard K. Stern took part in a commitment ceremony to each other in the Bahamas. Photographs of the event were beamed worldwide and people questioned not only the timing of the ceremony, so close to her son's death, but also the genuineness of the love between the couple. Still, they assured people that their relationship was genuine and denied that it had been made in a bid to halt paternity charges brought by Larry Birkhead in relation to Dannielynn. So determined were they to stop Birkhead having access to the child that Stern even appeared on *Larry King Live*, declaring that he and Anna had been in a relationship for a long time and that the child was most certainly his own.

The couple decided to settle permanently in the Bahamas; another decision apparently made to avoid the looming paternity tests that awaited them in the United States. Anna Nicole was happy to be a mother again, and caring for her daughter became the only bright spark in the last months of her life. Outwardly she seemed to be coping relatively well, considering, but once again this was an illusion and she was still so distraught at the death of Daniel that shortly after his death she was found floating face down in her swimming pool. She was saved by her partner, Howard K. Stern. She also started telling friends that she just could not get over the idea that Daniel was somehow calling to her from beyond the grave.

"I dream of him every day and every night" she said, and added that she was frightened he was stuck in purgatory, lost and unsure where to go. "He comes to me in my sleep; he's calling me to come to him," she told *Entertainment Tonight*. She also became inconsolable when told that her estranged mother, Virgie, had been to visit Daniel's grave. Anna claimed that her mother had only visited because she was paid by a magazine, and that she could not believe that the woman had decided to pay the visit on Daniel's birthday. "It makes me sick to my stomach," she cried.

To add to her worries, it became apparent that Larry Birkhead – not surprisingly – was not going to stand by and watch his daughter being raised by another man. The stress became too much and she told friends that she didn't know how long she could cope with it all. Her life was spiralling out of control. Having lost her son and now threatened with worry of losing her daughter too, Anna's heart was broken; she had no more fight left.

Tragically, on 8 February 2007, during a trip to Hollywood, Florida, Anna Nicole Smith was found unconscious in room 607 of the Seminole Hard Rock Hotel and Casino. Friends and staff tried desperately to revive her, before paramedics arrived and rushed her to Memorial Regional Hospital. Paramedics were seen trying to save her as her body was wheeled into the ambulance, but unfortunately she could not be resuscitated and was pronounced dead on arrival, shortly before 3 p.m. It was later decided that Smith had died of an accidental drug overdose, with chloral hydrate being the major component. Other drugs were found in her system included Valium and benzodiazepines but no illegal substances were discovered.

As soon as Anna died, a legal battle raged to decide where she should – and should not – be buried. Howard K. Stern insisted she should be buried next to her son in the Bahamas, while her estranged mother Virgie wanted her back in Texas. Even Larry Birkhead became involved, and although it wasn't related to the case at all, found himself answering questions about the paternity of Dannielynn. The real-life drama was beamed all over the world and Judge Larry Seidlin became famous not only for his one-liners during proceedings, but also for breaking down in tears on giving his verdict that he wanted to give custody of Anna's remains to Richard Milstein, the lawyer for Dannielynn. He specifically wished for Anna to be buried with her son, Daniel: "I want them to be together," he cried.

Both he and Stern got their wish and Anna's body was eventually buried next to that of her son, Daniel Smith. The ashes of her late husband J. Howard Marshall were also laid with her and a huge, black granite marker with photographs of Smith and her son was placed over the plot.

Meanwhile, on 10 April 2007 the paternity case was finally resolved when it was declared that Larry Birkhead was indeed the father of Anna's daughter. Dannielynn was handed over to her father in order to begin her new life in the United States. She paid tribute to her mother in November 2012 by becoming a model for Guess Jeans. Looking remarkably like Anna Nicole, the girl posed happily for the cameras, and her father later told reporters that it was entirely her decision to take part in the campaign – that she wanted her photograph on the Guess bags, just like her mother had done many years before her.

While Howard K. Stern claimed to be the father of Dannielynn and took part in a commitment ceremony with the little girl's mother, in the end he lost both and resigned himself to life without them. However, before he was able to move on completely, it was announced that he and other members of Smith's entourage – her psychiatrist and her doctor – would be charged with "crimes of prescribing, administering and dispensing controlled substances to an addict". There were also questions raised about whether or not there had been a conspiracy to use fake names in order to acquire drugs for Smith, and by the time the case went to court in August 2010, the media was once again full of Anna Nicole news, three and a half years after her sudden death.

By the end of the trial, Smith's doctor was acquitted of all charges, but Stern and the psychiatrist were found guilty and due to be sentenced in January 2011. When that day came the judge surprisingly decided that there was insufficient evidence to show that they intended to break the law and threw the case out of court. The only conviction that remained was a charge of fraud against the psychiatrist, though that was later reduced to a misdemeanour.

This decision angered many fans who believed – rightly or wrongly – that Stern had something to do with Anna Nicole's wild behaviour and the drug abuse which eventually led to her death. They were not the only ones, it would seem, as in October 2012 – two years after the initial guilty verdict – a California court made the decision that the judge had been wrong to throw out the case and that the convictions should be looked at again. Judge Robert Perry was then given the unenviable task of deciding what to do next: to consider Stern's request for a new trial (which would mean that the original case would have to be dismissed as the new trial could constitute double jeopardy); to find another grounds for dismissal; or to sentence the former lawyer to prison or probation based on the original conviction. As of March 2013, no decision has been made as to what the outcome will be, though if the former court appearances of Anna Nicole Smith are anything to go by, the case could run and run.

And what of Anna? Much has been said about her life and personality, though most of it is derogatory and untrue. Her life was so full of twists and turns that it is almost hard to believe it really happened. One thing that is not often reported, however, is that in spite of all the scandal and intrigue, she had a very big heart, lavishing her friends and children with attention and love in equal measure.

She was also extremely generous to her fans, as demonstrated when she lived for a time at 12305 Fifth Helena Drive, the last home of her idol, Marilyn Monroe. She didn't stay long, due to her son's apparent distaste for the property, but while she was there Marilyn's fans would often write and tell her how much the actress meant to them. Instead of ignoring the fan mail that came for her idol, she would often reply and send photographs of herself inside the home. These photos regularly appear on the internet, a testimony not only to how she appreciated her fans, but also how much she adored Marilyn Monroe.

It is a tragedy that, in the end, the woman who wanted so much to be like Marilyn, who dressed in replica costumes and rented her home to be "close" to her idol, ended up passing away in a strikingly similar situation. But then, given her tragic life, perhaps that was always inevitable.

55

Michael Jackson, the Man from Neverland

"The King of Pop", "Wacko Jacko" ... whatever you want to call him, the fact remains that Michael Jackson was one of the biggest pop superstars of the twentieth century. A dancer, singer, actor and all-round performer, he dazzled audiences across the globe with hits such as "Thriller", "Bad" and "The Way You Make Me Feel". However, it cannot be denied that away from the thrills of his music and stage presence, it was his personal life and death that caused the most sensation – and the circumstances of both are still furiously discussed and argued by fans today.

Born on 29 August 1958, Jackson was the eighth of ten children born to Katherine and Joe Jackson. The family was raised in a small house in Indiana, where Michael's father – who played in a band – had dreams of his children following in his footsteps. He got his wish, and in 1964 some of the brothers (including Michael) began performing together and eventually the Jackson Five (later the Jacksons) was born. The band was a huge success, signing to Motown and performing such hits as "I Want You Back" and "ABC". But in spite of the success of the band itself, it was "Little Michael" that got the most attention, and ultimately, while still young, he ended up releasing several albums and singles as a solo artist, including "Ben" and "Rockin' Robin".

Michael's childhood was traumatic and he was constantly bothered by the fact that he was unable to have the regular upbringing enjoyed by other children. There was little – if any – time for playing with friends, visiting the park or riding his bike in the street. Instead, the children were all expected to practise their dance routines day and night, under the ever-watchful eye of their father Joseph.

In several later interviews Michael claimed that his father would become emotionally and physically abusive while supervising rehearsals. He also said that as a child he was exceptionally lonely and often watched other children playing outside the building where he was working, unable to go down and take part because he had to record his latest single or album. Added to that, it is also said that the child was told on numerous occasions that he had a big nose and spots; a result of which – it would seem – was the obsession Jackson developed with undertaking plastic surgery procedures during the latter part of his life.

By the time he was a fully grown adult, Michael Jackson had the world of pop at his feet. A phenomenal superstar, his albums with the Jacksons were still huge hits, but he was ready to branch off on his own. He made a film – a box-office disaster – called *The Wiz* (1978) and then in 1979 he released his own album, *Off the Wall*, which went on to sell a staggering twenty million copies and introduced the world to a more mature Michael Jackson. More albums followed, including the astronomically successful *Thriller* in 1982 and *Bad* in 1987. He also toured the world extremely successfully, but while his professional life was nothing short of amazing, his personal life was heading towards disaster.

In January 1984 Jackson had been filming an advert for Pepsi Cola, when some pyrotechnics set his hair on fire. Footage of the episode shows Jackson dancing without realizing that his head is ablaze, and finding out too late to prevent second-degree burns to his scalp. This seems to have been a real turning point for the singer, and as a result he undertook various plastic surgery procedures and began taking tablets to ease the pain. Unfortunately, it would seem that this was to be his undoing, and Michael Jackson never truly recovered from the trauma inflicted that day.

After that tragic episode, certain elements of Jackson's life began to develop in ways that outsiders may describe as somewhat odd. He owned a chimpanzee – Bubbles – which slept in a crib by his bed and travelled the world with him on a private jet. Not only that, but it was also reported that it did everything with the singer – from watching movies in a private cinema to sitting at the table to eat his dinner. This seems to have been the start of the "Wacko Jacko" era; the media absolutely loved the Bubbles stories and rumours, and photographed the pair together at every opportunity.

It was not just fun stories being reported in the media, though. By summer 1993, rumours of a very different kind were circulating that involved Jackson being accused of the sexual abuse of a thirteen-year-old boy named Jordan Chandler. Money was said to have been demanded by the family of the boy, which Jackson refused to give, and then the matter of the alleged abuse was reported to the police. By Christmas 1993 Jackson's home had been investigated and the singer had been strip-searched. Jackson released a video statement, protesting his innocence. "Don't treat me like a criminal," he begged, and asked the media to wait for the truth before labelling him. "I am innocent," he said.

In January 1994 the matter was settled out of court with Michael still protesting his innocence and a rumoured $22 million being paid to the Chandler family. Then in early summer the entire matter was dropped by the police and Jackson was able to continue with his life, which – in May 1994 – included marrying Lisa Marie Presley, the daughter of Elvis Presley.

If the media had enjoyed a field day with the Bubbles stories and then the sexual abuse rumours, they really went to town on the marriage between Michael and Lisa Marie. How on earth had this come about, they wondered? And why were they suddenly so close? Actually, the pair had met in 1975 at a concert, and had reconnected in 1992 when they became friends after meeting to discuss a demo tape that Lisa Marie had recently recorded. Unknown to the media, the two then became friends. Michael took to phoning Elvis's daughter at every opportunity and was in constant contact with her throughout the child abuse accusations.

Lisa apparently believed she could somehow "save him" and fell in love with the singer to such a degree that when the possibility of marriage was brought to the table, she ultimately said yes. The two waited until the child abuse scandal passed, and then without making a big deal of it to anyone, decided to make their relationship official by marrying in the Dominican Republic. Unfortunately this did not sit well with Lisa Marie's mother, Priscilla, who knew nothing about the relationship at all; the first she heard of the marriage was when helicopters were buzzing around her house and she saw a news report on television. Priscilla was understandably suspicious and extremely confused by what was going on with her daughter and the King of Pop, and later said that at that particular time she was deeply worried that Lisa Marie was somehow being used.

Reports about the marriage of Jackson and Elvis's daughter were fuelled with rumour and gossip from the very first day. Once the story got out, the media wanted to know if the whole thing was a carefully manipulated scenario designed to rebuild Michael's reputation, and felt that maybe he was marrying in order to get closer to the Elvis back catalogue, since he was a huge fan himself. Members of the public, meanwhile, had other things on their mind and became obsessed with whether or not Michael and Lisa Marie were husband and wife in every sense of the word, or were they merely platonic friends? It seemed that everyone had their own ideas as to the basis of the relationship, and things were made no better after an embarrassing appearance at the MTV awards, where the pair stood on the stage with virtually nothing to say, before finally sharing an awkward kiss and leaving.

It is fair to say that in light of the way the media reported on it, everything about the relationship seemed a little contrived, but Lisa Marie laughed off the allegations and assured everyone that they were just like every other married couple out there – physically and otherwise. Yet people continued to remain doubtful that Michael had ever been intimate with anyone, though in all honesty, without knowing the man personally, this seems to be an unfair assumption.

It was not long before rumours began to surface that the marriage was on the rocks; that the couple were arguing and would no doubt separate soon. Of course, this meant that reporters crowded around the couple's home, spoke to their friends and tried to dig the dirt in order to find anything they could. However, because of the heavy secrecy surrounding Jackson's life, no one could really give much of an insight at all. Michael later shed some light on it when he explained to an interviewer that he and his fiancée had agreed to have children as soon as they got married, but after the wedding his new wife had changed her mind. Michael declared himself to be "broken-hearted" and gave this as the reason why the marriage started to break down.

Of course, as often happens, the other party – in this case, Lisa Marie – had a different version of the reasons why the marriage ended when she spoke to Oprah Winfrey some years after the divorce. In several recorded interviews the singer described that she had indeed planned to have children but wanted to make sure that everything was strong between the couple, as she had no intention of getting into a custody battle with Michael Jackson.

She also described the time she was married as "insane" and explained that during their relationship she was blindsided and naive. Finally – after enduring times when Michael would disappear for weeks on end and collapsed mysteriously during the making of an HBO special – she decided that she'd had enough. Added to that, Jackson was surrounded by a number of people whom she felt were sucking the life from him, and yet he seemed to choose them over her in his life. Eventually the young woman woke up and knew that in circumstances such as these, she was not able to carry on trying to "save" him and just wanted out.

The couple eventually went their separate ways in 1996, though they apparently stayed in touch and got back together several times. But when the affair finally breathed its last breath, Jackson began another relationship, this time with a nurse called Debbie Rowe, whom he married in November 1996. Not surprisingly, from the very start it seemed like a complicated relationship. Rowe had apparently met the singer during a dermatology appointment at the surgery where she worked. She felt sorry for him and the two became friendly. The story goes that during their friendship, Jackson shared his concerns over the break-up of his marriage to Lisa Marie and confided that he believed he would never have children – a revelation which prompted Rowe to suggest that she might be able to give him a child herself.

Michael agreed, but not before telling Lisa Marie that if she wasn't interested in having his baby then Rowe was more than willing. His ex-wife could not be swayed, however, and eventually a baby was conceived with Rowe (some claim by artificial insemination) and a son, Michael Joseph Jackson (known as Prince Michael), was born on 13 February 1997. Another child followed a year later when Paris Michael Katherine was born, and Jackson caused controversy by later claiming that he had literally taken the baby straight from the delivery room back to his home.

It was statements like this that led people to believe that Debbie Rowe had merely acted as a surrogate to Jackson, especially when she was said to have given up her rights to the children when the couple divorced in 1999. This supposed decision was later revoked, however, and it is said that as of 2012, Rowe does have visitation rights with her teenage children and is frequently quoted in newspapers as being concerned over their current welfare.

Jackson's next child was not conceived with Rowe, and instead an unknown woman gave the singer a child in 2002. Named Prince Michael Jackson II (but known to everyone as Blanket), the child became famous when his father took him out on to the balcony of his Berlin hotel room when he was just a few months old, in order to greet shouting fans. What he was thinking is not clear, but he ended up dangling the blanket-covered baby over the balcony for a split second before coming to his senses and taking the child back inside. Although Jackson later apologized for what he described as a mistake, the action of putting his son in danger caused controversy in the media and people wondered about the state of his mental health.

Added to that, Jackson's reputation took a nosedive once again when he insisted that his children went out in public wearing elaborate masks and veils to hide their faces; they were home-schooled, apparently to avoid them socializing with other children their age. Bizarre rumours also began to appear that suggested the children had to throw away their toys every night for fear that they would catch germs from their "used" play things. Since their father had long since been rumoured to sleep in an oxygen tent and was often seen wearing a surgical mask in public, the idea of his germ phobia did not seem too far-fetched, though a look through home movies, which were later released, seems to show this particular rumour to be false. In one revealing snippet, the small children can quite clearly be seen sitting on a wooden floor and playing with a jigsaw that has certainly seen better days, with the box collapsing with age – it certainly had not just been opened that day.

Of the masks and home-schooling, both Debbie Rowe and Michael Jackson said that it was for the children's safety and to protect their identity from the masses. That was fair enough, but given that other huge stars such as Madonna and Whitney Houston were raising their children without the aid of veils in public, this seemed a rather moot point. Further confusion was added when he told *At Large with Geraldo Rivera* that he would soon bring his children on stage with him, which would surely rule out any possibility of keeping them incognito for security's sake. It would seem that by this time, whether he liked it or not, Michael's "Wacko Jacko" persona seemed very much set in stone as far as the media were concerned.

From 2002 to 2003 Michael Jackson made the ill-fated decision to allow the filming of an in-depth television special with investigative journalist Martin Bashir. During the feature-length presentation, the singer was seen travelling around the world with his veil-covered children; going on huge shopping sprees to buy elaborate vases; and shaking wildly when trying to bottle-feed his youngest son. Unfortunately it did not stop there, and towards the end of the programme Jackson was seen holding hands with a teenage boy who he said had been very ill and had stayed at his Neverland ranch on several occasions. The singer explained that they had sleepovers at his home, and given the child molestation claims of just a few years before, this statement caused a riot in the newspapers.

Of course, the claims of having children stay overnight was not only of interest to the media and public, but to the authorities too. After an investigation into the matter, Jackson was arrested in November 2003 and charged with a number of offences, including child molestation and giving alcohol to a minor. Jackson, of course, denied the charges and called his ex-wife Lisa Marie, and as she had never seen any wrongdoing during their marriage, she encouraged her former husband to stay strong.

The trial of Michael Jackson began on 31 January 2005 in Santa Maria, California. It was extremely long-winded – as one might expect – and seemed to involve interviews with almost everyone who had known Michael Jackson over the years. The child at the centre of the case was called to testify, along with his brother and interviewer Martin Bashir. Then Macaulay Culkin, the former child star of the *Home Alone* films spoke of his friendship with the star but denied being molested himself and described the allegations as "absolutely ridiculous".

Every day Jackson would appear at the courthouse with his family, looking weaker and weaker as time went on. He would shuffle into the building shielded by umbrellas, but in spite of the unconventional surroundings, would always find time to wave to his ever-present fans. Then one day photographs of the star were beamed around the world when he arrived at court straight from a stint in hospital, still wearing pyjama bottoms and a pair of slippers. It is fair to say that this incident did nothing for the man's image and many media outlets used the photographs to "prove" that he was losing his sanity and finally going off the rails.

The trial rumbled on until finally, on 13 June 2005, Jackson was acquitted on all counts, and fans outside the courtroom cheered, wept and freed white doves in his honour. The visibly broken singer then made the painful decision to move from his beloved Neverland ranch in California in a bid to regain his life. For many years he had created a life behind the gates of the mansion where he would never have to leave. If he wanted to see a movie, he had a theatre in his home; if he wanted to visit a zoo there was one of those in the grounds. A theme park? Yes, that was there too. So to leave Neverland behind was a genuinely painful experience for the singer, but after the trauma and expense of the court case, it was unfortunately one that was deemed absolutely necessary.

From that moment on, the Jackson family led something of a nomadic existence and travelled the world to various places including Ireland and the Persian Gulf. Finally, they arrived back in the United States and settled into a leased, rambling mansion at 100 North Carolwood Drive, Los Angeles, which – by coincidence or not – was just steps away from the former California home of Elvis Presley, Jackson's idol and father of his ex-wife Lisa Marie. There he hoped to live a quiet life with his family, but it was not to be.

Suffering from various health problems, including an addiction to prescription pills, the singer was short of money and needed to earn some fast. To that end he was persuaded to do a series of shows in London, which were designed to get his life and his finances back on track once again. Initially, Michael Jackson agreed to do just a handful of shows, but by early 2009 this had grown into a staggering fifty concerts, which were due to kick off in July of that year and continue until March 2010.

To announce the concerts, which were to be called the "This Is It" tour, a huge event took place at the O2 arena in London, which saw Michael Jackson himself take to the stage to speak to his fans. The crowd were kept waiting quite some time but when Jackson eventually walked on, none of that seemed to matter. Grown men and women were seen jumping up and down in the crowd, screaming and crying as the singer walked around the stage, wearing a black and silver shirt and dark glasses.

Finally, after giving the cheering crowd a peace sign, he stopped at the podium to speak, telling the audience that he planned to do a series of concerts at the O2 arena, and described the events as the "final curtain call". "I'll see you in July," he cried, before leaving the stage.

The fans were beside themselves with excitement but unfortunately, as it turned out, the press conference given that day was the real "final curtain call" and he never did make it to London or anywhere else in July. On 25 June 2009 the world heard the shocking news that Michael Jackson, the King of Pop, had passed away, and a new mystery was about to begin . . .

The evening before his death, Jackson was feeling poorly but managed to do a late-night rehearsal at the Staples Center in Los Angeles for the forthcoming O2 concerts. He finished after midnight and then headed home to bed where he was unable to sleep and asked his doctor, Conrad Murray, to administer a drug called Propofol, which is an anaesthetic used in hospitals while performing surgery. To an outsider this would seem to be an absurd thing to administer, but in the world of Michael Jackson it appeared that this was just a regular occurrence. Certainly on 25 June, when Jackson was unable to sleep, Propofol was apparently administered; the singer fell into a deep sleep and he never woke up again.

That afternoon Murray is said to have found Michael Jackson in bed, not breathing and unresponsive. The doctor panicked and tried to revive him without success, before finally calling for members of the singer's security team to come and help. Strangely, it would seem that in order to try and provoke breathing, the doctor was not performing CPR on the floor, which is standard practice, and instead was attempting the procedure on the soft bed, making it extremely difficult to administer. Michael Jackson's bedroom was in total uproar by this time, with personal belongings and all manner of paraphernalia all over the room.

Added to the chaos came the distressing realization that Jackson's young daughter Paris had appeared at the door and was in total sight of the distressing events that were unfolding all around her. She was quickly taken away by staff members, though the sights already seen by the child that day were likely to stay in her mind for a great many years to come. Once she had been taken away from the room, work continued on Jackson, but by the time paramedics arrived at the property, things were not looking good at all. While they hoped to find Michael Jackson responding to treatment, they instead found that the singer was not breathing at all. They took over from the doctor and continued efforts to revive him for a full forty-two minutes before taking him by ambulance to the Ronald Reagan UCLA Medical Center. There, Jackson was worked on for over an hour before finally being pronounced dead at 2.26 p.m.

The news of Michael Jackson being rushed to hospital spread around the world to such an extent that many search engines and social media outlets crashed under the pressure of the worldwide public trying to find out what was going on. At first it looked as though the star had suffered a heart attack but was still alive; eventually an official statement was released by the family which confirmed what people were dreading – the

King of Pop had died. However, until an autopsy was performed, it could not be determined exactly why or how it had happened.

While police were investigating the circumstances surrounding the death of the world's most famous pop singer, a memorial for Michael Jackson was held and included a mix of tributes, songs and stories from friends and colleagues. The emotional climax came when the family surprised everyone by taking to the stage themselves, along with the Jackson children minus the veils and masks they had always worn in the past. While Prince and Blanket stayed in the background, Paris, supported by Michael's brothers and sisters, expressed her love and gratitude for the man who had raised her. Through her tears and despair, she made it clear that Michael Jackson had been a close, loving and very real father to her.

The children then went to live with their grandmother, where as of March 2013 they still remain – living a somewhat less guarded life, going to school, and attending clubs and activities like other children their age. Still, even this move into "normal" life has encountered some difficulties that have piqued media interest, including the time in summer 2012 when their grandmother apparently briefly went missing from the family home. The children took to Twitter to ask where she had gone, but it was soon revealed that she had merely been taken to a spa by several members of the Jackson family who were concerned that she was becoming too stressed over the legalities of running the Michael Jackson estate and caring for his children.

Back in 2009 the investigation into the circumstances surrounding Michael Jackson's death continued with searches of his home and the offices of his doctor, Conrad Murray. Many rumours about Jackson's private life flooded the newspapers, mainly regarding his children, questioning their paternity and whether or not they would be returned to their natural mothers. Several men stepped up to claim that they – not Michael Jackson – were the biological father but in the end no proof was ever forthcoming.

More than two years later, on 27 September 2011, the trial of Conrad Murray for the involuntary manslaughter of the singer began in earnest. The trial brought up all kinds of startling information, including photographs of Jackson's dead body; pictures of his dishevelled bedroom full of medical equipment; and the revelation that the insomniac would often beg his doctor to administer drugs powerful enough to bring on sleep.

It was revealed that when other powerful sedatives did not work, the singer would often be given Propofol and it was this, in conjunction with the other drugs in his system, that had finally pushed Jackson's body over the edge, inducing his untimely death. The trial ran until November 2011 when the jury eventually found Murray guilty of involuntary manslaughter and he was sentenced to four years in prison.

In the end, away from the tales of drugs and the trials and tribulations over what went on during that fateful day in June 2009, Michael Jackson's death was shockingly tragic, a conclusion to a life that could hardly have been stranger. During his almost fifty-two years on earth, he dazzled audiences around the world with his songs, his dance and his energy, but finally he seemed to become a shadow of the person he had once been, apparently surrounded by a team of hangers-on and yes-men. Perhaps it can be said that if more people had dared to say no to him, then the singer might still be alive today.

But while Jackson may have gone, he has left behind not only a body of work unlike anything that anyone had ever seen and heard before, but also three children who seem determined to do their father proud and carry on his legacy. The eldest, Prince Michael, has started work as a correspondent for *Entertainment Tonight*, while Paris has seemingly always wanted to follow in her father's footsteps as a performer. In a family video shot when she was very young, she was asked what she would like to be when she grew up. "Just like you, Daddy" was her reply. Now a teenager, she has already appeared in one movie and has plans to make many more in the years to come.

Finally, while they may no longer have their father around them, it is abundantly clear that in shielding the children from the paparazzi and giving them the early childhood that he himself never received, Jackson has enabled his daughter and sons to develop their own personas and be comfortable in their own skin. If only he had been given the same privilege – surely everything would have been very different for Michael Jackson, the King of Pop.

56

The Marriage Break-up of Kelsey and Camille Grammer

In October 2010, the successful *Real Housewives* television franchise was expanded with the release of *The Real Housewives of Beverly Hills*. The show catapulted six women to worldwide fame, and while only two of them were actually successful actresses, it did not matter, as the scandal provided by the women was more than enough to fill the pages of any Hollywood gossip magazine.

The reality show focused on the trials and tribulations of Taylor Armstrong, Adrienne Maloof, Camille Grammer, Kim Richards, Kyle Richards and Lisa Vanderpump. The six women all experienced their fair share of drama throughout the series, with numerous arguments, altercations and tragedies in their private lives.

The entire cast had many dramatic, real-life scenes, with one of the most memorable stories involving Taylor Armstrong, who was seen in a physically abusive marriage with her husband Russell before he shockingly committed suicide (thankfully off screen) during the making of series two. Former child star Kim Richards was seen fighting a battle with alcohol and becoming involved with a man deemed unsuitable by her friends and family, while Adrienne Maloof went into series three by going through a divorce from her plastic surgeon husband, Paul. Lisa Vanderpump moved out of her home, only to see it burn in an almighty blaze several months later, while Kyle Richards was often seen in tears, worried about the behaviour of her older sister Kim.

But while the series was full of dramas from beginning to end, perhaps the most talked about was the on-screen breakdown of Camille Grammer's marriage.

Camille was probably the most well-known of all the women when the programme began – not in her own right perhaps, but as the wife of television heavyweight Kelsey Grammer. Kelsey had been the star of *Cheers* and *Frasier* for two decades, and the two had married amid much fanfare in 1997. They went on to have two children and were frequently seen together at premieres and parties. They even worked together when Camille appeared in an episode of *Frasier*, dressed as Lady Godiva. During the show, the two are seen at a fancy dress party where Frasier tries desperately to flirt with her, while all the time trying to avoid the mix-ups and double entendres happening all around him.

Unfortunately, away from the fun of filming *Frasier*, the marriage also had its bleak spots, including a disastrous holiday to Hawaii, where Grammer suffered a heart attack while paddle-boating with Camille. Thankfully the episode was a mild one, though Camille is said to have supported him through this anxious time. To all intents and purposes, they seemed happily committed to each other.

Sadly, it would seem that while the couple seemed content enough, it was all an illusion, and this soon became apparent while making *The Real Housewives of Beverly Hills*. While he was still in the marriage, it may be true to say that emotionally Kelsey had already left, and he later claimed that he had encouraged his wife to be part of the reality show as his "parting gift" to her. He also later sarcastically told chat show host Oprah Winfrey that he had presented the "gift" because Camille had "given up so much to endure this life with me".

For the first few episodes of *The Real Housewives*, Camille happily talked about Kelsey while planning a trip with the other women to see him in the Broadway show, *La Cage aux Folles*. However, by the time they all hit New York, it had become very apparent that something was not right within the marriage, and after seeing the show, there then followed an awkward scene where Camille visited her husband backstage.

Looking as though he does not want her to be there, Kelsey could be seen greeting his wife as though she were merely a fan, the tension apparent for all to see. Kissing her briskly on the cheek, he says, "Thanks for coming", before she giggles nervously and is brushed out of the changing room on the pretext that he wants to freshen up after the show.

Camille later admitted that shortly before the trip, Kelsey had shocked her by telephoning to say he was finished with the marriage. She was upset but then surprised when Kelsey seemed to backtrack by requesting her presence in New York in order to attend the Tony Awards with him. Camille later said that her husband had suggested it could possibly be something of a romantic trip, though given his recent disclosure of being "finished" with the marriage, this could be seen as a rather odd statement.

For her part, Camille said that she did not want the marriage to end and asked that they both attend marriage counselling together, though this ultimately fell on deaf ears. Kelsey did not want to work on the marriage at all – he merely wanted out – but for the sake of their children Camille was not going to make it easy for him to go.

Believing that he was suffering a midlife crisis, she had gone along with the plan to fly to New York with the other ladies from *The Real Housewives* series, and continued the charade of pretending to be happily married. However, when the cameras rolled, it was obvious that Kelsey was most uncomfortable in his wife's presence in his new domain. First, there was that backstage awkwardness at the show, and then there was a particularly revealing scene in Camille's hotel room, where she made it clear that she would not be prepared to just fade into the background. Wearing a stunning red gown, Camille was seen kissing her husband and wishing him good luck for the awards. "I love you," she said, to which he replied, "Thank you."

Of course, television programmes can be cleverly edited and can obscure the full truth. However, in one particularly uncomfortable scene the programme shows the couple surrounded by people, raising a glass to Kelsey's success. Camille makes a toast to "love" and to their thirteen years of marriage, before her husband responds in kind but with an obvious hesitation in his voice. She gives him a knowing smile and raises her eyebrows, and then declares "Cheers" before walking away, leaving Kelsey to follow her with a look that says everything about how he was feeling at that precise moment in time.

Once they arrived at the Tony Awards ceremony that evening, the couple were photographed incessantly by waiting paparazzi, and while at first glance they looked perfectly happy together, their body language said something quite different. It was at this point that Camille later said she knew in her heart that the marriage was clearly over, and it was not long afterwards that she made the discovery that her husband of thirteen years was involved with another woman.

According to Kelsey, he first met British flight attendant Kayte Walsh – who is twenty-five years his junior – while on a flight to London in 2009, and the two met up in the city for a two-hour date shortly afterwards. In September 2012, Kelsey told talk-show host Conan O'Brien that the relationship had begun very innocently and the two shared a kiss but nothing else for several months.

During the interview, Conan stated how difficult that must have been, not to take things further, to which the *Frasier* star claimed that after a decade of not having sex, it was not a hard thing to have to wait. Since he had been married to Camille for thirteen years, this was obviously a thinly disguised dig at his ex-wife, though the comment was quickly denied by his ex, who tweeted "this is simply not true!" to her many followers.

At the end of the day, the sex life of Kelsey and Camille is most certainly no one's business but their own. What is important to note, however, is that while he claimed to resist sleeping with Kayte Walsh for some months after their first meeting, the actor had most certainly begun a relationship – and quite openly admitted kissing her – while he was still married to Camille.

After he and Kayte had gone on several dates together, they began conducting their affair in secret, while Kelsey was living alone in New York and appearing in his show on Broadway. If they met in late 2009, as Kelsey says, then the romance was most certainly already going on during the Tony Awards ceremony that Kelsey and Camille attended together, and throughout the first part of *The Real Housewives of Beverly Hills*.

Finally, however, despite trying to keep the whole thing secret, Camille apparently received word from a friend that Kelsey was behaving in a manner she found distasteful. This news came as a severe blow for Camille, who deep down still wondered if the marriage could be saved by counselling and communication. However, after an admission from her estranged husband shortly afterwards, she was forced to reassess the break-up, and in the end had no option but to agree that the marriage was well and truly over.

Shortly after the discovery of infidelity, the news broke publicly that the Grammers had split, and Camille announced on 1 July 2010 that she had filed for divorce, citing irreconcilable differences as the reason.

While the separation had come as a surprise to fans, this was nothing compared to the disclosure of Kelsey's relationship with Kayte Walsh and the announcement on 12 August 2010 that she was pregnant with his child. Congratulations began to pour in, though sadly in October the news came that Kayte had actually miscarried shortly after the news had first broken in August.

The breakdown of the marriage had a huge effect on Camille Grammer and this was clear for everyone to see during the latter part of the first series of *The Real Housewives*. Many arguments erupted, particularly between her and co-star former child-actress Kyle Richards, which did not present Camille in the best light, and at times her behaviour could be construed as rather bitchy, hard and sarcastic. This was something which was later seen to be untrue of her real self in the second series, where she was shown as a fairly calm and well-mannered individual, but the bad press was good news for Kelsey Grammer's camp as it placed him in a very good light indeed.

After watching each episode of the first series, many people took to Twitter and Facebook where they openly discussed the relationship and perhaps unfairly surmised that it was little wonder he had left such a mean-tempered woman as the one being portrayed. Since the first news of the split, some people had already begun bombarding Kelsey's Twitter page with negative comments about his estranged wife. In a surprising mark of respect, the actor issued several tweets of his own, asking fans to remember that while they might be separated, Camille was still the mother of his children and did not deserve to be spoken about in that way. Meanwhile, it seemed that Kelsey could do no wrong, and he was frequently seen out with Kayte during the autumn of 2010. Then on 25 February 2011, they were married during a ceremony in New York, where friends of the couple – including *Frasier* co-star David Hyde Pierce – came together to wish them both the best.

Since the messy divorce, both Kelsey and Camille have gone on various talk shows, discussing the marriage and what led to the break-up. Kelsey has spoken to the likes of Oprah Winfrey and Conan O'Brien, and his interviews involve a great deal of praise for his new wife, but he now seems to offer nothing but angst towards his former partner. In fact, such is his distaste that it is claimed the two only ever speak through lawyers and third parties.

A great deal of fighting has also taken place between the two regarding custody of their two children – son Jude and daughter Mason – with rumours abounding that while he was anxious to have his son come live with him in New York, Kelsey would allow his daughter to remain in Los Angeles. However, the intricate details of the custody issues have not been revealed (and are unlikely to be) so it is impossible to say what is true and what is merely unsubstantiated fodder for the tabloids.

On 13 July 2012, Kayte Walsh Grammer gave birth to a baby daughter, Faith, though the arrival was tinged with sadness when it was announced that Faith's twin brother had died prior to the birth. While the couple are obviously still mourning the loss of one baby, it is clear to see that the two are happily devoted parents to their daughter, with the *Frasier* star apparently even changing his fair share of nappies along the way. His career has also continued in a positive way: he won a Golden Globe award for his portrayal of Tom Kane, the Mayor of Chicago, in political TV drama *Boss*. The show was cancelled in November 2012, which came as a blow to the actor, but a film is now being discussed, which will see him reprise the role of Kane and finish off the storylines portrayed in the show.

Kelsey Grammer seems to be finding peace in his personal life, though his relationship with his ex-wife clearly still bothers him. During the interview with Oprah he would not refer to Camille by name, and then in September 2012 he caused a storm by refusing to be interviewed by Piers Morgan. Both interviewer and star met backstage and all appeared to be friendly, though it did not last when, in the moments before the interview was due to begin, Grammer saw a photograph of his ex-wife which he thought was about to be broadcast. The picture seemed to unnerve him and apparently without stopping for an explanation, the actor stormed from the building, leaving a shocked Piers Morgan without a guest.

The interviewer later called the episode "strange" and "unprofessional", adding that he had no intention of actually asking him about his ex-wife. However, Grammer's representatives did not believe the statement and released one of their own to website TMZ, declaring that Piers Morgan needed to take responsibility for his actions. "It's called accountability," they said.

More controversy came during Halloween 2012 when Grammer and Kayte were spotted at a party at the Playboy mansion. The actor was dressed as Dracula in a black cloak and T-shirt, while his wife was outfitted slightly more provocatively in a black lace dress, long blonde wig and a plaster on her nose. Was this a direct dig at Camille and the rumours that she had undergone plastic surgery? Some newspapers and public seemed to think it was, and so it seemed did several of Camille's *Beverly Hills* co-stars.

When one comment was made on Twitter about the possibility of Kayte dressing up as the former Mrs Grammer, Camille retweeted it, showing exactly what she thought about the situation. The whole episode got so out of hand, in fact, that the actor himself released a statement, denying any wrongdoing and claiming that Kayte had actually gone to the party dressed as a witch, but it had been so hot that she had needed to take her hat off. There weren't many people who believed this story, though Camille herself seemed determined to remain publicly tight-lipped.

Halloween costumes aside, since the break-up of the marriage Camille's reputation seems to have been fully mended and her personal life is most certainly on the up. During the making of the second series of *The Real Housewives of Beverly Hills*, she began a relationship with Dimitri Charalambopoulos, a young, toned, Greek gentleman who seems to be the complete opposite of her ex-husband. Professionally she has continued her adventure into reality television with guest appearances in the third series of *Real Housewives*, and is building up a huge following on Twitter. If Kelsey Grammer did indeed put her forward for the show as his parting gift, perhaps it wasn't such a bad thing after all; at the moment, her star certainly seems to be on the rise.

57

Arnold Schwarzenegger's Love Child

Perhaps one of the most ambitious and driven men who ever walked the earth, by 2011 Arnold Schwarzenegger had been a highly successful bodybuilder, action hero, governor of California and husband to Kennedy daughter Maria Shriver. Together they had four children and a beautiful California home, until one day it all came tumbling down when it was discovered that Arnie had not only been unfaithful, but had also fathered a child with his former housekeeper.

Born 30 July 1947 in Thal, Austria, Arnold was the son of Gustav Schwarzenegger, a local police chief, and his wife Aurelia. Together they were extremely strict parents who raised their son with a stern hand and a deep interest in religion. With a passion for school sports, Arnold enjoyed football but by the time he entered his teens he had discovered bodybuilding. The training was extremely exciting for the young man and this love of toning his body would ultimately lead Schwarzenegger from Austria to the bright lights of Hollywood.

After serving for a year in the Austrian Army (during which time he won the Junior Mr Europe contest), he went on to win several Mr Universe titles, which propelled him into fame. He used this opportunity to further his career by moving permanently to the United States, where he told friends he was going to become a huge movie star. He wasn't wrong.

Schwarzenegger continued with his bodybuilding and won the Mr Olympia title a staggering seven times. However, his adventures into film-making were slow, with his accent, body shape and long name becoming a major hurdle to success. One such example of this was when he was chosen to act in the movie *Hercules in New York* (1970): his name was changed to Arnold Strong and his lines were later dubbed after it was decided his accent was just too thick. This did not bode well for a successful movie and in the end it turned out to be a disaster, notorious with fans only because of its unintentional humour.

However, things picked up when Arnold won a Golden Globe award for New Male Star of the Year after his part in *Stay Hungry* (1976), and his star continued to climb throughout the 1980s with films such as *Conan the Barbarian* (1982), *Conan the Destroyer* (1984) and the hugely successful *The Terminator* in 1984. The late 1980s and early 1990s even introduced the actor to comedy, and he scored hits with both *Twins* (1988) and *Kindergarten Cop* (1990).

The coming years were just as successful, with *True Lies* (1994), *Terminator 2: Judgment Day* (1991) and *Junior* (1994) all proving to be huge hits at the box office. However, by the time the turn of the century rolled round, Arnie was seemingly growing tired of acting and was ready to try his hand at another of his passions – politics.

Schwarzenegger had always been interested in government business, and in 1977 had begun a relationship with Maria Shriver, a television reporter and niece of John F. Kennedy. Although she was a Democrat and he was a Republican, the two hit it off and in 1986 they married and went on to have four children together: Katherine, Christina, Patrick and Christopher. By the early 2000s, it was rumoured that the actor had plans to one day run for governor of California, though he denied this at the time, citing his successful career as an actor as the reason why he would not run.

However, by 2003 he had made up his mind and after announcing his intentions on *The Tonight Show with Jay Leno*, Schwarzenegger was well and truly in the race to become the next California governor, and by November his dreams came true when the public voted him in and he finally took office. It all moved extremely fast, but that wasn't the only thing that was fast if rumours are to be believed.

Going into politics has always been a ticket for people to go delving into past affairs, and "The Governator" was not immune to this. By his own admission, Schwarzenegger is no angel and in 1977 he jokingly boasted about smoking marijuana and attending orgies as a young man. It perhaps didn't come as much of a surprise, then, when during his campaign women began coming forward to complain that the actor-turned-politician was allegedly guilty of inappropriate behaviour. According to them, he had groped their breasts, put his hand up a woman's skirt and asked one lady to flash him in an elevator. The stories were potentially damaging, but in good faith Arnold responded to the allegations by apologizing and admitting that while he had behaved badly at times in the past, a lot of the stories were simply untrue.

However, while he was able to brush aside these particular rumours of sexual misconduct, he would not be so lucky in 2011 when his wife, Maria, began to suspect that Arnold had fathered a child – Joseph – by their housekeeper, Mildred "Patty" Baena. This wasn't a recent event; instead, it was something that had happened fourteen years before, at the same time as Maria was pregnant with their child, Christopher. In fact, so close were the conceptions that the two boys were actually born just days apart, towards the end of 1997.

According to Mildred, she was unaware that the father of her son was definitely Arnold until she started to notice a resemblance between the two. She later told *Hello* magazine that if Arnold noticed the similarity too, he most certainly did not mention it to her in the early days of the child's life. It would seem that while Arnold tried to believe that the child was not his, it did play on his mind that there was a distinct possibility he could be his son. In spite of any suspicions he may privately have had, the actor still attended Joseph's baptism with Maria in tow. He later spent time teaching him to play golf while he was playing with the Schwarzenegger children in their home.

By the time Joseph hit school age, the actor had come to accept the fact that the child was his – there was just too much of a resemblance to deny it – and Arnold went about paying not only towards Joseph's upbringing, but for that of the housekeeper's other children too. The child himself was not told who his real father was until some time around 2010 – a year before the episode was finally revealed publicly – and until then had always believed his mother's estranged husband Rogelio was his real father.

At first, Maria knew nothing about either the affair her husband had enjoyed with Mildred or the possibility that she had given birth to his child. This was demonstrated by her taking part in such events as the baptism and various other social gatherings. However, as he got older and began to resemble the action-hero-turned-politician, rumours started to go around the staff that Arnold must surely have fathered the child. Maria heard these whispers and her suspicions were raised enough for her to become very concerned indeed, asking her husband if he had fathered the child and then half-heartedly accepting his answer that he had not.

Arnold must surely have hoped his denial would put paid to any concerns his wife had, but of course this couldn't be further from the truth. Rumours still continued to swirl around the household and what went through Maria's mind as she saw the likeness herself can only be guessed at. It would be true to say, however, that it must have surely thrown her world into free-fall. Not wishing to cause a huge scandal and perhaps not wanting to hear the awful truth herself, Maria had no wish to ask the housekeeper about the truth of the rumours so instead started to drop small hints. When these did not elicit discussion, she eventually she got up enough nerve to ask Mildred directly, "Is my husband the father of your son?"

Unfortunately for Maria, she was met by the answer she most dreaded: yes indeed, Arnold Schwarzenegger was the father of Joseph Baena. According to Mildred, in an interview with *Hello* magazine, she then fell to her knees and cried while admitting the truth. She also claimed that Maria cried also, before they hugged and discussed how it wasn't entirely Schwarzenegger's fault; that it took two to get into the mess they were in.

On hearing the admission by Mildred Baena, Maria could have been forgiven for firing her immediately, but she did no such thing. Instead it was actually Mildred who suggested she leave early, knowing that she was due to retire very shortly anyway. However, showing a great deal of self-restraint and compassion, Maria told the shocked woman that she should stay in the household until Christmas was over and the time came for her to retire.

So now the secret was out between Maria and Mildred, and in his 2012 autobiography, *Total Recall: My Unbelievably True Life Story*, Arnold Schwarzenegger described how he too eventually had to come clean while attending marriage counselling with Maria. The session was scheduled for the day after he had left office in January 2011, and the former governor was led to believe that the purpose of the session was to help him make the transition from that of political dynamo back to "normal" family life. However, moments after he had sat down, the counsellor revealed the sole real reason for the meeting – to address the issue of whether or not he had fathered a child with the housekeeper way back in 1997.

Schwarzenegger had no option but to admit to what his wife had known for some time, and ended up telling her everything, even going so far as to list a number of reasons why he had not ever wanted to come clean about his indiscretion. Once the truth was confirmed by Schwarzenegger, Maria moved out of the family home and into another property nearby, so that the children could easily have access to both parents. They kept the scandal quiet for four months until finally the newspapers got wind of the story in May 2011, and the actor was forced to admit to the world and his children that he had fathered a child outside of marriage.

The press went wild at the revelations and eagerly tried to snap a picture of Joseph Baena. Despite the boy being forced into hiding, the photographers were successful and it was revealed that the child most certainly had a clear similarity to Arnold. This news understandably did not please Rogelio, the man who had believed himself to be Joseph's father for all those years. Rumours swirled round that he would be taking legal action against both his ex-wife and the former governor for falsifying the birth certificate, while it was hinted that Maria was doing her own investigations to see if Joseph was indeed the only child fathered by her husband.

An active member of Twitter, the former news anchor took to the social networking site to release her statement on 13 May 2011. In it Maria thanked everyone for their kindness, support and compassion. "I am humbled by the love. Thank you." She also released a brief statement, declaring, "As a mother, my concern is for the children", before then asking for "compassion, respect and privacy" as both herself and her children set about healing and rebuilding their lives.

Arnold gave his own short statement about why the marriage had ended, but decided to keep quiet about the full story until a year and a half later, during the publicity for his autobiography. In an interview with *60 Minutes* he was asked about the affair and revealed that he believed it to be the stupidest thing he had done during his relationship with Maria. "It was terrible," he said. "I inflicted tremendous pain on Maria and unbelievable pain on the kids." He answered the questions candidly and without embarrassment, and to his credit the actor refused point blank to answer anything directly related to his children – either the ones fathered with Maria or the son by Mildred Baena.

Although obviously estranged, the couple were forced to come back together briefly when their youngest son Christopher was involved in a surfing accident in July 2011.

The poorly youngster suffered a collapsed lung and broken bones, which saw him being admitted to intensive care, much to the horror of his parents. Putting their differences aside for a moment, the ex-couple released a statement which described the episode as scary, though they did say that he was expected to make a full recovery. But if Arnold hoped that this time together would change his wife's mind about the separation, he was wrong. While he did make it clear that he would happily rejoin the marriage, Maria had other ideas and finally filed for divorce in July 2012, though the two continue to co-parent their children.

While it is clear that Maria may have been more than sympathetic to her husband's rumoured indiscretions in the past, she seems determined to move on with her future and rebuild her life. It has also been said that she told friends she was not in the least bit happy about her former husband's autobiography being released, with her concerns made more acute by the fact that Arnold refused to send her an advance copy.

In fairness to Schwarzenegger, while he no doubt knew that the book would cause pain for his family, he had been placed in a difficult situation, primarily because he had been writing it for a very long time with the intention that it would be predominantly about his career achievements. Having his private life forced into the limelight in such a way changed all that, and he knew that the people buying the volume would be doing so not only to read about his career, but to get the dirt on his private life too. In September 2012 he told *60 Minutes* that he just could not write an autobiography that centred on his triumphs – he had to share the negative parts too.

Still, in spite of any concerns that the former couple may or may not have had, the book was published in October 2012 and went on to become a huge bestseller. Several months later, in January 2013, the actor made headlines once again when he was asked by a reporter about his family life. "I have four wonderful children," he said, and then quickly changed his mind. "Well, actually I have five."

It is clear that with a bestselling book under his belt and several important movies due for release, Schwarzenegger's acting career is back on track. It would also be fair to say, however, that with a divorce going through the courts and an illegitimate child now revealed, at the present moment his personal life can be described as nothing short of complicated.

58

The Very Public Meltdown of Charlie Sheen

Charlie Sheen is renowned for the various scandals in which he has been involved during his life and career, including being associated with the Heidi Fleiss vice case; rumoured domestic violence; very public divorces from Denise Richards and Brooke Mueller; and alleged drug addiction. However, his name really became synonymous with scandal during a very highly publicized few months in the early part of 2011.

At the time, Sheen was the star of *Two and a Half Men*, which by then was into its eighth season. Sheen was earning a record a $1.8 million an episode for his role as Charlie Harper, the loveable, jingle-writing bad boy, but in January 2011 shooting of the programme was suspended while Charlie Sheen went into rehab. The programme makers were happy to wait for their star to get back to good health, but unfortunately for all involved, while Sheen was on hiatus he began making derogatory comments about Chuck Lorre, the series' creator. The press went wild that the actor was biting the hand that feeds, and as the scandal built up and up, the studio took the massive decision of firing Sheen and banning him from the Warner Brothers lot, effective immediately. The actor retaliated by filing a wrongful termination lawsuit against his employers, though this was eventually settled on 26 September.

Although the firing of Charlie Sheen caused headlines, as it turned out it wasn't the biggest scandal. That came in the form of a very public meltdown during the months leading up to and after the firing, which was then seen live on the internet and on television by fans, foes and onlookers alike. Sheen's remarks in public were outrageous and at times incomprehensible; interviewers swarmed to his home in order to speak to him, hopeful that his comments would be shocking enough to gain column inches around the world. They weren't disappointed. To one interviewer he claimed that he was tired of pretending he wasn't special: "I'm tired of pretending I'm not a total bitchin' rock star from Mars." He also made comments about being a warlock and tiger blood dripping from his veins, and – in an outburst that earned him the most notoriety – made the repeated declaration that, despite losing his job, he was "winning!"

Sheen's whole life seemed to play out in front of the cameras – either controlled by news teams or himself. He opened a YouTube channel where he posted films of himself in conversation with his girlfriends, the "goddesses" Rachel Oberlin and Natalie Kenly. Despite his claims of being clean and healthy, he appeared gaunt and underweight, and many worried that his life was spiralling out of control. He most certainly did not appear to be "winning" though he continued to use the slogan so much that it soon appeared on T-shirts and bumper stickers around the world.

Sheen seemed to delight in uploading every aspect of his life on to the internet, from telephone calls to fake cooking shows, to even a disturbing video of his twin sons being removed from the family home by the authorities late one night. He also posted messages to his ex-colleagues on *Two and a Half Men* and took part in his own YouTube radio show, *Sheen's Korner*, where he was surrounded by staff and friends, all cheering themselves on with chants of how "winning" they were, though few viewers actually agreed. The show was at times incomprehensible, extremely hard to watch and did not last long, though old episodes are still available on Sheen's YouTube channel even now.

Then came Twitter, where Sheen broke records for gaining the most followers in the shortest time, and this continued to grow until numbers had reached the very impressive total of 7.7 million in 2012. So addicted to Twitter was he, apparently, that his girlfriend later complained that he even tweeted while making love – although what he chose to share remains a mystery.

Charlie's rants on both Twitter and YouTube were quick to draw onlookers, anxious to see what infamous quip he would come out with next. He even began a Facebook page and shared news and his "'winning" strategy with his 3.1 million "friends". Through the social network he was inundated with support from fans, though in truth he also suffered with his share of internet "trolls" too. His reaction? "They all suffer from Sheenis Envy."

The climax of his months of meltdown came in March 2011 when Charlie Sheen announced that he was embarking on a nationwide tour. Entitled "My Violent Torpedo of Truth/ Defeat Is Not an Option", it kicked off on 2 April in Detroit. Unfortunately for Sheen, however, the trolls did not stay behind their computers and came out in droves, eager to pour scorn over the highly publicized appearance. As he sat slumped in a chair on stage, Sheen was heckled and booed by members of the crowd. "Maybe it's more appropriate to sit up here and tell stories about crack," he reportedly told the audience, though very few knew how to take the remark. Footage reveals the content of the show to be shaky at best, and uncomfortable at worst, though after some adjustments, it did have a better reception during later dates on the tour.

Unfortunately for Sheen, the media spotlight and disappointing tour reviews did nothing for his relationship with the "goddesses" and by June 2011 they had both flown from his life, with reporters in hot pursuit, ready to hear their stories of life at Sheen's home, christened, rather ironically, "Sober Valley Lodge". But while his love life was on the rocks, by September 2011 Sheen seemed to have calmed down somewhat and, for the most part, his unconventional life was at last being played out behind closed doors.

It was also rumoured that the actor had been asked back to *Two and a Half Men*, but it was not to be and he eventually made peace with the fact that his career on the show was over. Ashton Kutcher was hired to replace him and the rumour mill went into overdrive, predicting (quite rightly as it turned out) that the character of Charlie Harper would be killed off. People wondered what Sheen would think of this new development, and finally his feelings on the matter were made loud and clear when presenting an award at the Primetime Emmy Awards. During his appearance, he made a heartfelt speech to everyone involved in the show.

"From the bottom of my heart," he said. "I wish you nothing but the best for this upcoming season." He then went on to say how they had all spent "eight wonderful years together and I know you will continue to make great television".

Meanwhile, season nine of *Two and a Half Men* premiered in September 2011 with Kutcher playing the character of Walden Schmidt, a heartbroken billionaire. Walden buys the late Charlie Harper's beach house and finds himself soon sharing it with two companions – Charlie's brother Alan and his son Jake.

The format was successful and attracted a whole new audience, but unfortunately for the programme makers, Ashton Kutcher's reputation hit the skids somewhat when it was alleged he had been cheating on his wife, Demi Moore. However, the show weathered the storm and on 12 May 2012 it was renewed for a tenth season, shortly before one of its other stars – Angus T. Jones, who plays teenager Jake – made the headlines himself.

The story was that Jones, who was earning $300,000 an episode at the age of just eighteen, had recently found God and no longer wanted to play the role of Jake. Not only that but he then decided to launch a scathing attack in a video rant, calling the programme "filth" and urging fans not to watch it. He described how he no longer wanted to be involved in the series; lectured about the effects of television on a person's brain; and declared the medium "bad news". The video was then posted online for the entire world – including CBS executives – to see.

They refused to comment about the video, though after the debacle of the Sheen scandal, it was clear to everyone that they would not be in the least bit pleased. An apology quickly came from the Jones camp in which he said sorry for any remarks that "reflect me showing indifference to and disrespect of my colleagues". Charlie Sheen was quick to jump to his former co-star's defence, however, and told newspapers that he could completely understand what the young actor was going through and said he was fairly certain the show was cursed. He then reached out to Angus and offered him a role in his new show, *Anger Management*, though whether or not the young actor will ever accept the offer is unknown.

In the meantime it remains to be seen if *Two and a Half Men* can struggle on much longer, given the scandals and negative comments that have been associated with its stars over the past few years. But for Sheen his life and career continues, living fairly quietly and starring in *Anger Management*, a comedy where he plays – of all things – an unconventional therapist specializing in controlling anger. The show attracted a record 5.74 million views for its debut episode, though reviews were mixed and it is not yet known if it will match the success of *Two and a Half Men*.

Still, there is no denying that the show proved to be a new beginning for Sheen, and it looked like he had set about moving up and away from the memories of his very public meltdown. This included deleting his highly successful Twitter account on 13 July 2012 with a photograph showing a bottle of Tabasco sauce on the dashboard of a plane. It was accompanied with a heartfelt but mystifying message which read: "Reach for the stars everyone. Dogspeed cadre. C out."

The reason Sheen gave for deleting the account was that he was not getting "anything out of the social network". However, fans need not have worried, as just a month later he was back, promoting his *Anger Management* show; welcoming back his 7.7 million followers; urging them to follow him on Facebook; and giving away signed scripts and other items. A week after rejoining Twitter, he posted a tweet thanking everyone for their support and ending with the catchphrase which is set to be with him forever: "Winning!" Let's hope for his sake that this time he really is.

59

The Relationship of Demi Moore and Ashton Kutcher

When Demi Moore married Ashton Kutcher in 2005, it created quite a stir. The bride was fifteen years older than her groom, but while they seemed to laugh in the face of their critics by making their marriage a good one, it ultimately ended in scandal, disgrace and very nearly tragedy.

Demi Moore is no stranger to controversy. In 1986 the actress starred in *About Last Night* with actor Rob Lowe, which not only showed her nude, but included an abundance of graphic sex scenes, the likes of which had very rarely been seen in a mainstream Hollywood film. Her love for pushing the envelope when it came to films continued in 1993 when she co-starred in *Indecent Proposal* with Woody Harrelson, playing a woman who sleeps with a playboy (Robert Redford) for the sum of $1 million.

Both films raised eyebrows, but in 1991, two years before *Indecent Proposal*, it was her personal life that was causing sharp intakes of breath. Completely at ease with her body and while seven months pregnant with her daughter, Scout LaRue, Demi took to the cover of *Vanity Fair*, completely naked with a hand placed strategically over her breasts. The cover caused scandal the world over and all hell broke loose with discussions over whether or not it was appropriate to see a pregnant woman in such a revealing pose.

The photo session succeeded in breaking down barriers in terms of how pregnant women's bodies are perceived, and indeed various celebrities have shown off their nude bumps since then. But in 1991 it had never been done before and has gone down in history as being the most talked-about *Vanity Fair* cover ever created.

Other "body-related" scandals erupted when Demi stripped on an episode of the *Late Show with David Letterman* and starred in a controversial movie entitled *Striptease* (1996), but while all this was fodder for the tabloids, her relationship with the much younger actor Ashton Kutcher provided much more than that. While Demi's films were sometimes physically revealing, she had a good reputation as an actress in movies such as *Ghost* (1990), *A Few Good Men* (1992) and *The Juror* (1996). However, Kutcher was the madcap star of *Dude, Where's My Car* (2000) and TV show *Punk'd*, so when they began dating in 2003, it did not seem as though the pair would have anything much in common.

Critics determined that the relationship wouldn't last, and when they married on 24 September 2005, many journalists made reference to the age gap and predicted the end would be soon in coming. However, as the marriage went on, it looked as though the couple were going to prove their critics wrong, and it wasn't long before the age gap made no difference to anyone but reporters.

Moreover, the couple also seemed to have a great deal in common: Demi was a follower of the Kabbalah faith and Kutcher joined too; they both had an active interest in raising awareness of child sexual slavery; and always looked extremely comfortable with each other while out and about in public. They even showed how diplomatic they could be towards Demi's ex-husband, Bruce Willis, when they were all photographed together – with children – on the red carpet and holidayed frequently as one big happy family.

However, it was on Twitter that the couple received the greatest attention, and in 2009 Kutcher became the first person to reach a million followers. The two seemed to enjoy reporting every detail of their personal lives online; chatted to each other on the site despite frequently being in the same room, and posted many pictures. One of those photos – of Demi bending over in her underwear – was flashed around the world at an incredible rate in 2009. Kutcher accompanied the picture with a caption, "Shhh don't tell wifey", while she responded by tweeting, "He is such a sneak" and told followers that the picture was snapped while she was steaming his suit.

It all seemed jovial enough, but it was also on Twitter that one of the first tremors was detected in the marriage. It apparently all happened one weekend when the couple were out together and a young woman took it upon herself to slip Kutcher her phone number. It would seem that Ashton showed the note to Demi, who was incensed and immediately took to Twitter, berating the girl and then posting her number online for all to see. Unfortunately for Demi, many of her followers started to ring the number and then report the outcome on the social networking site. Many more decided to bombard the actress with messages, telling her how irresponsible she had been to post the woman's number in the first place. Demi must have thought twice about her knee-jerk reaction: the tweet was taken down within minutes and never reported in the press.

The couple continued their relationship until autumn 2011, when Kutcher landed the plum role of Walden Schmidt in the sitcom *Two and a Half Men*. The star enjoyed the infamy that came with involvement in the production, but unfortunately for him, it was for all the wrong reasons that he started to make headlines, shortly after shooting began. It was alleged that on the day before the couple's sixth wedding anniversary, instead of spending time with his wife, Ashton was partying in Las Vegas with a bevy of young women. Pictures soon emerged of the actor at the Hard Rock Hotel surrounded by the ladies in question; then Sara Leal, the woman at the centre of it all, came forward to tell her story of the "fling" she had enjoyed with the actor.

Things were made no better when rumours surfaced that Kutcher and Moore shared an "open" marriage and that he had previously been involved with a woman called Brittney Jones. This was denied by the couple, but it seemed that by this time the damage was already done.

Demi was heartbroken that her marriage was falling apart, but still the couple battled on, attending Kabbalah meetings and then deciding to go on a camping trip to Cachuma Lake near Santa Barbara. They were not alone, however, as they were accompanied not only by their Kabbalah teachers, but also members of the paparazzi who hid in bushes to take photos of the couple together.

The resulting pictures did little to assure the public that all was well, failing to show any intimacy between Demi and Ashton at all. In fact, the couple hardly seemed to know each other existed, and Demi – who had always been slim – was depicted stirring food over a camp fire looking extremely gaunt. Kutcher, meanwhile was photographed standing near to his wife, unshaven and visibly unhappy.

It came as no real surprise then, when Demi released a statement in November, announcing the end of the marriage. In it she said: "It is with great sadness and a heavy heart that I have decided to end my six-year marriage to Ashton." She then went on to describe how as a woman, a mother and a wife there were particular things that she had held sacred, such as values and vows. "It is in this spirit that I have chosen to move forward with my life," she said. The actress then begged the public and press for privacy and compassion, stating that it was a terribly trying time for both herself and her family, and that she would like to be given the same amount of privacy that anyone else would be afforded in that same situation.

Ashton meanwhile released his own statement through his favourite networking site, Twitter, which said that he would forever cherish his time with Demi. "Marriage is one of the most difficult things in the world," he said, before going on to say that, unfortunately, sometimes relationships fail.

After the announcement, Kutcher appeared to move on easily with his life – filming *Two and a Half Men* and being seen out with several different women. But Demi's life seemed to stall. She was reluctant to change her Twitter name – @ MrsKutcher – and chastised fans who asked her why. It would take over five months before she was finally ready to change. Asking fans to send in ideas, Demi finally chose @JustDemi and revealed the new handle in May 2012.

But back in November 2011, Demi was photographed looking even skinnier than she had been in the recent past, and "friends" told the press that she had not been eating or taking care of herself. Then in December, she was devastated to learn that her friend Patsy Rugg had passed away. Rugg had been Demi's sponsor at AA meetings and the two were exceptionally close. Unfortunately her death seemed to affect Demi in an acute way, and in the weeks ahead, she appeared to be going from one extreme to the other – one minute depressed, then at other times, according to friends, partying as if there were no tomorrow.

Finally, in January 2012 it all came crashing down. Demi was hosting a party at her home when she suddenly collapsed after suffering some kind of seizure. A friend called an ambulance and reported that the actress was semi-conscious, burning up, suffering convulsions and barely breathing. She shouted for the ambulance to hurry and reported that friends had to hold Demi down, such were the severity of the seizures. In a 911 tape released later that month, the friend is heard telling the operator that Moore had "smoked something – it's not marijuana, it's similar to incense".

It was later claimed that the substance could have been nitrous oxide, or laughing gas as it is better known. An ambulance raced to Demi's home and she was admitted to hospital before entering rehab in order to recover properly. Once she was discharged, a number of friends were seen going in and out of the actress's home, including first husband Bruce Willis, who had shown obvious concern for the health of the mother of his children.

The incident was a turning point for Demi, and afterwards she began trying to put her life back together; spending time with friends, putting on weight and embarking on a new TV show. *The Conversation* was an interview show that seemed to begin where Oprah left off. Talking to women about their experiences of life, the show was executively produced by Demi, and hosted by her friend Amanda de Cadenet. The brand worked and women from around the world began tweeting their delight with the show.

Demi was thrilled, though her personal life was still a problem, with rumours circulating that her children, Rumer, Scout and Tallulah, had distanced themselves from their mother, saying they needed space after a series of arguments concerning their ongoing friendship with Ashton Kutcher. The estrangement was an eerie reminder of Demi's troubled relationship with her own mother, Virginia Guynes, as the two did not speak to each other for many years. "Her life has come full circle," exclaimed friends, who remembered the troubles Demi had with Virginia, "and now her daughters just don't want to deal with the drama."

Other so-called friends declared that she had been an unwanted guest at Tallulah's graduation ceremony, and that her children had wanted Ashton to attend instead. Demi balked at such a request, and although she did indeed attend the graduation, it seemed apparent that things weren't going well, and none of the children were publicly photographed with their mother.

Also adding to the actress's worries was the media's continuing prodding into her relationship with estranged husband Ashton Kutcher. The couple – who were still legally married despite their very obvious and public separation – had bumped into each other at a party for their Kabbalah teacher in May 2012. The pair were civil and cordial to each other, but even this politeness was enough to prompt stories of a reconciliation. Immediately friends reported that the couple had hugged for "at least 60 seconds" in view of the other guests, and that they were obviously still comfortable in each other's company.

Rumours became rife when Demi "favourited" a tweet by singer Wiz Khalifa that explained how everyone makes mistakes and that shouldn't be the reason why you would give up on somebody. Then came another one saying that sometimes you have to love people from a distance in order to give them time to "get their minds right". Could these quotes be cryptic notes to Ashton? The media definitely thought so.

Unfortunately for them, however, Demi was in no mood to play the reporters' games and in response to their stories, she sent out a tweeted statement which described her feelings on the subject. In the comment she expressed how she had laughed at the need for the media to twist words and take tweets out of context "so they can create fictitious stories to sell to the public!" Of course, it was only a matter of time before the media jumped on this quote too and gleefully reproduced it in their publications.

As it later turned out, there was going to be no reconciliation between the estranged couple, as Ashton was soon being photographed kissing and cuddling with new love, actress Mila Kunis. Demi meanwhile was rumoured to be linked to actor Martin Henderson though it would seem that at the time of writing, the actress is far too busy working on the relationship with herself to put much time and energy into a relationship with another person. She is also said to be fairly content with the fact that her divorce from Kutcher is finally going through, showing that while the past few years have been a strain, she is looking forward to the future.

60

The Rise and Fall of Whitney Houston

The destruction and death of Whitney Houston is a painful story, made worse by the fact that during the first years of her career, people believed she was a clean-cut performer who could do no wrong. Unfortunately, her image as a gospel-singing good girl was not only exaggerated, but in the end, very much an illusion.

Born on 9 August 1963, Whitney grew up in a family full of unique talent: gospel singer Cissy Houston was her mother, Aretha Franklin was a close friend (though not her godmother as some have rumoured her to be) while soul legend Dionne Warwick was her cousin. It was, therefore, seemingly inevitable that Whitney would follow in their footsteps and from the moment she sang "Saving All My Love For You" in 1985, she became a star.

Her initial success was followed up by hits such as "How Will I Know?", "So Emotional", "I Wanna Dance with Somebody" and "Didn't We Almost Have it All", and award followed award as she raced her way quickly up the ladder of fame. It was at an award show on 12 April 1989 that Whitney met soul singer Bobby Brown, who after a long friendship went on to become the love of her life. She later told *Rolling Stone* magazine that Brown was the first male in show business who she could really talk to and be her real self with, and from the start it became apparent that for Brown, the feeling was mutual.

After turning down Bobby's first marriage proposal, the singer eventually said yes and the two were married on 18 July 1992 in the grounds of Whitney's house in New Jersey, in front of 800 guests. For a time they seemed a happy couple, and when Whitney gave birth to their daughter Bobbi Kristina in 1993, it seemed to seal the relationship in the eyes of the public.

Unfortunately their marriage was soon to deteriorate amid rumours that Whitney was secretly in love with her female assistant and friend, Robyn Crawford. The stories were never proved, though that has not stopped the gossip, even after Houston's death. Regardless of rumours and hearsay about the status of their friendship, what does seem pretty clear is that Brown and Crawford disliked each other intensely. Such was their distaste, in fact, that eventually Crawford gave up her job, which resulted in the end of her friendship with the singer. However, the former assistant always held a place for Whitney in her heart and in 2012 she shared her feelings with *Esquire* during a poignant tribute to her recently deceased friend.

Once Robyn had departed the Houston/Brown home, the couple continued their marriage, though the relationship was always volatile and made no better when the two apparently acquired an interest in narcotics and illegal substances. According to Houston, during the years of worldwide fame after her movie *The Bodyguard* (1992) and song "I Will Always Love You" were released, both she Bobby Brown became heavily into drugs, with cocaine being their substance of choice. This was kept secret from her adoring public for some time, until the bubble finally burst on 11 January 2000 when marijuana was discovered in their baggage while at Hawaii airport.

No charges were brought due to the couple jetting off in their plane before the authorities could arrive, but rumours flew and it wasn't long before all kinds of stories were reported in the press of cancelled interviews, erratic behaviour and even of Whitney being fired from an Academy Award show performance. There were also rumours of abuse within the marriage; of affairs and profound unhappiness; but the couple remained silent. For now.

Though still occasionally releasing records and movies, as well as enjoying a record-breaking music deal, Whitney's career took a definite back seat during this fraught time. The success of *The Bodyguard* could have led to Whitney matching her singing success with a high-profile Hollywood career, and she did make a couple more films such as *Waiting to Exhale* (1995) with Angela Bassett and *The Preacher's Wife* (1996) with Denzel Washington. However, it seems that her burgeoning acting career may have been sacrificed as a consequence of her drug-fuelled life with Brown.

In 2002 she sat down to an interview with Diane Sawyer for *ABC News*. It quickly became known as the "Crack is Whack" interview, when the singer declared she made too much money to ever smoke that particular drug, as it was so cheap. When asked if it was true that she had spent $730,000 on drugs, Whitney bizarrely declared "I want to see the receipts!" before going on to admit that she had used a variety of substances. "I don't like to think of myself as addicted," she said. "I'd rather think that I have a bad habit, which can be broken."

By 2006 one habit that she did want to break was her apparently abusive and destructive marriage to Bobby Brown. It had been on the rocks for many years and a car-crash TV show, *Being Bobby Brown*, did nothing for their relationship, showing them frequently fighting and taking part in what can only be described as erratic behaviour. Things were made much worse when leaked photographs of their drug-filled bathroom were splashed around the world and it was claimed that, during drug-fuelled episodes, Whitney would spend days at a time in her bedroom, sleeping, taking substances, so out of control she wouldn't know what day it was.

It was said that it was the leaked photographs, coupled with stories of Bobby Brown's infidelity and emotional abuse, which led Whitney to want to regain control of her career and clean up her life. Despite Brown's protests, Whitney moved out of the family home and flew to California with their daughter, Bobbi Kristina, where she set about rebuilding her life, spending quality time with her daughter and doing simple things such as the school run and pottering around her home.

She filed for divorce from Brown, which became final in early 2007, and for a time things started to look up. Desperate to get her career back on track, Whitney entered the recording studio and the album that was created, *I Look to You*, was released in 2009. Unfortunately the big comeback left fans disappointed when it was noticed that there was a significant change in her voice. No longer could she hold long notes; her voice sounded deeper, as though she had a bad cold or had smoked too many cigarettes. In public Whitney did not seem to notice – or did not wish to accept – any difference, but when she was booed on stage during a shambolic concert tour, she surely must have known she was not the singer she once was.

Giving her first interview in seven years, Whitney appeared on *The Oprah Winfrey Show* in September 2009, where she opened her heart and admitted having formerly laced marijuana with rock cocaine on an everyday basis. She also went over the details of her marriage, telling Winfrey how she and her husband would sit for days on end, doing drugs and never once talking to each other – just sitting in the room watching television and never uttering one word. "It was that bad," she admitted. When Oprah asked if she thought she'd ever go back to drugs, she seemed uncertain. "Don't think I don't have desires for it . . . I have to pray it away. One day at a time."

Unfortunately, after taking things one day at a time for the next few years, the demons that had haunted Houston for so long returned. She was photographed looking dishevelled and rumours began to surface that she was back on drugs. Fans prayed that they were wrong, but when pictures surfaced of her coming out of a nightclub covered in sweat and in obvious distress, it could not be denied any longer; Whitney was in trouble once again.

On 6 February 2012, the singer checked into room 434 of the Beverly Hilton Hotel for a week of Grammy Award-related parties and celebrations. On Saturday, 11 February, she complained to her assistant of a sore throat that had been bothering her for a few days, and was told to take a bath and relax for a while. The assistant then went to run some errands, leaving her employer alone to ready herself for the party that was due to take place in the hotel that night. The time was approximately 3 p.m., but tragically by the time she returned at 3.36 p.m. Whitney Houston was dead.

The scene that greeted the assistant when she returned to the room was her boss face down in a bathtub which was filled to the top with water; the taps had been turned off but water was spilling all over the floor. The devastated employee immediately alerted a bodyguard and Houston was pulled out of the bath and an ambulance was called. It was too late, however, and when the paramedics arrived, Whitney Houston was pronounced dead at the scene. The time was 3.55 p.m. – just an hour since the singer had complained to her assistant that she had felt a little unwell and decided to take a bath.

When police arrived on the scene, they were shocked to discover the disarray that greeted them. Tablets, medication bottles, capsules and a spoon with "a white crystal-like substance in it" were all present in the room, along with "a rolled up piece of white paper". The water in the bathtub was so hot that at 00.25 a.m. – a staggering nine hours after her death – the temperature still tested at an incredible 89 °F (30 °C).

When Whitney's daughter Bobbi discovered that her mother had died, she was so distraught that she collapsed and was rushed to hospital. Staff members were seen weeping in the corridors, while downstairs a television crew who were due to interview the star were shocked when told the reason they could no longer film the segment.

Whitney Houston's death was announced to the world, but while the news spread like wildfire, the pre-Grammys party that was being planned downstairs went ahead while Whitney's body was apparently still lying just floors above. The event was turned into a tribute to the tragic singer, though understandably some guests refused to attend, citing that the episode was in bad taste and should have ultimately been cancelled or postponed.

Whitney's body was eventually removed from the hotel and an autopsy was performed. After toxicology tests were run, it was eventually determined that her death was caused by accidental drowning, due to the effects of atherosclerotic heart disease and cocaine use. However, in December 2012, Paul Huebl, a Los Angeles private investigator, revealed that he believed the singer had been murdered by drug dealers wishing to collect a debt of $1.5 million. Information relating to the case was said to have been turned over to the FBI, though whether or not they are investigating the theory seriously is not yet known.

On Saturday, 18 February, Whitney's four-hour funeral took place at the New Hope Baptist Church in Newark, New Jersey. Dionne Warwick officiated, while friends such as Stevie Wonder and Alicia Keys performed, and Whitney's *Bodyguard* co-star Kevin Costner spoke a moving eulogy. Even her funeral, however, was tinged with scandal when her ex-husband Bobby Brown stormed from the church after a problem with the seating arrangements.

The next day, on 19 February 2012, Whitney was laid to rest in Fairview Cemetery, Westfield, New Jersey. She lies next to her father, apparently wearing her favourite dress, personal jewellery and gold slippers. Her ability to rest in peace, however, remains questionable, with concerns over enthusiastic fans and grave-robbers prompting the hiring of security guards to conduct round-the-clock patrols at the location where the once amazing singer now lies.

61

The Marriage of Tom Cruise and Katie Holmes

Actor Tom Cruise was no stranger to marriage: the first Mrs Cruise was actress Mimi Rogers, whom he divorced in 1990, and the second was Nicole Kidman, from whom he separated in February 2001. However, at the time he began dating actress Katie Holmes in April 2005, it seemed that this time the actor was well and truly smitten, and destined to live happily ever after . . .

By this time Tom Cruise was a global superstar, while Katie Holmes was the sweetheart of teen romance television drama, *Dawson's Creek*. They made an interesting couple, and for several weeks rumours swirled that they were more than just good friends. Fans, reporters and the curious waited for an official announcement of their love, which eventually came in the shape of an appearance together in Rome.

Dressed casually in jeans and shirts, the couple were photographed for the first time on 27 April 2005, holding hands and greeting fans. Then two days later, on 29 April, they were snapped in far more glamorous attire as they arrived at the David di Donatello Award ceremony, where they thrilled onlookers with a very public kiss – something which was to become a frequent occurrence during the course of their relationship.

By the time the couple returned to the United States, the press had already christened them "TomKat" and began reporting every tiny detail of their lives for all to see. The public were intrigued; fans discussed the relationship on internet forums and photographers recorded their every move; but it was Tom's appearance on *The Oprah Winfrey Show* on 23 May 2005 that really demonstrated how much the actor had fallen for his new love.

During the interview, Tom giggled like a lovestruck schoolboy; excitedly shook a gobsmacked Oprah; laughed uncontrollably when asked questions about Katie; and bizarrely punched the ground while crouching on the floor. But it was what came next that got everyone talking: Cruise suddenly leapt on to Oprah's couch and began jumping up and down with his arms in the air. The crowd when wild, but the newspapers even more so, nicknaming Cruise "The Sofa Jumper" and wondering what he was going to do next. During the show he even ran off stage to drag his shy girlfriend on to meet the talk-show host, and once again enjoyed a very public kiss and cuddle in front of the delighted audience.

The press continued to report the couple's every move to a hungry public, until finally on 6 October 2005 came the announcement that they were expecting a baby. Many people wished the couple well, but there were the odd few who did not, and internet trolls came out of the woodwork to create rumours that Katie wasn't actually with child; that the pregnancy was nothing more than a false stomach made by Hollywood special-effects artists. In Katie's case, whole forums began to pop up, discussing whether or not the couple were faking the entire thing. Photographs then appeared not only on the internet but in newspapers and magazines too, showing Katie's bump frequently changing size and citing this as a reason why the pregnancy could not possibly be real. The entire thing was ridiculous, of course, as a pregnant woman's bump changes size and shape throughout the average day, but this knowledge seemed lost on the trolls and most certainly did nothing to stop the rumours.

One day, when out on a windy street, Katie's dress was caught in a breeze, resulting in the front of her outfit puffing out over her pregnancy bump and making it look as though the actress's stomach was a rather distorted shape. Of course, someone was there to record the event, and immediately the gossip-mongers went into overdrive, refusing to believe that the photo was the result of a windy day, and declaring that it was definite "proof" that the pregnancy was fake.

Finally, Katie was photographed wearing a slightly cut-off top with the hint of stretch marks on her stomach. The photograph was blown up and published in magazines the world over, though even this was not enough to put paid to the rumours. "They've faked those too; it's the work of make-up artists," screamed crazed posters on internet sites.

When Tom and Katie's daughter Suri was born on 18 April 2006, the couple sensibly decided to keep her from the prying eyes of the public, which sent conspiracy theorists into overdrive. "Where is the baby?" they asked, while they took to internet forums to accuse the pair of not actually having a baby at all. But Katie and Tom could not be pressured into showing her off until finally famed photographer Annie Leibovitz snapped the family for the October 2006 edition of *Vanity Fair*. The fact that Suri was the image of her father, Tom Cruise, quietened many of the theorists, though even seven years later there are still the odd few who still like to discuss the far-fetched notion that the pregnancy was the creation not of a couple, but of a team of Hollywood professionals.

On 18 November 2006, Tom Cruise and Katie Holmes tied the knot in a fifteenth-century castle in Bracciano, Italy. Tom Cruise is a faithful and dedicated member of the Scientology religion, and before the wedding it was said that Katie Holmes took part in courses in order to change her religion from that of Catholic to Scientologist. As a result of Cruise's support of the faith, the wedding was a Scientology ceremony, though publicists later assured the public that they had celebrated an official wedding in Los Angeles the day before. The bride wore a beautiful white gown, and the couple were photographed looking happy with daughter Suri and Cruise's other children, Connor and Isabella.

For the next five years the couple were reported to be blissfully happy in their marriage, frequently photographed holding hands, kissing and carrying their daughter out and about in New York. However, it seems that what the public saw was somewhat different to what was going on inside the marriage, at least towards its conclusion. Although in April 2012 rumours started to swirl that Katie Holmes was pregnant with her second child, the claim was vehemently denied by her spokesperson. Instead, in the privacy of her home, Katie was planning quite a different surprise: the announcement that she was leaving Tom Cruise to start a new life with their daughter Suri.

According to sources, the actress had been unhappy in her marriage for quite some time and had quietly moved into an apartment in New York, away from the family home. There, she confided her plans to friends and family; changed her phone numbers and email addresses; and finally – on 29 June 2012 – made the shock announcement that she and Tom Cruise would be divorcing after five-and-a-half years of marriage.

Tom was said to have been blindsided by the decision, which appears to have been revealed to him just moments before it was announced to the entire world. He had no idea it was coming, his spokesperson said, and indeed just weeks before, the couple had been seen out and about, holding hands in full view of the cameras.

When the news broke, the actor was in Iceland making a movie and planning a huge party for his fiftieth birthday. After the news, all plans for celebrating were immediately thrown out of the window, and instead he spent the evening quietly with his children, Connor and Isabella. He also chose to remain tight-lipped about the break-up, leaving it to his lawyer Bert Fields to tell reporters, "It's not Tom's style to do this publicly. He is really sad about what's happening."

As soon as the divorce became public, newspapers were filled with headlines about the apparently warring couple. According to some they were fighting because Tom Cruise wanted Suri to attend a Scientology school while Holmes wanted her raised a Catholic. Meanwhile, other sources claimed that was not the case at all, and that Katie had been quite happy to live her life as a Scientologist, embracing the religion and visiting the Scientology Centre in Los Angeles even when her husband was out of town.

For several days after the announcement, Katie and Suri were kept away from the cameras in the safety of their apartment. There was concern when a large white car was seen sitting near the apartment block, with several men inside, taking a particular interest in the property. Some said that they were private detectives, sent to spy and report on Cruise's estranged wife, though if that was the case they were not very good at their job since they were spotted on more than one occasion and photographed openly by the press.

Others came up with the idea that the men were actually Scientologists, sent to persuade Katie against the divorce, though in reality it would seem that they were actually a team of security professionals who had been hired by Katie to not only protect her and Suri from unwanted attention, but to keep at bay the hordes of press photographers who were camped day and night outside her apartment. When Katie finally left to undertake a pre-booked work commitment, the photographers went crazy, snapping her every move and reporting on everything from what she was wearing to how skinny she appeared and whether or not she looked happy. Shortly after, she was seen taking Suri for ice cream, though the all-too-familiar press crowded them to such a degree that the child had to cling to her mother for support, her eyes screwed up tight, obviously wondering what was going on.

As gossip heated up, speculation was rife that the divorce proceedings would be public knowledge, cracking open the carefully shrouded mystery of Scientology for all to see. However, everyone was surprised when Katie's lawyer announced on 9 July 2012 that the divorce had already been settled and, what's more, the details would be kept entirely private. Any stories reporting otherwise were absolutely false, he assured reporters. He then released a statement which read: "We are thrilled for Katie and her family and are excited to watch as she embarks on the next chapter of her life."

Meanwhile, Tom Cruise and Katie Holmes released a joint statement as a conclusion of their marriage. In it they said that they were committed to working together as parents to accomplish what was in Suri's best interests: "We want to keep matters affecting our family private and express our respect for each other's commitment to each of our respective beliefs and support each other's roles as parents."

And with that the marriage of TomKat was ended, and the two went on with their separate lives. In September 2012, while Tom was in London, Suri Cruise took her first tentative steps into education, enrolling in a school in New York. But while Tom may not have been able to wave her off, hundreds of paparazzi did show up, leaving the child even more distressed than a child of her age would normally be when facing their first day at school.

Since then newspapers have reported every detail of Suri's life to and from school, such as what the child was wearing that day; what cartoon character she sported on her bag; and whether or not she was hanging out with friends. The intrusion into both her life and that of her parents is extreme, and it would therefore seem that while the relationship between Katie and Tom may be over, the public's fascination with the former family looks set to run and run for many years to come.